ESL WORKS & LESSON PLANS
Supplementary Lessons

By Paul J. Hamel

Copyright © 2017 by Paul J. Hamel

All rights reserved

No part of this publication may be stored in a retrieval system or transmitted in any form or by any means electronically, mechanical, recording, or otherwise without the prior permission of the copyright owner.

This book is available at Amazon.com.

For more information concerning this publications contact the author at paulhamel@twc.com or (310) 991-2374.

ESL WORKSHEETS & LESSON PLANS

Supplementary Lessons

By Paul J. Hamel

These worksheets have been developed to supplement English-as-a-Second-Language textbooks and curriculum--not to replace them. They are meant to enhance and bring variety to an already-existing school English language teaching program. The worksheets are designed to be duplicated and distributed to students. The worksheets can be used at home, school, or in any other independent setting. They can also be used to make overhead transparencies or be projected onto a whiteboard or smart board on which students can see the worksheet and write directly onto the projected image. Each worksheet is accompanied by a detailed step-by-step lesson plan and suggested teaching techniques to assist the instructor in providing an interesting and successful lesson. The lessons can also provide a useful resource for substitute teachers and tutors.

TABLE OF CONTENTS

	PAGE
Introduction	1
Key Word List	2
A Few, A Little, A Lot of, Pair Practice, Fill In	5
Above, Beside, Below, Behind, In Front of, In Back of, Next To, Pair Practice	7
Across, Along, Around, Over, Under, Through, Around, Pair Practice, Writing	9
Adjectives and Adverbs of Manner, Pair Practice, Writing, Vocabulary Building	11
Adverbs of Frequency, Pair Practice, Writing, Vocabulary Building	13
Adverbs of Manner Using How And -ly Ending, Student Mixer, Discussion	15
Anything, Something, Nothing, Indefinite References, Pair Practice, Writing	17
Apartment Ads, Reading, Vocabulary Building, Pair Practice	19
Basic Written Directions and Instructions, Filling out an application	21
Better and Worse, Pair Practice, Vocabulary Building, Fill in, Class Discussion	23
Body Parts, Pair Practice, Vocabulary Building, Fill-In, Class Discussion	25
Body Parts, Crossword Puzzle, Vocabulary Building	27
Breaking a Work Rule, Values Clarification, Discussion	29
Bulletin Board Ads, Reading, Writing, Pair Practice, Dictation, Vocabulary Building	31
Can and Can't, Animal Names, Common Verbs, Writing, Class Discussion	33
Can, Modal Verb, At The Shopping Center, Vocabulary Building	35
Clothing Items, Student Mixer, Class Discussion, Vocabulary Building	37
Clothing, Find The Differences In Clothing, Discussion, Games, Vocabulary Building	39
Clothing and Accessories, Crossword Puzzle, Vocabulary Building	41
Common Materials, What Kind Of, Vocabulary Building, Word Order	43
Common Verbs 1, Crossword Puzzle, Vocabulary Building	45
Common Verbs 2, Crossword Puzzle, Vocabulary Building	47
Comparative and Superlative, Pair Practice, Fill In, Class Discussion	49
Comparative and Superlative, Geographical Terms, Pair Practice, Writing, Class Discussion	51
Comparative and Superlative, Student Mixer, Class Discussion	53
Comparative and Superlative, Facts About The USA	55
Could & Would, Pair Practice, Writing, Class Discussion	57
Could, Modal Verb, Asking Polite Questions, Pair Practice, Writing	59
Counting, U.S. Money, Reading, Counting, Oral Drill	61
Days, Months, & Seasons, Expressions Of Time, Vocabulary Building	63
Direct and Indirect Speech, Discussion, Writing, Discussing Drug Abuse	65

Do & Don't, Imperative, Basic School Rules, Reading, Writing, Class Discussion	67
Do & Don't, Present Tense, Reading, Fill In, Vocabulary Building	69
Do or Make Expressions, Crossword Puzzle, Vocabulary Building	71
Does and Doesn't, Present Tense, Reading, Fill In, Vocabulary Building	73
Driving Directions, Reading And Listening Comprehension, Vocabulary Building	75
Employment Application, Fill In, Vocational ESL, Pair Practice	77
Family Relationships, Vocabulary Building, Class Discussion, Fill In	79
Filling Out a Simple Form, Personal Information, Reading, Writing	81
Following Simple Directions, Operating Common Machines, Reading Comprehension	83
Food Ads, Use of Present Tense, Pair Practice, Common Abbreviations	85
Food Containers, Portions & Packaging, Crossword Puzzle, Vocabulary Building	87
Food Menu Items, Crossword Puzzle, Vocabulary Building	89
Fruit Names, Crossword Puzzle, Vocabulary Building	91
Gerunds, Common Tools, Vocational ESL Vocabulary	93
Going To, Future, Expressions of Time, Writing, Vocabulary Building	95
Have To, Reading an Appointment Book, Pair Practice, Writing, Class Discussion	97
Him, Her, It, Them, Object Pronouns, Common Verbs, Pair Practice, Writing, Common Verbs	99
His, Her, Their, Possessive Adjectives, Pair Practice, Writing, Vocabulary Building	101
Home Furnishings and Appliances, Crossword Puzzle, Vocabulary Building	103
Household Chores 1, Crossword Puzzle, Vocabulary Building	105
Household Chores 2, Crossword Puzzle, Vocabulary Building	107
How Much & How Many, Pair Practice, Writing, Fill In, Vocabulary Building	109
How Used With By, With, & On, Prepositions, Pair Practice, Writing, Vocabulary Building	111
Imperative, Common Verbs, Household Chores, Ordinal Numbers, Reading, Writing	113
In, For, Until, By (Expressions of Future Time), Pair Practice, Writing, Class Discussion	115
In, On, At, Prepositions of Location, Abbreviations In Addresses	117
Irregular Adverbs of Manner, Reading, Writing, Class Discussion, Vocabulary Building	119
Irregular Verbs In The Past Tense 1, Spelling, Crossword Puzzle, Vocabulary Building	121
Irregular Verbs In The Past Tense 2, Spelling, Crossword Puzzle, Vocabulary Building	123
Job Ads, Pair Practice, Vocabulary Building	125
Job Interview Questions, Discussion, Vocational ESL Vocabulary	127
May, Modal Verb, Asking Permission, Pair Practice, Writing	129
Might, Modal Verb, Expressing Indecision, Pair Practice, Writing	131
Modal Verbs (Review), Giving Advice, Reading, Writing, Class Discussion	133
More and Less, Pair Practice, Fill In, Class Discussion, Vocabulary Building	135
Not Understanding, Values Clarification, Discussion	137

Numbers, Listening And Reading Comprehension	139
Occupations, Crossword Puzzle, Vocabulary Building	141
Opposites, Common Adjectives, Vocabulary Building, Writing	143
Opposites Concepts, Crossword Puzzle, Vocabulary Building	145
Parts of A Car, Prepositions Of Location, Vocabulary Building	147
Parts of A Car, Crossword Puzzle, Vocabulary Building	149
Parts of The Day, Expressions Of Time, Vocabulary Building	151
Passive Voice (Past Tense), Listening Comprehension, Writing Activity	153
Passive Voice in Newspaper Headlines, Rewriting Newspaper Headlines	155
Passive Voice, Opening a Small Business, Vocational ESL Vocabulary	157
Past Continuous & Simple Past Tense Review, Pair Practice, Fill-in, Discussion, Role Play	159
Past Continuous Tense, Pair Practice, Writing	161
Past Participle Endings, Crossword Puzzle, Vocabulary Building	163
Past Tense Irregular Verbs, Pair Practice, Vocabulary Building	165
Past Tense Regular Verbs 1, Expressions of Time, Pair Practice, Common Verbs	167
Past Tense Regular Verbs 2, Pair Practice, Dictation, Vocabulary Building	169
Past Tense Review, Rewriting a Picture Story, Reading Comprehension, Writing	171
Past Tense Review, Telling a Story, Reading, Writing	173
Possessive ('s), Student Mixer, Vocabulary Building, Class Discussion	175
Prepositions of Location, North, South, East, West, Far From, Near, Close To, Pair Practice, Writing	177
Prepositions of Location Review, Listening, Drawing, Vocabulary Building	179
Present Continuous Tense, Common Verbs, Pair Practice, Writing, Vocabulary Building	181
Present Continuous and Simple Present Review, Pair Practice, Writing, Vocabulary Building	183
Present Perfect Tense 1 , A Job Interview, Pair Practice, Writing, Class Discussion	185
Present Perfect Tense 2, Shopping Survey, Pair Practice, Writing, Discussion	187
Past Perfect Tense, Group Discussion, Writing, Dealing with AIDS	189
Present Tense & Household Responsibilities, Common Verbs, Writing, Class Discussion	191
Present Tense, Student Mixer, General Information, Questions, Pair Practice, Discussion	193
Professions, Crossword Puzzle, Vocabulary Building	195
Question Word Review, TV and Movie Survey, Writing, Class Discussion	197
Reading a Newspaper, Information Search, Reading, Discussion, Vocabulary Building	199
Reading Body Language - Hand Gestures, Reading, Discussion, Role Playing	201
Safety Signs, Speaking, Writing, Pair Practice Dictation	203
Say & Tell, Past and Present Tense Review, Writing, Discussion	205
Say, Spell, Pronounce, Pair Practice, Language Clarification, Vocabulary Building	207
School Items, Crossword Puzzle, Vocabulary Building	209

Should, Modal Verb, Giving Opinions And Advice, Pair Practice, Writing	211
Social Language, Role Playing, Vocabulary Building	213
Some and Any 1, Reading, Pair Practice, Ordering from a Menu, Vocabulary Building	215
Some and Any 2, Pair Practice, Fill In, Writing, Role Playing, Vocabulary Building	217
Spelling Words with Silent Letters, Spelling, Crossword Puzzle, Vocabulary Building	219
Still, Anymore, Just, Ago, Already, Yet, Present Perfect, Pair Practice, Writing, Discussion	221
Street Directions, Vocabulary Building, Pair Practice	223
Suffixes Used In Occupations, Writing, Vocational ESL Vocabulary Building	225
Telling Time, Pair Practice, Fill In, Vocabulary Building	227
That, Relative Pronoun, Basic Employment Vocabulary, Pair Practice, Writing, Class Discussion	229
To Be, Short Answers, Pair Practice, People Categories, Vocabulary Building, Fill In	231
Tools, Crossword Puzzle, Vocabulary Building	233
Topics for Conversation 1: about Law, Education, Government, Environment, Discussion	235
Topics for Conversation 2: Business Related, Group Disccussion	237
Topics for Conversation 3: Personal Questions	239
Traffic Signs, Pair Practice Dictation, Vocabulary Building	241
Transportation, Crossword Puzzle, Vocabulary Building	243
Trivia 1 Game, Discussion	245
Trivia 2 Game, Discussion	247
Trends: Current & Future, Group Discussion	249
Understanding Directions, Values Clarification, Discussion, Role Playing	251
Using The Library, Internet, or New Media, Information Search	253
Vegetables, Crossword Puzzle, Vocabulary Building	255
Want & Want To, Use of The Infinitive, Pair Practice, Writing, Vocabulary Building	257
Was & Were, Emotions, Pair Practice, Writing	259
When, Where & What Time, Expressions Of Time, Pair Practice, Fill In	261
Who & That, Relative Pronouns, Which, Pair Practice, Writing, Discussion	263
Who & What, Question Words, Reading An Office Directory, Pair Practice, Fill In	265
Who, Relative Pronoun, Basic Employment Vocabulary, Pair Practice	267
Would, Asking Hypothetical Questions using the Conditional, Group Discussion	269
Why? (Because, To, and For), Pair Practice, Writing, Class Discussion	271
Will (Future Tense), Taking a Trip, Pair Practice, Vocabulary Building	273
Word Order, When, How, Pair Practice, Writing, Class Discussion	275

INTRODUCTION

Reproducible worksheets have unquestionably played a prominent role in education beginning with the invention of the ditto machine or spirit master, photocopier, overhead projector, and now the "smart board."

Worksheets serve as an important tool in supplementing, reinforcing, and expanding your lessons. No matter how good or complete the content of your textbook or curriculum may be, there will always be a need to fill in the gaps in knowledge and skills your students need to learn.

The value of worksheets in teaching English as a Second Language is clear.

Worksheets help students:

- review and understand already-taught materials in a new way
- learn through a variety of different methods
- develop writing and spelling skills
- have fun in doing challenging grammar and vocabulary building assignments
- keep their minds active and engaged
- learn new words and phrases on a topic
- make inferences, evaluating choices, and drawing conclusions
- refresh and help retain grammar points and vocabulary they have just learned
- visualize the new words through photos
- continue learning outside of the classroom

Crossword puzzles help teachers:

- supplement textbooks and curriculum
- extend and reinforce existing lessons
- keep students' interest
- provide extra homework or classroom assignment to improve English skills
- employ additional methods of presenting grammar and vocabulary
- reinforce already-taught structures and vocabulary words
- review and test students with a less intimidating and threatening tool

KEYWORD LIST

Find a lesson by using these keywords.

a few 5
a little 5
a lot of 5
abbreviations 117, 125
above 7, 179
accessories 41
across 9
adjectives 119
adjectives of manner 11
ads 125
adverbs 119
adverbs of frequency 13
adverbs of manner 11, 15
advice 211
ago 221
along 9
alphabet song 208
already 221
always 13
any 215, 217
anybody 17
anymore 221
anything 17
apartment ads 19
appliances 103
application 21
application form 77
appointment book 97, 261, 273

around 9
at 117
because 271
behind 7, 179
belong to 102, 175
below 179
beside 7
better 23
between 179
body language 201
body parts 25, 27
bulletin board 31
business 157, 237
buy 33
by 111, 115
calendar 167, 169
can 33, 35
can't 33
cars 147, 149, 263
chores 71, 105, 107, 113, 191, 193
classroom items 209
close to 177
clothing 37, 39, 41
common materials 43
common tools 93
common verbs 45, 46, 83
comparative 49, 51, 53, 55
containers 86

could 57, 59
counting money 61
days 63
descriptive adjectives 43
direct speech 65
directions 83, 223, 251
do 67, 69, 71
does 73
doesn't 73
don't 67, 69
down 9
draw 179
driving directions 75
drug abuse 65
east 177
education 235
emotions 259
environment 235
ever 13
expressions of time 22, 261
facts about the USA 55
family 79
family tree 80
far from 177
find 33
fire report 161
follow directions 83
food ads 85

food containers 87
food items 87, 89, 215, 217
food menu 89
for 115, 271
frequently 14
fruit 91
future 95, 115, 273
generally 14
geographic terms 53
gerunds 93
giving advice 133, 211
going to 95
government 235
hand gestures 201
hardly ever 14
have to 97
headlines 155
her 99, 101
him 99
his 101
home furnishing 103
household chores 105, 107, 113, 191
how 11, 15, 111, 119, 207, 275
how many 5, 109
how much 5, 109
how often 13
hurt 25
imperative 67, 113
in 115, 117
in back of 7

in front of 7, 179
indirect speech 65
information search 199, 253
internet 253
interview questions 127
interview rating form 78
irregular adverbs of manner 119
irregular past tense 121, 123
irregular verbs 165
it 99
job ads 125
job interview 127, 185
just 221
law 235
left 179
less 135
library 253
liquid measure 88
lost 31
make 71
map 177
materials 43
may 129
meals 215, 217
menu 89, 215, 217
middle 179
might 131
modal verb review 133
money 61
months 63

more 135
near 177
never 13
news media 253
newspaper 155, 199
next to 7, 179
nobody 17
north 177
not ever 14
not understanding 137
nothing 17
numbers 139
object pronouns 99
occasionally 14
occupations 141, 225
office directory 265
often 13
on 111, 117, 179
opinion 211
opposites 143, 145
ordinal numbers 113
over 179
over 9
packaging 87
pain 25
parts of the day 151
passive voice 153, 155, 157
past continuous tense 159, 161
past participles 163
past tense 159, 165, 167, 169, 171, 173, 205

personal 239
picture story 171
portions 87
possessive 175
possessive adjectives 101
prepositions of location 7, 9, 117, 177, 179
present continuous 181, 183
present perfect 185, 187, 189, 221
present tense 183, 191, 205, 231
professions 195
pronounce 207
question words 197
rarely 13
registration form 81
relative pronouns 229, 263, 267
responsibilities 191
right 179
safety signs 203
say 205, 207
school items 209
school rules 67
seasons 63
seldom 13
shopping survey 189
should 211
signs 203, 241
silent letters 219
simple directions 83

simple machines 83
social language 213
some 215, 217
somebody 17
something 17
sometimes 13
south 177
spell 207
sport verbs 70
still 221
street directions 223
suffixes 225
superlative 49, 51, 53, 55
survey 189
tell 205
telling time 227
than 23
that 229, 263
their 101
them 99
through 9
time 227
to 271
to be 231, 259
tools 233
tools 93
traffic signs 75, 241
transportation 243
trends 249
trip 273
trivia game 245, 247
under 9, 179
understanding directions 251

until 115
usually 13
values clarification 27
vegetables 255
want 257
was 259
weight 88
were 259
west 177
what 265
what kind of 11, 119
what time 261
when 261, 275
where 261
who 263, 265, 267
whose 101
why 271
will 115, 273
with 111
won't 115
word order 275
work rules 27
worse 23
would 57, 269
writing notes 31
written directions 21
yet 221

ESL Beginning Level   Pair Practice • Vocabulary Building • Fill In

A little, A few & A lot of

① Directions: *Read and pronounce the names of the items below.*

water • tickets • bread • milk • cash • homework • pencils • friends • coffee • coins

sugar • people • gas • books • dollars • problems • food • relatives • hours • hair

Directions: *List the items above under* **A FEW** *or* **A LITTLE** *below.*

A FEW
(Count)

tickets _____

_____ _____

_____ _____

_____ _____

_____ _____

A LITTLE
(Non-count)

water _____

_____ _____

_____ _____

_____ _____

_____ _____

② Directions: *Practice asking with another student with* **"How much?"** *and* **"How many?"** *Answer using* **"a little,"** **"a few,"** *and* **"a lot of."** *See the examples ▶*

Student 1: *How much/How many _____ do you see?*

Student 2: *I see _____ .*

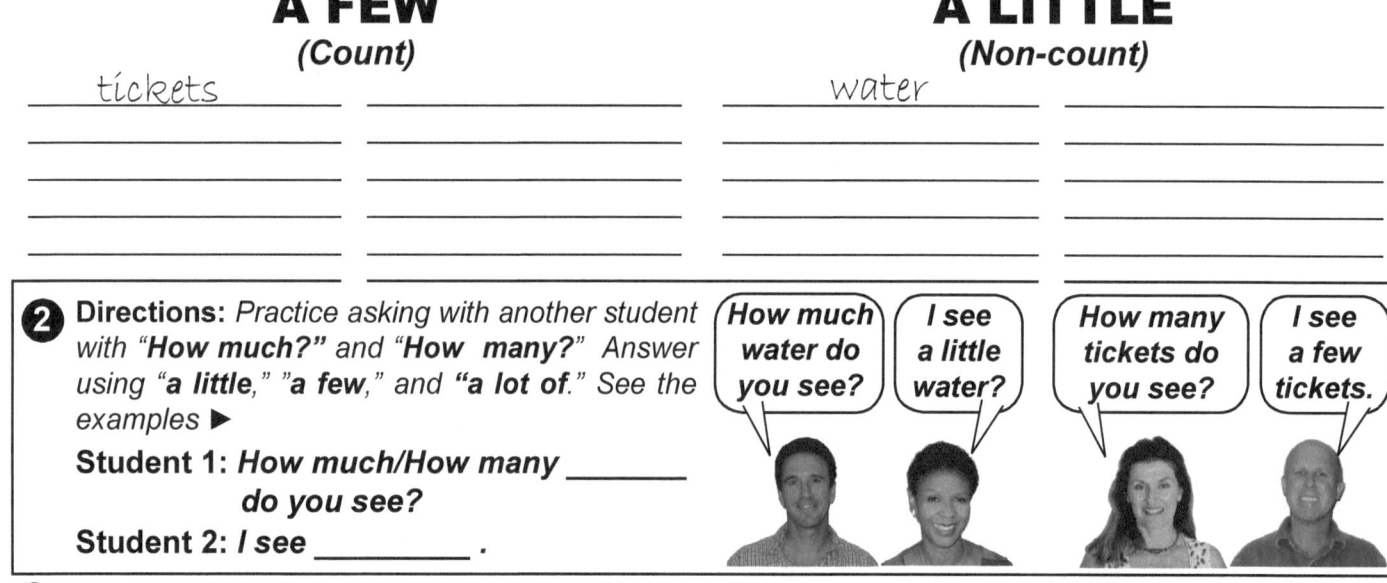

③ Directions: *Write "a few," "a little," or "a lot of" below.*

1 How many apples are there? There are _a few_ **apples.**

2 How much tea do you drink? I drink _____ **tea.**

3 How many people are there? I see _____ **people.**

4 How many children are there? There are _____ .

5 How much fruit do you eat? I eat _____ **fruit.**

6 How much cash is in the photo? It's _____ **money.**

④ Interview: *Ask another student the questions below. Write the answers using "a few," "a little," or "a lot of."*

Student Survey

1. How many brothers/sisters do you have? _____
2. How many relatives do you have? _____
3. How much money does gas cost? _____
4. How many hours do you sleep? _____
5. How many books do you read in a year? _____
6. How many close friends do you have? _____
7. How many hours do you study? _____
8. How much do you like _____ ? _____
9. How much _____ ? _____
10. How many _____ ? _____

ESL Beginning Level   Pair Practice • Vocabulary Building • Fill In

Teacher's Notes

1 Before distributing the worksheet, begin the lesson with a conversation using "**how much**" and "**how many**" to determine how much the students already know about how these expressions are used. (See lesson **How much & How many**, Item #0098).

2 Distribute the worksheet. Introduce the vocabulary and pronounce the names of the items for each photo. Have the students model the pronunciation of the words after you. Make sure that the students know the following countable nouns: *glass, carton, cup, slice, spoon, liter, gallon, lock* (of hair), and *plate.* Point out that these words are countable and can be used with non-countable words in expressions with "**of**." Examples: *a glass of water, a carton of milk, a cup of coffee, a slice of bread, a spoon of sugar, a liter/gallon of gas, a lock of hair,* and *a plate of food.*

3 Explain that we use "**a few**" for items that can be counted and "**a little**" for items that cannot be counted. Then, direct the students to list the items in the photos under the columns "**A FEW**" or "**A LITTLE**".

4 Introduce the structure by asking questions such as the examples below. Continue asking similar questions about the remaining photos.

    How much water do you see in the photo?   *I see a little water.*
    How many tickets do you see?   *I see a few tickets.*

5 Vary the questions by using other verbs such as "**want**," "**have**, "**need**," "**eat**," "**drink**," "**study**," "**like**," etc.

    Examples: *How much money do you want?*   *How much coffee do you drink?*
                       How many friends do you have?   *How much food do you eat for dinner?*
                       How much do you like ice cream?   *How many hours do you study?*

6 Explain that "**a lot of**" is the opposite of "**a little**" and "**a few**" and is used with both count and non-count nouns.

    Examples: *How many friends do you have?*   *I have a lot of friends.*
                       How much money do you want?   *I want a lot of money.*

Repeat the drill in exercise 2 eliciting answers with "**a lot of.**" Ask about friends, relatives, cousins, the cost of a car, gas, etc.

7 Direct students to exercise 3 on the worksheet. Identify the items in the photos and have students repeat them after you. As a oral exercise ask the students to use "**a little**," "**a few**," and "**a lot of**" in the blank spaces below the photos. Expand the activity by asking for volunteers to pose original questions using "**How much**" and "**How many**" using "**a little**," "**a few**," or "**a lot of**" in the answers. Finally, have the students write the expressions on the blank lines provided. (**Answers:** 1. a few; 2. answers will vary; 3. a lot of; 4, a lot of; 5. answers will vary; 6. a lot of)

8 Direct the students to the **Student Survey** in exercise 4 at the bottom of the worksheet. As an active listening and reading exercise, read the questions to the class orally and have the students underline any unknown words. Then, explain any unfamiliar vocabulary. Ask the students to provide two original questions at the end of the survey. Finally, discuss the answers in a class discussion.

FOLLOW UP ACTIVITIES

9 Emphasize the use of such words as "*food*," "*money*," "*work*," "*furniture*," and "*hair*" with the question "*How much?*" Some students tend to use the question "*How many?*" with these words. It may be useful to drill these in the following types of contrasts:

    How much money? A little money.   *How much work? A little work.*

Stress that the use of the article "**a**" is essential. Lack of the article produces a negative impression.

10   Compare: *I have little time.* (almost none)   *I have few friends.* (almost none)
                      I have a little time. (a small quantity)   *I have a few friends.* (some)

ESL Beginning Level — Prepositions of Location • Pair Practice • Writing

Above, Beside, Below, Behind, In Front of, In Back of, Next To

1 *Read the sentences.*

1. The students and teacher are in the classroom.

2. The chalkboard is behind Jim.

3. Betty is next to Joyce.

4. Paul and Rita are in the back of the classroom.

5. The alphabet is above the maps.

6. The maps are below the alphabet.

7. The teacher is in front of the classroom.

8. Joyce is between the teacher and Rita.

---

2 **Pair-Practice:** *Practice answering and asking questions with another student. See examples.* ▶

Student 1: **Who's** _____?
Student 2: _____ is.
Student 1: **Where's** _____?
Student 2: **He/She** _____.

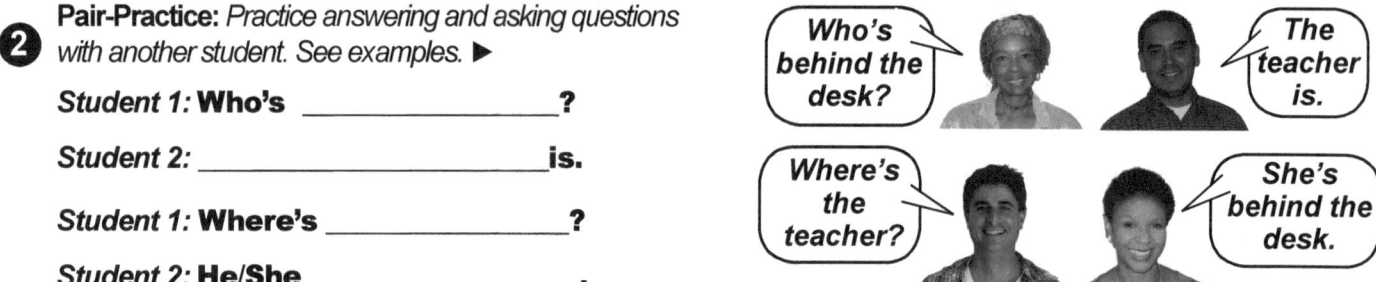

Who's behind the desk? — The teacher is.
Where's the teacher? — She's behind the desk.

---

3 *Write the answers to the questions below the photos.*

| 1. Where are the people? | 2. Where's Jack? | 3. Where's the umbrella? | 4. Where are the girls? |

   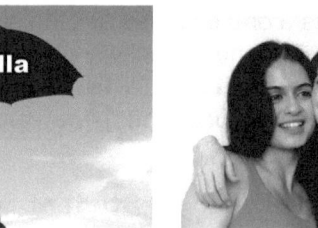

They're in front of the house.

| 5. Where are the clouds? | 6. Where's Kim? | 7. Where's the baby? | 8. Where's Carl? |

7

ESL Beginning Level   Prepositions of Location • Pair Practice • Fill In

Teacher's Notes

1 Before distributing the worksheet, start the lesson with a conversation. To assess your students' knowledge of the use of prepositions of location, ask personalized questions asking the locations of people and things in your classroom. Elicit answers in which the students must use a preposition *in front of*, *in back of*, *behind*, *above*, *below*, *next to*, and *between*. Ask questions modeled after the questions in exercise 3 at the bottom of the worksheet.

2 Distribute the worksheet. Identify the people and objects in the photo. Have the students repeat the words after you.

3 Ask individual students yes/no questions such as, "*Is the teacher standing in front of the classroom?*" Model the response, "*Yes, she is.*" Ask similar questions using all the prepositions listed in the picture.

4 As a variation, drill the prepositions in questions using "*who*" such as, "*Who's behind the desk?*" Model the response, "*The teacher is.*" Have one student ask a similar question and another student supply an appropriate answer.

5 Drill the prepositions through questions using "*where*" such as, "*Where's Rita?*" Model the answer, "*She's between Susan and Ray.*" Continue this activity using the methodology described in item 3 above.

6 Ask yes/no questions, and questions with "*who*" and "*where*." Use the questions in exercise 2 as a guide. Have students continue this activity by having them ask one another.

7 Ask three volunteers to come to the front of the class. Introduce them. As you walk around the three students, have other students describe where you or one of the three students is. Model a few examples such as "*You're in front of Mary. You're behind John. John's beside Mary.*"

8 As a listening comprehension exercise, have individual students follow directions such as, "*Go and stand between John and Mary.*"

9 Direct the students to exercise 2. Have them use the patterns and the examples given in the pair practice activities. With the help of a student, demonstrate how to do the pair practice exercises using the pictures at the top of the page. Then have your students continue by working in pairs. Walk around the classroom listening to the pairs of students. Correct their pronunciation as needed.

10 Read the questions in exercise 3 and ask volunteers to answer them orally. Then, have students answer the questions in writing below the photos.

11 Draw a simple landscape consisting of three hills, a road, a tree, and a house on the chalkboard. Have the class tell you or a student volunteer what item to add to the picture and where to place it. Tell students to use the prepositions from the box on the worksheet. Model a few examples such as:

> *Draw a bird above the tree.*
> *Draw a flower between the tree and the house.*
> *Draw a cat next to the tree.*
> *Draw a table in front of the house.*
> *Draw two chairs behind the table. etc.*

12 After all the prepositions have been used, reverse the exercise by having the students tell you what to erase.

Model the examples:

> *Please erase the bird (that's) above the house.*
> *Please erase the flower (that's) between the tree and the house.*

This is an effective way to subtly introduce and drill the relative pronoun "*that*."

8

ESL Beginning Level Prepositions of Location • Pair Practice • Writing

Across, Along, Around, Over, Under, Up, Down, Through

1 *Read about Joanne's hike with her friends.*

Joanne and her friends like to hike. They ...

• run **along** a path

• go **under** a tree

• walk **over** a bridge

• walk **across** a creek

• jog **through** a tunnel

• climb **up** and **down** stairs

• rest **around** a tree.

2 **Pair-Practice:** *Practice answering and asking questions with another student. See examples.* ▶

Student 1: **What does Joanne do before she _____?**

Student 2: **She _____ .**

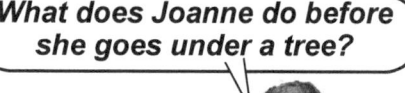
What does Joanne do before she goes under a tree? She runs along a path.

3 **Pair-Practice:** *Practice answering and asking questions with another student. See examples.* ▶

Student 1: **What do the hikers do after they _____?**

Student 2: **They _____ after they _____ .**

What do the hikers do after they walk over a bridge? They walk across a creek.

4 *What are the people doing in the photos? Write your answers below the photos.*

Rita is walking along a path.

Beth (cliff)

Joe

Joyce (river)

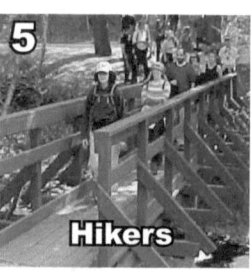
Hikers

ESL Beginning Level   Prepositions of Location • Pair Practice • Writing

Teacher's Notes

1 Distribute the worksheet. Read the captions below each photo. Describe and drill each segment of the hike. For example, have the students repeat, "*Joanne and her friends (hikers) go along a path.*" Little by little add subsequent steps until the entire course of the hike can be described as follows:

> *The hikers run along a path,*　　*jog through a tunnel,*
> *go under a tree,*　　*climb up and down stairs,*
> *walk over a bridge,*　　*and rest around a tree.*
> *walk across a creek,*

2 Ask for volunteers to describe the complete sequence of the hike.

3 Continue drilling the prepositions by asking questions using "*before*" and "*after*." For example, ask, "*What does Joanne do before she goes under a tree?*" or "*What do the hikers do after they go under a tree?*" Model a few sample responses. Then have individual students ask similar questions to other students.

4 Direct the students to exercises 2 and 3. Have them use the patterns and the examples given in the pair practice activities. With the help of a student, demonstrate how to do the pair practice exercises using the pictures at the top of the page. Then have your students continue by working in pairs.

5 Ask your students to describe what the people in the photos at the bottom of the worksheet are doing. Have students complete exercises in writing using the present continuous tense. Answers:

> 1. Rita is walking *along* a path.
> 2. Beth is climbing *up* a cliff.
> 3. Joe is walking *through* a tunnel.
> 4. Joyce is walking *across* a river.
> 5. The hikers are walking *over* a bridge.

6 Play the game "*Simon says*." Have students stand up. Tell them that they have to do whatever you tell them to do except when you do not begin the command with the words "*Simon says*." Students who do so are eliminated from the game and have to sit down. Tell students to take a piece of paper that has a hole in it. Give commands such as:

> • *look under the desk*
> • *look through the hole*
> • *put your hand over the hole*
> • *look around the room*
> • *look up/down*
> • *look over your shoulder*

7 **Follow Up Activity:** Pantomime can be used as a game. Divide the class into two teams. Have the students guess the action. Have a student keep count of each team's correct guesses. Some examples are: *jumping over a puddle of water, climbing a mountain, looking under a bed for a shoe,* and *going through a window.*

8 Explain that the "*gh*" in the words "*right*" and "*through*" is silent.

ESL Intermediate Levels   Pair Practice • Writing • Vocabulary Building

Adjectives & Adverbs of Manner

1 *Read the sentences below the photos.*

| A careful driver drives carefully. | A careless driver drives carelessly. | A polite employee acts politely. | A rude employee acts rudely. | A safe rider rides safely. | An unsafe rider rides unsafely. |

    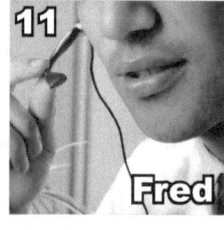 

| A loud speaker speaks loudly. | A soft speaker speaks softly. | An honest player plays honestly. | A dishonest player plays dishonestly. | A clear speaker speaks clearly. | An unclear speaker speaks unclearly. |

2 **Pair-Practice:** *Practice answering and asking questions with another student. See examples.* ▶

  Student 1: **What kind of** _____ **is** _____?

  Student 2: **He/She is a** _____.

3 **Pair-Practice:** *Practice answering and asking questions with another student. See examples.* ▶

  Student 1: **How does** _____?

  Student 2: **He/She** _____.

4 **Class Discussion:** *Practice answering and asking questions with other students in your class. See examples.* ▶

  What kind of _____ are you?

  How do you _____?

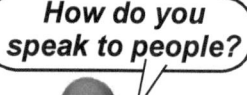

5 *Answer the questions in writing. Use the adjectives and adverbs above.*

1. What kind of person are you? *I'm an honest person.*
2. How do you speak to people? *I speak to people politely.*
3. What kind of person is a judge? _____
4. How does your teacher speak? _____
5. What kind of card player are you? _____
6. How do you play games? _____
7. What kind of driver are you? _____
8. How do you ride a bicycle? _____
9. What kind of friends do you have? _____
10. How do your friends speak to you? _____

ESL Intermediate Levels   Pair Practice • Writing • Vocabulary Building

Teacher's Notes

1 Before distributing the worksheet, start the lesson with a conversation. To assess your students' knowledge of the use of descriptive adjectives and adverbs of manner, ask personalized questions like the ones at the bottom of the worksheet.

2 Distribute the worksheet. Review and explain the sentences below each photo.

3 Introduce the adverbial forms of the words below the photos by asking questions with "*How?*" and "*What kind of...?*" Model the following questions and answers.

   What kind of driver is Jill? She's a careful driver.   *How does Jill drive? She drives carefully.*

4 Continue asking similar questions about each photo. Have the students repeat both the questions and answers.

5 Pose yes/no questions that elicit a negative answer. For example, ask "*Is Jill a careless driver?*" Model the response, "*No, she isn't. She's a careful driver.*" Ask, "*Does she drive carelessly?*" Model the response, "*No, she doesn't. She drives carefully.*" Continue drilling using the remaining photos.

6 In activity 2, the first pair-practice exercise, direct the students to ask and answers questions using "*What kind of person is [name]?*" Model responses using adverbs of frequency. Have the students continue the activity by working in pairs asking one another questions based on the information in the phrases at the top of the worksheet.

7 In activity 3, the second pair-practice exercise, have the students use the question "*How does [name] [verb]?*" Then, model a few responses using an adverb of manner. Let the students work in pairs.

8 Expand the activity by asking the class personalized questions such as the ones listed at the bottom of the worksheet. Then, as a class discussion in activity 4, encourage the students to ask one another original questions.

9 After reviewing the questions in activity 5, have students complete the questions in writing. Ask them to share some answers with the whole class.

NOTE

10 Explain that adjectives generally precede nouns and the adverbs of manner follow verbs. Point out that many common adverbs are formed by adding the suffix "**-ly**" to adjectives.

11 Present spelling and pronunciation rules progressively over several class sessions. Drill both orally and in writing. Utilize a chalkboard drill to reinforce spelling changes. Have students transform adjectives into corresponding adverbial forms.

   a. "*y*" changes to "*i*" before adding "*-ly*." The spelling change results in a difference in the vowel quality. Drill the following examples contrastively:

easy → easily	lucky → luckily	noisy → noisily
busy → busily	temporary → temporarily	lazy → lazily
angry → angrily	happy → happily	steady → steadily

   b. When an adjective ends in "l," students may have a tendency to incorrectly spell the adverb with a single "l." the following are some examples of this type of adjective-adverb pair:

beautiful → beautifully	official → officially	individual → individually
careful → carefully	equal → equally	legal → legally
cheerful → cheerfully	accidental → accidentally	normal → normally

   c. When a word ends in "*le*," drop the "*e*" and simply add "*y*." The letter "*e*" is no longer pronounced. Note the examples below:

simple → simply	gentle → gently	horrible → horribly
capable → capably	comfortable → comfortably	sensible → sensibly
legible → legibly	honorable → honorably	terrible → terribly

12 Introduce and drill other adjective-adverb pairs such as:

calm → calmly	clear → clearly	false → falsely
bad → badly	nice → nicely	correct → correctly
sad → sadly	nervous → nervously	perfect → perfectly

13 Point out that there are some common adjectives end in "*-ly*:" costly, deadly, friendly, kindly, likely, lively, manly, timely.

12

ESL Intermediate Level   Pair Practice • Writing • Vocabulary Building

Adverbs of Frequency

1 *Read the phrases below.*

Linda

Steve

Linda	Frequency	Steve
• arrives at work on time • greets her co-workers	**Always** 100%	• arrives 10 minutes before work • wears a uniform
• works on a computer at work • drinks tea on her break	**Usually** 90%	• works in a warehouse • drinks coffee on his break
• checks her e-mails at lunch • takes a bus to work	**Often** 75%	• makes phone calls at lunch • drives to work
• has lunch at a restaurant • works overtime	**Sometimes** 50%	• has lunch at work • works on weekends
• gets sick • drives to work	**Seldom** 20%	• sees Linda at work • take a bus to work
• makes mistakes • works on the weekend	**Rarely** 5%	• leaves work early • works late
• forgets her keys • eats at her desk	**Never** 0%	• gets hurt at work • complains about his job

Other Expressions
all the time
annually
bimonthly
daily
every two weeks
four times a month
from time to time
monthly
most of the time
now and then
once in a while
several times
twice a day
weekly
yearly

2 **Pair-Practice:** *Practice answering and asking questions with another student. See examples.* ▶

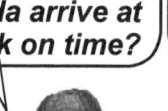 

How often does Linda arrive at work on time?   *She always arrives on time.*

Student 1: **How often does** _____?

Student 2: **He/she** _____.

3 **Pair-Practice:** *Practice answering and asking questions with another student. See examples.* ▶ *Use some of the expressions in the box to the right.*

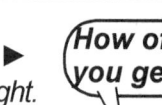 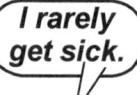

How often do you get sick?   *I rarely get sick.*

Student 1: **How often do you** _____?

Student 2: **I** _____.

4 *Answer the questions in writing. Use an adverb of frequency or one of the expressions in the box above.*

1. How often do you call your friends? *I call my friends twice a week.*
2. How often do you arrive late to school or work? *I never arrive late.*
3. Do you ever get sick? How often? _____
4. What do you usually eat for breakfast? _____
5. What kind of music do you often listen to? _____
6. How often do you forget your keys? _____
7. How often do you make mistakes? _____
8. How often do you take a bus? _____
9. Do you ever sleep late? How often? _____
10. How often do you speak English as home? _____

ESL Intermediate Level   Pair Practice • Writing • Vocabulary Building

Teacher's Notes

1 Before distributing the worksheet, start the lesson with a conversation. To assess your students' knowledge of the use of the adverbs of frequency, ask personalized questions like the ones below.

How often do you eat at a restaurant?   *How often do you get sick?*
How often do you use your cell phone?   *Do you ever arrive at school or work late? How often?*
Do you speak English at home? How often? *Do you ever make mistakes? If so, how often?*

2 Distribute the worksheet. Review and explain the phrases in the chart at the top of the worksheets so that the students understand any new vocabulary. Then, drill the adverbs of frequency by asking questions about Linda and Steve.

3 Ask questions such as "*How often does Linda arrive at work late?*" and "*How often does Steve wear a uniform?*" Continue asking similar questions about each activity in the chart. Have the students repeat both questions and answers.

4 Ask questions with "*ever*" such as "*Does she ever greet her co-workers?*" Model the responses using short answers, "*Yes she does?*" Then follow up with the question, "*How often?*" Model the corresponding answer, "*She always greets her co-workers.*"

5 Explain that adverbs of frequency precede the main verb of the sentence, but follow the verb "*to be.*"

  Examples: *I <u>often</u> go to school.*   *He has <u>seldom</u> worked.*
                  I'm <u>always</u> hungry.   *She is <u>never</u> late.*

6 In activity 2, the first pair-practice exercise, direct the students to ask and answers questions using "*How often does Linda/Steve...?*" Model responses using adverbs of frequency. Have the students continue the activity by working in pairs asking one another questions based on the information in the phrases at the top of the worksheet.

7 Review and explain the time expressions in the box at the right of the worksheet and make sure that the students understand the new vocabulary. Explain that adverbial expressions of time generally come at the end of the sentence.

8 In activity 3, the second pair-practice exercise, have the students use the question *"How often do you...?"* Then, model a few responses using the adverbs of frequency or the time expressions in the box at the right of the worksheet. Let them work in pairs.

9 Expand the activity by asking the class personalized questions such as the ones listed in activity 4 at the bottom of the worksheet. Then, as a class discussion, encourage the students to ask one another original questions.

10 After reviewing the questions in activity 4, have students complete the questions in writing.

11 Contrast the word order for adverbs of frequency and for adverbial (time) expressions by asking questions as those found in activities 2 and 3. For example, ask, "*How often do you eat in a restaurant?*" Compare the responses:

  I <u>seldom</u> eat in a restaurant.   *I eat in a restaurant <u>twice a month</u>.*

12 You may want to expose the students to other common adverbs of frequency:

  frequently   *generally*   *hardly ever*   *not ever*   *occasionally*

13 Explain that some adverbs of frequency may also appear as the initial word of the sentence. They include "*usually,*" "*generally,*" "*frequently,*" "*sometimes,*" and "*occasionally.*"   Compare:

  <u>Sometimes</u> *Tom and Jerry fight.*   *Tom and Jerry <u>sometimes</u> fight.*
  <u>Usually</u> *I come to work early.   I <u>usually</u> come to work early.*

ESL Intermediate Level   Student Mixer • Adverbs of Manner (-ly) • How

Adverbs of Manner

*Directions: Walk around the room and find the students with the information below.
Write the students' names on the lines.*

1 _____
learns fast.

7 _____
drives safely.

2 _____
studies seriously.

8 _____
listens quietly.

3 _____
talks to people politely.

9 _____
dresses beautifully.

4 _____
follows directions correctly.

10 _____
speaks clearly.

5 _____
works hard.

11 _____
makes friends easily.

6 _____
does the homework carefully.

12 _____
teachers well.

ESL Intermediate Level   Student Mixer • Adverbs of Manner (-ly) • How

Teacher's Notes

Review all the vocabulary and the use of the adverbs of manner. Explain the following:

❶
- Adverbs of manner usually answer the question **How?**
- Most adverbs usually follow the verb.
- Most adverbs are formed by simply adding the suffix **-ly** to an adjective (Example: quick**ly**)
- The letter **y** changes to **i** before adding **-ly**. (Example: bus**y**--bus**ily**)
- When a word ends in **le**, drop the **e** and simply **y**. The letter **e** is no longer pronounced. Example: comfortabl**e**--comfortabl**y**

❷
- Do NOT drop the final **l** when adding **-ly**. (Example: careful--carefu**lly**)

❸
- Unlike most adverbs, **well**, **fast**, and **hard** are irregular forms and do not end in **-ly**.
- Point out that **hard** is also used as an adjective meaning **difficult** as well as the opposite of **soft**.
- Do NOT confuse **hard** with **hardly**. **Hardly** is an adverb of frequency and is often used with **ever**. **Hardly** answers the question **How often...?** It means **almost never**.

❹
- **Well** can also be an adjective meaning **healthy**.

Use this group activity as a mixer exercise in which students have to talk to each other to get the necessary information. This is an excellent way for students to get to know one another especially at the beginning of a new term. Have the students get up and walk around the room to collect the names of other students who match the descriptions on the worksheet. Allow at least 15 minutes.

❺
Have the students practice asking and answering questions about the information collected. Ask questions such as **Who...?** or **How does...?**

Have the students ask one another personalized questions as:	How do you plan games?
	How do you swim/run?
How do you work	How do you study?
How do you do your homework?	How do you dance?
How do you speak?	How do you sleep?

❻ Follow-up by having the class make up an additional list of other kinds of personal information. For example: works accurately, listens attentively, runs quickly) Make a list of the new phrases and repeat the lesson using them.

As an additional activity, you may want to show that well can be used with verbs to form compound adjectives such as:

❼
well-mannered person	well-cooked meal
well-dressed man	well-perpared speech
well-educated woman	well-written letter
well-done meat	well-made dress

ESL Intermediate Level — Indefinite References, Pair Practice, Writing

Something, Nothing, Anything, Somebody, Nobody, Anybody

1 Directions: *Read and pronounce the names of the items below.*

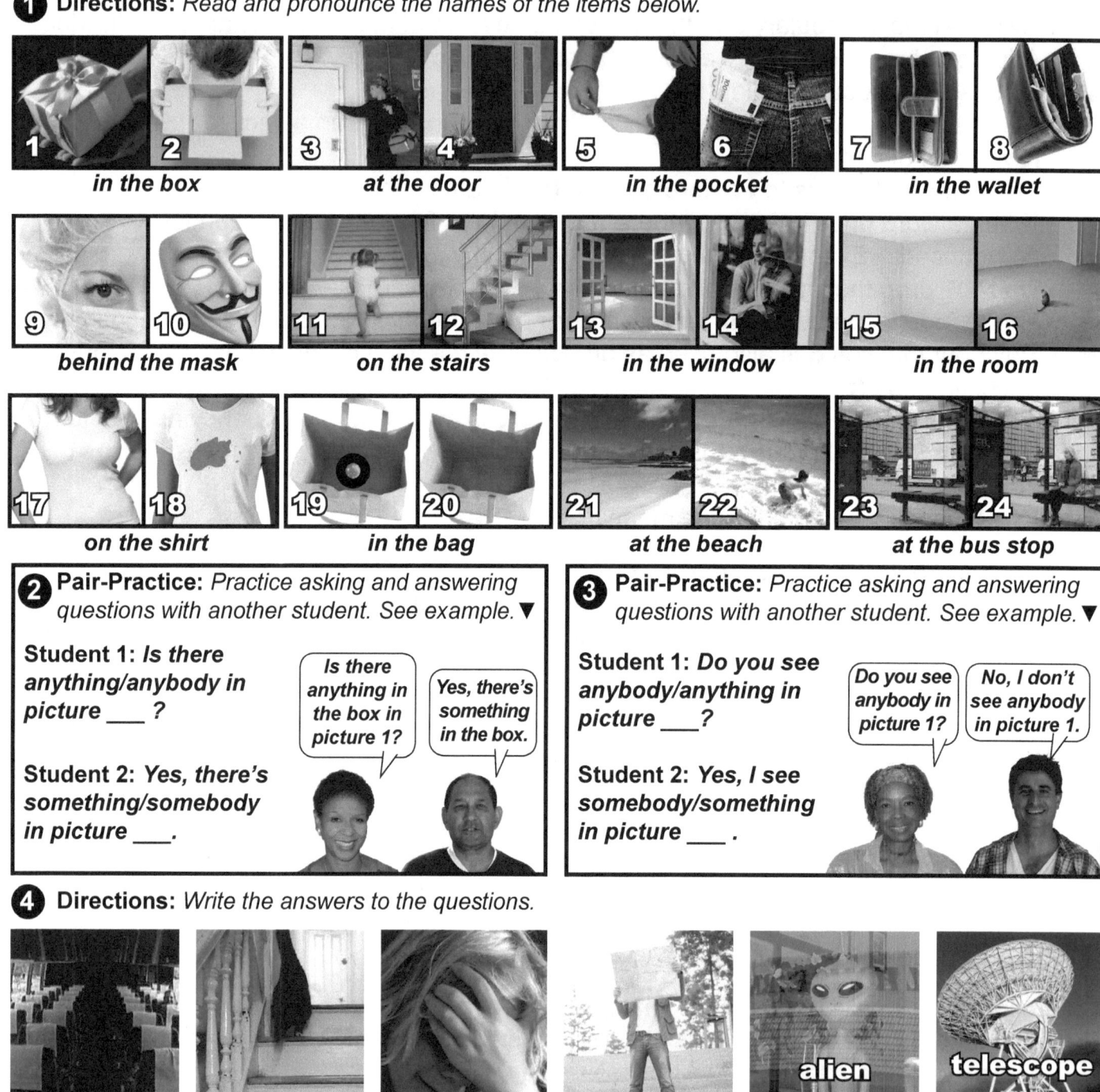

1, 2	3, 4	5, 6	7, 8
in the box	at the door	in the pocket	in the wallet

9, 10	11, 12	13, 14	15, 16
behind the mask	on the stairs	in the window	in the room

17, 18	19, 20	21, 22	23, 24
on the shirt	in the bag	at the beach	at the bus stop

2 Pair-Practice: *Practice asking and answering questions with another student. See example.* ▼

Student 1: *Is there anything/anybody in picture ___ ?*

Student 2: *Yes, there's something/somebody in picture ___ .*

Is there anything in the box in picture 1?
Yes, there's something in the box.

3 Pair-Practice: *Practice asking and answering questions with another student. See example.* ▼

Student 1: *Do you see anybody/anything in picture ___?*

Student 2: *Yes, I see somebody/something in picture ___ .*

Do you see anybody in picture 1?
No, I don't see anybody in picture 1.

4 Directions: *Write the answers to the questions.*

1. Is there anyone on the bus?
2. Do you see anything?
3. Is something the matter?
4. Who's sitting on the stairs?
5. Do you see anybody?
6. Is there anything/anybody out there?

17

ESL Intermediate Level · Indefinite References, Pair Practice, Writing

Teacher's Notes

1. Before distributing the worksheet, begin the lesson with a conversation using "**What**" and "**Who**" and eliciting the responses "**something**" and "**nothing**" to determine how much the students already know about how these expressions are used. Using the classroom ask questions such as *"What's under the desk?"*, *"Who's at the door?"*, *"What's in your pocket?"* and the expression, *"What's the matter?"*

2. Distribute the worksheet. Introduce the vocabulary by modeling the pronunciation of the names of the items and the prepositional phrases below the pictures. Have the students repeat the pronunciation of the phrases after you. While you are reading, ask the student to underline any unfamiliar words, then explain them.

3. Referring to the pictures, pose questions using the word "**What**" and "**Who**." For example, ask questions and have the students repeat. Then model the responses. **Examples:**

"What is in the box in picture 1?" "Something is."   *"Who's at the door in picture 3?" "Somebody is."*
"What's in the box in picture 2? "Nothing is."   *"Who's at the door in picture 4? "Nobody is."*

4. Next, ask yes/no questions using "**anybody**" and "**anything**" such as *"Is there anybody at the window?"* Have the students refer to the pictures, and then reply with either the short answer, *"Yes, there is"* or *"No, there isn't."*

Repeat the activity above. Have the students expand their answers to include the words "**somebody**," "**anybody**," "**something**," "**anything**."

"Is there anybody at the door in picture 3?"   *"Yes, there's somebody."*
"Is there anything in the wallet in picture 7?"   *"No, there isn't anything."*

5. Expand the questioning by asking the question, *"Do you see anything in picture___ ?"* After examining the picture, the students should give either the affirmative response, *"Yes, I see something."* or the negative response, *"No, I don't see anything."* Drill "**somebody**" and "**anybody**" in a similar manner.

6. Have the continue the drill by asking the students to pair up with another student to continue the drill in pair-practice exercises 2 and 3.

7. For maximum effectiveness, drill both affirmative and negative forms in contrast. Ask the question, *"Who do you see on the stairs in picture 12?"* Model the response, *"I don't see anybody on the stairs in picture 12, but I see somebody on the stairs in picture 11."* Have the class repeat the structure and elicit similar responses from individual students.

8. Using the sample questions such as *"Is there anything on the desk?"*, *"Do you see anybody at the door?"*, and *"Is there anyone at your home now?"*, have the students ask each other questions relating to persons and objects in the classroom.

9. Have students ask each other personalized questions using the following sample structures: *"Do you know anybody famous?"* and *"Do you see anything strange?"* Write the adjectives below on the chalkboard. Have the students use these words to formulate a variety of questions. Note that the adjective follows such words as "**somebody**," "**anybody**," "**nobody**."

ANYBODY: *strange, important, tall, short, pretty, handsome, rich, poor, sick*
ANYTHING: *special, funny, sad, interesting, red, blue, green, big, small, important*

10. In exercise 4, have the students answer the questions in writing at the bottom of the worksheet. *(Answers: 1. There isn't anybody in the bus. 2. There's something on the stairs. 3. Yes, something is the matter. 4. No, there isn't anyone sitting on the stairs. 5. Answers will vary. 6. Answers will vary.)* You may want to use the last question as the basis of a class discussion.

NOTE

• The words "**anybody**" and "**anything**" cannot be the subject of a negative verb.

• Stress the spelling of "**some**" and "**any**." It may be helpful to point out that such words as "**nobody**" and "**something**" are made up of two elements. Pay particular attention to the students' pronunciation of the letter "**o**" in "n<u>o</u>thing" which has the same value as the "**o**" in "n<u>o</u>ne."

• Although words formed with "**some**" are occasionally found in questions, words formed with "**any**" are more common in such patterns.

• Additional vocabulary: *someone, anyone, no one, somewhere, anywhere, nowhere.*

ESL Intermediate & Advanced Levels • Vocabulary Building • Pair Practice • Writing

Apartment Ads

1 Study the newspaper ads. Then cover the ads in the middle box. Read the ads on the left aloud.

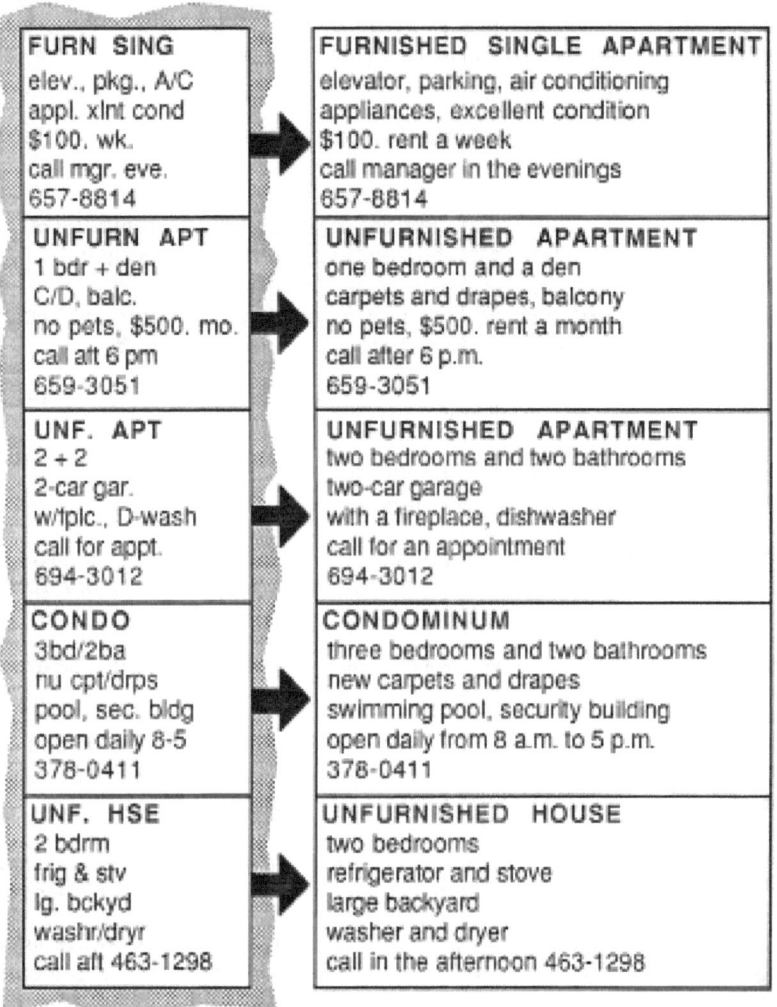

FURN SING	**FURNISHED SINGLE APARTMENT**
elev., pkg., A/C	elevator, parking, air conditioning
appl. xlnt cond	appliances, excellent condition
$100. wk.	$100. rent a week
call mgr. eve.	call manager in the evenings
657-8814	657-8814
UNFURN APT	**UNFURNISHED APARTMENT**
1 bdr + den	one bedroom and a den
C/D, balc.	carpets and drapes, balcony
no pets, $500. mo.	no pets, $500. rent a month
call aft 6 pm	call after 6 p.m.
659-3051	659-3051
UNF. APT	**UNFURNISHED APARTMENT**
2 + 2	two bedrooms and two bathrooms
2-car gar.	two-car garage
w/fplc., D-wash	with a fireplace, dishwasher
call for appt.	call for an appointment
694-3012	694-3012
CONDO	**CONDOMINUM**
3bd/2ba	three bedrooms and two bathrooms
nu cpt/drps	new carpets and drapes
pool, sec. bldg	swimming pool, security building
open daily 8-5	open daily from 8 a.m. to 5 p.m.
378-0411	378-0411
UNF. HSE	**UNFURNISHED HOUSE**
2 bdrm	two bedrooms
frig & stv	refrigerator and stove
lg. bckyd	large backyard
washr/dryr	washer and dryer
call aft 463-1298	call in the afternoon 463-1298

OTHER COMMON ABBREVIATIONS USED IN APARTMENT ADS

bach.	bachelor apartment
beaut.	beautiful
bltins	built-in cabinets
dec.	decorated
dep.	deposit
din. rm.	dining room
fam. rm.	family room
1st/last	first and last month's rent
flrs.	floors
fwy.	freeway
gard.	garden
gd.	good
hdwd. flrs.	hardwood floors
hr.	hour
jac.	jacuzzi
kit.	kitchen
lse.	lease
loc.	location
lux.	luxury
mgr.	manager
nr.	near
own.	owner
pd.	paid
p/p; prvtprty	private party
refs. req.	references required
sep.	separate
twnhse.	townhouse
utils.	utilities
vu.	view
yd.; yrd.	yard

2 Talk with another student about the ads above.

Student 1: Does the .... have ....?
Student 2: Yes, it does. / No, it doesn't.

 Does the condo have a fireplace?

 No, it doesn't.

3 Write the full words for the abbreviations to the left.

UNF. APT _____	utils. pd. _____
3 + 2 _____	lg. yrd. _____
stv/frig _____	nu D/C _____
xlnt cond. _____	1st mo. dep. _____
call mgr. eve. _____	A/C _____

19

ESL Intermediate & Advanced Levels • Vocabulary Building • Pair Practice • Writing

Teacher's Notes

1. • Read the ads to the left. Then read the corresponding ads in the middle box. Point out and discuss the abbreviations.

• Tell the students to cover the ads in the middle box. Ask for volunteers to read the ads using only the abbreviations. (You may want to use an overhead projector to project only the abbreviations.)

2. • Teach the short dialog. Show how to do this activity with the help of a student. Then have the students continue the exercise by working in pairs or small groups.

3. • Answers:

UNF. APT	=	Unfurnished apartment
3 + 2	=	three bedrooms and two bathrooms
stv/frig	=	stove and refrigerator
xlnt cond	=	excellent condition
call mgn. eve.	=	call the manager in the evening

utils. pd.	=	utilities paid
lg. yrd.	=	large yard
nu D/C	=	new draps and carpets
1st mo. dep.	=	first month's deposit
A/C	=	air conditioning

4. • Read and explain other common abbreviations used in apartment ads in the box at the right of the handout.

5. • As a follow-up activity, have the students write an original ad for an apartment on a piece of paper. Put their names on the back of the paper. Then have the students role-play choosing an apartment they would like to rent. The students must discuss the rental arrangements with the author of the ad, who acts as the owner of the apartment.

6. • For more advanced students, you may want to teach additional vocabulary:

appliances	garden	smoke detector
attic	heater	stairs
basement	laundry room	trash bin
chandelier	patio	Venetian blinds
closet	radiator	wet bar
fence	security locks	
fireplace	shades	

ESL Beginning & Intermediate Levels — Filling out a Simple Application

Basic Written Directions & Instructions

1 *Read Sybil Lopez's application.*

APPLICATION
(Please Print)

1. Name *(Cross out three.)* ~~Mr.~~ ~~Mrs.~~ ~~Ms.~~ Miss
   _Lopez,_____ _Sybil,_____ _Maria_____ _N/A_____
   Last   First   Middle   Maiden
2. Address: ____123_____ ____Clark Street_____ ____#101_____
   Street Number   Street   Apartment Number
   ____Los Angeles_____ ____California_____ ____90048_____
   City   State/Province   ZIP Code/Postal Code
3. Telephone: (810) 987-1234   (323) 370-4321   E-mail: _sybil.lopez@xyz.com_
   Home   Work or Cell number
4. Place of Birth: _Los Cabos, Mexico_   5. Date of Birth: _11_ / _29_ / _1980_
   City, Country   Month/Date/Year
6. Sex: *(Check one.)* ☐ Male (♀)   7. Age: *(Check one.)* ____ Under 18
   ☑ Female (♂).   _✓_ Over 18
8. Hair color: *(Circle one.)* Black, (Dark Brown), Light Brown, Brunet(te), Blond(e), Red, Gray, White.
9. Eye color: *(Circle one.)* (Brown), Blue, Green, Hazel, Black
10. Marital Status: *(Underline one.)* Married, <u>Single</u>, Divorced, Separated, Widowed, Domestic Partner
11. Are you a citizen of this country? *(Circle one.)* Yes (No)
12. What is your occupation? _Dental assistant_
13. Signature: _Sybil M. Lopez_   Today's date: _March 20, 2010_

Sybil Lopez

2 *Fill out the application with your personal information.*

APPLICATION
(Please Print)

1. Name *(Cross out three.)* Mr.   Mrs.   Ms.   Miss
   _____
   Last   First   Middle   Maiden
2. Address: _____
   Street Number   Street   Apartment #   City   State   Zip Code
3. Telephone: (___)_____   (___)_____   E-mail: _____
   Home   Work or Cell number
4. Place of Birth: _____   5. Date of Birth: ___ / ___ / ___
   City, Country   Month/Date/Year
6. Sex: *(Check one.)* ☐ Male (♀)   7. Age: *(Check one.)* ____ Under 18
   ☐ Female (♂).   ____ Over 18
8. Hair color: *(Circle one.)* Black, Dark Brown, Light Brown, Brunet(te), Blond(e), Red, Gray, White.
9. Eye color: *(Circle one.)* Brown, Blue, Green, Hazel, Black
10. Marital Status: *(Underline one.)* Married, Single, Divorced, Separated, Widowed, Domestic Partner
11. Are you a citizen of this country? *(Circle one.)* Yes   No
12. What is your occupation? _____
13. Signature: _____   Today's date: _____

ESL Beginning & Intermediate Levels   Filling out a Simple Application

Teacher's Notes

1 Before distributing the worksheet, start the lesson with a conversation. To assess your students' knowledge of the vocabulary used in filling out an simple application, ask personalized questions such as: "*What's your name, address, marital status, place of birth, date of birth, hair/eye color, and occupation?*"

2 Demonstrate on the chalkboard the meaning of "*check*," "*underline*," "*print*," "*circle*," and "*cross out*."

3 Have students take a piece of paper. Dictate each instruction below. Then demonstrate each appropriate action on the chalkboard.

- *a. On line one, print your name.*
- *b. On the second line, write the numbers 1 to 10.*
- *c. Underline your last name.*
- *d. Circle your first name.*
- *e. Check the first line.*
- *f. Cross out number 6.*
- *g. Underline number 9.*
- *h. Circle number 1.*
- *i. Cross out number 10.*
- *j. Check the second line.*

4 Distribute the worksheet and ask information questions about the application form at the top of the worksheet. Ask the following questions and mode the corresponding responses:

Who's filling out the application?	*Sybil Lopez is.*
What's her last name?	*It's Lopez.*
What's her address?	*It's 123 Clark Street, Apartment 101.*

Continue asking similar questions about the information in the application.

5 Ask yes/no questions about the application such as "*Is Sybil's home telephone number 323-370-4321?*" Model the response, "*No, it isn't. It's 310-987-1234.*"

6 Have individual students ask questions of other students about the application.

7 Vary the exercise by having students ask each other personalized questions based on the application.

NOTES

8 Point out the following items that may cause confusion before having students fill out the application:

- The meaning of "*Mr.*" "*Mrs.*," "*Miss*," and "*Ms.*"
- The last name preceding the first name on many forms and applications.
- The street number preceding the street name.
- "*N/A*" means "*Not Applicable*," but can also mean "*Not Available*."
- Apartment numbers written as "*#6*," "*Apt. 6*," "*Apt. #6*" or "*Unit 6*" are placed after the street name.
- Telephone: cell phone, home phone, work phone, area codes, prefixes, and text messages.
- The e-mail symbols "*@*" (*at*), "*.com*," and "*.net*."
- Symbols for **Male** (♀) and **Female** (♂).
- Marital Status: *Married, Single, Divorced, Separated, Widowed,* and *Domestic Partner*
- The month as the first element of the date which is expressed either by word or number. Caution students not to use Roman numerals.
- Hair colors: *black, dark brown, brown, light brown, brunet(te), blond(e), red, gray, white*
- Eye colors: *brown, blue, green, hazel, black*

In the United States, it is against the law to ask certain questions on employment applications (i.e., *race, religion, sex and age*).

9 Have students fill out the application form. Insist on printing and accuracy. Walk around the classroom giving assistance.

10 After completing and reviewing the application, arrange students into small groups and have them ask one another questions based on their applications. Finally, as a class discussion, ask students to share some of their answers.

Cultural Notes:

- "*Separated*" is when a husband and wife are living apart often leading to divorce.

- In English-speaking countries, a "*last name*" normally refers to the family name of the father or husband. A "*middle name*" is selected like a "*first name.*" The concept and order of first, middle and last names vary from culture to culture.

- A "*maiden*" name is the woman's family or sir name before her marriage.

- Discuss the meaning of the words "*minor*" and "*adult*" as they relate to local and national laws.

ESL Beginning Level • Vocabulary Building • Pair Practice • Fill In • Class Discussion

Better & Worse

1 *Listen to your teacher and repeat the words below.*

dresses

plays basketball

drives

cooks

feels

sings

2 **Pair-Practice:** *Practice answering and asking questions with another student. Use the photos. See examples.* ▶

Student 1: **Who _____ better/worse, ___[name]___ or ___[name]___?**

Student 2: __[name]__ ___ better/worse than ___[name].

 Who dresses better, Dave or Ivan?

 Ivan dresses better than Dave.

---

3 *Complete the sentences with "**better than**" or "**worse than**."*

1. Dave dresses ___worse than___ Ivan.
2. Ivan dresses ___better than___ Dave.
3. Casey plays basketball _____ Kurt.
4. Kurt plays basketball _____ Casey.
5. Jill drives _____ James.
6. James drives _____ Jill.
7. Ben cooks _____ Amy.
8. Amy cooks _____ Ben.
9. Sam feels _____ Ron.
10. Ron feels _____ Sam.
11. Lucy sings _____ Ted.
12. Ted sings _____ Lucy.

4 **Pair-Practice:** *Practice answering and asking questions with another student.. Use some of the words on the chalkboard below.*

Student 1: **What's better/worse, _____ or _____?**

Student 2: _____ **is better/worse than** _____.

 What is better, coffee or tea? — Tea is better than coffee.

a movie/a book	dogs/cats	Italian/Chinese food
big/small car	fall/spring	long/short hair
classical/modern music	football/cards	money/happiness
coffee/tea	fruit/vegetables	red/blue
daytime/nighttime	hot/cold weather	vanilla/chocolate

ESL Beginning Level • Vocabulary Building • Pair Practice • Fill In • Class Discussion

Teacher's Notes

1 Before distributing the worksheet, start the lesson with a conversation to assess your students' use of "***better***" and "***worse***." Ask questions such as, "***Which is better/worse, a book or a movie?***" You may want to use some of the vocabulary at the bottom of the worksheet to ask additional questions.

2 Distribute the worksheet and read the vocabulary and the names below each photo. Elicit the comparative forms "***better***" and "***worse***" by posing the following kinds of questions about each pair of photos:

Who's a worse dresser? *Who's a better dresser?*
Who dresses worse? *Who dresses better?*

3 Continue the exercise by having students ask each other questions using "***better***" or "***worse***."

4 In activity 2, the first pair-practice exercise, direct the students to ask and answers questions using "***What is better/worse, _____ or _____?***" Model responses using "***better than***", or "***worse than***." Have the students continue the activity by working in pairs asking one another questions based on the information in the photos at the top of the worksheet.

5 Next, have the students ask one another personalized questions such as "*In your opinion, what's better/worse, stealing or lying?*" The following gerunds can be used as nouns in such questions:

reading/watching TV *playing/working* *being married/single*
walking/riding a bike *crying/laughing* *having a big/small family*
giving/receiving a present *washing/ironing* *having a big/small car*

6 Direct students to activity 3 and show how to fill in the blanks with "***better than***" and "***worse than***." Tell the students to complete the remaining sentences. Answers:

1. Dave dresses *worse than* Ivan.
2. Ivan dresses *better than* Dave.
3. Casey plays basketball *better than* Kurt.
4. Kurt plays basketball *worse than* Casey.
5. Jill drives *better than* James.
6. James drives *worse than* Jill.
7. Ben cooks *better than* Amy.
8. Amy cooks *worse than* Ben.
9. Sam feels *worse than* Ron.
10. Ron Feels *better than* Sam.
11. Lucy sings *better than* Ted.
12. Ted sings *worse than* Lucy.

7 In activity 4 the second pair-practice activity have the students ask one another personalized questions such as "*In your opinion, what's better/worse, a movie or a book?*" using the vocabulary at the bottom of the worksheet.

a movie/a book *dogs/cats* *Italian/Chinese food*
big/small car *fall/spring* *long/short hair*
classical//modern music *football/cards* *money/happiness*
coffee/tea *fruit/vegetables* *red/blue*
daytime/nighttime *hot/cold weather* *vanilla/chocolate*

8 As a class discussion encourage the students to continue the activity by posing original questions to you, the teacher, and other students.

ESL Beginning Level   Vocabulary: Body Parts • Pair Practice Activity

Body Parts

Directions: *Study the body parts.*

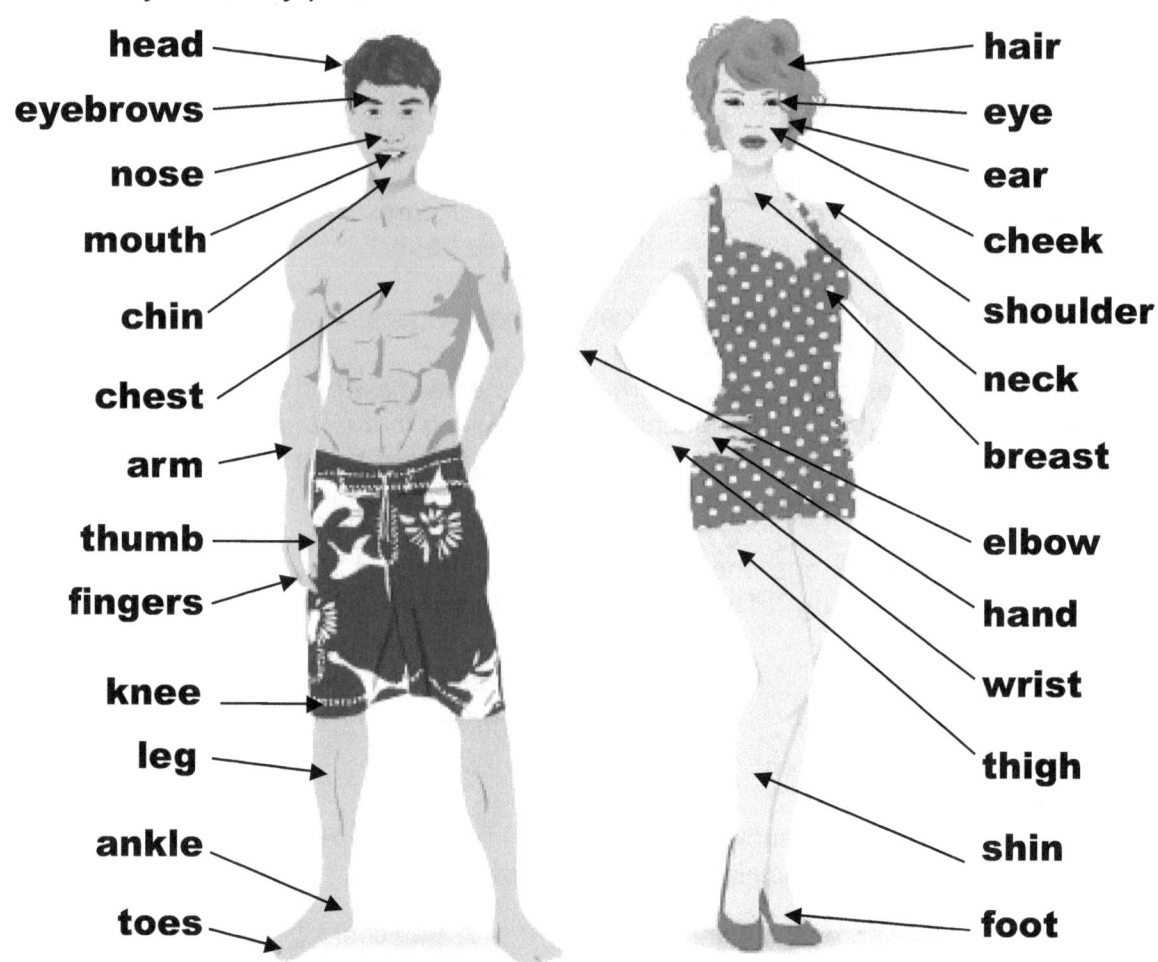

Pair Practice: *Talk with another student. Use the dialog and the vocabulary in the picture.*

Student 1: *Where does it hurt?*   Student 1: *What's the matter?*
Student 2: *My _____ hurts.*   Student 2: *I have a pain in my _____ .*

25

ESL Beginning Level — Vocabulary: Body Parts • Pair Practice Activity

Teacher's Notes

1 Read and explain the different parts of the body. Practice the pronunciation of the vocabulary. Flash cards are useful in this activity.

2 Have volunteers go to the chalkboard or whiteboard and draw parts of the body. As they draw a part, they have to name it.

3 Play "Simon Says." Have all the students stand up. The leader says, *"Simon says to touch your ..... ."* The students have to obey. If the order is not preceded by the words *"Simon says,"* then the students must not move. If they do, they are out of the game and have to sit down. The person who remains standing wins. Make the game more challenging by having the leader touch one part of the body and call another.

4 Using an overhead transparency, practice the pair practice activity as a whole-class oral drill.

5 After the students are familiar with the phrases, have them do the pair practice activity. Pairing activities give the students time, especially in large classes, to practice important speaking skills. Have each student choose a partner. (The first few times, you will probably have to go around the classroom and pair up students.) Encourage the students to pair up with different partners each time. While students are doing the exercise, walk around the room, listen to individuals, and correct their pronunciation.

6 As a follow-up activity, you might want to teach some additional body parts.

Body: face, forehead, armpit, waist, abdomen, buttocks, hip, calf
Hand: knuckle, fingernail, index finger, middle finger, ring finger, little finger, palm
Head: sideburns, nostril, beard, mustache, tongue, tooth/teeth, lip
Eye: eyelid, eyelashes, iris, pupil
Foot: heel, instep, ball, big toe, little toe toenail

7 On a subsequent day, make photo copies of the drawing below and have the students fill in the words as a quiz.

Body Parts Quiz

Directions *Write the words for the body parts below.*

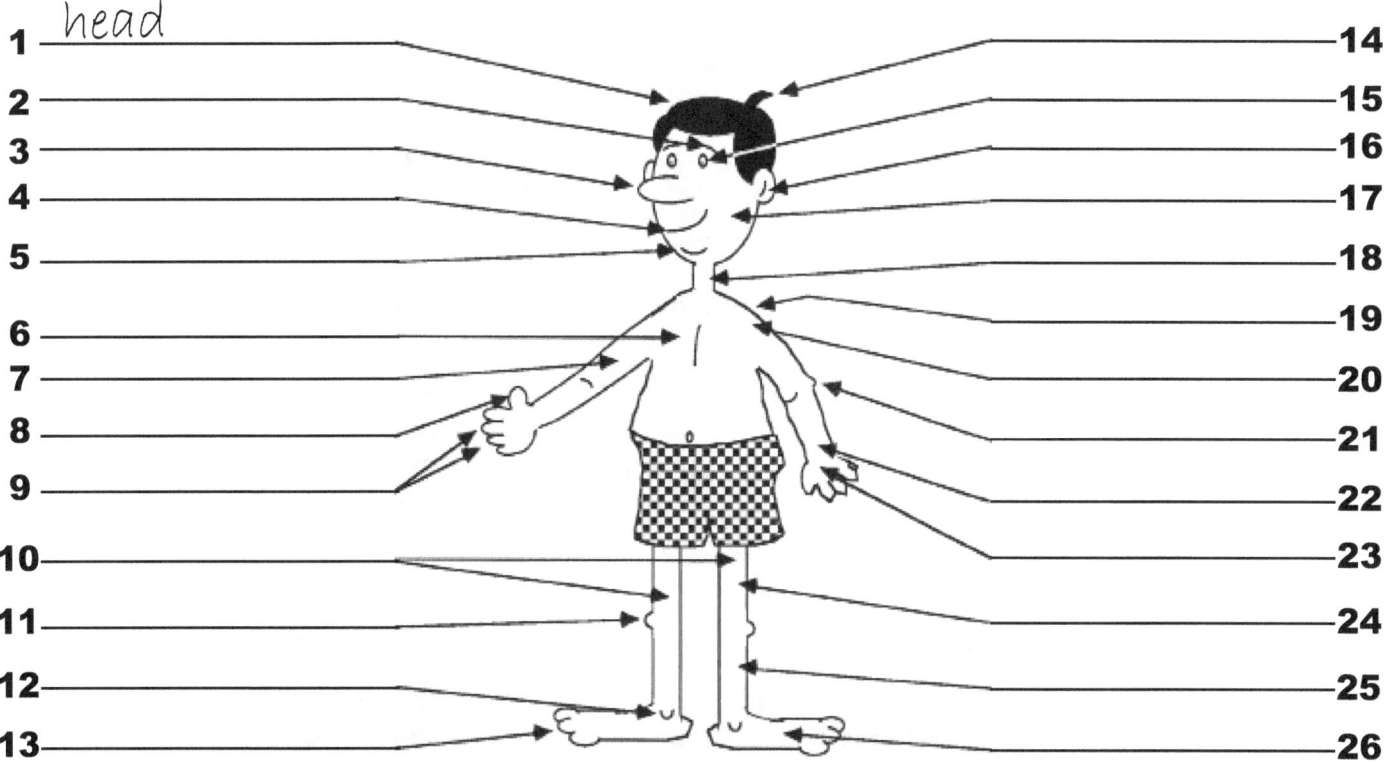

1. head
2. ___
3. ___
4. ___
5. ___
6. ___
7. ___
8. ___
9. ___
10. ___
11. ___
12. ___
13. ___
14. ___
15. ___
16. ___
17. ___
18. ___
19. ___
20. ___
21. ___
22. ___
23. ___
24. ___
25. ___
26. ___

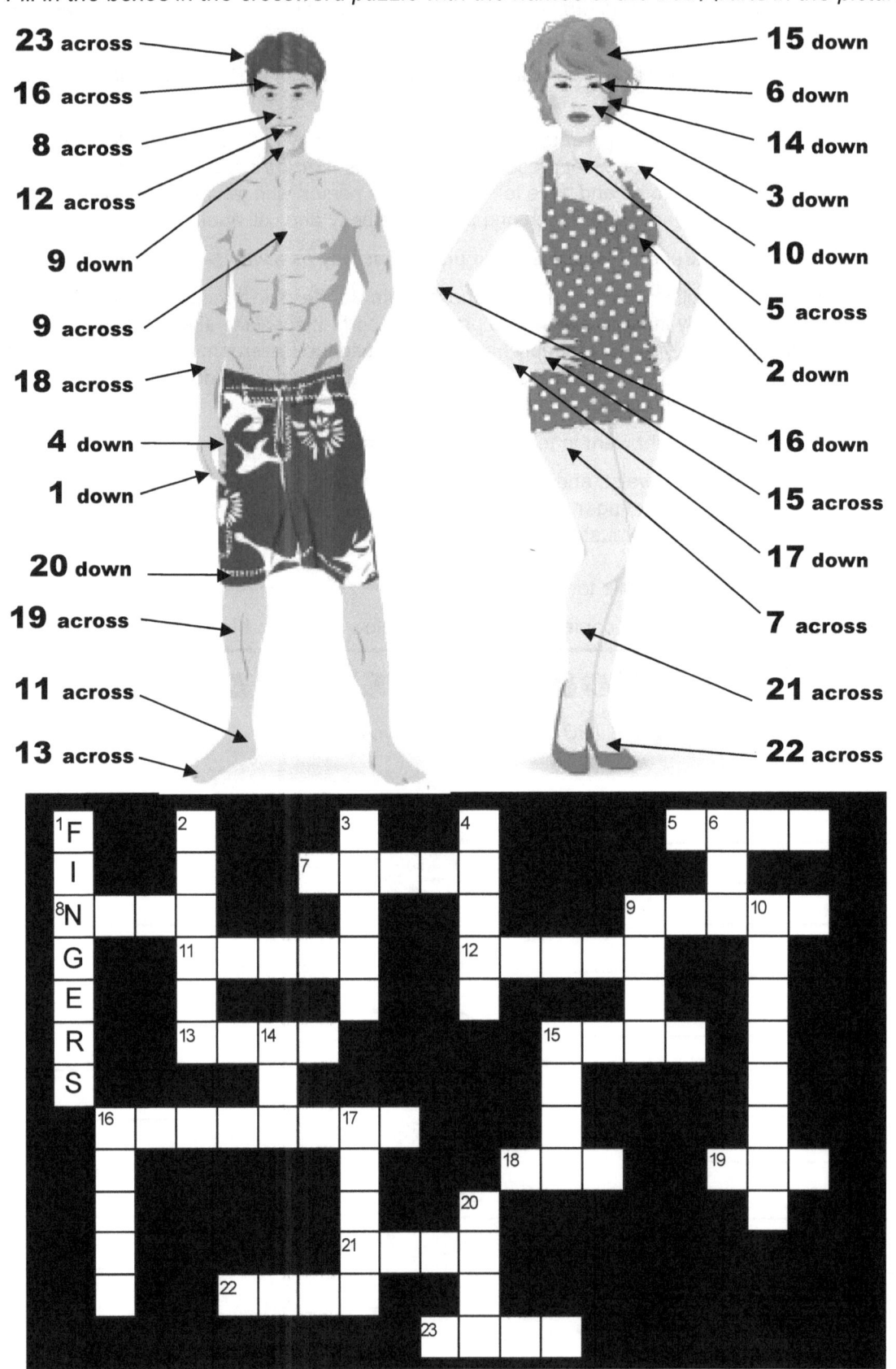

ESL Beginning Level   Vocabulary Building: Body Parts • Crossword Puzzle

Teacher's Notes

1 Before distributing the worksheet, begin the lesson with a conversation. Ask your students to name common body parts. Ask them to name and point out as many body parts that they can. List them on the board. Make sure that the lists include some of the following:

ankle	chest	eye	hair	leg	shin	toes
arm	chin	eyebrows	hand	mouth	shoulder	wrist
breast	ear	fingers	head	Neck	thigh	
cheek	elbow	foot	knee	Nose	thumb	

2 You may want to teach lesson 0019 (Vocabulary: Body Parts) before handing out this worksheet.

3 Distribute the worksheet and identify each body part.

4 Demonstrate how to do a crossword puzzle. Explain the concept of **DOWN** and **ACROSS**. Then, show the students how to fill in the puzzle using the visual clues. Do a few examples with the whole class.

5 Allow some time for your students to complete the crossword puzzle. You may want to have students work in pairs or assigning it as a homework assignment.

6 Correct the answers by projecting an overhead transparency image directly onto the board on which students can take turns writing the answers on the board. See solution below.

7 As a follow-up activity, you might want to teach some additional body parts.

Body: face, forehead, armpit, waist, abdomen, buttocks, hip, calf
Hand: knuckle, fingernail, index finger, middle finger, ring finger, little finger, palm
Head: sideburns, nostril, beard, mustache, tongue, tooth/teeth, lip
Eye: eyelid, eyelashes, iris, pupil
Foot: heel, instep, ball, big toe, little toe, toenail

8 Play a crossword puzzle game. Draw or project a grid onto the board or screen as well as a list of the new body parts. Divide the class into two teams and flip a coin to determine which team goes first. Have the first student of the first team go to the chalkboard and write a word that uses one letter of an existing word in the crossword. If the word fits and is correctly spelled, then give one point for every letter of the new word. Then, go on to the first student of the other team. If the word is incorrect, erase it and go to the opposite team.

9 Play "*Simon Says*." Have all the students stand up. The leader says, *"Simon says to touch your ...."* The students have to obey. If the order is not preceded by the words *"Simon says,"* then the students must not move. If they do, they are out of the game and have to sit down. The person who remains standing wins. Make the game more challenging by having the leader touch one part of the body and call another.

10 As a follow-up activity, drill the following mini dialogs to practice using the new vocabulary. Have your students point to the appropriate body part. Examples:

Student 1: ***Where does it hurt?***   Student 2: ***My _____ hurts.***
Student 1: ***What's the matter?***   Student 2: ***I have a pain in my _____ .***

CROSSWORD PUZZLE SOLUTION:
ACROSS: 5 neck, 7 thigh, 8 nose, 9 chest, 11 ankle, 12 mouth, 13 toes, 15 hand, 16 eyebrows, 18 arm, 19 leg, 21 shin, 22 foot, 23 head;
DOWN: 1 fingers, 2 breast, 3 cheek, 4 thumb, 6 eye, 9 chin, 10 shoulder, 14 ear, 15 hair, 16 elbow, 17 wrist, 20 knee

ESL Intermediate Level — Values Clarification • Discussion • Role Playing

Breaking A Work Rule

1 *Read the situation below.*

THE SITUATION

Troy is going to be late to work today. He calls you at home and asks you to punch his time card so that the employer will not know he was late. What should you do?

2 *Read the possible solutions to the problem above. Rank the solutions in order from the best to the worst. (The top box is the best and bottom box is the worst.) Write your ranking in the column* **MY RANKING** *to the left below. Please feel free to come up with other practical solutions.*

MY RANKING ← BEST / WORST →

POSSIBLE SOLUTIONS

1.
Tell Troy that you would be happy to do this for him.

2.
Tell Troy that you cannot do it. Suggest that he explain to the employer why he is late and try to arrange for a time to make up the time.

3.
Tell Troy you will do it this time only, but never again in the future.

4.
Tell Troy that you are very sorry, but you are uncomfortable doing this for him.

5.
Tell your employer that Troy asked you to punch in for him.

6.
Do nothing at all.

7. (Other)

_____
_____

GROUP RANKING ← BEST / WORST →

3 *Break up into small groups and discuss your ranking with the rankings of the other members in your group. Feel free to discuss other practical possibilities. Finally, decide on a group ranking. Again, rank the possible solutions in order from the best to the worst. All members of the group must agree before you write the numbers in the column* **GROUP RANKING**.

4 *As a whole class, discuss the best and worst solutions to the situation.*

ESL Intermediate Level • Values Clarification: Breaking a Work Rule • Discussion

INTRODUCTION

These lessons are appropriate for students in English-as-a-Second-Language (ESL) and Vocational ESL classes as well as for native English speakers entering the work force. The goal of this book is to help people make ethical decisions in the work place. Each lesson presents a commonly-found work situation that requires discussing and clarifying individual and group values. These lessons are not meant to provide a right or wrong response to a decision. They are only a means to clarify an individual's or a group's choices in making an ethically-based decision. Instead of a right or wrong answer, the decision made about a specific situation might be a question between different views of what is right. The lessons help the participants explore the different reasons for their views. Instead of asking the participants to make generalized decisions about ethical questions, the lessons present specific situations in which a variety of good decisions can be made. Some participants may disagree among different versions of what appears right. Participants are encouraged to discuss different perspectives, values, and actions to the same situation. Also be aware that our actions also tend to rely on our experiences, social status, culture, and assumptions. Hopefully, the participants will respond to each other with respect and increase mutual recognition of each other as persons who want to do the right thing.

TEACHING NOTES

1. Before distributing the handout, read the situation and ask basic comprehension questions to check for understanding.

2. Distribute the worksheet to the student, and read the situation to the class. Discuss any unfamiliar vocabulary and expressions.

3. Read the possible solutions to the problem. Again, discuss any unfamiliar vocabulary and ask basic questions to check for understanding. Tell the students that they are free to come up with other practical possibilities in addition to the ones presented.

4. Direct the students to rank the possibilities in order from the best solution to the worst, the best being the box at the top and the worst at the bottom. Have the students prioritize their personal ranking in the column named "**MY RANKING**."

5. Then, gather in groups of four or five students.

6. Tell each group of students to discuss their ranking. Instruct them that they must come up with a single ranking that they must all agree on. Identify one person in each group to record the group's ranking in the column labeled "**GROUP RANKING**." Tell students to talk about what should be done, state the other practical possibilities, and ask about the reasons that support these proposals: observations, values, and assumptions.

7. Have each group report on its ranking to the whole class. You may also want to write the various rankings on the blackboard/whiteboard or overhead transparency for comparison.

8. Discuss other possible solutions with the students and write them on the chalkboard.

8. Finally discuss the pros and cons of each ranking, and lead the class in coming to a general consensus.

9. Write other possible solutions to the problems --on the blackboard as a follow-up exercise.

10. As a follow-up activity, use the exercises as a basis for role playing. When doing a role playing exercise, allow students to .prepare themselves in pairs or small groups before having them perform before the whole class. Give the students the freedom to vary the situation and be creative. Don't over-correct. Note major mistakes; discuss and correct them later. To practice active listening, have the other students in the class note the errors, too. Discuss the role-playing exercises afterwards for students' reaction and interpretations.

ESL Advanced Level • Reading, Writing, Vocabulary Building • Pair Practice • Dictation

Bulletin Board Notes

Directions: *Fold the page down the middle on the dotted line and choose a side. Do this activity with a partner. Look at your side of the handout only. Read the messages on the notes on your side of the sheet to your partner, who will write the message in the blank note paper on the other half of the handout. Then, reverse the activity by writing the message that your partner dictates to you on the blank note paper on your side. Compare your messages only after you both finish.*

Student 1   Student 2

BULLETIN BOARD

Student 1:

1. [blank note]

2. To English Conversation Club members. Let's have lunch together. Meet here Monday at noon.

3. LOST
Red handbag.
REWARD!
Return to Ann Long in Room 1A or call extension 237

4. [blank note]

5. [blank note]

6. JOB WANTED
Part-time sales clerk. Experienced and hard-working.
E-mail Angela at angela@abcd.org

Student 2:

1. FOUND
Dark blue sweater. See secretary in office.

2. [blank note]

3. [blank note]

4. Room & Board in exchange for light housework and babysitting. Call Rita at 371-0412

5. FOR SALE
Sports car, 5 years old. Excellent condition. Make offer.
jimscar@aabb.com

6. [blank note]

ESL Advanced Level • Reading, Writing, Vocabulary Building • Pair Practice • Dictation

Teacher's Notes

1 Present and discuss the following vocabulary before students do the activity:

found	handbag	excellent condition	e-mail
lost	Reward!	part-time	extension
Room and Board	in exchange for	sales clerk	secretary
For Sale	light housework	hardworking	make offer
Job Wanted	babysitting	experienced	office

2 Distribute the worksheet and read the directions to the class. Tell students to fold the sheet down the middle. Next, tell them to find a partner. Have each pair of students select a side of the bulletin board on the worksheet. Explain that each partner will read the messages on his or her side of the sheet, and that the partner will write the message in the blank box on the other side of the worksheet. Next, reverse rolls. Have the students compare their messages only after they have both completed the exercise.

3 On a subsequent day dictate the notes as a short quiz.

4 **Follow-Up Activities**

• Have the students write one another notes modeled on those in the exercise.

• Make a bulletin board in the classroom.

• Develop a one-page class newsletter made up of student's notes.

• Review how to read and write cursive script.

• Read the LOST & FOUND section of your local newspaper and flyers.

• Study common abbreviations used in lost and found classified advertisements:

5

ext.	=	extension		exp.	=	experienced
eve.	=	evening		gd.	=	good
hr.	=	hour		loc.	=	local
immed.	=	immediate		pt/ft	=	part time/full time
max.	=	maximum		nec.	=	necessary
pri.	=	private		req.	=	required
p.p.	=	private party		@	=	at
nr.	=	near		#	=	number
pd.	=	paid		$	=	dollar
yr.	=	year		%	=	percent
w/	=	with		+	=	plus
info.	=	information		&	=	and
xlnt.	=	excellent		=	=	equals

ESL Beginning Level • Animal Names • Common Verbs • Writing • Class Discussion

Can & Can't

1 parrots	2 dog	3 horse	4 pig	5 bird	6 cat
talk	read	see	sing	fly	swim

1 **Pair-Practice:** Practice answering and asking questions with another student. See the examples. ▶

Student 1: **Can .... ?**

Student 2: **Yes, it/they can.**
or **No, it/they can't.**

Can parrots talk? Yes, they can. Can this dog read? No, it can't.

2 Answer the questions orally and in writing.

1. Can the dog see?
No, the dog can't see, but the cat can see.

2. Can dogs drive?
No, they can't, but they can ride in the car.

3. Can this monkey speak?

4. Can this dog jump high?

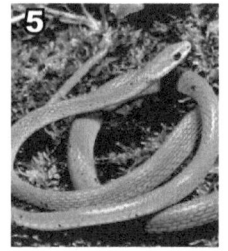

5. Can this snake walk?

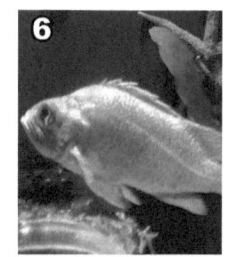

6. Can this fish live on land?

7. Can these cats dance?

8. Can this dog play music?

9. Can this puppy fly?

10. Can this kitten sing?

11. Can this bird talk?

12. Can cows swim like dolphins?

3 Answer the questions orally and in writing. Discuss the answers with the other students in class.
1. How well can you cook? _____
2. Can you drive a car? _____
3. How many languages can you speak? _____
4. Can you swim well? _____
5. What instruments can you play? _____

ESL Beginning Level • Animal Names • Common Verbs • Writing, Class Discussion

Teacher's Notes

1 Before distributing the worksheet, begin the lesson with a conversation about commonly known animals. Ask general questions to determine how many animals the students can already name. Make a list on the chalkboard or whiteboard.

2 Distribute the worksheet and identify and practice the pronunciation of all the animals' names on the worksheet: *bird, cat, cow, dog, dolphin, fish, horse, hummingbird, kitten, monkey, parrots, pig, puppy, snake.* Then, ask the students what these animals can do. Make sure to cover the following common verbs: *see, drive, speak, run, walk, live, dance, play, fly, sing, swim, crawl, meow, purr, bark,* and *jump*.

3 Introduce structures by means of the following types of yes/no questions and answers using the photos in the first exercise. Examples: *Can parrots speak? Yes, they can. Can the dog read? No, it can't.*

Have students repeat the appropriate questions and answers for each item. Then ask individual students similar questions requiring answers of the type "*Yes, it/they can.*" and "*No, it/they can't.*" Drill questions and answers by having one student ask another.

4 Next ask questions with the word "**what**" such as, "*What can parrots do*?" Model the response, "They can speak." Pose similar questions to individual students.

5 Continue the drill by having individual students ask questions to other students. For variety, direct one student to ask another student a question with the pronoun "**you**," for example, "*Can you swim?*" The second student must respond with the appropriate answer, "*Yes, I can.*" or "*No, I can't.*" Next, expand the exercise by letting students ask original questions with such verbal expressions as "*sing,*" "*drive,*" "*speak English,*" "*ride a bicycle/motorcycle,*" "*work,*" "*draw well,*" "*make a pizza,*" "*spell the number 8,*" "*play the guitar.*" You may want to stimulate questions by writing this list on the chalkboard.

6 Read the sentences below each photo in Exercise 2 and ask students to answer each question orally using the structure below. This is an oral exercise and students should not be writing anything at this point. Each question requires a negative answer followed by a positive rejoinder. Allow for different answers.

Can the dog in photo number one see?   *No, it can't, but the cat can see.*
Can dogs drive?   *No, they can't, but they can ride in the car.*

After the oral activity direct the students to write their answers below each photo.

7 As a class discussion activity, discuss the written questions at the bottom of the worksheets with the students. Finally, ask the students to write their personal answers to each question.

NOTE

8 • Point out that "**can**" is usually unstressed and the vowel is pronounced like the "**i**" in "p**i**n." The pronunciation of "**can**" rhymes with "**man**" when used emphatically in a short answer or in contrast. For example: **Yes, I can** *(short answer)*. He **can't** drive, but I **can**. *(contrast)*. The vowel in "**can't**" never weakens and always rhymes with "**pant**." The quality of the vowel is essential to the distinction between "**can**" and "**can't**."

• Show that "**can**" does not take an "**s**" after the third person singular. Contrast: "*He drives a car.*" and "*He can drive a car.*"

• Point out that "**can**" is only followed by the verb and not the infinitive. Contrast: "*I want to drive.*" and "*I can drive.*"

• The expression "**to be able to**" is the equivalent of "**can**." You may want to drill this expression as a variation.

• The contraction "**can't**" is normally used in conversation. The non-contracted form "**cannot**" is more commonly found in writing. Unlike the grammatical forms "**is not**," "**are not**," "**do not**," and "**does not**," the word "**cannot**" is written together as one word.

Follow-Up Activities

9 Drill the association between the contracted and non-contracted forms by means of a brief written activity. On the chalkboard write various sentences using contractions. Have the students copy these sentences replacing the contractions with the corresponding non-contracted forms. For example, "**He can't drive.**" would become "**He cannot drive.**"

With the aid of your students, make a list of job titles (*mechanic, doctor, electrician, etc.*) on the chalkboard. Pose questions of the type, *"What can a mechanic do?"* Ask for volunteers to answer.

ESL Beginning Level • Modal Verb • At the Shopping Center • Vocabulary Building

Can

1 Directions: Read the names of the places and the items below.

1 Bakery	2 Pharmacy	3 Market	4 Shoe Store	5 Pet Shop	6 Post Office	7 Theater	8 Bank
9 Bookstore	10 Electronics Store	11 Beauty Salon	12 Furniture Store	13 Clothing Store	14 Coffee Shop	15 Hardware Store	16 Video Store

2 Directions: Practice asking and answering questions with **can**, **buy**, **find**, and **get**. See the examples below:

Student 1: Where **can** I **buy** a stamp?   Student 2: You **can buy** a stamp at the post office.
Student 1: Where **can** I **find** a doll?   Student 2: You **can find** a doll at a toy store.
Student 1: Where **can** I **get** a dictionary?   Student 2: You **can get** a dictionary at a book store.

1 a dog collar	 2 a cup of tea	3 a cake	 4 a computer	  5 fruit	 6 a haircut	 7 a chair	8 a stamp
 9 shoes	10 a dictionary	 11 a DVD	 12 socks	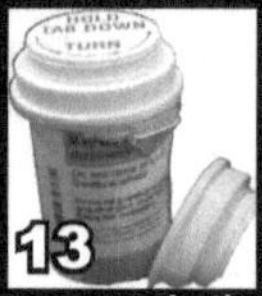 13 a prescription	 14 a flashlight	15 movie tickets	16 an ATM

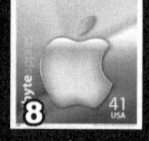

3 Directions: Read the samples below, then write sentences with **buy**, **find**, and **get**.

1. Where can I buy a magazine. / You can buy a magazine at the bookstore.
2. Where can I find a man's shirt? / You can find a shirt at the clothing store.
3. Where can I get a loaf of bread? / You can get a loaf of bread at the bakery.
4. _____ a cell phone. / You _____
5. _____ a sofa. / You _____
6. _____ some money. / You _____

35

ESL Beginning Level • Modal Verb • At the Shopping Center • Vocabulary Building

Teacher's Notes

1 Before distributing the worksheet, begin the lesson with a conversation about shopping. Ask general questions to determine how much they already know about local stores and what they can buy in each.

Distribute the worksheet and identify the stores in the photos at the top of the page. Practice the pronunciation of the store names under each photo by having the students repeat after you.

Bakery	**Clothing Store**	**Furniture Store**	**Post Office**
Bank	**Coffee Shop**	**Market**	**Shoe Store**
Beauty Salon	**Hardware Store**	**Pet Store**	**Theater**
Bookstore	**Electronics Store**	**Pharmacy**	**Video Store**

2 Repeat the same for the names of the store items in the photos in the middle of the page.

a cake	**a dictionary**	**a haircut**	**fruit**
a chair	**a dog collar**	**a prescription**	**movie tickets**
a computer	**a DVD**	**a stamp**	**shoes**
a cup of tea	**a flashlight**	**an ATM**	**socks**

3 Introduce the word "**can**" by asking the question, *"Where can I buy a stamp?"* Model the answer, *"You can buy a stamp at the post office."* Continue the activity by posing similar questions to individual students about various store items.

4 Ask another question, *"Where can I find an ATM?"* Model the answer, *"You can find an ATM at a bank."* After drilling the example several times, pose similar questions to individual students using various store items. Finally, repeat the same activity with the word "**get**."

5 Have students continue the drill by directing pairs of students to ask each other similar questions using the remaining objects in the lesson. Encourage the students to expand the lesson by having them ask about the other items that do not appear on the worksheet.

6 In Item #3, read the sentences in the balloons at the bottom of the page with the students. Then, direct them to fill in the balloons at the bottom of the page using the sentences in the balloons as examples.

NOTE

7 You may want to point out that In many English-speaking countries with historical ties with Great Britain, words ending in "**-er**" are usually spelled "**-re**." In the United States, there is a general tendency to use this alternate spelling in signs and in advertising. Examples of this usage include: ***center — centre; theater — theatre.***

In conversation, the vowel in "**can**" is often unstressed and pronounced as the "**i**". in "**p*i*n**." The verb following "**can**" receives the major stress.

Follow-Up Activity

8 Divide the class into two teams. Tell one person on the first team to ask another person on the second team, ***"What can you find/buy in a [name of a store]?"*** The student on the second team must name as many objects as he/she can in 30 seconds. The teacher or another student should time the student and count the number of responses. Reverse the roles by having a student on the second team ask a student on the first team a similar question. Continue until everyone has had a chance to participate. List the stores and the items found in them on the chalkboard, whiteboard, or project onto the board using an overhead projector. Do not allow duplicate answers. At the end of the game, the team with the most responses wins.

ESL Beginning Level   Student Mixer • Vocabulary • Clothes

Clothing Items

Directions: Walk around the room and find the students with the clothes below. Write the students' names on the lines.

1 _____
is wearing brown shoes.

2 _____
is wearing a long-sleeved shirt.

3 _____
is wearing a black belt.

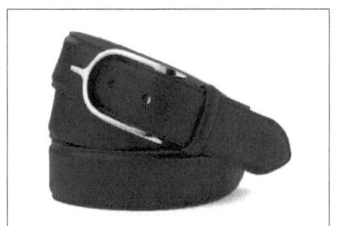

4 _____
is wearing a red jacket.

5 _____
is wearing green socks.

6 _____
is wearing a skirt.

7 _____
is wearing glasses.

8 _____
is wearing a dress.

9 _____
is wearing a blouse.

10 _____
is wearing a tie.

11 _____
is wearing tennis shoes.

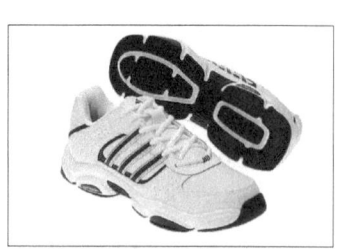

12 _____
is wearing blue pants.

ESL Beginning Level   Student Mixer • Vocabulary • Clothes

Teacher's Notes

1 Use this group activity as a mixer exercise in which students have to talk to each other to get the necessary information. This is an excellent way for students to get to know one another especially at the beginning of a new term. Have the students get up and walk around the room to collect the names of other students who match the clothes description on the worksheet. Allow at least 15 minutes.

2 Distribute the worksheet and read the directions at the top of the handout to the students.

3 Review the vocabulary below:

shoes	**socks**	**tie**	**long-sleeved**	**green**
shirt	**shirt**	**pants**	**brown**	**blue**
belt	**glasses**	**tennis shoes**	**black**	**red**
jacket	**blouse**	**dress**	**white**	**to wear**

4 Review and practice the following phrases:

What's your name? Please spell it.   *Who has a ....?*
What are you wearing?   *What color is/are the ....?*
Are you wearing ....?   *What kind of .... are you wearing?*
Who is wearing ....?

5 Have the students practice asking and answering questions about the information collected.

Who is wearing ....? (Introduce the words **nobody** and **no one** if necessary.)
Who has a .... at home?
What color is your ....?

6 **Follow-Up Activities**

Practice the general sequence of adjectives: size, color, then noun.

7 *Examples:* **small white shirt**   • **short blue skirt**   • **long black belt**

Have students describe some of the following:

   • their favorite outfits

   • their country's traditional clothing

   • appropriate outfits for work

   • appropriate outfits for a wedding and other events

ESL Beginning Level • Vocabulary Building (Clothes) • Discussion • Games

Find the Differences in Clothing

① Directions: How many differences can you find in the two pictures? See the examples below.

The girl is wearing a dress in Picture #2 and a white blouse and black skirt in Picture #1.

The boy is wearing a white shirt in the second picture, but no shoes in the first picture.

Vocabulary

shirt	under-	glasses	slippers	ered
blouse	wear	socks	dress	polka dot
skirt	jacket	shoes	solid	plaid
pants	sweater	necklace	color	print
jumper	earrings	buttons	striped	zigzag
suit	tie	buckle	check-	

The man is wearing black shoes in the first picture and white shoes in the second picture.

The man is wearing pants in Picture #1, but no pants in Picture #2.

② Describe four differences in writing in the pictures above.

Example: _The woman is wearing glasses in the first picture, but not in the second picture._
1. _____
2. _____
3. _____
4. _____

39

ESL Beginning Level • Vocabulary Building (Clothes) • Discussion • Games

Teacher's Notes

1 Before handing out the worksheet, review the name of the colors and the following vocabulary:

Vocabulary				
shirt	suit	tie	buttons	striped
blouse	underwear	glasses	buckle	checkered
skirt	jacket	socks	slippers	polka dot
pants	sweater	shoes	dress	plaid
jumper	earrings	necklace	solid color	print
				zigzag

2 Practice the vocabulary above by identifying the various types of clothes in the classroom. For example, ask the question "Who's wearing _____?"

3 Have students identify the person. Gradually, have students ask one another.

4 Expand the exercise to include the designs or color of the clothes. For, example, ask who is wearing a blue, polka dot blouse.

5 Hand out the worksheet and have the students find as many differences as possible. This should be an oral exercise and students should not be writing at this point.

6 As a variation, play a game. Have the students work in pairs or small groups. Tell them to list on a piece of paper as many differences as possible. The pair or group with the most differences wins. If there is a tie, check for spelling.

7 As a writing activity ask the students to write four examples of differences between the first and second pictures. To correct the sentences have the students write them on the board so that all of the students can take part in the correction. You may want to distribute an overhead transparency and have the students write their sentences on it. Then, project it onto the chalkboard for correction.

Follow-up Activities

8 Cut out pictures of clothing from magazines, newspapers or department store catalogs. Paste the pictures to cardboard for use in drilling, spelling bees or games. Write the name of the object on the back of the card.

9 Play a game based on 20 questions. A student stands in front of the class with a picture hidden from the view of the rest of the class. The student is allowed to answer only "yes" or "no." The rest of the class asks yes/no questions until someone guesses what kind of clothes is shown in the picture. The person who guesses correctly, takes the next turn in front of the class.

10 Practice the general sequence of adjectives: size, color, then noun.

Examples: **small white shirt • short blue skirt • long black belt**

Have students describe some of the following:

- their favorite outfits
- their country's traditional clothing
- appropriate outfits for work
- appropriate outfits for a wedding and other events

ESL Beginning Level   Crossword Puzzle • Vocabulary Building

Clothing & Accessories

Directions: *Fill in the boxes with the names of the clothes and accessories in the photos.*

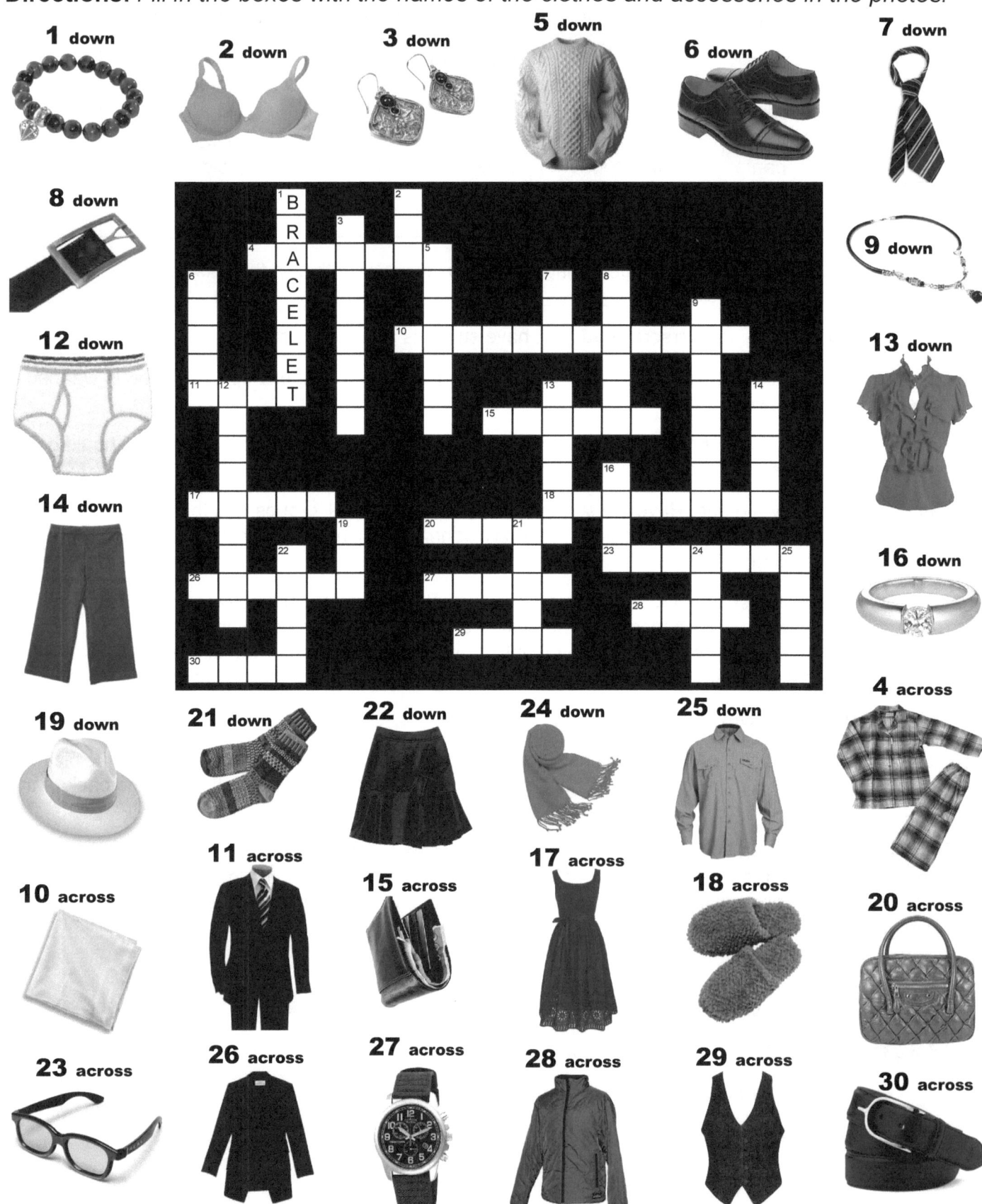

1 down
2 down
3 down
5 down
6 down
7 down

8 down
9 down
12 down
13 down
14 down
16 down

4 across
19 down
21 down
22 down
24 down
25 down

10 across
11 across
15 across
17 across
18 across
20 across

23 across
26 across
27 across
28 across
29 across
30 across

41

ESL Beginning Level   Crossword Puzzle • Vocabulary Building

Teacher's Notes

1 Before distributing the worksheet, begin the lesson with a conversation. Ask your students general questions about common clothing and accessories. Ask them to name and describe as many as they can. List them on the board. Make sure that the lists include some of the following items:

belt	buckle	glasses	necklace	ring	skirt	sweater	wallet
blouse	coat	handkerchief	pajamas	scarf	slippers	tie	watch
bra	dress	hat	pants	shirt	socks	underwear	
bracelet	earrings	jacket	purse	shoes	suit	vest	

2 Distribute the worksheet and identify and discuss each clothing and accessory item. Ask simple questions about shapes, sizes, colors, cost, where they are bought, worn, and any other distinguishing features.

3 Review and practice the following phrases:

What are you wearing?   *Who has a _____?*
Are you wearing _____?   *What color is/are the _____?*
Who is wearing _____?   *What kind of _____ are you wearing?*

4 As a class discussion have your students practice asking and answering questions about the information collected. *(Introduce the words* **nobody** *and* **no one** *if necessary.)*

   Who is wearing_____?   Who has a _____ at home?   What color is your _____?

5 Expand the activity by practicing the general sequence of adjectives: *size*, *color*, then *object*.

   Examples: **small white shirt • short blue skirt • long black belt**

   Have students describe some of the following:
   • their favorite outfits   • appropriate outfits for work
   • their country's traditional clothing • appropriate outfits for a wedding and other events

6 Demonstrate how to do a crossword puzzle. Explain the concept of **DOWN** and **ACROSS**. Then, show the students how to fill in the puzzle using the visual clues. Do a few examples with the whole class.

7 Allow some time for your students to complete the crossword puzzle. You may want to have students work in pairs or assigning it as a homework assignment.

8 Correct the answers by projecting an overhead transparency image directly onto the board on which students can take turns writing the answers on the board. See solution below.

9 Play a crossword puzzle game. Draw or project a grid onto the board or screen as well as a list of the new clothing and accessories. Divide the class into two teams and flip a coin to determine which team goes first. Have the first student of the first team go to the chalkboard and write a word that uses one letter of an existing word in the crossword. If the word fits and is correctly spelled, then give one point for every letter of the new word. Then, go on to the first student of the other team. If the word is incorrect, erase it and go to the opposite team.

CROSSWORD PUZZLE SOLUTION:

DOWN: 1 bracelet, 2 bra, 3 earrings, 5 sweater, 6 shoes, 7 tie, 8 buckle, 9 necklace, 12 underwear, 13 blouse, 14 pants, 16 ring, 19 hat, 21 socks, 22 skirt, 24 scarf, 25 shirt;

ACROSS: 4 pajamas, 10 handkerchief, 11 suit, 15 wallet, 17 dress, 18 slippers, 20 purse, 23 glasses, 26 jacket, 27 watch, 28 coat, 29 vest, 30 belt

ESL Intermediate Level   What kind of ...? • Vocabulary Building • Word Order

Common Materials

1 Directions: *Read and pronounce the names of the items below.*

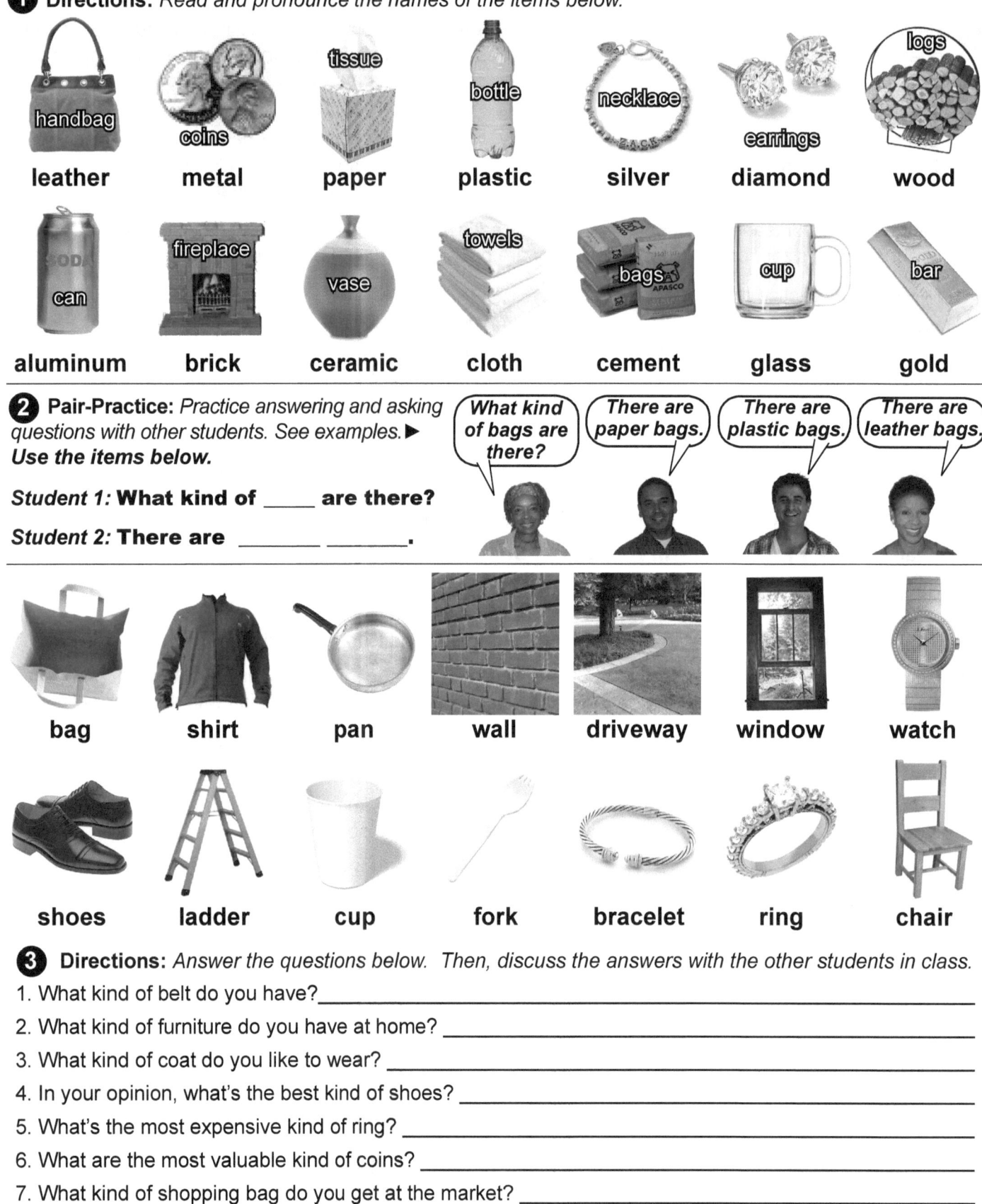

| leather | metal | paper | plastic | silver | diamond | wood |

| aluminum | brick | ceramic | cloth | cement | glass | gold |

2 Pair-Practice: *Practice answering and asking questions with other students. See examples.* ▶ *Use the items below.*

What kind of bags are there?
There are paper bags.
There are plastic bags.
There are leather bags.

Student 1: **What kind of _____ are there?**
Student 2: **There are _____ _____ .**

| bag | shirt | pan | wall | driveway | window | watch |

| shoes | ladder | cup | fork | bracelet | ring | chair |

3 Directions: *Answer the questions below. Then, discuss the answers with the other students in class.*

1. What kind of belt do you have? _____
2. What kind of furniture do you have at home? _____
3. What kind of coat do you like to wear? _____
4. In your opinion, what's the best kind of shoes? _____
5. What's the most expensive kind of ring? _____
6. What are the most valuable kind of coins? _____
7. What kind of shopping bag do you get at the market? _____

ESL Intermediate Level   What kind of ...? Vocabulary Building • Word Order

Teacher's Notes

❶ Before distributing the worksheet, begin the lesson with a conversation using "**What's the ___ made of?**" to determine how much the students already know about common materials. Using classroom items ask questions such as "**What's the chair made of?**" Model the responses, *"It's made of wood."* Have the students repeat both question and answer. Then direct the question to individual students.

❷ Distribute the worksheet. Introduce the vocabulary by modeling the pronunciation of the names of the fourteen items in and below the pictures. Have the students repeat the pronunciation of the words after you. While you are reading, ask the student to underline any unfamiliar words, then explain them.

❸ After the students have had the opportunity to practice the questions *"What's the ___ made of?"* several times, ask similar questions about the items illustrated at the top of the worksheet (i.e., *leather handbag, metal coins, paper tissue, plastic bottle, silver necklace, diamond earrings, wood longs, aluminium can, brick fireplace, ceramic vase, cloth towels, cement bags, glass cup, gold bar*).

❹ Direct the students to the fourteen objects illustrated in the second section of the lesson. Pose the question, *"What kinds of bags are there?"* "Model possible responses, *"There are paper bags," "There are plastic bags,"* and *"There are leather bags."* After drilling the examples several times, ask questions to individual students about a few more objects. Continue the drill by directing individual students to ask questions of other students using the remaining objects.

❺ Have students expand the exercise by asking one another personalized questions such as:

What kind of ___ do you have?   *What's the best type of ___?*
What's the least expensive ___?   *What's the least useful kind of ___?*
What kind of ___ do you like?   *What's the: most economical ___?*
What's the most practical kind of ___ ? *What's the cheapest type of ___?*

❻ Read over the questions at the bottom of the worksheets and discuss the answers as a class discussion. Encourage students to pose their own original questions to others in the class. Finally have them write their own answers.

NOTE

• Nouns such as "**plastic**" and "**paper**," which denote materials, may be used as adjectives to describe other nouns.

• Note the existence of two parallel forms: "**gold/golden**," and "**wood/wooden**." Usage often leads to a preference of one form over the other. Although the words "**gold**" and "**wood**" may be us as either nouns or adjectives, the words "**golden**" and "**wooden**" may only be used as adjectives.

• You may want to expand the activity to include additional descriptive words and colors. The following examples show the correct word order for such adjectives.

descriptive adjective	color	material	thing
small	brown	wooden	spoon
long	green	plastic	comb

Additional vocabulary: *big, small, long, short, heavy, light, hard, soft, new, old, strong, weak, broken, used, clean, dirty.*

• Have the students expand this activity by asking them to describe the items in the photos on the worksheet.

Cultural Note: The adjective "**cheap**" has two meanings. It may signify an item selling at a low price or a product of inferior quality. Due to this dual meaning, many people tend to use the words "**economical**" and "**inexpensive**" when referring to price.

• You may wish to incorporate the following vocabulary into the oral and written activities:

pearl necklace	*dirt road*	*cotton blouse*	*cardboard box*
wool sweater	*fur coat*	*steel pipe*	*silk stockings*

ESL Beginning Level   Crossword Puzzle • Vocabulary Building

Common Verbs 1

Directions: *Fill in the boxes with the verbs in the photos.*

1 across   **4** across   **5** across   **7** across   **10** across   **12** across

13 across   **14** across

16 across   **17** across

18 across   **19** across

1 down   **2** down   **3** down   **6** down   **7** down   **8** down

9 down   **11** down   **12** down   **14** down   **15** down   **17** down

45

ESL Beginning Level   Crossword Puzzle • Vocabulary Building

Teacher's Notes

1 Before distributing the worksheet, begin the lesson with a conversation to assess your students' knowledge of some commonly used verbs. Ask questions using the present continuous tense such as:

What are you doing?   *Are you sitting/standing?*
Is [a student's name] sitting/standing?   *Are [two student's names] listening?*
What are they doing? (pointing to someone)? *What am I (the teacher) doing now?*

2 Distribute the worksheet. Identify the people and what they are doing in the photos. Ask the question, "***What's _____ doing?***" Model the response, "***He/She's _____.***" Have the students repeat both question and answer. Continue asking similar questions about the people in the photos. For variety, have students ask each other questions with the word "***where***" such as "***Where's _____?***" Students should reply, "***He/she's _____.***"

3 Ask your students general questions about other common activities. Ask them to name and describe as many as they can. List them on the board. Make sure that the lists include some of the following items:

ask	eat	listen	ride	study	wait
count	exercise	look	shop	take	walk
cut	help	play	show	tie	watch
drive	laugh	read	sing	touch	write

4 Demonstrate how to do a crossword puzzle. Explain the concept of **DOWN** and **ACROSS**. Then, show the students how to fill in the puzzle using the visual clues. Do a few examples with the whole class.

5 Allow some time for your students to complete the crossword puzzle. You may want to have students work in pairs or assigning it as a homework assignment.

6 Correct the answers by projecting an overhead transparency image directly onto the board on which students can take turns writing the answers on the board. See solution below.

7 Play a crossword puzzle game. Draw or project a grid onto the board or screen as well as a list of the common verbs. Divide the class into two teams and flip a coin to determine which team goes first. Have the first student of the first team go to the board and write a word that uses one letter of an existing word in the crossword. If the word fits and is correctly spelled, then give one point for every letter of the new word. Then, go on to the first student of the other team. If the word is incorrect, erase it and go to the opposite team.

8 As an additional activity, play Tic-Tac-Toe: Draw a Tic-Tac-Toe grid and fill it in with common verbs. Divide the class into two teams, each team assigned the symbol "X" or "0." Then flip a coin to determine which team begins. Have the students take turns in an orderly fashion by going down the rows. Tell the first student of the first team to use any word from the grid in a sentence. If the sentence is correct, replace the word with the team's symbol (X or 0), otherwise, leave the word. Go on to the first person on the other team. Continue in this manner until one team wins by having three consecutive X's or 0's in a row vertically, horizontally or diagonally. Keep score by giving one point for each game won. After each game, replace all the words in the grid with a different group of verbs.

9 Expand the activity by teaching additional common verbs: *drink, write, sit, run, work, swim, stand, speak, make, wear, smile, hold, hear, understand, visit, turn, need, see, steal, type, read, relax,* and *meet*.

CROSSWORD PUZZLE SOLUTION:

ACROSS: 1 walk, 4 look, 5 show, 7 ride, 10 take, 12 study, 13 cut, 14 listen, 16 shop, 17 touch, 18 drive, 19 help; **DOWN:** 1 watch, 2 play, 3 count, 6 wait, 7 read, 8 exercise, 9 ask, 11 eat, 12 sing, 14 laugh, 15 write, 17 tie

ESL Beginning Level — Crossword Puzzle • Vocabulary Building

Common Verbs 2

Directions: *Fill in the boxes with the verbs in the photos.*

1 across
3 across
4 across
6 across
7 across
8 across

9 across
11 across
13 across
14 across
15 across
16 across

19 across
1 down
2 down
3 down
4 down
5 down

6 down
10 down
12 down
13 down
17 down
18 down

47

ESL Beginning Level Crossword Puzzle • Vocabulary Building

Teacher's Notes

1 Before distributing the worksheet, begin the lesson with a conversation to assess your students' knowledge of some commonly used verbs. Ask questions using the present continuous tense such as:

What are you doing? *Are you sitting/standing?*
Is [a student's name] sitting/standing? *Are [two student's names] listening?*
What are they doing? (pointing to someone)? *What am I (the teacher) doing now?*

2 Distribute the worksheet. Identify the people and what they are doing in the photos. Ask the question, "*What's _____ doing?*" Model the response, "*He/She's _____.*" Have the students repeat both question and answer. Continue asking similar questions about the people in the photos. For variety, have students ask each other questions with the word "*where*" such as "*Where's _____?*" Students should reply, "*He/she's _____.*"

3 Ask your students general questions about other common activities. Ask them to name and describe as many as they can. List them on the board. Make sure that the lists include some of the following items:

Break	Hear	Read	See	Speak	Type
Drink	Hold	Relax	Show	Stand	Visit
Feed	Make	Rest	Sit	Swim	Wear
Fly	Meet	Run	Smile	Turn	Work

4 Demonstrate how to do a crossword puzzle. Explain the concept of **DOWN** and **ACROSS**. Then, show the students how to fill in the puzzle using the visual clues. Do a few examples with the whole class.

5 Allow some time for your students to complete the crossword puzzle. You may want to have students work in pairs or assigning it as a homework assignment.

6 Correct the answers by projecting an overhead transparency image directly onto the board on which students can take turns writing the answers on the board. See solution below.

7 Play a crossword puzzle game. Draw or project a grid onto the board or screen as well as a list of the common verbs. Divide the class into two teams and flip a coin to determine which team goes first. Have the first student of the first team go to the board and write a word that uses one letter of an existing word in the crossword. If the word fits and is correctly spelled, then give one point for every letter of the new word. Then, go on to the first student of the other team. If the word is incorrect, erase it and go to the opposite team.

8 As an additional activity, play Tic-Tac-Toe: Draw a Tic-Tac-Toe grid and fill it in with common verbs. Divide the class into two teams, each team assigned the symbol "X" or "0." Then flip a coin to determine which team begins. Have the students take turns in an orderly fashion by going down the rows. Tell the first student of the first team to use any word from the grid in a sentence. If the sentence is correct, replace the word with the team's symbol (X or 0), otherwise, leave the word. Go on to the first person on the other team. Continue in this manner until one team wins by having three consecutive X's or 0's in a row vertically, horizontally or diagonally. Keep score by giving one point for each game won. After each game, replace all the words in the grid with a different group of verbs.

9 Expand the activity by teaching additional common verbs: *ask, count, cut, drive, eat, exercise, help, laugh, listen, look, play, read, ride, shop, show, sing, study, take, tie, touch, wait, walk, watch,* and *write*.

CROSSWORD PUZZLE SOLUTION:

ACROSS: 1 sit, 3 show, 4 fly, 6 make, 7 smile, 8 read, 9 drink, 11 visit, 13 turn, 14 break, 15 hold, 16 hear, 19 speak; **DOWN:** 1 swim, 2 relax, 3 see, 4 feed, 5 work, 6 meet, 10 run, 12 stand, 13 type, 17 rest, 18 wear

ESL Intermediate Level, Pair Practice • Fill In • Class Discussion • Vocabulary Building

Comparative & Superlative

1 *Read the sentences below.*

Geography

Science

Math

Mrs. Boxer is 65 years old. She is a geography teacher. She has a new car.

Ms Garcia is 30 years old. She is a scientist. She has an expensive car.

Jack Carter is 21 years old. He is a math student. He has an old car.

2 **Pair-Practice:** *Practice answering and asking questions with another student. Use some of the words in the box to the right. See examples.* ▶

Who's taller, Mrs. Boxer or Ms. Garcia?

Ms. Garcia is taller than Mrs. Boxer.

Adjectives

easy	attractive
hard	beautiful
heavy	confusing
light	difficult
long	economical
new	expensive
old	helpful
poor	important
rich	interesting
short	modern
tall	popular
thin	practical
young	useful

Student 1: **Who's/What's** ____, ____ or ____?

Student 2: _____ is _____ than _____.

3 **Pair-Practice:** *Practice answering and asking questions with another student. See examples.* ▶ *Use some of the words in the box to the right.*

Who's the tallest of the three?

Jack Carter is the tallest of the three.

Student 1: **Who's/What's** ____ of the three?

Student 2: _____ is the _____ of the three.

4 *Complete the sentences with the comparative or superlative form of the adjective in parentheses in red.*

1. Jack Carter (tall) *taller* than Ms Garcia, and Mrs. Boxer is the (short) *shortest* of the three.
2. A smaller car is usually (economical) _____ _____ than a bigger car.
3. Is math (difficult) _____ _____ than science? No, I think science is (easy) _____ than math.
4. Is geography (hard) _____ than math? Yes, it's (easy) _____ than math.
5. Ms. Garcia's car is the (expensive) _____ _____ and (beautiful) _____ car of the three.
6. Mrs. Boxer is the (short) _____ and (old) _____ of the three people.
7. Mrs. Boxer's car is (small) _____ than Jack's car, and it's (practical) _____ _____ , too.
8. Ms. Garcia is (tall) _____ than Mrs. Boxer, but Ms. Garcia is (short) _____ than Jack Carter.
9. Jack Carter is (poor) _____ than Mrs. Boxer, but Ms. Garcia is the (rich) _____ of all.

5 **Class Discussion:** *Answer the questions in writing on the back of this worksheet and share the answers in class.*

In your opinion ...
1. What's the more interesting to you, books or movies?
2. What's easier for you, math or science?
3. What's more important to you, money or happiness?
4. Who's the most famous actor in the world?
5. What's your biggest challenge?
6. What more difficult for you, speaking or writing English?
7. Who's the taller of the two, your mother or father?
8. Who's the most economical car of all?
9. What's the largest animal in the world?
10. What the biggest holiday of the year?
11. Who's the most important person in your life?

ESL Intermediate Level, Pair Practice • Fill In • Class Discussion • Vocabulary Building

Teacher's Notes

1 Before distributing the worksheet, begin the lesson with a conversation to determine how well your students can use the comparative and superlative forms of adjectives. Ask questions similar to those at the bottom of the worksheet.

2 Distribute the worksheet. Introduce the vocabulary by asking yes/no questions about the people, objects, and school subjects in the pictures. For example, ask, "*Is Mrs. Boxer old?*" Model the response, "**Yes, she is.**" Have students repeat both question and answer. Continue asking questions using the adjectives in the box to the right of the worksheet..

3 On the chalkboard, whiteboard, or overhead projector present a list of only the one-and two-syllable adjectives, which can be found in the first row of words in the box to the right of the worksheet. Introduce the comparative structure "*-er than*" (used with the one-and two-syllable words). Ask questions such as "**Who's older, Mrs. Boxer or Ms. Garcia?**" Model the correct answer and have students repeat, "**Mrs. Boxer is older than Ms. Garcia.**" After giving several examples, have an individual student ask another student a similar question using one of the one-syllable word list.

4 Do the same as above with longer multi-syllable adjectives, which can be found in the second row of adjectives in the box at the right of the worksheet. Introduce the comparative structure "*more .... than*" (used with longer words).

5 Introduce separately the two superlative structures "*-est*" (e.g., the oldest) and "*the most*" (e.g., the most beautiful) following the methodology described above. Note that "*-est*" is used with the list of short adjectives and "*the most*" is used with the list of long adjectives.

6 Ask questions using the various comparative and superlative structures. Then have individual students ask other students questions patterned after the examples given in the pair practice activities in exercises 2 and 3. With the help of a student, demonstrate how to do the pair practice exercises using the pictures at the top of the page. Then have your students continue by working in pairs.

7 Next, the students complete the sentences in exercise 4 in writing. Answers:
1. Jack Carter *__taller__* than Ms. Garcia, and Mrs. Boxer is the *__shortest__* of the three.
2. A smaller car is *__more economical__* than a bigger car.
3. Is math *__more difficult__* than science? No, I think science is *__easier__* than math.
4. Is geography *__harder__* than math? Yes, it's *__easier__* than math.
5. Ms. Garcia's car is the *__most expensive__* car of the three.
6. Mrs. Boxer is the *__shortest__* and *__oldest__* person of the three.
7. Mrs. Boxer's car is *__smaller__* than Jack's car, and it's *__more practical__*, too.
8. Ms. Garcia is *__taller__* than Mrs. Boxer, but is *__shorter__* than Jack Carter.
9. Jack Carter is *__poorer__* than Mrs. Boxer, but Ms. Garcia is the *__richest__* of all.

8 Read through the questions in exercise 5 to make sure that your students understand any unfamiliar vocabulary. Then, ask them to write the answers to the questions on the back of the worksheet. Finally, have the students share some of their answers as a class discussion.

9 Explain the spelling rules:

• "*y*" changes to "*i*" before "*-er*" or "*-est.*" Example: *easy, easier, easiest*.

• When the original word ends in a consonant-vowel-consonant pattern and the final vowel is stressed, the final consonant is doubled before adding "*-er*" or "*-est.*" Example: *big, bigger, biggest*. Note: The letters "*w*" and "*y*" are never doubled.

• If the word ends in "*e*," only add "*-r*" or "*-st.*" Example: *nice, nicer, nicest*.

Words ending in "*ng*" undergo a minor pronunciation change in the comparative and superlative forms. For example, the final "*g*" in a word such as "*long*" is absorbed into the nasal combination "*ng*" and is not pronounced with a hard "*g*" as in "*big.*" However, in the comparative and superlative forms the "*g*" is pronounced.

10 Many students tend to confuse "*than*" with "*that*," especially in writing. Compare "**He is the tallest person that I know.**" and "**He is taller than Alice.**"

11 As a follow-up activity introduce the expressions below:

of the two:	Who's the taller of the two, your mother or father?
of all:	In your opinion, who's the most famous person of all?
in the world:	What's the largest animal in the world?
of the year:	What's the biggest holiday of the year?
in your life:	Who's the most important person in your life?

12 Ask three students to come up in front of the class. Ask questions contrasting age, height and weight. For example: Teacher: *Is Juan taller than Martha?* Student: **Yes, he is.** Teacher: **Compare Juan and Martha.** Student: **Juan's taller than Martha.**

ESL Intermediate Level • Geographical Terms, Pair Practice • Writing • Class Discussion

Comparative & Superlative Review

1 Listen to the text below.

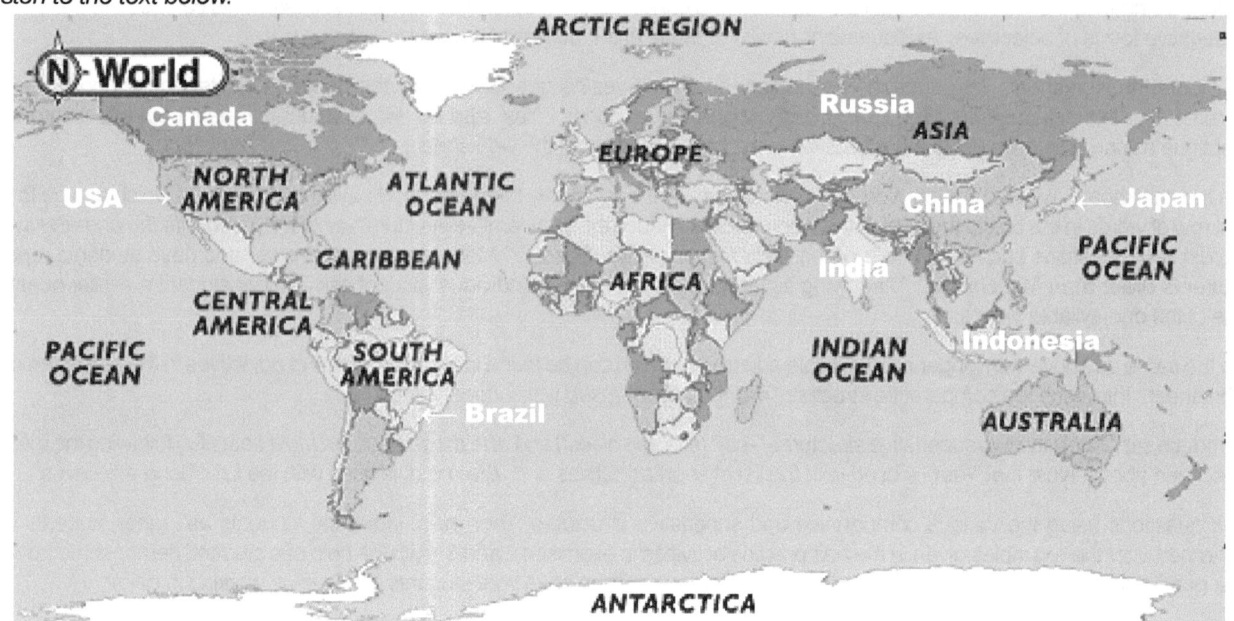

The world has seven continents with more than 192 countries. The largest continent is Asia and the smallest is Australia. The United States is one of the biggest and one of the most populous. Only Russia, Canada, and China are bigger than the U.S.A. China is smaller than Russia and Canada, but China has a larger population than both of them together. Japan is not a big country, but it is one of the most industrial and developed nations in the world. Tokyo has the largest population of all the cities in the world and is the most crowded, too. Some of the tiniest countries are in Europe: San Marino, Andorra, and Monaco. Most of the oldest countries are in Asia: Iran, Iraq, Vietnam, Korea and China. The newest countries are islands in the South Pacific: Tonga, Tuvalu, and Nauru, which is the smallest island country in the world. Countries that are near the equator have the warmest climates, and the countries near the Arctic and the Antarctic regions have the coldest climates.

CONTINENTS* (sq. kilometers)		COUNTRIES* (sq. kilometers)		COUNTRIES* (By Population)		CITIES* (By Population)	
Asia	44,000,000	Russia	17,000.000	China	1,700,000,000	Tokyo Japan	34,000,000
Africa	30,000,000	Canada	10,000,000	India	1,500,000,000	Canton, China	24,500,000
North America	24,500,000	China	9,800,000	USA	300,000,000	Seoul, Korea	24,000,000
South America	18,000,000	USA	9,500,000	Indonesia	250,000,000	Mexico City	23,500,000
Antarctica	14,000,000	Brazil	8,500,000	Brazil	200,000,000	Delhi, India	23,000,000
Europe	10,000,000						
Australia	9,000,000	* Numbers are approximate.					

2 Pair-Practice: Practice asking and answering questions with another student. Use the information above. See examples. ▶

What's the biggest country in the world?

Russia is the biggest country in the world.

Student 1: **What's the** _____ **in the world?**

Student 2: _____ **is the** _____ **in the world.**

Student 1: **Which** _____ **is** _____, _____ **or** _____?

Student 2: _____ **is** _____ **than** _____.

Which city is larger, Tokyo or Delhi?

Tokyo is larger than Delhi.

3 Answer the questions in writing on the back of this worksheet.

1. What's the biggest country in the world by size?
2. What's the largest country in the world by population?
3. Which country is smaller in size, Canada or the USA?
4. Which city in the world is the most populous?
5. Which continent has a warmer climate, Europe or Africa?
6. What's the tiniest island country in the world?
7. Where are the oldest and youngest countries?
8. Which city of the world is the most crowded?
9. Which is larger, Mexico City or Delhi, India?
10. Is your country larger or smaller than the USA?

ESL Intermediate Level • Geographical Terms, Pair Practice • Writing • Class Discussion

Teacher's Notes

1 Before handing out the worksheet, begin the lesson with a conversation to assess your students' use of the comparative and superlative forms of adjectives and geographical terms. You may want to use some of the questions at the bottom of the worksheet. Use a large wall map if available.

2 Distribute the worksheet and have the students fold it so that only the map is visible. Repeat the names of the continents, geographical areas, and the countries on the map. Have the students repeat the names.

3 As a listening comprehension activity, tell your students to listen to you read the text below the map. Then, Ask general comprehension questions such as

How many countries are there in the world? *Name a small country in Europe.*
Name a city in Japan. *What continent do we live on?*

4 Have students look at the text. Tell them to underline the words that they don't understand as you read it aloud a second time. Explain any unknown vocabulary. Then have individuals read parts of the text. Then, ask comprehension questions using the questions above as a guide.

5 Ask individual students to retell the text in their own words.

6 Have individual students ask questions to other students based on the map and text.

7 Direct students to the first chart below the map. Have them repeat each country name and land area.

8 Ask questions with "*how big*" such as, "*How big is Russia?*" Model the answer, "*It's 17 million square kilometers.*" Have students repeat both questions and answers.

9 Have individual students ask other students questions about the charts below the map. Then, have the students work in pairs. Refer to the sample questions and examples as a guide in exercise 2.

10 Pose questions about the students' native or adopted country. Ask about the country's biggest city, longest river, highest mountain, largest lake, most beautiful place, most interesting tourist attraction, most important products, and most famous personalities. Encourage individual students to ask other students similar questions.

11 Tell the students to give you the names of countries and write them on the chalkboard with the nationality and language for each. In the following list, the common suffixes used with nationalities and languages are underlined:

Country	Nationality	Language	Country	Nationality	Language
Mexico	Mexican	Spanish	Netherlands	Dutch	Dutch
Spain	Spanish	Spanish	France	French	French
Japan	Japanese	Japanese	Thailand	Thai	Thai
England	English	English	Greece	Greek	Greek
Israel	Israeli	Hebrew	Philippines	Filipino	Pilipino (Tagalog)
Egypt	Egyptian	Arabic	Switzerland	Swiss	French, German, Italian

12 Have students answer the questions at the bottom of the worksheet in writing on the back of the worksheet. Ask your students to share their answers. Answers:
1. The biggest country in the world by size is Russia.
2. The largest country by population is China.
3. The USA is smaller in size than Canada.
4. Tokyo is the most populous city in the world.
5. Africa has a warmer climate than Europe.
6. The tiniest island country is Nauru.
7. The oldest countries are in Asia and the youngest countries are in the South Pacific.
8. Tokyo is the most crowded city in the world.
9. Mexico City is larger than Delhi.
10. (Answers will vary.)

NOTE

• Stress the capitalization of geographical locations. The article "*the*" and prepositions "*of*" are not capitalized.

• Commas are used to separate hundreds, thousands, and millions.

Other related worksheets: Comparative and Superlative, More & Less, Better & Worse, Facts about the USA

ESL Intermediate Level   Student MIxer

Comparative & Superlative

Directions: Walk around the room and find the students with the information below. Write the students' names on the lines.

1 _____
is the youngest person in the room.

2 _____
has an older brother.

3 _____
has the most brothers and sisters.

4 _____
has the most experience.

5 _____
gets up the earliest every morning.

6 _____
the politest person in the room.

7 _____
has the longest hair.

8 _____
speaks the most languages.

9 _____
has a younger sister.

10 _____
is the best student in the room.

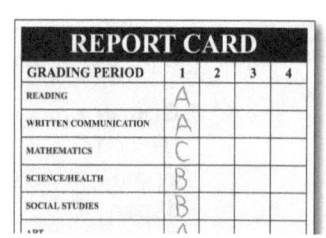

11 _____
lives the nearest to a school.

12 _____
takes the longest breaks.

ESL Intermediate Level   Comparative & Superlative, Student Mixer

Teacher's Notes

1 Review all the vocabulary and the use of the comparative and superlative.

The Comparative
- Use the comparative to compare two objects or people.
- Use the suffix **-er** after short adjectives or adverbs with one or two syllables.
- Use **more** before long adjectives with three or more syllables.
- Always place **than** after the comparative.
Examples: *February has **fewer** days **than** January.*
            *Rhode Island is **more industrial than** Alaska.*

The Superlative
- The irregular superlative forms are as follows:

| good/well | → | the best | a little | → | the least |
| bad | → | the worst | much/many | → | the most |

Spelling Changes
- Most words do not change spelling when we add **-er** or **-est**.
    Example: small • smaller • smallest
- We change **y** to **i** before we add the suffixes **-er** or **-est** to adjectives and adverbs.
    Example: dry • drier • driest
- When a word ends in a consonant-vowel-consonant pattern and the final vowel is stressed, we double the final consonant before adding **-er** or **-est**. We never double the letters **w** or **y**.
    Example: big • bigger • biggest
- If the word ends in **e**, only add **-r** or **-st**.
    Example: large • larger • largest

2 Read the directions at the top of the handout with the students.
- Use this group activity as a "mixer" exercise in which students have to talk to each other to get the necessary information. Have students get up and walk around the room to collect the names of other students who match the description on the handout. Allow at least 15 minutes. This is an excellent way for students to get to know one another especially at the beginning of a new term.

Have students practice asking and answering questions about the information collected.

3 Follow-up by having the class make up an additional list of other kinds of personal information (i.e., has a younger brother, older sister, etc.) and repeat the exercise.

4 For additional practice:

5 - To practice the words **best**, **worse**, **more**, and **less**, have students ask one another personalized questions such as *"In your opinion, what's better/worse, stealing or lying?"* The following gerunds can be used as nouns in such questions:

coffee/tea	football/cards	a movie/a book
blue/red	money/happiness	daytime/nightime
dogs/cats	big/small cars	long/short hair
fruit/vegetables	vanilla/chocolate	Italian/Chinese food
fall/spring	hot/cold weather	classical/modern music

- Supplementary Vocabulary: Practice the comparative and superlative by usisng the phrases below with the students. Encourage them to come up with additional examples.

of the two	*Who's the taller **of the two**, you or your father?*
of all	*In your opinion, who's the most famous person **of all**?*
in the world	*What the largest country **in the world**?*
of the year	*What's the biggest holiday **of the year**?*
in your life	*Who's the most important person **in your life**?*

ESL High Intermediate & Advanced Levels   Reading • Fill In • Geography of USA

Comparative & Superlative

❶ *Fill in the spaces below with the comparative or superlative form of the word under the line.*

Facts about the USA

The United States is a big country, but it is not the _____ country in the world.
                                                                big

Russia, Canada, and China are _____ than the United States. Th USA has fifty
                               big

states. Alaska is the _____ state and Rhode Island is the _____ state.
                      large   **small**

Rhode Island is _____ and has a _____ population than Alaska. Of all
               industrial   **great**

the fifty states, Alaska has _____ people. California has the _____ people.
                            few   **many**

Massachusetts and Virginia are the _____ states. Hawaii and Alaska are the
                                   old

_____ states. The United States has many great cities. New York City is the
new

_____ city. Los Angeles is the second _____, and Chicago is the third.
big   **big**

Some people believe that San Francisco is the _____ city in the country. Other
                                              beautiful

people say that Seattle is the _____, _____, and _____ city to live
                               clean   **safe**   **good**

in. The weather is not the same everywhere in the country. The North is generally

_____ than the South, and the West is usually _____ than the East.
cold   **dry**

❷ *Draw lines from the names of the states and cities to the correct places on the map.*

Seattle   Chicago
San Francisco   Massachusetts
Los Angeles   Rhode Island
California   New York City
Hawaii   Virginia
Alaska   Florida

❸ *Locate your state and city on the map.*

55

ESL Advanced Level • Writing • Past Tense Review • Reading • Listening

Teacher's Notes

1 As an introduction pose questions about the student's native or adopted country. Ask about the country's biggest city, longest river, highest mountain, largest lake, most beautiful place, most interesting tourist attraction, most important products, and most famous personalities. Encourage students to ask one another questions.

Review the uses of the comparative and superlative:

2 **The Comparative**
- Use the comparative to compare two objects or people.
- Use the suffix **-er** after short adjectives or adverbs with one or two syllables.
- Use **more** before long adjectives with three or more syllables.
- Always place **than** after the comparative.
Examples: *February has **fewer** days **than** January.*
            *Rhode Island is **more industrial than** Alaska.*

The Superlative
- The irregular superlative forms are as follows:

| good/well | → | the best | a little | → | the least |
| bad | → | the worst | much/many | → | the most |

Spelling Changes
- Most words do not change spelling when we add **-er** or **-est**.
    Example: small • smaller • smallest
- We change **y** to **i** before we add the suffixes **-er** or **-est** to adjectives and adverbs.
    Example: dry • drier • driest
- When a word ends in a consonant-vowel-consonant pattern and the final vowel is stressed, we double the final consonant before adding **-er** or **-est**. We never double the letters **w** or **y**.
    Example: big • bigger • biggest
- If the word ends in **e**, only add **-r** or **-st**.
    Example: large • larger • largest

3 Explain how to fill in the words in the story about the United States. Read the directions and do a few examples with the whole class. Correct the exercise and have volunteers read the text. Answer key:
Line 1: biggest

Line 2: bigger
Line 3: largest, smallest
Line 4: most industrial, greater

Line 5: fewest, most
Line 6: oldest
Line 7: newest
Line 8: biggest, biggest

Line 9: most beautiful
Line 10: cleanest, safest, best
Line 12: colder, drier

4 Instead of the teacher asking comprehension questions about the text, play a game. Divide the class into two teams. Teams take turns asking difficult questions about the text. If one team asks a question that the second team cannot answer, then it gets a point. If the answer is correct, then no points are given. The team with the most points wins.

5 Have students draw lines from the names of the states and cities to the correct place on the map. As a follow-up activity, have the students find the location of their city, state, or country on a wall map.

6 For a student mixer exercise use the Student Mixer lesson using the comparative and superlative in the ESL Worksheets and Lesson Plans collection, Item #0004.

ESL Intermediate Level   Modal Verbs • Pair Practice • Writing • Discussion

Could & Would

1 *Read the expressions below the photos.*

1. Open the door!
2. Be quiet!
3. Help!
4. Stop!
5. Open the door.
6. Be quiet.
7. Help.
8. Stop.

2 **Pair-Practice:** *Practice asking polite questions with another student. Use the list of expressions to the right. See examples.* ▶

Student 1: _____.

Student 2: Could you please _____.

Open the window.
Could you please open the window.

Other Expressions
1. Pass the salt.
2. Explain this word.
3. Close the door.
4. Repeat that.
5. Speak slowly.
6. Cash this check.
7. Lend me some money.
8. Tell me the time.
9. What a minute.
10. Call me later.
11. Do me a favor.
12. Show me the way.

3 **Pair-Practice:** *Practice asking polite questions with another student. Use the list of expressions to the right. See examples.* ▶

Student 1: _____.

Student 2: Would you _____.

Be quiet.
Would you be quiet.

4 *Write polite questions using "**would**" and "**could**." Then, share your questions with the rest of the class.*

1. _____
2. _____
3. _____
4. _____
5. _____

57

ESL Intermediate Level   Modal Verbs • Pair Practice • Writing • Discussion

Teacher's Notes

1 Before distributing the worksheet, start the lesson with a conversation using "*Would*" and *Could*" to determine how well the students understand basic polite requests and to introduce new vocabulary. Use the following expressions:
Open the window.

Be quiet.   *Pass the paper. Give*   *Hand me the ...*   *Tell me the time.*
Help me.   *me change for...*   *Open this ...*   *Go to the door.*
Stop talking.   *Explain this word.*   *Hold this ...*

2 Distribute the worksheet and read the words in the balloons in the top row of photos. Exaggerate your pronunciation of the exclamation. Be sure to point out that with a strong command an exclamation point (!) is used.

3 Read the words in the balloons in the second row of photos, but this time, do not exaggerate the pronunciation. These are called rhetorical questions. Use the intonation used to express a polite request, which is similar to that of a question.

4 Elicit the commands from individual students. Prompt the command for the first four pictures by using a structure such as *"Tell the soldier to open the door,"* Students should respond appropriately, *"Open the door!"*

5 The last four pictures reflect polite requests. Prompt the polite request by using a structure such as *"Politely ask the man to open the door."* Model the response, *"Would you please open the window."* Have students repeat the structures. Continue by asking individual students.

6 As a variation, prompt the request with "*could*." For example, drill a structure of the type, *"Could you please open the window."*

7 Read and discuss the sample phrases in the balloons in Pair Practice in exercise 2. With the help of a student, demonstrate how to do the pair practice exercise using the phrases in the box at the right of the worksheet. Then have the students continue by working in pairs.

8 Use exercise 3 as an extension to the first Pair Practice exercise, drill polite requests by having students use "**could**" and would with the phrases in the box at the right side of the worksheet.

9 Expand the drill of polite requests by having students use "**would**" and "**could**" with the following sentences in addition to the ones in the box at the right of the worksheet:

Pass the butter.   *Hold on. (wait on the phone)*   *Give me a ride.*
Lower the volume.   *Tell me how much this costs.*   *Lend me [object]*
Open this for me.   *Wrap the present.*   *Tell me how I can get to [place]*
Give me a form.   *Fill 'er up. (gas for a car)*   *Tell me if there are any vacancies.*

10 Direct the students to Exercise 4 at the bottom of the page. Ask them to write original sentences on the lines in the balloons in the photos using "*could*" and "*would*". Afterwards, ask students to write some of their sentences on the board and discuss them with the whole class.

FOLLOW-UP ACTIVITIES

11 You may want to familiarize the students with some additional polite forms such as the following:

I'd like ... [a polite request]   *May I...? (asking permission)*
Please ...   *Shall I/we... ? (seeking approval/agreement)*

12 Show the students how to translate exclamations into a polite request by using some of the following expressions:

Exclamation Polite Request   **Exclamation Polite Request**
Shut up!   *Would you please be quiet.*   *Give me the pen!*   *Could I have the pen.*
Come here!   *Please come here.*   *Get out!*   *Would you please leave.*
I want some coffee!   *I'd like some coffee.*   *We're going!*   *Shall we go.*

NOTE

"**Could**" and "**would**" are two of many modal verbs. • Other modal verbs are: **can, may, might, shall, should, will, must, ought to**. Modal verbs do not change form, so we cannot add the **-s** ending to the third person singular. We use modal verbs with the simple form of the verb (an infinitive without **to**).

ESL Intermediate Level • Modal Verbs • Asking Polite Questions • Pair Practice • Writing

Could

Read: *Practice the phrases below the photo with another student.*

We use the word **could** to ask a polite question.
Examples:

Could you please help me? Yes, I **could**.
Could you tell me the time? Yes, it's 9 o'clock.

Pair Practice: *Practice asking and answering questions with the word* **could**. *See the example to the right. Use the expressions below.*

Student 1: **Could** you please ...?

Student 2: Yes, I **could**. or No, I **couldn't**.

... help me?
... tell me the time?
... show me the way out?
... change twenty dollars?
... repeat that?
... have lunch with me?
... come for dinner?
... direct me to Room 101?

Could you please help me?

Yes, I could.

Write: *Write polite questions using* **could** *for the situations below.*

1. Could you please help me find my way?
Vera is lost.

2.
Ann needs a phone number.

3.
Helen didn't hear the answer.

4.
Mark didn't understand.

5.
Mary wants some coffee.

6.
Troy is hungry.

7.
Al needs a ride home.

8.
Kim wants a cookie.

59

ESL Intermediate Level • Modal Verbs • Asking Polite Questions • Pair Practice • Writing

Teacher's Notes

1 Read and explain the use of **could** in the box at the top of the page.

Explain that **could** is one of many modal verbs. • Other modal verbs are: **can, could, may, might, shall, should, will, would, must, ought to**. Modals do not change form, so we cannot add the **-s** ending to the third person singular. We use modals with the simple form of the verb (an infinitive without **to**).

2 Read and discuss the vocabulary in the items in the Pair Practice exercise. With the help of a student, demonstrate how to do the pair practice exercise using the phrases. Then have the students continue by working in pairs.

As an extension to the Pair Practice exercise, drill polite requests by having students use **could** with the following phrases:

pass the butter	lower the volume
give me change for ...	open this jar for me
give me an application	hold (wait on the telephone)
explain this word	tell me how much this costs
wrap this present	do me a favor
fill 'er up (gas for a car)	tell me the time
check the oil and fluids	lend me...
give me a ride	hand me the ...
tell me how I can get to ... (place)	how to do this

3 Describe situations in which the students must respond with **"Could you...?"**

Stimulus	Response
The door is open. It's cold.	**Could** you please close the door?
You lost your watch and you don't know the time.	**Could** you please tell me the time?
You are at a restaurant with a friend and you don't have any money.	**Could** you lend me some money?

4 Explain how to write questions with **could** in the speech balloons on the handout. Correct the answers by having volunteers write them on the chalkboard. Discuss other possible answers.

Follow-Up Activities

5 • Repeat the pair practice exercise using the expression *"Would you please...?"*

6 • Practice using "could" as the past tense of **can**. Practice the phrases: *"Could you ....* *when you came to this country?*

"Yes, I could ..." or *"No, I couldn't ..."*

ESL Beginning Level   Reading • Oral Drill • Vocabulary Building

Counting U.S. Money

1 Read and pronounce the names of the coins and bills below.

COINS
a penny   = 1 cent
a nickel   = 5 cents
a dime   = 10 cents
a quarter   = 25 cents
a half dollar = 50 cents

a penny
a half dollar 
a quarter 
a dime
a nickel

NOTES *(Paper Money)*
One twenty-dollar bill = a twenty (a 20)
Two five-dollar bills = two fives (two 5s)
Three ten-dollar bills = three tens (three 10s)

2 Count the money in the boxes and fill out the balance sheet to the right.

BALANCE SHEET

Number of Coins   Amount

_____ pennies   _____

_____ nickels   _____

_____ dimes   _____

_____ quarters   _____

_____ half dollars _____

Total: $ _____

3 What combination of coins is correct to pay for the items below? Place the letter in box next to the number.

1 The newspaper costs a dollar.

2 The parking meter costs a half dollar per hour.

3 The magazine cost two dollars and thirty-six cents.

A a twenty-dollar bill, a one-dollar bill, a penny and a quarter

B two quarters

C a quarter, a penny, two nickels, and a dime

D three quarters, a dime, five pennies, and two nickels

E

F a quarter, a dime, a penny, and a dollar bill

ESL Beginning Level　　　　　　Reading • Oral Drill • Vocabulary Building

Teacher's Notes

① Distribute the handout and pronounce the names of the coins and bill. (If possible, bring actual coins and pass them around in the class.) You can even use the paper money from the Monopoly game.

• Read and explain the information in the note.
• Practice the names of the coins by doing a simple drill:

   Student #1: *How much is a (penny) and a (nickel)?*
   Student #2: *It's (six) cents.*

• Practice the use of the short form for bills:

   Student #1: *How much are (2 tens) and (3 fives)?*
   Student #2: *(35)   dollars.*

• Do an additional drill:

   Student #1: *Can you change a (20 or twenty dollar bill)?*
   Student #2: *Yes, I can. Here you are.* or *No, I can't. I only have (2 fives).*

② Read the directions and ask the students to fill out the balance sheet in the middle of the worksheet.

• You may want to project a copy of the handout that has been transferred to an overhead transparency directly onto the chalkboard where students can write the correct answers.

③ Teach the names of the symbols for the following: **+ plus**, **- minus**, and **= equals** (or "**is**."). Practice using the symbols **+**, **-**, and **=** by having students count the money they have in their pockets or purses.

④ Reading Comprehension

BALANCE SHEET

Number of Coins		Amount
6	pennies	.06
5	nickels	.25
7	dimes	.70
3	quarters	.75
0	half dollars	.0
	Total: $	1.76

• Read the directions with the students and have them choose which of the six combinations of coins and bills are correct to purchase a newspaper, parking meter, and magazine.

Answers

1. D (Three quarters, a dime, five pennies, and two nickels equals one dollar.)
2. B (Two quarters equal 50 cents or a half dollar.)
3. E (two dollar bills, a quarter, a dime, and a penny)

⑤ Have the students calculate the amounts in each box:

A = $21.26 (Twenty-one dollars and twenty-six cents);   D. = $1.00 (One dollar);
B = $0.50 (Fifty cents);   E = $2.36 (Two dollars and thirty-six cents);
C = $0.46 (Forty-six cents);   F = $1.36 (One dollar and thirty-six cents)

⑤ Challenge: Ask the students to find the names of the people on U.S. bills. (Answers:

1 dollar bill: George Washington　　　　　　20 dollar bill: Andrew Jackson
5 dollar bill: Abraham Lincoln　　　　　　　 50 dollar bill: Ulysses S. Grant
10 dollar bill: Alexander Hamilton　　　　　　100 dollar bill: Benjamin Franklin

ESL Beginning Level — Expressions of Time

Days, Months, and Seasons

1 *Read and pronounce the words in the boxes.*

Days of the Week (on)	Seasons (in the)	Months (in)
Monday Friday Tuesday Saturday Wednesday Sunday Thursday	Spring Summer Fall (Autumn) Winter	January May September February June October March July November April August December

2 *Practice answering and asking questions with another students. Use the expressions above.*

Student 1: **When do you .... ?** or **When is...?**   Student 2: **I ....**

- I relax _____
- My birthday is _____
- I go to school _____
- I go to the market _____
- My favorite holiday is _____
- I have free time _____
- I visit my family _____
- I don't work _____
- I have free time _____
- I take a vacation _____
- I see my friends _____
- I go to the movies _____

3 *Complete the sentences with the words in boxes above.*

63

ESL Beginning Level Expressions of Time: Days, Months, Seasons

Teacher's Notes

1 Before distributing the worksheet ask simple questions eliciting the days of the week, seasons, and months. Ask questions using "**when**" and the new vocabulary (*relax, birthday, market, favorite, holiday, free time, homework, movies, TV program, work, visit,* and *friends*). Ask the following questions to determine how much the students already know.

When do you relax?	*When do you visit your family?*
When is your birthday?	*When don't you work?*
When do you go to school?	*When do you have free time?*
When do you go to the market?	*When do you take a vacation?*
When is your favorite holiday?	*When do you see your friends/family?*
When do you have free time?	*When do you go to the movies?*

2 Distribute the handout. Read the names of the days and months in the box at the top of the page. Have the students repeat the names several times for correct pronunciation. *(Bring a calendar to class if possible.)*

3 Explain that we use "**in**" with months, seasons, and years, "**on**" dates and the days of the week. (Teach the phrase, "**I was born...**" as an expression although this lesson deals with using the present tense.)

Examples:

I was born	**in**	November.
I was born	**in**	1980.
I was born	**on**	November 29th.
I was born	**on**	November, 29, 1980.

You may want to present variations for dates.

I was born	**on**	the twenty-ninth of November.
I was born	**on**	Thursday, November 29th.

4 Ask the students to circle the name of today's day and the month of their birthday on the worksheet. Practice vocabulary by asking the questions "**What day is today/tomorrow/ etc.?**" and **"When is your birthday?"**

5 Read the directions for the Pair Practice exercise #2, and do a few examples with the whole class. Use the incomplete sentences in the cartoon balloons as cues. Then, have the students continue by practicing in pairs. *(Tell the students not to write; this should be a time for oral practice.)* Expand the activity by asking the students to provide original questions and answers.

6 Next, direct the students to complete the sentences in the balloons in writing, and do a few examples with the whole class. *(You may want to give this as a homework assignment.)*

7 Correct the sentences by projecting a copy of the handout that has been transferred to an overhead transparency directly onto the chalkboard or whiteboard where students can write the correct answers.

8 **Follow-Up Activities**

• Teach ordinal numbers: first, second, third, etc.

• Discuss important local, state, and national holidays; special occasions such as weddings, anniversaries, Mother's Day, Father's Day; religions holidays; and other holidays specific to the native country of the students.

ESL High-Intermediate, Advanced Levels — Discussion • Writing • Drug Abuse

Direct & Indirect Speech

1 Directions: Read and discuss the grammar rules below.

Affirmative
Pronouns must change to agree with the new sentence and the usual sequence of tenses must be followed. Examples:
Direct: *Jim said, "I'm hungry."*
Indirect: *John said (that) he was hungry.*

Imperative
Use the infinitive *(to + verb)* to express a command.
Examples:
Direct: *Anna told me, "Go home!"*
Indirect: *Anna told me to go home.*

Interrogative
Express the original question in statement form.
Examples:
Direct: *Mary asked, "Does John work here?"*
Indirect: *Mary asked where John worked.*

If or whether
Introduce a question with "if" of "whether" if the sentence does NOT begin with a question word. Examples:
Direct: *Mary asked, "Does John work here?"*
Indirect: *Mary asked if John worked here.*

---

2 Directions: Write an ending using direct speech.

Drug Abuse?

Miki could hardly believe her good luck when her friend, Nana, invited her to a party that Ana Dion was giving. Ana and her friends were the most popular students at school. Miki had always dreamed of being in their circle, and of meeting Brad, Ana's brother, because she had a crush on him.

Miki was having a wonderful time at the party when she suddenly saw a marijuana cigarette being passed around. She whispered to Nana, "What are they smoking?"

"Oh, just a little pot," said Nana. "What's wrong with that?"

"It's just that I've never been with people who use drugs. I'm not sure it's right," replied Miki.

"Ana's group thinks it's OK, and you'd better, too, if you want to be part of it."

At that point, Brad came up to them, holding a joint.

"Hey, Miki," he said, "how about a hit?"

_____
_____
_____
_____
_____
_____
_____

Continue on another sheet.

ESL Advanced Level · Discussion • Writing • Drug Abuse

Teacher's Notes

1 Begin the lesson with a discussion. Do not distribute the worksheet yet. Use the following questions as a guide:

- *Do you belong to a club, group, or circle of friends?*
- *What kind of people are in your circle of friends?*
- *What qualities do you look for in new friends?*
- *What do you and your circle of friends have in common?*
- *Are strangers easily accepted into your circle of friends?*
- *Is there a group that you would like to be part of? If so, what would you have to do to become a part of that group?*
- *How strong is peer pressure in your circle of friends?*
- *How do your group feel about alcohol, tobacco, and drugs?*
- *Do you know anyone who takes drugs? If so, what kind?*
- *What affect do they have on people?*
- *How could you help a friend on drugs?*
- *How has drug abuse affected your community? What can be done?*
- *Should some drugs be legalized? Why or why not?*

Language Activities

2 Distribute the worksheet and review the use of direct and indirect speech in the balloons at the top of the sheet. Explain that direct speech consists of reporting <u>exact</u> words of the speaker. Direct quotes are set off by quotation marks (") and with commas (,) if they appear in sentences. Place all punctuation within the quotation marks. Example: **"I'm not sure it's right," replied Jenny.**

3 Do an active listening comprehension exercise by having the students circle any unfamiliar words in the story as you are reading it. You may want to review the following vocabulary: **hardly, grass (marijuana), pot (marijuana), a hit (a puff), a joint (a marijuana cigarette), to have a crush on someone, to whisper, to pass around,** and the expression **"You'd better."**

4 Then ask simple questions beginning with question words (what, where, when, why, etc.) to test the students' comprehension.

5 Discuss the story by asking students how they would continue it.

6 Have students write an ending to the story using direct speech.

7 After the exercise has been corrected, ask for volunteers to share their stories with the class.

8 On the back of the worksheet or on another piece of paper, have students rewrite their stories using indirect speech.

9 **Follow-up Activity**

Ask students to role-play the situations in their stories.

ESL Beginning Level — Imperative: Do & Don't • School Rules

Do & Don't

Directions: Help Mike decide. Write **Do It!** *or* **Don't do it!** *under the photos.*

1. Listen to the teacher. — *Do it!* 
2. Talk on your cell phone in class. — *Don't do it!* 
3. Do your homework.
4. Work quietly. 
5. Arrive late. 
6. Ask permission to speak.  
7. Chew gum.   
8. Argue with other students. 
9. Forget your books. 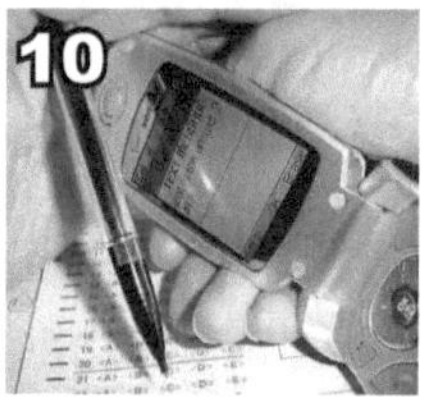
10. Cheat on a test.
11. Make noise. 
12. Dress neatly. 
13. Pay attention. 
14. Treat people with respect. 
15. Play fair. 
16. Text messages in class. 
17. Follow directions. 
18. Eat and drink in class. 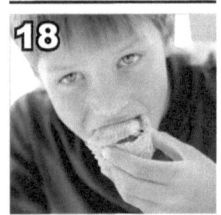 
19. Keep your desk clean. 
20. Correct your mistakes. 
21. Come to class regularly.
22. Talk quietly.

ESL Beginning Level   Imperative: Do & Don't • School Rules

Teacher's Notes

1 Before distributing the worksheet, begin the lesson with a conversation to assess your students' knowledge of general school rules. On the chalkboard list as many rules as you can elicit from your students. Make two lists, one under the word "**DO**" and the other "**DON'T**." Make sure that you cover some of the phrases below:

DO		**DON'T**	
Ask permission to speak.	Keep your desk clean.	Argue with other students.	Make noise.
Come to class regularly.	Listen to the teacher	Arrive late.	Run in the hall.
Correct mistakes.	Pay attention.	Cheat on a test.	Sit on the desk.
Do your homework.	Play fair.	Chew gum.	Smoke at school.
Dress neatly.	Talk quietly.	Eat and drink in class.	Talk on your cell phone in class.
Follow directions.	Treat people with respect.	Forget your books at home.	Text messages in class.
Help the teacher	Work quietly.	Forget your books.	Write on the desk.

2 Distribute the worksheet. Identify what the people are doing in the photos by reading the expression below the photos. Tell the students to say "*Do it!*" or *Don't do it!*" for each phrase.

3 Ask questions in the simple present tense using "*Do*." Model the short answers, "**Yes, I do.**" and "**No, I don't.**" Have your students repeat both the questions and short answers.

Expand the activity by asking the students to respond to the same questions with full sentences. Ask questions such:

Do you listen to the teacher?   *Yes, I listen to the teacher.*
Do you do your homework?   *Yes, I do my homework.*
Do you eat in class?   *No, I don't eat in class.*
Do you chew gum in class?   *No, I don't chew gum in class.*

4 Explain how to write "*Do it!*" and "*Don't do it!*" on the blank line below the photo and phrases. *(See examples.)* In correcting the activity, try projecting a copy of the worksheet onto the chalkboard where students can go up to the board and write the answers.

5 Expand the exercise by doing an oral drill using the following mini-dialog, the commands on the worksheet, and the additional commands below.

Student #1: *Hold it!*
Student #2: *What's the matter?*
Student #1: *Don't .... or ....(imperative form).........!*

Open the window.	Pick up the desk.	Chew gum.
Close the door.	Drink in the classroom.	Eat in class.
Run in the hall.	Do your homework.	Write on the walls.

Follow-Up Activities

6 • Play a pantomime game. Divide the class into two teams. Have members of each team take turns acting out a series of actions. The opposite team must guess the actions. Keep count of each team's correct guesses.

7 • As an additional activity, teach other common expressions in the imperative:

Take care!	Don't do that!	Keep out!
Watch out!	Wait!	Do not enter!
Look out!	Stop!	Handle with care!

ESL Beginning Level   Reading • Fill In • Vocabulary Building

Do & Don't

1 *Read the story about George, Will, Helen, and Ann.*

George and Will like sports.
They play basketball.
They play soccer.
They play baseball.
They don't play football.
They don't play hockey.

Helen and Ann like sports, too.
They go to a gym.
They do aerobics.
They swim.
They don't play football.
They don't lift weights.

Ann   Helen   **George   Will**

2 *Write the missing words.*

1. __Do__ George and Will play basketball?   __Yes,__ , they __do.__ .
2. __Do__ George and Will play football?   __No__ , they __don't__ .
3. _____ George and Will play soccer?   _____, they _____ .
4. _____ they play hockey?   _____, they _____ .

5. _____ Helen And Ann play football?   _____, they _____ .
6. _____ Helen and Ann do aerobics?   _____, they _____ .
7. _____ they go to a gym?   _____, they _____ .
8. _____ they lift weights?   _____, they _____ .

3 *Read the story about Bob and Harriett.*

Bob and Harriett don't work.
They are retired.
They exercise often.
They walk.
They ride. They bicycle.
They don't jog.
They don't run.

4 *Write the missing words.*

9. _____ Bob and Harriett exercise?   _____, they _____ .
10. _____ Bob and Harriett walk?   _____, they _____ .
11. _____ they jog?   _____, they _____ .
12. _____ they run?   _____, they _____ .

ESL Beginning Level • Present Tense: DO & DON'T • Reading • Fill In • Vocabulary Building

Teacher's Notes

1 Before distributing the worksheet, begin the lesson with a conversation to assess your students' knowledge of the use of "***do***," "***don't***," and the names of some sports and individual physical exercises. On the chalkboard list as many sports and activities as you can elicit from your students. Make sure that you include some of the phrases below:

basketball	*hockey*	*lift weights*	*jog*
soccer	*aerobics*	*walk*	*run*
baseball	*swim*	*ride a bicycle*	

2 Distribute the worksheet and read the story about George, Will, Helen, and Ann to the students as a listening comprehension exercise. *(If possible, project a copy of the worksheet onto a screen or chalkboard so that your students do not write at this point in the lesson.)*

3 Ask simple "yes/ no" comprehension questions using "***Do***." Example: Question: ***"Do George and Will like sports?"*** Have students answer ***"Yes, they do."*** or ***"No, they don't."***

4 Read the stories again while the students underline unfamiliar vocabulary. Then explain the vocabulary.

5 Use the fill-in exercises in Section 2 as oral drills. *(Discourage students from writing. This should be a time for oral practice.)* Continue the drill by having students ask questions using "***do***."

6 Next, have students write in the missing words. *(See examples.)*

7 Correct the sentences. You may want to project a copy of the handout that has been transferred to an overhead transparency directly onto a chalkboard or whiteboard where students can write and see the correct answers.

8 Repeat the same procedure for Sections 3 and 4.

Follow-Up Activities

9 • As a class, write a four-line text modeled on the stories on the worksheet about two students in your class. Practice asking and answering questions about the new story.

10 • Discuss the verbs that are associated with sports:

play hockey	*hike*	*ice skate*
play baseball	*swim*	*ski*
play basketball	*surf*	*water ski*
play football	*jog*	*bowl*
play soccer	*run*	*box*
play tennis	*walk*	*do aerobics*
play volleyball	*exercise*	*do gymnastics*
play racquetball	*ride bicycles*	*lift weights*
play handball	*golf*	
play ping-pong	*roller skate*	

11 • On a subsequent day, give the stories as a dictation.

ESL Beginning Level
Crossword Puzzle • Vocabulary Building
"Do" or "Make" Expressions

Directions: *Fill in the boxes with the expressions used with "do" or "make" in the photos.*

1 across — Do the _____ 
4 across — Make a _____ 
6 across — Make a _____ 
7 across — Do the _____ 
9 across — Do the _____ 
14 across — Do the _____ 
17 across — Make a _____ (two words)  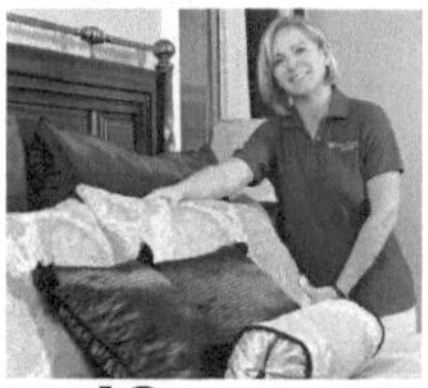
19 across — Make the _____ 
20 across — Do the _____ 
22 across — Do the _____ 
23 across — Do one's _____

2 down — Do the _____
3 down — Make a _____ 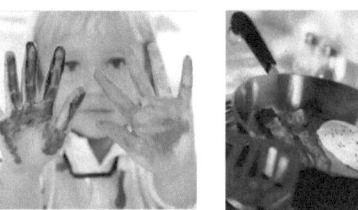
4 down — Do the _____ 
5 down — Make a _____ 
8 down — Do the _____ 
10 down — Do the _____ 
11 down — Do one's _____ 
12 down — Do the _____ 
13 down — Do the _____ 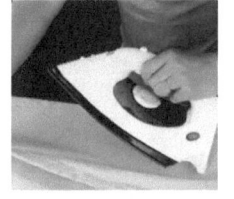
15 down — Do one's _____ 
16 down — Do the _____ 
18 down — Do the _____ 
21 down — Do one's _____ 

1 across: WEEDING
2 down: DRAPES

71

ESL Beginning Level · Crossword Puzzle • Vocabulary Building

Teacher's Notes

1 Before distributing the worksheet, begin the lesson with a conversation to assess your students' knowledge of some common expression using "do" and "make." Ask questions using the simple present tense such as:

What do you do at home?
Do you do the laundry, shopping, cooking?
Do you make your bed, meals, a mess?

What is a man's/woman's/children's chores?
What don't you do at home?
Who does the [chore] at your home?

2 Distribute the worksheet. Identify what the people are doing in the photos. Ask the question using the present continuous tense, "**What's [person] doing?**" Model the response, "**He/She's doing/making _____.**" Have the students repeat both question and answer. Continue asking similar questions about the other people in the photos.

3 Ask your students general questions about other common chores. Ask them to name and describe as many as they can. List them on the board. Make sure that the lists include some of the following items:

Do one's best	Do the carpets	Do the dusting	Do the laundry	Make a meal
Do one's hair	Do the cleaning	Do the floors	Do the shopping	Make a mess
Do one's homework	Do the cooking	Do the gardening	Do the yard work	Make a phone call
Do one's nails	Do the dishes	Do the housework	Do the windows	Make a reservation
Do the bathroom	Do the drapes	Do the ironing	Make a cake	Make the bed

4 Grammar Note: Explain to your students that we usually use the verb "*do*" for most household chores except for "*make the bed.*" "*Do*" is widely used when referring to all types of work. We usually use the verb "*make*" when describing work that is done by one's hands, construction, and building. Using "*make*" implies that what was made can be touched.

5 Demonstrate how to do a crossword puzzle. Explain the concept of **DOWN** and **ACROSS**. Then, show the students how to fill in the puzzle using the visual clues. Do a few examples with the whole class. Allow some time for your students to complete the crossword puzzle. You may want to have students work in pairs or assigning it as a homework assignment.

6 Correct the answers by projecting an overhead transparency image directly onto the board on which students can take turns writing the answers on the board. See solution below.

7 Play a crossword puzzle game. Draw or project a grid onto the board or screen as well as a list of expression using either "*do*" or "*make.*" Divide the class into two teams and flip a coin to determine which team goes first. Have the first student of the first team go to the board and write a word that uses one letter of an existing word in the crossword. If the word fits and is correctly spelled, then give one point for every letter of the new word. Then, go on to the first student of the other team. If the word is incorrect, erase it and go to the opposite team.

8 As a follow-up activity have a class discussion about the kinds of household duties are done by men and women in your students' households. Have your students make a list of their household chores on the back of the handout. Discuss and compare the students' chores in class.

CROSSWORD PUZZLE SOLUTION:

ACROSS: 1 weeding, 4 cake, 6 reservation, 7 dishes, 9 dusting, 14 cleaning, 17 phone call, 19 bed, 20 shopping, 22 laundry, 23 homework;

DOWN: 2 drapes, 3 mess, 4 cooking, 5 meal, 8 housework, 10 carpets, 11 best, 12 gardening, 13 ironing, 15 nails, 16 bathroom, 18 floors, 21 hair

ESL Beginning Level   Present Tense • Reading • Fill In • Vocabulary Building

Does & Doesn't

❶ Read the story about Mike and Tom

Mike lives in Canada.
Tom lives in Brazil.
Mike rents a house.
Tom rents an apartment.
Mike works outside.
Tom works in an office.
Mike drives a truck.
Tom drives a car.

❷ Write the missing words.

1. Mike _____ in Canada; he _____ _____ in Brazil.
2. Mike _____ a house; he _____ _____ an apartment.
3. Mike _____ outside; he _____ _____ in an office.
4. Mike _____ a truck; he _____ _____ a car.
5. __*Does*__ Mike __*live*__ in Canada? __*Yes,*__, he __*does*__.
6. __*Does*__ Mike __*rent*__ an apartment? __*No*__, he __*doesn't*__.
7. _____ Mike _____ outside? _____, he _____.
8. _____ Mike _____ a car? _____, he _____.
9. _____ Mike _____ a truck? _____, he _____.
10. _____ Mike _____ in New York? _____, he _____.

---

❸ Read the story about Ella and Kana.

Ella lives in Moscow.
Kana lives in Tokyo.
Ella works in a store.
Kana works in a factory.
Ella eats lunch at home.
Kana eats lunch at work.

❹ Write the missing words.

11. Ella _____ in Moscow; she _____ _____ in Tokyo.
12. Kana _____ in Tokyo; she _____ _____ Moscow.
13. Ella _____ in a store; she _____ _____ in a factory.
14. Kana _____ lunch at work; she _____ _____ at home.
15. _____ Ella _____ in Moscow? _____, she _____.
16. _____ Ella _____ in Tokyo? _____, she _____.
17. _____ Ella _____ in a store? _____, she _____.
18. _____ Ella _____ at work? _____, she _____.

ESL Beginning Level • Present Tense: DOES & DOESN'T • Reading • Fill In • Vocabulary Building

Teacher's Notes

1 Before distributing the worksheet, begin the lesson with a conversation to assess your students' knowledge of the use of "*does*" and "*doesn't*." Ask questions about some of your students in class. Ask questions such as

Does [name] live in this country?   *Does [person] drive a car?*
Does [name] rent an apartment?   *Does [person] drive a truck?*
Does [person] work?   *Does [person] eat lunch at school?*

2 Distribute the worksheet and read the story about Mike and Tom to the students as a listening comprehension exercise. *(If possible, project a copy of the worksheet onto a screen or chalkboard so that your students do not write at this point in the lesson.)*

3 Ask simple "yes/ no" comprehension questions using "***Does***." Example: Question: ***"Does Mike rent a house?"*** Have students answer ***"Yes, he does."*** or ***"No, he doesn't."***

4 Read the stories again while the students underline unfamiliar vocabulary. Then explain the vocabulary.

5 Use the fill-in exercises in Section 2 as oral drills. *(Discourage students from writing. This should be a time for oral practice.)* Continue the drill by having students ask questions using "***does***."

6 Next, have students write in the missing words. *(See examples.)*

7 Correct the sentences. You may want to project a copy of the handout that has been transferred to an overhead transparency directly onto a chalkboard or whiteboard where students can write and see the correct answers.

8 Repeat the same procedure for Sections 3 and 4.

9 **Grammar Notes:** Explain the spelling rules for the third person singular ending:

• Add "***-es***" to verbs that end with "***s***," "***sh***," "***ch***," "***z***," and "***x***" sounds.

• When words end in "***y***" preceded by a consonant, change the "***y***" to "***i***" and add "***-es***." This is the same rule for forming plural nouns.

• Add "***-s***" to most other verbs.

Examples: "***She punches in at 8 a.m.***"; "***She finishes at 5 p.m.***"; and "***He studies in the evening.***" (Other verbs include: ***change, catch, teach, wash, watch, dress, miss, marry,*** and ***study***.)

Follow-Up Activities

10 As a class, write a six-line text about two students in your class modeled on the stories on the handout. Practice asking and answering about the new story using "***does***" and "***doesn't***."

11 Locate Canada, Brazil, Moscow, Russia, and Tokyo, Japan on a map.

12 Locate the homes of the students in the class on a map or by using "Google Earth."

13 On a subsequent day, give the stories as a dictation.

ESL Advanced Level   Vocabulary Building • Reading Comprehension

Understanding Driving Directions

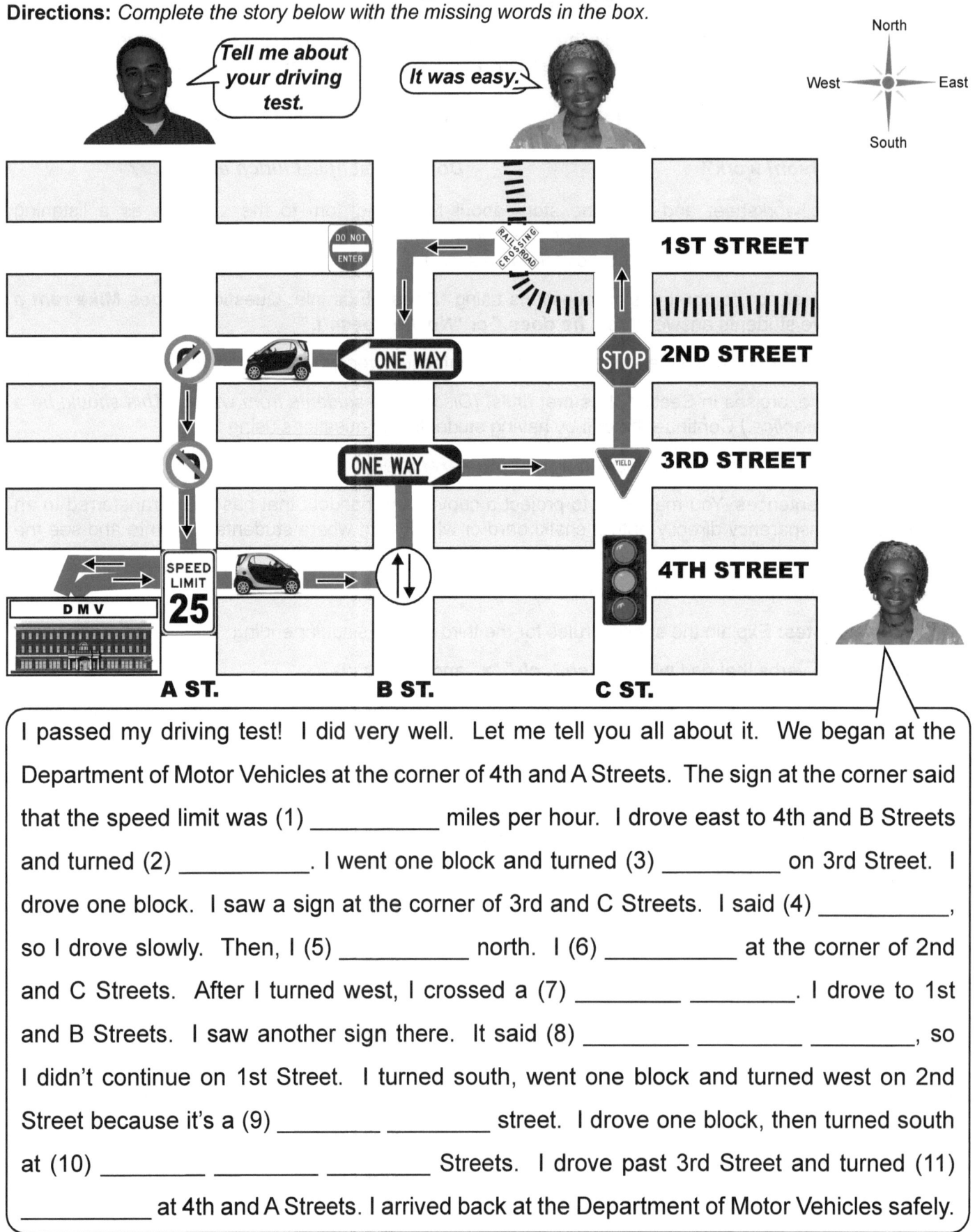

Directions: *Complete the story below with the missing words in the box.*

I passed my driving test! I did very well. Let me tell you all about it. We began at the Department of Motor Vehicles at the corner of 4th and A Streets. The sign at the corner said that the speed limit was (1) _____ miles per hour. I drove east to 4th and B Streets and turned (2) _____. I went one block and turned (3) _____ on 3rd Street. I drove one block. I saw a sign at the corner of 3rd and C Streets. I said (4) _____, so I drove slowly. Then, I (5) _____ north. I (6) _____ at the corner of 2nd and C Streets. After I turned west, I crossed a (7) _____ _____. I drove to 1st and B Streets. I saw another sign there. It said (8) _____ _____ _____, so I didn't continue on 1st Street. I turned south, went one block and turned west on 2nd Street because it's a (9) _____ _____ street. I drove one block, then turned south at (10) _____ _____ _____ Streets. I drove past 3rd Street and turned (11) _____ at 4th and A Streets. I arrived back at the Department of Motor Vehicles safely.

75

ESL Advanced Level   Vocabulary Building • Reading Comprehension

Teacher's Notes

❶ Review the meanings of the traffic signs in the map at the top of the handout. (You may want to contact your local Department of Motor Vehicles for driver handbook that contains pictures of all traffic signs or use the lesson on traffic signs on page 241 to review traffic signs before doing this lesson.

❷ Explain how to fill in the words in the fill-in exercise. Read the words in the box at the top of the page, read the directions, and do a few examples with the whole class. Correct the exercise by having volunteers read parts of the text aloud.

Answers

1. 25	5. turned	9. ONE WAY
2. left	6. stopped	10. Second and A
3. right	7. Railroad Crossing	11. west
4. YIELD	8. DO NOT ENTER	

❸ Have students change the story from the past to the imperative.

Example:

- *Begin at the Department of Motor Vehicles at the corner of 4th and A Streets.*
- *Drive east to 4th and B Streets and turn left.*
- *Go one block and turn right on 3rd Street.*
- *Drive one block.*
- *Turn north.*
- *Stop at the corner of 2nd and C Streets, then go to 1st and C Streets.*
- *After you turn west, cross a railroad crossing.*
- *Drive to 1st and B Streets.*
- *Turn south, go one block, and turn west on 2nd Street.*
- *Drive one block, and then turn south at 2nd and A Streets.*
- *Drive past 3rd Street and arrive back at the Department of Motor Vehicles.*

❹ Practice giving directions by having students explain how to go from school to various places in your community.

❺ For additional practice, try arranging desks, tables, and chairs as an obstacle course. Have one students direct a blind-folded student through the course by giving oral directions.

❻ Follow-up Activity

Ask the students to bring in a map of the city. Ask them to find government buildings, fire department, hospital, schools, religious institutions, airports, bus stations, cultural and recreation facilities. Have them explain how to get to each place from the school and what kind of service each place provides.

ESL Advanced Level   Vocational ESL • Discussion • Fill-in

Employment Application

"We'll keep your application and call you about the job after we finish all the interviews."

APPLICATION FOR EMPLOYMENT

All applicants will be considered for employment without regard to race, religion, color, sex, national origin, age, marital status, disability, sexual orientation, veteran status or any other status protected by law. We are an Equal Opportunity Employer.

PERSONAL INFORMATION
(Please print or type)   Date __2/3/16__

Name __Vince Cartelli__   Soc. Sec# __032-66-2526__
Address __13 Theater Drive, #1__ City __L.A.__ State __CA__ Zip __90038__
Telephone No. __213-421-9605__   Referred By: __Joanne Vordale__
Are you legally eligible for permanent employment in the U.S.? __Yes__
Position(s) applied for __salesperson__   Full Time __x__   Part Time ☐
Seasonal Help only ☐ Yes   ☒ No
If part time, specify days/hours available __N.A.__
Rate of pay desired: $ __15__ per __hr.__
Have you worked for us before? __x__ If YES, when? ____ Position ____
Indicate special qualifications or skills __I have experience with lumber, paint, and hardware.__

EDUCATION NAME & LOCATION OF SCHOOL	COURSE OF STUDY	DID YOU GRADUATE?	IF YOU DIDN'T GRADUATE YEARS COMPLETED OR ATTENDED
ELEMENTARY Solis Elem., Puerto Rico		Yes	
HIGH SCHOOL Kennedy H.S.		Yes	
		No	

(employment subject to legal age verification)

APPLICATION FOR EMPLOYMENT

All applicants will be considered for employment without regard to race, religion, color, sex, national origin, age, marital status, disability, sexual orientation, veteran status or any other status protected by law. We are an Equal Opportunity Employer.

PERSONAL INFORMATION   Date _____
(Please print or type)

Name _____   Soc. Sec# _____
Address _____ City _____ State _____ Zip _____
Telephone No. _____ Referred By: _____
Are you legally eligible for permanent employment in the U.S.? _____
Position(s) applied for _____ Full Time ☐   Part Time ☐
Seasonal Help only   ☐ Yes   ☐ No
If part time, specify days/hours available _____
Rate of pay desired: $ _____ per _____
Have you worked for us before? _____ If YES, when? _____ Position _____
Indicate special qualifications or skills _____

EDUCATION NAME & LOCATION OF SCHOOL	COURSE OF STUDY	DID YOU GRADUATE?	IF YOU DIDN'T GRADUATE YEARS COMPLETED OR ATTENDED
ELEMENTARY			
HIGH SCHOOL			
COLLEGE			
OTHER			

SPECIAL QUESTIONS
Are you over 18 years of age? _____ If NO, state your age: _____ *(employment subject to legal age verification)*

"Thank you for your time."

Write
Fill out the application for the job, too. Use the application at the top as an example.

ESL Advanced Level Vocational ESL • Discussion • Fill-in

Teacher's Notes

1 Before having the students fill out the form on this page, demonstrate on the board the meaning of check, *underline, print, circle,* and *cross out.*

2 Have the students take a piece of paper. Dictate each instruction below. Then demonstrate each appropriate action on the board.

1. On line one, print your name.
2. Write 1-10 on the second line.
3. Underline your last name.
4. Circle your first name.
5. Check the first line.
6. Cross out number 6.
7. Underline number 9.
8. Circle number 1.
9. Cross out number 10.
10. Check the second line.

3 Read through the application and explain any unfamiliar vocabulary.

4 Instead of the teacher asking comprehension questions about the dialog, play a game. Divide the class into two teams. Teams take turns asking difficult questions about the application. If one team asks a question that the second team cannot answer, then it gets a point. If the answer is correct, then no points are given. The team with the most points wins.

5 Have the students fill out the job application. Correct the application with a transparency and overhead projector if available.

6 Have the students do a role-play job interview in front of the class. Use volunteers. One student is the employer and the second is an applicant. Use some of the items on the application. The rest of the class rates the interview with the raiting form below.

	Very Good	Good	Fair	Poor	Bad
Posture					
Manners					
Language					
Voice					
Eye Contact					
Attitude					
Personality					
Self-Confidence					
Personal Appearance					

ESL Beginning Level — Vocabulary Building • Class Discussion • Fill In

Family Relationships

Panel 1: What's the relationship between Yvonne and Wilfred? — They're husband and wife.

Panel 2: Who does Mark look like? — He looks like his grandfather.

Panel 3: Who is Audrey's father? — Leo is Audrey's father.

Panel 4: What are Joey and Audrey? — They're cousins.

❶
Practice asking and answering questions with another student about the relationships in the family tree below. Use the dialogs above as models and

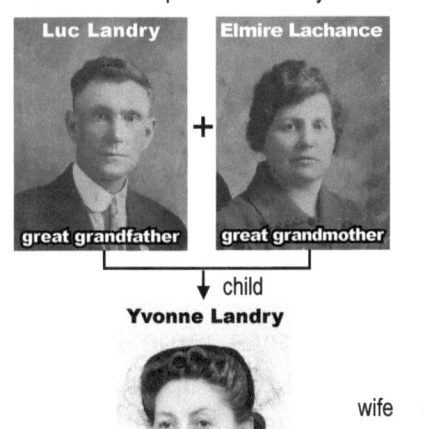

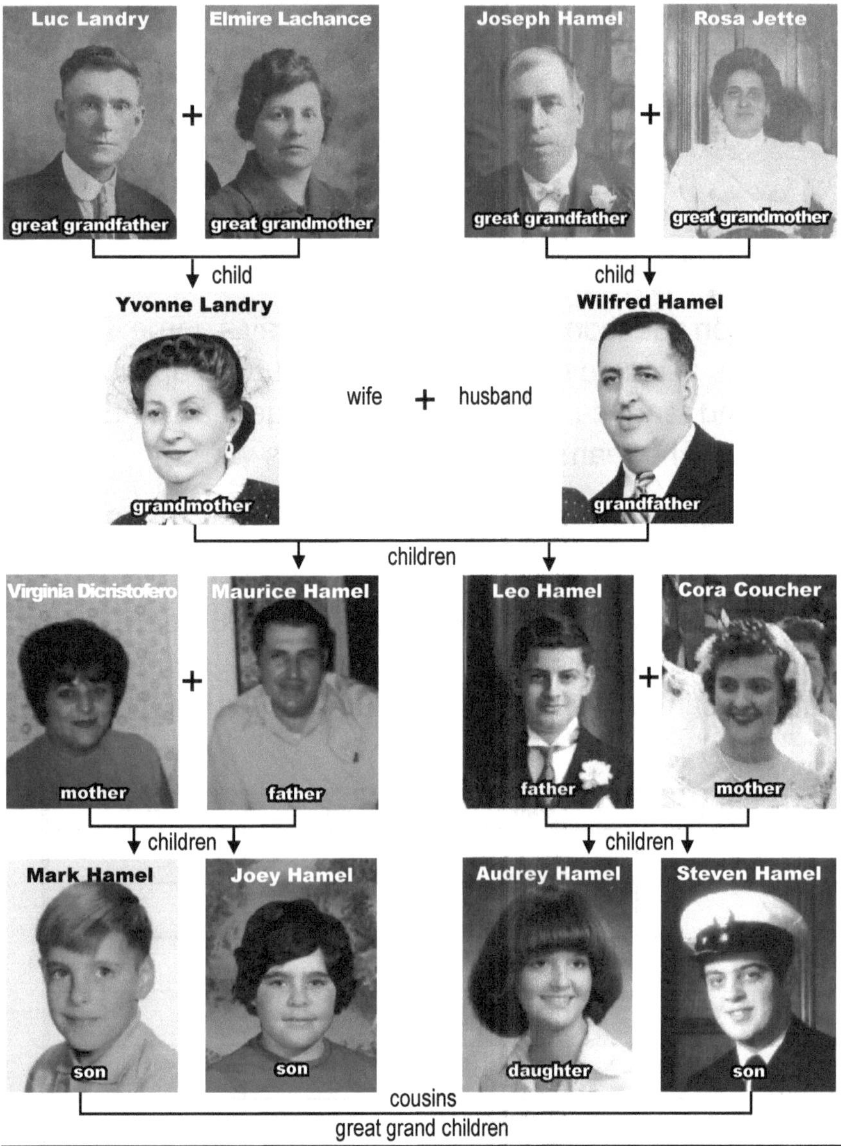

Family Tree:

- Luc Landry (great grandfather) + Elmire Lachance (great grandmother) → child: Yvonne Landry
- Joseph Hamel (great grandfather) + Rosa Jette (great grandmother) → child: Wilfred Hamel
- Yvonne Landry (wife, grandmother) + Wilfred Hamel (husband, grandfather) → children:
  - Virginia Dicristofero (mother) + Maurice Hamel (father) → children: Mark Hamel (son), Joey Hamel (son)
  - Leo Hamel (father) + Cora Coucher (mother) → children: Audrey Hamel (daughter), Steven Hamel (son)
- cousins; great grand children

❷ Class Discussion

Discuss the following questions in class.

1. How many people are there in your family?
2. How many brothers and sisters do you have?
3. Do all your family members live together?
4. How many family members do you life with?
5. Do you live with your parents?
6. Are your parents living?
7. Are your grand parents living?
8. Where do your relatives live?
9 Who do you look like in your family?
10. Who is your oldest living relative?

❸ Write: Fill In

Fill in the blanks below with one of the words in the list at the bottom of the worksheet.

My cousin's father is my (1) _____ and my uncle's wife is my (2) _____ and my aunt's children are my (3) _____ and my father's mother is my (4) _____ and my mother's father is my (5) _____ and my grandparent's son is my (6) _____ .

My uncle and (7) _____'s daughter is my cousin, and my brother and (8) his _____'s children are my niece and nephew, and my (9) _____'s sister is my sister-in-law, and my (10) _____'s husband is my brother-in-law, and you are my (11) _____ and I am your (12) _____!

Family	son	sister	uncle	relative(s)	brother-in-law	distant relative
husband	daughter	grandfather	aunt	father-in-law	sister-in-law	first name
wife	father, dad	grandmother	nephew	mother-in-law	step-father	middle name
parents	mother, mom	grand daughter	niece	son-in-law	step-mother	last/sir name
child/children	brother	grand son	cousin(s)	daughter-in-law	step-children	maiden name

ESL Beginning Level • Family Relationships • Vocabulary Building • Class Discussion • Fill In

Teacher's Notes

1 Before distributing the handout ask simple questions about the students' families to determine how much vocabulary they know about family relationships. You may want to use the questions in Section 3: Class Discussion.

2 Review the use of the possessive ('s). **See Worksheet #0016: Student Mixer • Using the Possessive ('s)**

3 Distribute the handout and read the mini-dialogs at the top of the page. Discuss the meaning and practice the pronunciation of the vocabulary at the bottom of the handout.

4 Read the names and relationships in the family tree.

5 Practice asking questions based on the mini-dialogs to the students. After the students have learned how to ask the questions, ask for volunteers to pose similar questions with the following structures:

- **What is the relationship between _____ and _____?**
- **Who is _____'s _____?**
- **What are _____ and _____?**
- **Who does _____ look like?**

Gradually begin asking the students personal questions with the same structures. Finally, have the students ask one another original questions using the questions in Section 2 as samples.

6 As a reading comprehension and simple writing activity, direct the students to read the text silently in Exercise 3, then fill in the missing words using the vocabulary at the bottom of the page.

Answers: 1. uncle, 2. aunt, 3. cousins, 4. grandmother, 5. grandfather, 6. father or uncle, 7. aunt, 8. sister, 9. husband, 10. sister, 11. son/daughter, 12. mother

7 **Follow-Up Activity: Homework Assignment**

Make enlarged copies of the outline of the family tree below, and distribute it to the students to fill in. On a subsequent day, make copies of a few of the students' family tree and project them one at a time onto the chalkboard using an overhead projector. Also, ask the students to bring in personal photos of their families.

8 Have students practice the following questions and answers about their family tree and photos:

Student 1: *What's your _____'s name?*   **Student 2:** *His/her name is _____ .*

Student 2: *Who's ___(name)___ ?*   **Student 2:** *That's my _____ .*

Directions: Make your own family tree. Fill in the spaces with the names of the members of your family. Add spaces if necessary.

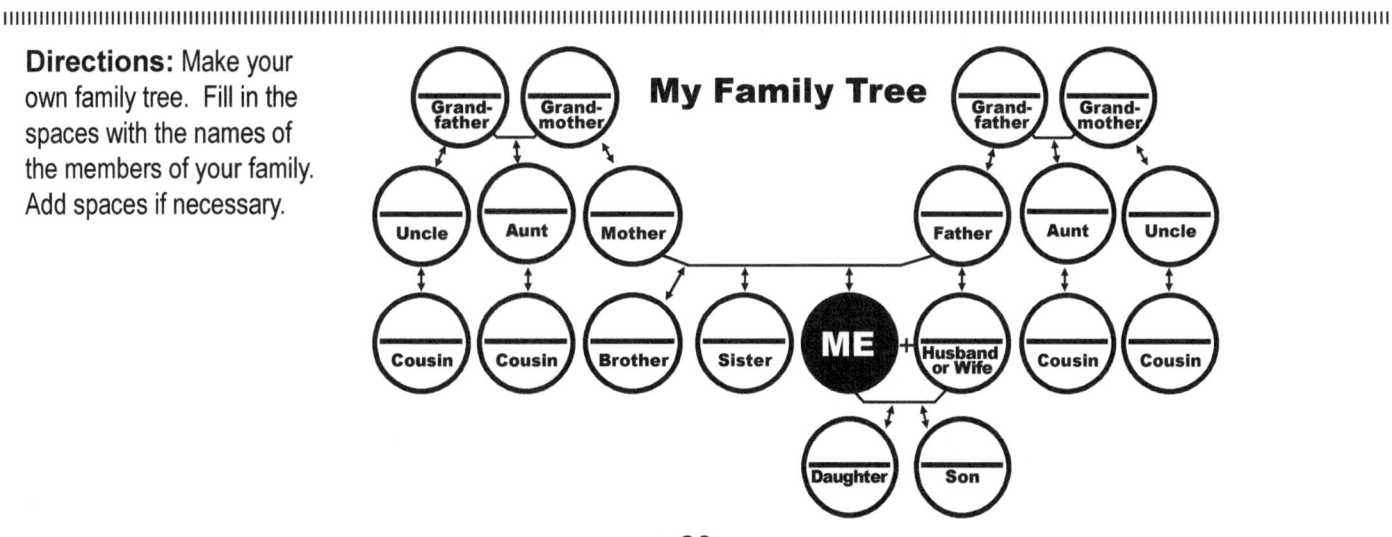

My Family Tree

(family tree diagram with: Grandfather, Grandmother, Uncle, Aunt, Mother, Father, Aunt, Uncle, Cousin, Cousin, Brother, Sister, ME, Husband or Wife, Cousin, Cousin, Daughter, Son)

80

ESL Beginning & Intermediate Levels   Personal Information • Writing • Reading

Filling Out a Simple Form

1 *Read the registration card and the abbreviations below.*

"I want to register for a class."

Wanda Perry

REGISTRATION FORM
Print Firmly

NAME ____Perry_____Wanda_____Marie____
           Last   First   Middle

ADDRESS ____3300 Brown Street, Apt. 101____
              Number   Street   Apartment

CITY _Los Angeles_ STATE _CA_ ZIP CODE _90046_

DATE OF BIRTH _6/21/1976_ NATIONALITY _French_

COURSE _ESL_ LEVEL _3_ TELEPHONE _323-213-0987_

SIGNATURE _Wanda Perrie_ DATE _1/7/2009_

Abbreviations
St. = Street
Ave. = Avenue
Blvd. = Boulevard
Dr. = Drive
Rd. = Road
Apt. = Apartment
# = Number
N. = North
S. = South
E. = East
W. = West

2 *Fill out the registration form for Ramon Perez.*

REGISTRATION FORM
Print Firmly

NAME _____
           Last   First   Middle
ADDRESS _____
           Number   Street   Apartment
CITY _____ STATE _____ ZIP CODE _____
DATE OF BIRTH _____ NATIONALITY _____
COURSE _____ LEVEL _____ TELEPHONE _____
SIGNATURE _____ DATE _____

"I'm Ramon Perez. My middle name is Juan. I want to study English. I'm from Peru. I want to be in level two ESL class. I passed a placement test for level two. I live at 1133 Woodman Ave., La Mesa, California. My zip code is nine-two-zero-four-one. My phone number is six-one-nine-four-six-nine-three-one-five-seven. I'm thirty-one years old. My birthday is July second."

3 *Fill out your own registration form.*

REGISTRATION FORM
Print Firmly

NAME _____
           Last   First   Middle
ADDRESS _____
           Number   Street   Apartment
CITY _____ STATE _____ ZIP CODE _____
DATE OF BIRTH _____ NATIONALITY _____
COURSE _____ LEVEL _____ TELEPHONE _____
SIGNATURE _____ DATE _____

ESL Beginning & Intermediate Levels   Personal Information • Writing • Reading

Teacher's Notes

1 Distribute the handout and read the registration card at the top of the page. Make students aware of the street address patterns used in your community. In many English-speaking countries, cities are usually organized in blocks. Each block generally contains one hundred addresses. Odd numbers are used on one side of the street and evennumbers on the other side. Some cities, such as Washington, D.C., utilize a grid system dividing the city into N.E., N.W., S.E., and S. W.

2 On the chalkboard or whiteboard, list the abbreviations along with their non abbreviated forms. Drill for pronunciation. Allow the students sufficient time to study the list. Then erase the non abbreviated forms. Divide the class into two teams. Alternately have one member of each team come to the chalkboard. Have the student select a word from the list of abbreviations and write the word beside the corresponding abbreviation. For each correct answer, give one point to the appropriate team. Insist on complete accuracy including spelling and capitalization. You may want to use some of the additional words below.

CA	California	Hwy.	highway	Rm.	room
Cir.	circle	Jr.	junior	Ste.	suite
Co.	county, country	Ln.	lane	TX	Texas
Ct.	court	Pl.	place	NY	New York
D.C.	District of Columbia	P.O.	post office	L.A.	Los Angeles

3 Read the information about Roger Best in the speech balloons.

• Tell the students that they are responsible for filling out the registration card using the information in the speech balloon. Do the first few lines with them. (You may want to project an overhead transparency image directly onto the chalkboard where students can write their answers directly onto the form.)

4 Before having the students fill out the registration card at the bottom of the page, point out the following items that may cause confusion.

1. the meaning of Mr., Mrs., Miss, and Ms.

2. the last name preceding the first name on many forms and applications

3. the street number preceding the street name

4. apartment numbers written as #6, Apt. 6, or Apt. #6 and placed after the street name

5. telephone area codes and prefixes

6. the month as the first element of the date which is expressed either by word or number

ESL Beginning & Low Intermediate Levels — Word Building/Common Verbs

Following Simple Directions

Directions: Place the instructions below in the correct order.

Operating Simple Machines

❶ To operate a photocopier:

___2___ Open lid.

_____ Close lid.

_____ Wait for the light.

_____ Remove original paper and copy.

___3___ Place paper on glass surface.

___1___ Deposit money.

_____ Select size of copy.

_____ Press button to start.

❷ To operate a coin-operated washing machine:

_____ Close lid.

_____ Open lid.

_____ Deposit money.

_____ Push money to start.

_____ Remove clean clothes.

_____ Select water temperature.

_____ Wait until the machine stops.

_____ Place dirty clothes and detergent in the washer.

❸ To operate a microwave oven:

_____ Close door.

_____ Open door.

_____ Remove hot food.

_____ Press button to start.

_____ Place cold food in microwave.

_____ Select time and temperature.

_____ Wait for the buzzer when the food is cooked.

❹ To replace a printer cartridge

_____ Turn off printer.

_____ Remove old printer cartridge.

_____ Close cover.

_____ Use printer.

_____ Lift printer cover.

_____ Turn on printer.

_____ Replace old printer cartridge with new cartridge.

ESL Beginning & Low Intermediate Levels   Word Building/Common Verbs

Teacher's Notes

1 Introduce the vocabulary below before doing the exercise. Try using pantomime.

deposit	**press**	**use**	**operate**	**check**	**unplug**
open	**wait**	**lift**	**make**	**adjust**	**plug in**
place	**remove**	**turn on**	**position**	**follow**	**screw**
close	**push**	**turn off**	**tighten**	**include**	**unscrew**
select	**turn**	**replace**	**insert**	**attach**	**throw away**

2 Read through the sentences in the four exercises. Then explain how to put the sentences in the correct order. Do the first example with the whole class. You may want to project the image on the chalkboard using an overhead projector. Correct the exercise by having individuals read the right order aloud.

Answers
Photocopier: 2, 4, 7, 9, 3, 1, 5, 8, 6
Microwave: 7, 1, 6, 4, 2, 3, 5

Washing machine: 4, 1, 5, 6, 8, 3, 7, 2
Printer cartridge: 1, 3, 5, 7, 2, 6, 4

3 **Activities**

- Have students do a pantomine activity. Ask volunteers to act out the instructions without speaking.

- As a review of the present continuous tense, have the students act out the instructions using the present continuous. For example, I **am depositing** the money, I **am opening** the lid.

- Have the students practice the past tense by describing what they did. For example, Mary **deposited** the money. She **opened** the lid.

4 **Follow-Up Activities**

- For additional practice, place the instructions below out of order on the chalkboard and repeat the activities above.

To Operate a Coffee Machine

- Deposit money.
- Select item.
- Press button to start.
- Lift plastic door.
- Remove cup.

To Replace a Light Bulb

- Turn off the lamp.
- Disconnect the plug.
- Remove shade.
- Unscrew the old bulb.
- Screw in the new bulb.
- Replace the shade.
- Plug in the cord.
- Turn on the switch.

To Replace a Dirty Heater Filter

- Turn off the heater.
- Remove the heater cover.
- Remove the dirty filter.
- Replace it with a new filter.
- Close the cover.
- Turn on the heater.
- Throw away the dirty filter.

5 **Follow Up Activities**

- Ask the students to find a simple set of directions and bring them to class to share with the other students.

- Ask the students to mix up the order of the directions and place them on the board/overhead transparency so that other students can discuss them.

ESL Beginning Level • Pair Practice • Present Tense • Abbreviations • Vocabulary Building

Reading Food Ads

1 **Directions:** *Read the ads below. Then, answer the questions about the items in the supermarket ad below.*

1. How much do two pounds of apples cost?
2. Are tomatoes on sale?
3. How much do five cans of orange juice cost?
4. How much do you save on Swiss cheese?
5. How much does a bag of apples cost with a coupon?
6. How many rolls are there in a package of paper towels?
7. How much do two bags of potatoes cost?

LOWER PRICES
Shop at Breyer's Supermarket

APPLES — 75% off with coupon — 1 lb. bag $2.50

YOGURT — 8 oz. container .70¢

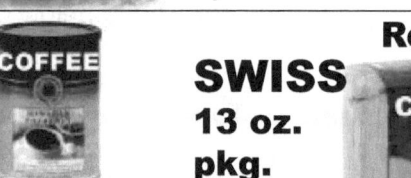

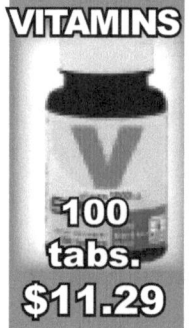

POTATOES — Buy one bag, get one free. — 2 lb. bag $3.99

TOMATOS on the vine — SALE — .88¢ per lb.

CHICKEN — 3.5 lbs. $5.92

EGGS — $1.79 — 1 doz. carton

TUNA — 12 oz. can — Solid White Albacore Tuna — Limited time offer — $3.69

ORANGE JUICE — 6 oz. can — $1 ea. — limit 5

PAPER TOWELS — 3 rolls for $2.99

COFFEE — 1 lb. can — $6.99

SWISS CHEESE — Reg. $6. — 13 oz. pkg. — SALE — $4.99

CANDY — 32 oz. jar — 7.89¢

FLOUR — 5 lb. sack — $3.09

DETERGENT — WASH — 96 oz container — $12.99

DEODORANT — 2 1/2 oz. stick — $3.49

VITAMINS — 100 tabs. — $11.29

Abbreviations
reg. = regular
oz. = ounce
ea. = each
lb. = pound
tabs. = tablets
pkg. = package
lb. = pound
per = each

Containers
cans
sack
boxes   jars
cartons
bottles

2 **Pair Practice:** *Ask and answer questions using the supermarket ad above. See examples below.*

Student 1: *How much does a ... cost?*
Student 2: *A ... cost ... $ ...*

How much does a can of tuna cost?

A can of tuna costs $3.69.

85

ESL Beginning Level • Pair Practice • Present Tense • Abbreviations • Vocabulary Building

Teacher's Notes

1 Distribute the handout. Read and explain any new vocabulary items and abbreviations in the newspaper food ad, their sizes, and the abbreviations. *(See box below the ad on the worksheet.)*

2 Have students practice making sentences modeled on the structure below.

A/an [quantity] of [item] costs [price].

Examples:

A pound of apples costs two dollars and fifty cents.
A twelve ounce can of tuna costs three dollars and sixty-nine cents.
A five pound sack of flour costs three dollars and nine cents.

3 Repeat the exercise above using the abbreviated form for reading prices.

Examples:

A pound of apples costs two fifty.
A twelve ounce can of tuna costs three sixty-nine.
A five pound sack of flour costs three 0 nine.

4 Explain and practice the present tense ("**do**," "**does**," and the suffix "**s**" at the end of the verb in the third person singular). Then practice the questions shown in the pair practice exercises at the bottom of the handout. *(Note that students are required to do simple addition.)*

5 With the help of a student, demonstrate how to do the pair practice exercise using the newspaper food ad. Then have the students continue by working in pairs.

6 As a follow-up exercise write the following on the chalkboard:

cans: _____ _____ _____ _____

boxes: _____ _____ _____ _____

jars: _____ _____ _____ _____

cartons: _____ _____ _____ _____

bottles: _____ _____ _____ _____

sacks: _____ _____ _____ _____

7 Challenge your students to name grocery store items that come in the containers listed above. Correct the exercise by having volunteers write the items in the lists on the chalkboard. Practice the pronunciation of the items.

8 Have students answer the questions around the ads. Tell them that they have to calculate the prices from the information in the ads.

9 To correct the activity, have volunteers come up to the front of the class and explain how to calculate the prices of one of the eleven questions.

ESL Beginning Level   Crossword Puzzle • Vocabulary Building

Food Containers, Portions & Packaging

Directions: *Fill in the boxes with the names of containers, portions and packaging.*

DOWN

1. a ___ of water
2. a ___ of lettuce 
3. a ___ of cheese 
4. a ___ of soap 
5. a ___ of fruit 
6. a ___ of food 
9. a ___ of cereal 
10. a ___ of meat 
11. a ___ of milk 
13. a ___ of bananas
14. a ___ of jam 
16. a ___ of tea
18. a ___ of tissue

Crossword grid: 1 Down starts with GLASS

ACROSS

3. a ___ of nuts
4. a ___ of groceries 
7. a ___ of paper towels 
8. a ___ of potatoes 
9. a ___ of wine 
10. a ___ of butter 
12. a ___ of tooth paste 
15. a ___ of bread 
16. a ___ of soda 
17. a ___ of ice 

87

ESL Beginning Level Crossword Puzzle • Containers, Portions & Packaging

Teacher's Notes

1 Before distributing the worksheet, ask the students general questions about common containers, portions, and packaging to find out what they already know. Ask them to name and describe as many as they can and list them on the chalkboard or whiteboard. Make sure that the lists include the following:

| bag | roll | bottle | tube | can | glass | piece | basket | bowl | carton | jar | box |
| package | sack | stick | loaf | cube | head | bar | plate | slice | bunch | cup | |

While you are eliciting the names of containers, portions, and packaging, be sure to include examples of food or products that accompany the new vocabulary. For example, when discussing the word "**bag**" include examples such as "**a bag of groceries, chips, food, flour, nuts**," etc.

2 Distribute the worksheet and identify and discuss each item. Ask simple questions about their shapes, sizes, colors, and tastes.

3 Demonstrate how to do a crossword puzzle. Explain the concept of **DOWN** and **ACROSS**. Then, show the students how to fill in the puzzle using the visual and written clues. Do a few examples with the whole class. Correct the answers by projecting an overhead transparency image directly onto the board on which students can write the answers. See solution below. Consider giving this worksheet as a homework assignment. Encourage the students to think of as many other containers, portions, and packaging that they can name. Make a list on the chalkboard or whiteboard. You may want to list some other common vocabulary not listed in the crossword puzzle:

    a pitcher of beer   a packet of ketchup   a tub of ice cream
    a jug of water   a grain of rice
    a pack of gum   a sheet aluminium foil

4 To expand the exercise, expose the students to expressions of measurements:

    a gallon of water   a tablespoon of salt   a bit of pepper
    a quart of juice   a teaspoon of spices   a scoop of ice cream
    a pint of ice cream   a kilogram of chicken   a pinch of salt
    a pound of meat   a spoon of sugar
    a ounce of cream   a drop of water

5 As a follow-up activity, compare US common liquid and dry measurements with the metric system.

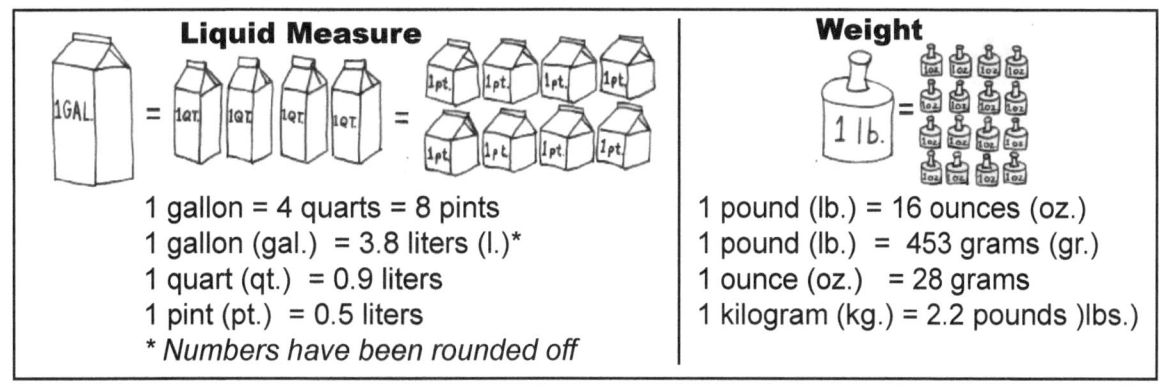

Liquid Measure

1 gallon = 4 quarts = 8 pints
1 gallon (gal.) = 3.8 liters (l.)*
1 quart (qt.) = 0.9 liters
1 pint (pt.) = 0.5 liters
* Numbers have been rounded off

Weight

1 pound (lb.) = 16 ounces (oz.)
1 pound (lb.) = 453 grams (gr.)
1 ounce (oz.) = 28 grams
1 kilogram (kg.) = 2.2 pounds)lbs.)

6 Ask the students in what weight and liquid measure can they find the following items: milk, butter, cream, blood, juice, gasoline, bag of sugar, sack of potatoes, gold, apple.

As a challenge exercise, ask the students to calculate their weight in pounds.

CROSSWORD PUZZLE SOLUTION:
DOWN: 1 glass, 2 head, 3 piece, 4 bar, 5 basket, 6 plate, 9 bowl, 10 slice, 11 carton, 13 bunch, 14 jar, 16 cup, 18 box **ACROSS:** 3 package, 4 bag, 7 roll, 8 sack, 9 bottle, 10 stick, 12 tube, 15 loaf, 16 can, 17 cube

Food Menu Items

ESL Beginning Level — Crossword Puzzle • Vocabulary Building

Directions: *Fill in the boxes with the names of the clothes and accessories in the photos.*

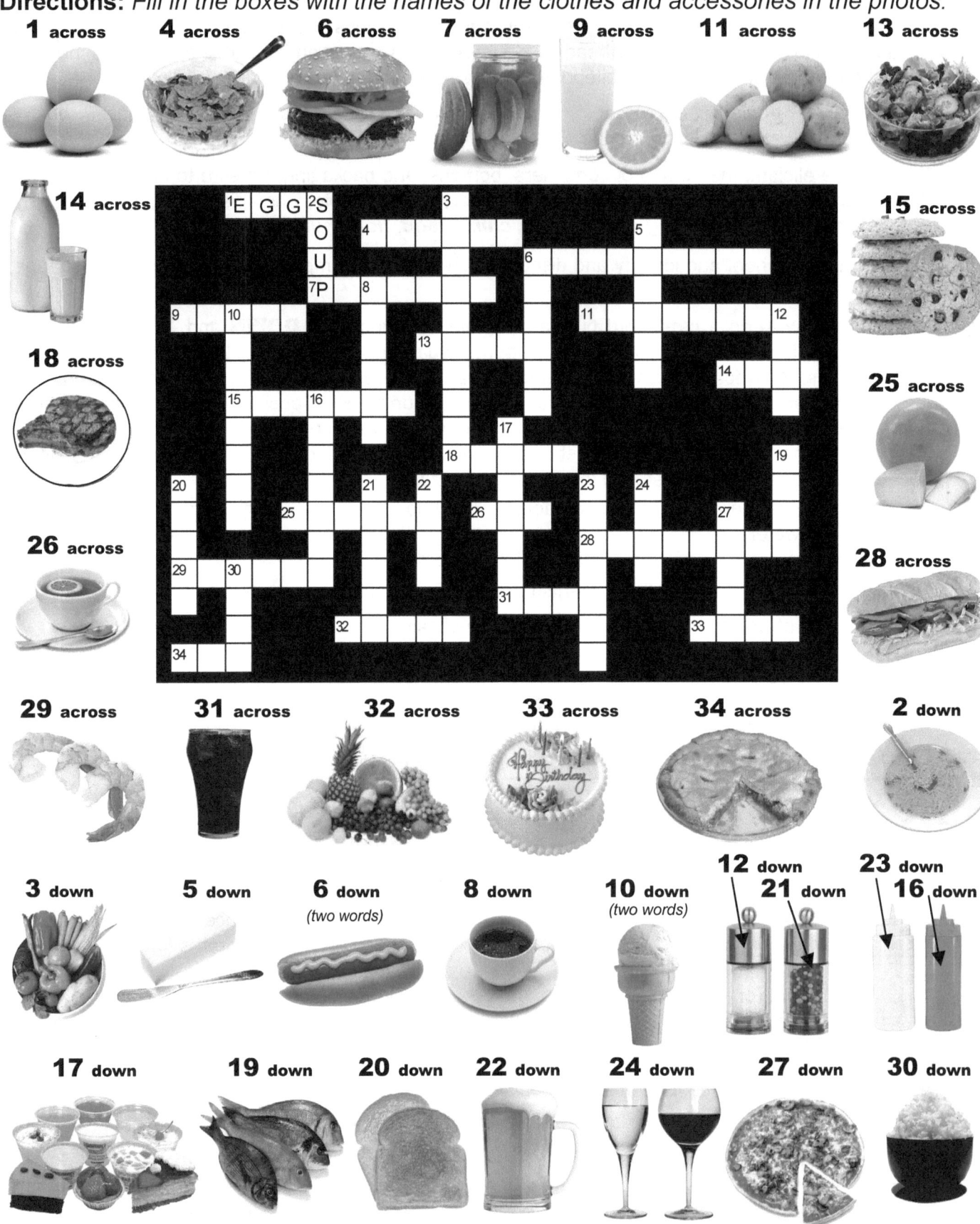

- 1 across
- 4 across
- 6 across
- 7 across
- 9 across
- 11 across
- 13 across
- 14 across
- 15 across
- 18 across
- 25 across
- 26 across
- 28 across
- 29 across
- 31 across
- 32 across
- 33 across
- 34 across
- 2 down
- 3 down
- 5 down
- 6 down (two words)
- 8 down
- 10 down (two words)
- 12 down
- 23 down
- 21 down
- 16 down
- 17 down
- 19 down
- 20 down
- 22 down
- 24 down
- 27 down
- 30 down

Filled letters in grid: 1 across = EGG; 2 down = SOUP; 7 across begins with P.

89

ESL Beginning Level Crossword Puzzle • Vocabulary Building

Teacher's Notes

1 Before distributing the worksheet, begin the lesson with a conversation. Ask your students general questions about common food menu items. Ask your students to name and describe as many as they can. List them on the board. Make sure that the lists include some of the following items:

Beer	Coffee	Fish	Ketchup	Pickles	Salad	Steak
Butter	Soda	Fruit	Milk	Pie	Salt	Tea
Cake	Cookies	Hamburger	Mustard	Pizza	Sandwich	Toast
Cereal	Deserts	Hot dog	Juice	Potatoes	Shrimp	Wine
Cheese	Eggs	Ice cream	Pepper	Rice	Soup	Vegetables

2 Distribute the worksheet and identify and discuss each menu item. Ask simple questions about taste, color, cost, origins, and any other distinguishing features.

3 This activity lends itself well to role playing in which you act as the waiter or waitress in a restaurant and the students respond as customers. Such role playing presents an excellent opportunity to introduce common expressions used in restaurants:

May I help you?
Are you ready to order?
Anything else?
Check, please.

Would you like any ...?
I'd like some ...
Could you bring me some ...?
Do you have any ...?

4 **Cultural Note**

Depending on the geographical area of the United States, the meals of the day are known as either breakfast, lunch, and dinner; or breakfast, dinner, and supper. The word brunch is a combination of words breakfast and lunch and refers to a late-morning meal especially on weekends.

5 Discuss other American type food such as the following:

Buffalo wings	Coleslaw	Ham	Onion rings	Sherbert
Caesar salad	Cottage cheese	Lemonade	Pancakes	Shrimp cocktail
Cheese cake	Fish & chips	Milk shake	Patty melt	Sundae
Chili	French toast	Nachos	Potato chips	Yogurt

6 As a follow-up activity ask students to make a menu of their favorite national or ethnic foods and explain them to the other students in the class.

7 Demonstrate how to do a crossword puzzle. Explain the concept of **DOWN** and **ACROSS**. Then, show the students how to fill in the puzzle using the visual clues. Do a few examples with the whole class.

8 Allow some time for your students to complete the crossword puzzle. You may want to have students work in pairs or assigning it as a homework assignment.

9 Correct the answers by projecting an overhead transparency image directly onto the board on which students can take turns writing the answers on the board. See solution below.

10 Play a crossword puzzle game. Draw or project a grid onto the board or screen as well as a list of the new food menu items. Divide the class into two teams and flip a coin to determine which team goes first. Have the first student of the first team go to the chalkboard and write a word that uses one letter of an existing word in the crossword. If the word fits and is correctly spelled, then give one point for every letter of the new word. Then, go on to the first student of the other team. If the word is incorrect, erase it and go to the opposite team.

CROSSWORD PUZZLE SOLUTION:

ACROSS: 1 eggs, 4 cereal, 6 hamburger, 7 pickles, 9 juice, 11 potatoes, 13 salad, 14 milk, 15 cookies, 18 steak, 25 cheese, 26 tea, 28 sandwich, 29 shrimp, 31 soda, 32 fruit, 33 cake, 34 pie;

DOWN: 2 soup, 3 vegetables, 5 butter, 6 hotdog, 8 coffee, 10 ice cream, 12 salt, 16 ketchup, 17 deserts, 19 fish, 20 toast, 21 pepper, 22 beer, 23 mustard, 24 wine, 27 pizza, 30 rice

ESL Beginning Level   Crossword Puzzle • Vocabulary Building: Names of Fruit

Fruit

Directions: *Fill in the boxes with the names of vegetables in the photos.*

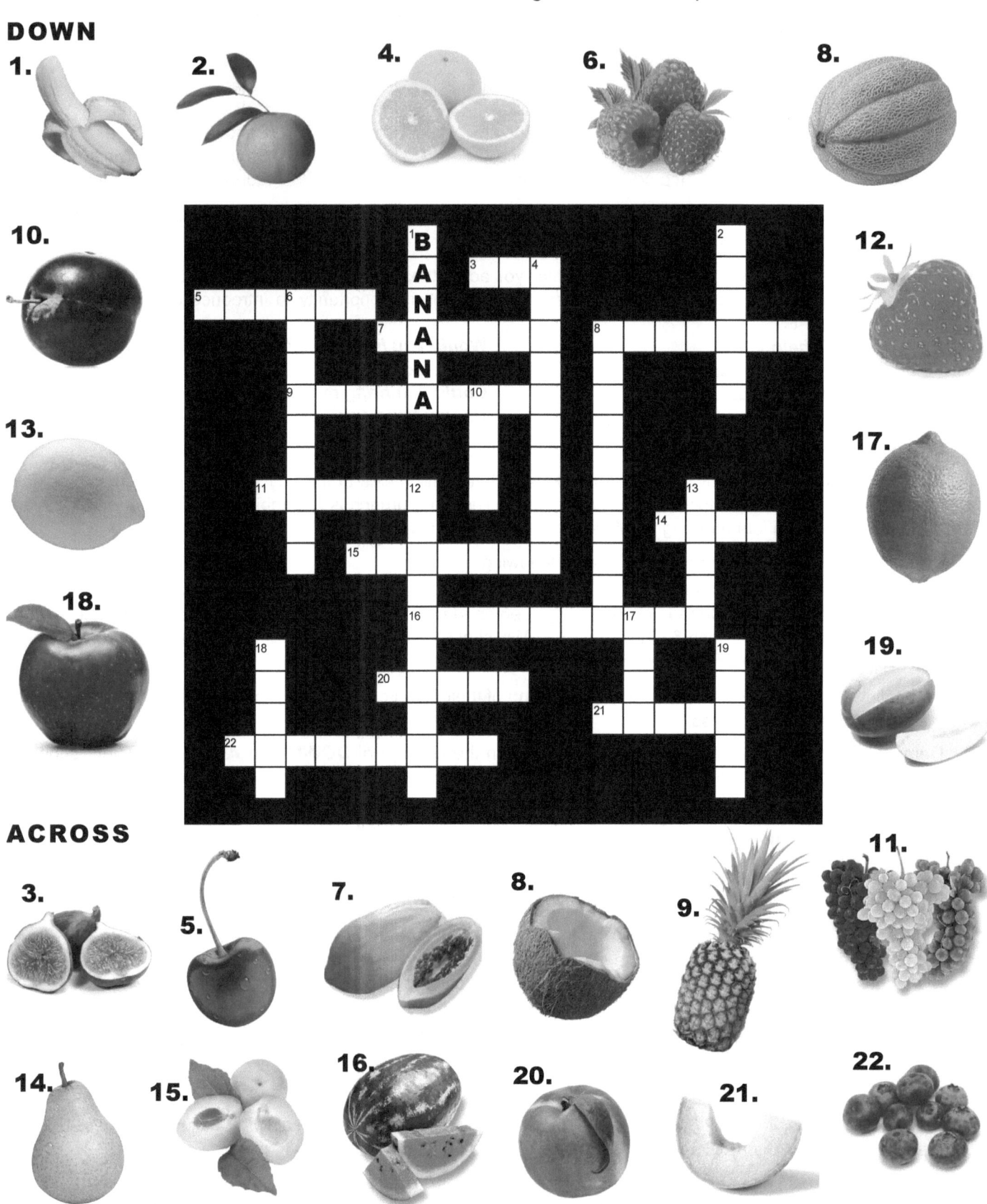

DOWN

1.
2.
4.
6.
8.
10.
12.
13.
17.
18.
19.

ACROSS

3.
5.
7.
8.
9.
11.
14.
15.
16.
20.
21.
22.

ESL Beginning Level   Crossword Puzzle • Vocabulary Building: Names of Fruit

Teacher's Notes

1 Before distributing the worksheet, ask the students general questions about fruit such as which ones they eat at home. Ask them to name and describe as many as they can and list them on the chalkboard or whiteboard. Make sure that the lists include the following fruit.

Apple	Cherry	Lemon	Pineapple	Raspberry
Apricot	Coconut	Lime	Plum	Strawberry
Banana	Fig	Melon	Peach	Watermelon
Blueberry	Grapes	Mango	Pear	
Cantaloupe	Grapefruit	Orange	Papaya	

2 Distribute the worksheet and identify and discuss each fruit item. Ask simple questions about their shapes, sizes, colors, and tastes.

3 Demonstrate how to do a crossword puzzle. Explain the concept of **DOWN** and **ACROSS**. Then, show the students how to fill in the puzzle using the visual clues. Do a few examples with the whole class.

4 Correct the answers by projecting an overhead transparency image directly onto the board on which students can write the answers. See solution below. Consider giving this worksheet as a homework assignment.

5 Encourage the students to think of as many other pieces of fruit that they can name, especially those from other cultures. Make a list on the chalkboard or whiteboard. You may want to list some common fruit not listed in the crossword puzzle.

Blackberry	Cranberry	Nectarine	Quince
Boysenberry	Guava	Persimmon	Tangerine
Cherimoya	Kiwi	Pomegranate	

6 Play a crossword puzzle game. Draw or project a grid onto the chalkboard or whiteboard as well as a list of fruit names. Divide the class into two teams and flip a coin to determine which team goes first. Have the first student of the first team go to the chalkboard and write a word that uses one letter of an existing word in the crossword. If the word fits and is correctly spelled, then give one point for every letter of the new word. Then, go on to the first student of the other team. If the word is incorrect, erase it and go to the opposite team.

7 As an additional activity, play Tic-tac-toe: Draw a tic-tac-toe grid and fill it in with the names of fruit. Divide the class into two teams, each team assigned the symbol "X" or "0." Then flip a coin to determine which team begins. Have the students take turns in an orderly fashion by going down the rows. Tell the first student of the first team to use any word from the grid in a sentence. If the sentence is correct, replace the word with the team's symbol (X or 0), otherwise, leave the word. Go on to the first person on the other team. Continue in this manner until one team wins by having three consecutive X's or 0's in a row vertically, horizontally or diagonally. Keep score by giving one point for each game won. After each game, replace all the words in the grid with a different group of fruit names each time.

CROSSWORD PUZZLE SOLUTION:

DOWN: 1 banana, 2 orange, 4 grapefruit, 6 raspberry, 8 cantaloupe, 10 plum, 12 strawberry, 13 lemon, 17 lime, 18 apple, 19 mango

ACROSS: 3 fig, 5 cherry, 7 papaya, 8 coconut, 9 pineapple, 11 grapes, 14 pear, 15 apricot, 16 watermelon, 20 peach, 21 melon, 22 blueberry;

ESL Advanced Level Common Tools • Vocational ESL Vocabulary

Gerunds

1 Directions: Practice asking and answering questions about the items below. Use a gerund after the preposition **for**. See example.

What is a broom used for?

A broom is used for sweeping.

broom	lock	tape measure	extension cord
shovel	thermostat	hose	fence
hand truck	ladder	calculator	flash light

2 Make a list of tools that you use. Then, explain what they are used for.

Tools	Use
1. hammer	A hammer is used for pounding nails.
2. _____	_____
3. _____	_____
4. _____	_____
5. _____	_____
6. _____	_____
7. _____	_____

ESL Advanced Level   Gerunds • Vocational ESL Vocabulary

Teacher's Notes

1 Before distributing the worksheet, explain the use of gerunds:
- A gerund is a form of a verb that ends in **-ing**.
- We can use gerunds after prepositions in the same way that nouns are used.

Examples:

I am responsible	**for**	**taking** care of my computer.
I am interested	**in**	**learning** more about computers.
I am thinking	**about**	**buying** a new computer.
I am looking forward	**to**	**using** my new computer.
I will take advantage	**of**	**having** a computer.

2 Distribute the worksheet and review the vocabulary. Practice the mini-dialog and read the directions aloud to the class. Next, show how to do this oral exercise with the help of a volunteer. Practice the activity until the students understand what to do. Then, tell the students to continue the exercise by working in pairs.

3 Extend this activity by having the students think of as many different gerunds as possible for each item on the worksheet. List the new vocabulary on the board or overhead transparency.

Examples: *A broom is used for sweeping.*
A lock is used for protecting valuables.
A tape measure is used for measuring.
An extension cord is used for connecting a distant electrical item to an outlet.
A shovel is used for digging.
A thermostat is used for controlling room temperature.
A hose is used for watering.
A fence is used for protecting property.
A hand truck is used for moving heavy items.
A ladder is used for climbing.
A calculator is used for adding, subtracting, multiplying, and dividing numbers.
A flash light is used for seeing in the dark.

4 Ask the students to think of tools that they use. Have them write the names of the tools on the worksheet. Then, have them explain what the tools are used for. You may want to make an overhead transparency of the handout that can be projected onto the board where students can write the list of tools and their use.

5 **Follow-up Activity**

Practice the following phrases with the students using gerunds. See example below.

What do you have experience in?
I have experience in working with computers.

Student 1: **What do/are you ....?**
Student 2: **I ....**

have experience in	**responsible for**
interested in	**waiting for**
thinking about	**talk about**
look forward to	**take advantage of**
looking forward to	**taking advantage of**

94

ESL Beginning Level   Future • Vocabulary Building: Expressions of Time

Going to

1	take an airplane
2	take a cruise
3	walk on the beach
4	swim in a pool
5	listen to music
6	read a book
7	relax
8	take a tour
9	take photos
10	go shopping
11	exercise
12	eat well
13	meet new friends
14	ride a bicycle

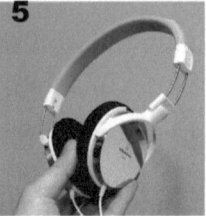

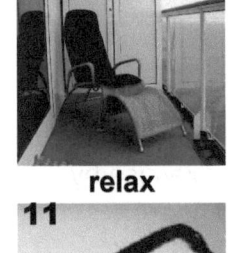

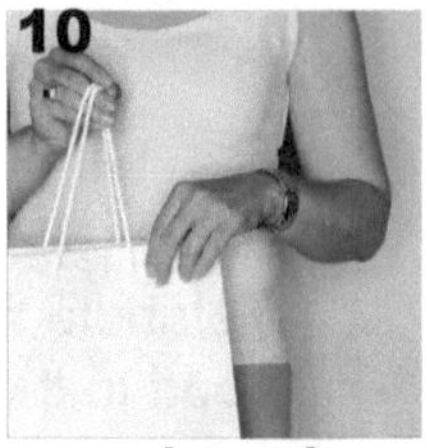

Susan

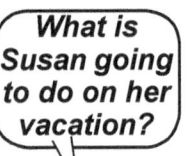

❶ Pair-Practice: *Practice answering and asking questions with another student. See examples.* ▶

Student 1: **What is Susan going to do on her vacation?**

Student 2: **She's going to _____.**

What is Susan going to do on her vacation?
She is going to take an airplane.

❷ Pair-Practice: *Practice answering and asking questions with another student. See examples.* ▶
Use the expressions of time in the box to the right.

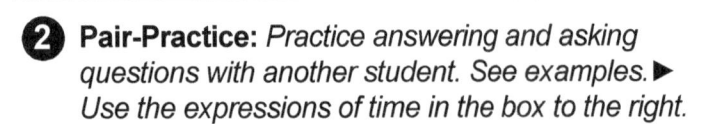

Student 1: **What are you going to do ___?**

Student 2: **I'm going to _____.**

What are you going to do next week?
I'm going to exercise next week.

Expressions of Time

after breakfast
after class
after dinner
after lunch
later
in a few minutes
in a while
in an hour
next month
next summer
next week
next year
soon
tomorrow afternoon
tomorrow evening
tomorrow morning
tomorrow night

❸ Write: *Fill in the sentences.*

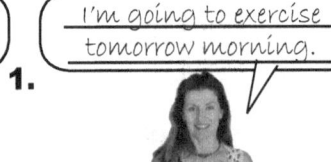

What are you going to do tomorrow morning?

1. I'm going to exercise tomorrow morning.

Where is your next vacation going to be?

2. _____

3.  _____   I'm going to go to _____.

What are you going to do there?

4. _____

95

ESL Beginning Level Future • Vocabulary Building: Expressions of Time

Teacher's Notes

1. Before distributing the worksheet, begin the lesson with a conversation about vacations. Ask general questions to determine how many vacation activities the students can already name. Make a list on the chalkboard or whiteboard. Be sure to include the following items: *take an airplane, take a cruise, walk on the beach, swim, listen to music, read a book, relax, take a tour, take photos, go shopping, exercise, eat well, meet new friends,* and *ride a bicycle.*

2. Distribute the worksheet. Introduce the vocabulary and pronounce the names of the activities below each photo. Have the students model each after you. (You may want to introduce the students to the names of some of the items in the photos such as *ship, headphones, lounge chair, balcony, tour bus, camera, shopping bag, table setting,* and *electronic reader.*)

3. Introduce the structure by asking yes/no questions such as *"Is Susan going to take an airplane?"* Model the short response, *"Yes, she is."* or *"No, she's not."* Continue posing questions to individual students.

4. Have the students ask other students personal questions using the pronoun "you" patterned after the examples above. *"Are you going to take a cruise?"* Model the short answers: *"Yes, I am."* or *"No, I'm not."*

5. Drill "**going to**" with the question words "**what**," "**where**," "**how**," and "**when**." For example, ask, *"Where's Susan going to walk?"* Model the response, *"She's going to walk on the beach."*

6. Expand the activity by having individual students ask *"What are you going to do on your vacation?"* to another student who must supply an appropriate answer. (**Note:** *In rapid conversation, the pronunciation of "***going to***" is "***gonna.***" Students should at least have a passive recognition of this form.*)

7. With the help of your students, make a list on the chalkboard or whiteboard of future expressions of time. Include *after breakfast, after class, after dinner, after lunch, later, in a few minutes, in a while, in an hour, next month, next summer, next week, next year, soon, tomorrow afternoon, tomorrow evening, tomorrow morning,* and *tomorrow night.*

8. Ask a question using one of the expressions of time such as *"What are you going to do next week?"* Have one student ask another student a similar question using a different expression of time. The second student should supply an appropriate answer. Encourage students to continue the exercise by expanding the list to include original questions and answers.

9. Explain that "**going to**" used in conjunction with another verb does not necessarily convey any sense of movement. Clarify this point by drilling "**going to**" with static verbs such as "**stay**," "**think**," "**see**," "**read**," "**listen to**," "**speak**," "**study**," "**buy**," and "**learn**."

10. Review the sentences in the balloons in Exercise 3 at the bottom of the page and explain how to fill in the missing words. Encourage students to continue the activity by providing original sentences in the last balloon. End the activity by having the students write a few original questions and answers on the board. When correcting the exercise, check carefully that the students have not omitted the verb "**to be**" (**am**, **is**, **are**) from the structure.

Follow-Up Activity

On a subsequent day, review "**going to**" using other expressions of a future time such as: *a week from today, a week from tomorrow, after school, in a day or two, after work, in a moment, in fifteen minutes, the day after tomorrow, the week after next,* and *next Saturday.*

ESL Intermediate Level • Appointment Booking • Reading • Pair Practice • Writing

Have To

1 *Read the text.*

If you want to make money, you have to get a job.
If you want to get a job, you have to look for a job.
If you look for a job, you have to prepare for an interview.
If you prepare for an interview, you have to know English.
If you want to know English well, you have to go to school.
If you go to school, you have to study.
If you study, you will make money.

A counselor is speaking to Moussa.

2 *Practice the dialogs below with another student. Use the words above.*

Student 1: What does Moussa have to do if he ...?
Student 2: He has to ...

(What does Moussa have to do if he wants to get a job?)
(He has to look for a job.)

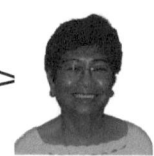

Student 1: What do you have to do if you ...?
Student 2: I have to ...

(What do you have to do if you want to make money?)
(I have to get a job.)

3 *Fill out the appointment book for next week.*

APPOINTMENT BOOK
WHAT I HAVE TO DO

Monday
___
___

Tuesday
___
___

Wednesday
___
___

Thursday
___
___

Friday
___
___

Saturday
___
___

Sunday
___
___

97

ESL Intermediate Level • Appointment Booking • Reading • Pair Practice • Writing

Teacher's Notes

1 Before distributing the worksheet, explain the use of **have to**:

- We use **have to** to show necessity or strong obligation.
- The third person affirmative singular is irregular: **has to**.
- **Have to** and **has to** are followed by the simple form of the verb.

Example: You have to get a job.

2 Distribute the worksheet and read the text at the top of the page, and explain or discuss the vocabulary.

3 As an active listening exercise, have students underline or circle **have to** as you read the text aloud.

4 Also explain the general impersonal use of the pronoun **you**. (Although used less, the word **one** can also be used.)

5 With the help of a student, demonstrate how to do the pair practice exercises using the text at the top of the page. Then have the students continue by working in pairs.

6 Expand the oral practice by having students practice the phrases below. Have students complete the mini-dialogs in their own words:

Person 1: Why can't you stay?
Person 2: I have to ...

Person 1: Before you leave, you have to ...
Person 2: Do I have to?
Person 1: Yes, you do!

Person 1: What's the matter?
Person 2: The ... is broken, I have to call a ...

Person 1: Why do I have to ...?
Person 2: Because ...

Person 1: Don't you want to ...
Person 2: Of course.
Person 1: Then, you have to ...

Person 1: What do you have to study to become a ...?
Person 2: You have to study ...

Person 1: What's you favorite day of the week?
Person 2: Sunday, because I don't have to ...

7 Have students fill out the appointment book at the bottom of the handout using sentences with **have to**.

Project a copy of the handout on an overhead transparency directly onto the chalkboard on which the students can write their sentences.

8 Repeat the pair practice exercise using the new sentences in the appointment book.

ESL Beginning Level • Object Pronouns • Pair Practice • Writing • Common Verbs

Him, Her, It, Them (Object Pronouns)

1 *Read the photo captions.*

1. Rita is speaking to Jerry, and Jerry is listening to Rita.

2. Joanne likes her dog, Penny. Penny likes Joanne.

3. Jeff is standing next to Paul. They are holding the award.

4. Bill is driving his old car. He likes his car very much.

5. Kim is looking at the camera. She is listening to the camera man.

6. The boy is writing in his book. We don't know his name.

7. Jim is sitting between Anna and Mary. He is holding a book.

8. The camera is in front of Ella. She is taking a photo of her friends.

2 **Pair-Practice:** *Practice answering and asking questions with another student. Use "in front of," "next to," "behind," and "between" in the answers. See examples.* ▶

Is Rita next to Jerry? — *Yes, she's next to him.*

Student 1: **Is [name] _____ [name]?**

Student 2: **Yes/No, he/she/it is/isn't _____ [name].**

3 **Pair-Practice:** *Practice answering and asking questions with another student. Use "in front of," "next to," "behind," and "between". See examples.* ▶

Does Joanne like her dog? — *Yes, she likes it.*

Student 1: **Is/Does [name] _____ [name]?**

Student 2: **Yes/No, _____.**

4 *Answer the questions with "him," "her," "it," and "them." Use the photo below.*

1. Is Carla sitting next to Adam?
   <u>Yes, Carla is sitting next to him.</u>
2. Is Adam in front of the table?
   _____
3. Do we know Amy?
   _____
4. Is Carla speaking to Will?
   _____
5. Do you see the children?
   _____

6. Is Adam looking at Amy?
   _____
7. Are they looking at the camera?
   _____
8. Do you like these photos?
   _____
9. Do you listen to your teacher?
   _____
10. Do you understand the lesson?
    _____

ESL Beginning Level • Object Pronouns • Pair Practice • Writing • Common Verbs

Teacher's Notes

1 Before distributing the worksheet, make sure that the students are familiar with the following vocabulary: **Prepositions:** *in front of, next to, behind, between.* **Common verbs:** *drive, hold, know, like, listen to, look at, see, sit, speak to, stand, take a photo of, understand, write.*

2 In the four corners of the room, position a male student, a female student, two students together, and an object such as a chair. Place yourself so that individual students may describe where you are. Model a few examples such as:

    You're in front of <u>her</u>.   *You're next to <u>him</u>.*   *You're behind <u>them</u>.*   *You're on <u>it</u>.*

3 Have your students pass a small object around the room. Have one student tell another student to give the object to a third person. Model the sentence, "***Give it to him/her.***" After the students have sufficiently mastered this structure, continue drilling the same sentence with the word "**them**" by having the students pass around two or more objects. Model the sentence, "***Give them to him/her.***" For maximum effectiveness, drill this structure for a few minutes on three consecutive class meetings. By the third meeting students should be able to utilize this structure without any help from the teacher. Use this drill when you have worksheets or handouts to distribute to the students.

4 Distribute the worksheet and read the captions below the photos. Identify the people, objects, and what is happening in the photos. Ask the question below. Model the response and have your students repeat both question and response. Continue drilling "***him***," "***her***," "***it***," and "***them***" by asking similar questions about the people, animals, and objects in the picture.

Photo 1
Is Rita speaking to Jerry? Yes, she's speaking to <u>him</u>.
Is Jerry listening to Rita? Yes, he's listening to <u>her</u>.
Photo 2
Does Joanne like the dog? Yes, she likes <u>it</u>.
Is Penny behind Joanne? No, Penny is in front of <u>her</u>.
Photo 3
Is Paul standing next to Jeff? Yes, he's standing next to <u>him</u>.
Are Jeff and Paul holding the award? Yes, they are holding <u>it</u>.
Photo 4
Is Bill driving his car? Yes, he's driving <u>it</u>.
Does Bill like his old car? Yes, he likes <u>it</u> very much.

Photo 5
Is Kim looking at the camera? Yes, she's looking at <u>it</u>.
Is she listening to the camera man? Yes, she's listening to <u>him</u>.
Photo 6
Is the boy writing in his book? Yes, he's writing in <u>it</u>.
Do we know his name? No, we don't know <u>it</u>.
Photo 7
Is grandfather holding the book? Yes, he's holding <u>it</u>.
Is he sitting between Anna and Mary? Yes, he's sitting between <u>them</u>.
Photo 8
Is the camera in front of Ella? Yes, it's in front of <u>her</u>.
Is Ella taking a photo of her friends? Yes, she's taking a photo of <u>them</u>.

5 In Exercise 2 practice the pronouns as objects of such prepositions as "*in front of*," "*next to*," "*between*," and "*behind*." For example, ask, "*Is Rita standing in front of Jerry?*" Model the response, "***No, Rita's standing next to <u>him</u>.***" Have individual students ask other students questions of a similar pattern. Then, have them practice in pairs.

6 In exercise 3 model and practice the sample question and answer given above. Drill the object pronouns in these structures using the photos as cues. Have individual students ask other students questions of a similar pattern. Then, have them practice in pairs.

7 Direct the students to exercise 4 at the bottom of the page. Read the questions about the photos and ask your students to answer them orally. For example, ask, "*Is Carla sitting next to <u>Adam</u>?*" Have a student give an answer containing the appropriate pronoun such as, "***Yes, she is sitting next to <u>him</u>.***" Next, have the students provide answers in writing. Answers: 1. Yes, she's sitting next to <u>him</u>.; 2. No, he's behind <u>it</u>.; 3. No, we don't know <u>her</u>.; 4. No, she isn't speaking to <u>him</u>.; 5. Yes, I see <u>them</u>.; 6. No, he isn't looking at <u>her</u>.; 7. Yes, they are looking at <u>it</u>.; 8. Answers will vary.; 9. Answers will vary.; 10. Answers will vary.

NOTE

Make sure that your voice consistently stresses the verb and not the pronoun. In rapid conversation, the pronouns "***him***," "***her***," and "***them***" weaken to "***im***," "***er***," and "***em***." Drill these conversational forms for passive recognition.

There are a limited number of contexts in which the word "***her***"/"***er***" is used to refer to inanimate objects, For example, the expression, "***Fill er up.***," refers to putting gasoline into the car.

"***Him***" and "***her***" are sometimes used to refer to pets such as a dog or cat.

Show that "***her***" serves as both object pronoun and possessive pronoun as in the example, "*I mailed <u>her</u> <u>her</u> photo.*"

You may further expand the use of object pronouns by introducing expressions such as "***the both of them/us***," and "***the three of them/us***."

ESL Beginning Level • Possessive Adjectives • Pair Practice • Writing, Vocabulary

His, Her, Their (Possessive Adjectives)

Pair Practice: *Practice the questions and answers orally with another student.*

Whose keys are they?
They are his keys.

Teresa & David
her → their ← his

Example:
Student 1: Whose keys are they?
Student 2: They are **David's** keys. They are **his** keys.

David's keys
❶ They are his keys.

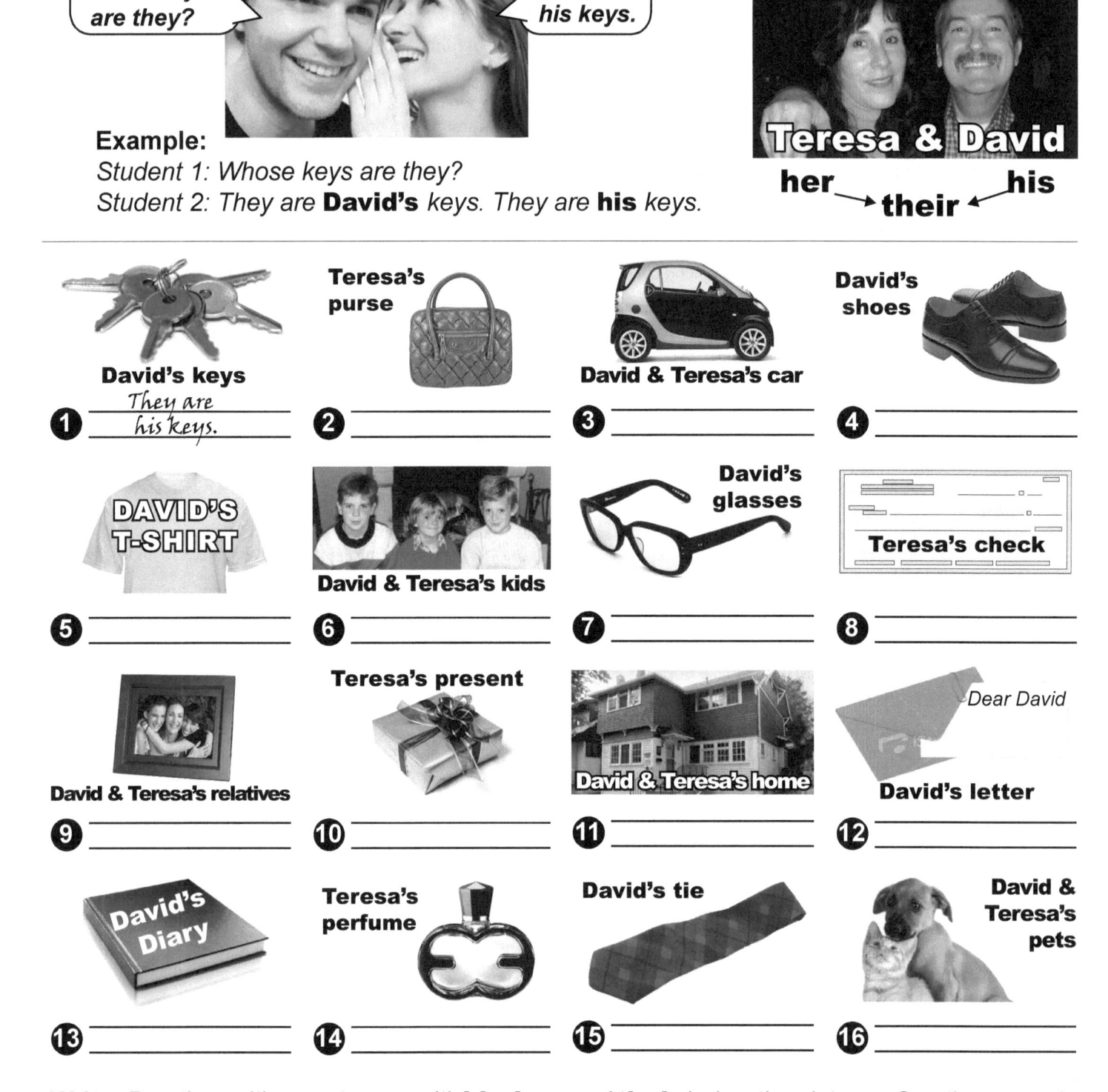

Teresa's purse
❷ _____

David & Teresa's car
❸ _____

David's shoes
❹ _____

DAVID'S T-SHIRT
❺ _____

David & Teresa's kids
❻ _____

David's glasses
❼ _____

Teresa's check
❽ _____

David & Teresa's relatives
❾ _____

Teresa's present
❿ _____

David & Teresa's home
⓫ _____

David's letter
⓬ _____

David's Diary
⓭ _____

Teresa's perfume
⓮ _____

David's tie
⓯ _____

David & Teresa's pets
⓰ _____

Write: *Practice writing sentences with **his**, **her**, and **their** below the pictures. See the example below number 1.*

ESL Beginning Level • Possessive Adjectives • Pair Practice • Writing, Vocabulary

Teacher's Notes

1 Review the use of the possessive **'s**. (Example: David**'s** keys).

2 Before doing the activity, read and pronounce the names and items below the pictures on the worksheet.

Read and practice the question and answer at the top of the page. *"Whose keys are they?" "They are Mike's keys." "They are his keys.* Continue the drill substituting the items in the photos. *(Discourage the students from writing. This should be a time for oral practice.)* Continue the substitution drill by pointing to items in the room.

3 Repeat the activity by using contractions: **It's** and **They're**. (Point out that **They're** and **their** sound the same.)

4 Pair up students and have them practice the drill again orally.

5 Have the students write sentences with the possessive (**'s**) beside each photo.

6 Correct the sentences. You may want to project a copy of the handout that has been transferred to an overhead transparency directly onto a chalkboard or whiteboard on which the students can write the correct answer.

7 **Follow-Up Activities**

- Practice the use of the expression "**belong to.**"
  Example: *Whose computer does it* **belong to**? *It* **belongs to** *David.*

- Review the use of the object pronouns: **me, you, him, her, it, us, them**.
  Use them with the expression **belong to**.
  Example: *Whose computer does it* **belong to**? *It* **belongs to** *her. (Point to a woman.)*

- Contrast possessive pronouns and adjectives: **my, your, his, her, our, its their**.
  Examples: *This is* **my** *pen. It belongs to* **me**.
  This is **her** *bag. It belongs to* **her**.
  These are **his** *books. They belong to* **him**.

- Practice the short form of the possessive.
  Example: *Whose computer is it? It's* **David's** *computer.*
  Excuse me, whose? **David's**.

Answers:
1. They are **his** keys.
2. It is **her** purse.
3. It's **their** car.
4. They are **his** shoes.
5. It's **his** T-shirt.
6. They are **their** sons.
7. They are **his** glasses.
8. It's **her** check.
9. They are **their** relatives.
10. It's **her** present.
11. It's **their** home.
12. It's **his** letter,
13. It's **his** diary.
14. It's **her** perfume.
15. It's **his** tie.
16. They are **their** pets.

ESL Beginning Level   Crossword Puzzle • Vocabulary Building

Home Furnishings & Appliances

Directions: *Fill in the boxes with the names of the home furnishings and appliances in the photos.*

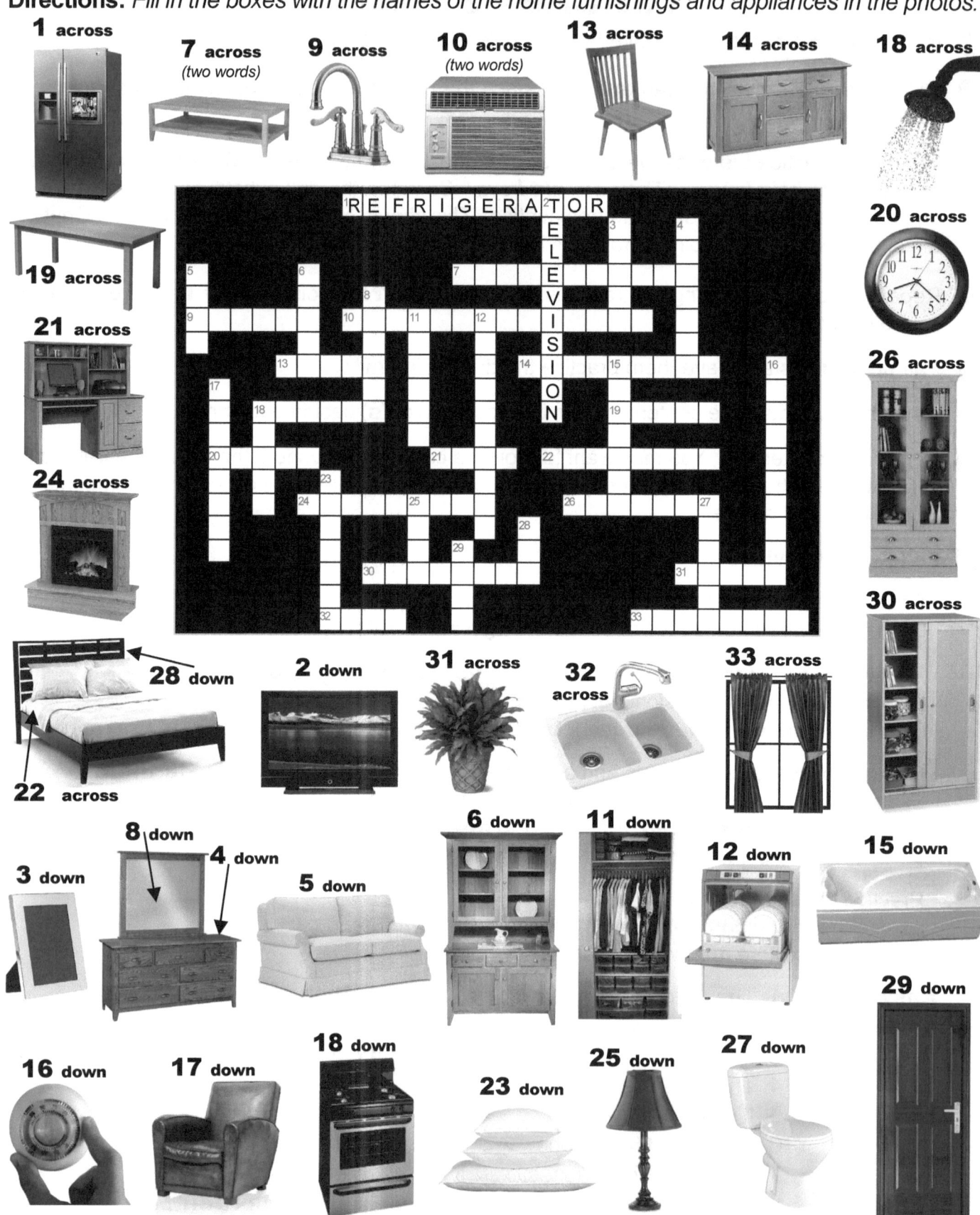

1 across

7 across (two words)

9 across

10 across (two words)

13 across

14 across

18 across

19 across

20 across

21 across

26 across

24 across

30 across

28 down

2 down

31 across

32 across

33 across

22 across

3 down

8 down

4 down

5 down

6 down

11 down

12 down

15 down

29 down

16 down

17 down

18 down

23 down

25 down

27 down

Across answers visible in grid:
- 1 across: REFRIGERATOR
- 2 down: TELEVISION

103

ESL Beginning Level • Crossword Puzzle • Vocabulary Building

Teacher's Notes

1 Before distributing the worksheet, begin the lesson with a conversation. Ask your students general questions about home furnishings and appliances. Ask them to name and describe as many as they can. List them on the board. Make sure that the lists include some of the following items:

Air conditioner	Chair	Curtains	Faucet	Mattress	Shower	Table
Armchair	Clock	Desk	Fireplace	Mirror	Sideboard	Television
Bathtub	Closet	Dishwasher	Frame	Pillows	Sink	Thermostat
Bed	Coffee table	Door	Hutch	Plant	Sofa	Toilet
Cabinet	Cupboard	Dresser	Lamp	Refrigerator	Stove	

2 Distribute the worksheet and identify and discuss each item. Ask simple questions about their use, size, where they are located in the home, and any other distinguishing characteristics. For example, ask questions such as:

Do you have _____ at home?   *In what room can you find _____?*
How big/small is _____?   *When do we use _____?*

3 Demonstrate how to do a crossword puzzle. Explain the concept of **DOWN** and **ACROSS**. Then, show the students how to fill in the puzzle using the visual clues. Do a few examples with the whole class.

4 Allow some time for your students to complete the crossword puzzle. You may want to have students work in pairs or assigning it as a homework assignment.

5 Correct the answers by projecting an overhead transparency image directly onto the board on which students can take turns writing the answers on the board. See solution below.

6 Play a crossword puzzle game. Draw or project a grid onto the board or screen as well as a list of the names of home furnishings and appliances. Divide the class into two teams and flip a coin to determine which team goes first. Have the first student of the first team go to the board and write a word that uses one letter of an existing word in the crossword. If the word fits and is correctly spelled, then give one point for every letter of the new word. Then, go on to the first student of the other team. If the word is incorrect, erase it and go to the opposite team.

7 As an additional activity, play Tic-Tac-Toe. Draw a Tic-Tac-Toe grid and fill it in with names of furniture and appliances. Divide the class into two teams, each team assigned the symbol "X" or "0." Then flip a coin to determine which team begins. Have the students take turns in an orderly fashion by going down the rows. Tell the first student of the first team to use any word from the grid in a sentence. If the sentence is correct, replace the word with the team's symbol (X or 0), otherwise, leave the word. Go on to the first person on the other team. Continue in this manner until one team wins by having three consecutive X's or 0's in a row vertically, horizontally or diagonally. Keep score by giving one point for each game won. After each game, replace all the words in the grid with a different piece of furniture or appliance each time.

8 Expand the activity by teaching additional vocabulary items such as: *blanket, computer, printer, drapes, space heater, lounge chair, paintings, vases, rocking chair, oven, VCR, sliding glass door, and vanity.*

CROSSWORD PUZZLE SOLUTION:

ACROSS: 1 refrigerator, 7 coffee table, 9 faucet, 10 air conditioner, 13 chair, 14 sideboard, 18 shower, 19 table, 20 clock, 21 desk, 22 mattress, 24 fireplace, 26 cabinet, 30 cupboard, 31 plant, 32 sink, 33 curtains;

DOWN: 2 television, 3 frame, 4 dresser, 5 sofa, 6 hutch, 8 mirror, 11 closet, 12 dishwasher, 15 bathtub, 16 thermostat, 17 armchair, 18 stove, 23 pillows, 25 lamp, 27 toilet, 28 bed, 29 door

ESL Beginning Level

Crossword Puzzle • Vocabulary Building

Household Chores 1

Directions: *Fill in the boxes with the names of the household chores in the photos.*

1 across _____ the washing machine

2 across _____ the vegetables

5 across _____ the lawn

6 across _____ the furniture

9 across _____ the window

11 across _____ dirty clothes in the hamper

13 across _____ a party

16 across _____ bookshelves

17 across _____ bathroom

20 across _____ the pets

22 across _____ the clothes

1 down _____ the clothes

3 down _____ the mail

4 down _____ the toys *(two words)*

5 down _____ the bed

7 down _____ the floor

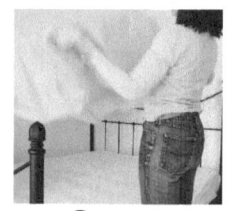

8 down _____ the sheets

10 down _____ a painting

12 down _____ the clothes

14 down _____ the door

15 down _____ the toilet

18 down _____ the garbage or trash

19 down _____ the pets

21 down _____ the bills

1 across answer fills in as: LOAD (shown in grid)

105

ESL Beginning Level   Crossword Puzzle • Vocabulary Building

Teacher's Notes

1 Before distributing the worksheet, begin the lesson with a conversation to assess your students' knowledge of some commonly household chores. Ask questions using the present continuous tense such as:

What do you do at home?   *What is a man's/woman's/children's chores?*
Do you wash the dishes/floor/windows?   *What don't you do at home?*
Who cooks, shops, makes dinner at home?   *What's an easy/hard chore?*

2 Distribute the worksheet. Identify what the people are doing in the photos. Ask the question, "**What's _____ doing?**" Model the response, "**He/She's _____.**" Have the students repeat both question and answer. Continue asking similar questions about the people in the photos. For variety, have students ask each other questions with the word "*what*" such as "**What's the person doing in _____?**" Students should reply, "**He/she's _____.**"

3 Ask your students general questions about other common chores. Ask them to name and describe as many as they can. List them on the board. Make sure that the lists include some of the following items:

Bathe the pets	Cut the lawn	Fix the toilet	Load the washing	Mow the lawn	Place dirty the
Change the bed	Dry the clothes	Get the mail	machine	Organize	clothes in the
sheets	Dust the furniture	Hang a picture	Lock the door	bookshelves	hamper
Clean the bathroom	Empty the trash	Iron the clothes	Make the bed	Pay the bills	Plan a party
Close the window	Feed the pets	Launder clothes	Mop the floor	Pick up the toys	

4 Demonstrate how to do a crossword puzzle. Explain the concept of **DOWN** and **ACROSS**. Then, show the students how to fill in the puzzle using the visual clues. Do a few examples with the whole class.

5 Allow some time for your students to complete the crossword puzzle. You may want to have students work in pairs or assigning it as a homework assignment.

6 Correct the answers by projecting an overhead transparency image directly onto the board on which students can take turns writing the answers on the board. See solution below.

7 Play a crossword puzzle game. Draw or project a grid onto the board or screen as well as a list of the common chores. Divide the class into two teams and flip a coin to determine which team goes first. Have the first student of the first team go to the board and write a word that uses one letter of an existing word in the crossword. If the word fits and is correctly spelled, then give one point for every letter of the new word. Then, go on to the first student of the other team. If the word is incorrect, erase it and go to the opposite team.

8 Expand the activity by teaching additional common household chores:

Dry the dishes	Polish the furniture	Recycle the garbage	Shop for food	Vacuum the carpet
Fill the bird feeder	Prepare the meals/	Replace the light bulb	Shovel snow	Walk the dog
Hang the clothes on	budget	Replace the toilet paper	Sort the clothes	Wash the dishes
hangers	Prune the trees	Rinse the dishes	Spray the shower	Water the plants
Keep one's room neat	Put away the groceries	Scrub the tiles	Sweep the floors	Weed the garden
Mend the clothes	Put the toys away	Set the table	Take out the garbage	Wipe down the cabinets
Plant flowers	Rake the leaves	Shampoo the carpets	Tidy the closet	

CROSSWORD PUZZLE SOLUTION:

ACROSS: 1 load, 2 cut, 5 mow, 6 dust, 9 close, 11 place, 13 plan, 16 organize, 17 clean, 20 bathe, 22 dry;

DOWN: 1 launder, 3 get, 4 pickup, 5 make, 7 mop, 8 change, 10 hang, 12 iron, 14 lock, 15 fix, 18 empty, 19 feed, 21 pay

ESL Beginning Level   Crossword Puzzle • Vocabulary Building

Household Chores 2

Directions: *Fill in the boxes with the names of the household chores in the photos.*

1 across _____ flowers 
4 across _____ the dishes 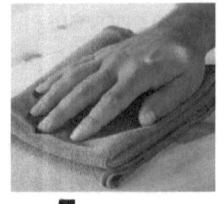
5 across _____ the table 
6 across _____ the table 
9 across _____ the trees 
10 across _____ the carpets

11 across _____ the light bulb
14 across _____ the carpet 
15 across _____ the shower
16 across _____ the floors 
18 across _____ the garden
20 across _____ the garbage *(two words)*

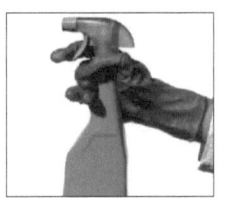

1 down _____ the car 
2 down _____ the closet 
3 down _____ the leaves 
6 down _____ for food 
7 down _____ the trash 
8 down _____ the clothes

9 down _____ the meals
10 down _____ the snow 
12 down _____ the counter 
13 down _____ the groceries *(two words)* 
17 down _____ the plants 
19 down _____ the dog 

1 across: POLISH (across: PLANT)

107

ESL Beginning Level   Crossword Puzzle • Vocabulary Building

Teacher's Notes

1 Before distributing the worksheet, begin the lesson with a conversation to assess your students' knowledge of some commonly household chores. Ask questions using the present continuous tense such as:

What do you do at home? *What is a man's/woman's/children's chores?*
Do you wash the dishes/floor/windows? *What don't you do at home?*
Who cooks, shops, makes dinner at home? *What's an easy/hard chore?*

2 Distribute the worksheet. Identify what the people are doing in the photos. Ask the question, "**What's _____ doing?**" Model the response, "**He/She's _____.**" Have the students repeat both question and answer. Continue asking similar questions about the people in the photos. For variety, have students ask each other questions with the word "*what*" such as "**What's the person doing in _____?**" Students should reply, "**He/she's _____.**"

3 Ask your students general questions about other common chores. Ask them to name and describe as many as they can. List them on the board. Make sure that the lists include some of the following items:

Plant flowers	Rake the leaves	Set the table	Sort the clothes	Tidy the closet	Water the plants
Polish the car	Recycle the trash	Shampoo the	Spray the shower	Vacuum the	Weed the garden
Prepare the meals	Replace the light	carpets	Sweep the floors	carpet	Wipe the table
Prune the trees	bulb	Shop for food	Take out the	Walk the dog	
Put away the groceries	Scrub the counter	Shovel the snow	garbage	Wash the dishes	

4 Demonstrate how to do a crossword puzzle. Explain the concept of **DOWN** and **ACROSS**. Then, show the students how to fill in the puzzle using the visual clues. Do a few examples with the whole class.

5 Allow some time for your students to complete the crossword puzzle. You may want to have students work in pairs or assigning it as a homework assignment.

6 Correct the answers by projecting an overhead transparency image directly onto the board on which students can take turns writing the answers on the board. See solution below.

7 Play a crossword puzzle game. Draw or project a grid onto the board or screen as well as a list of the common chores. Divide the class into two teams and flip a coin to determine which team goes first. Have the first student of the first team go to the board and write a word that uses one letter of an existing word in the crossword. If the word fits and is correctly spelled, then give one point for every letter of the new word. Then, go on to the first student of the other team. If the word is incorrect, erase it and go to the opposite team.

8 Expand the activity by teaching additional common household chores:

Bathe the pets	Dust the furniture	Hang clothes on hangers	Make the bed	Place dirty clothes in
Change the bed sheets	Empty the trash	Iron the clothes	Mend the clothes	hamper
Clean the bathroom	Feed the pets	Keep one's room neat	Mop the floor	Plan a party/menu
Close the window	Fill the bird feeder	Launder the clothes	Mow the lawn	Put the toys away
Cut the lawn/grass	Fix the toilet	Load the dishwasher/	Organize bookshelves	Replace the toilet paper
Dry the clothes	Get the mail	washing machine	Pay the bills	Rinse the dishes
Dry the dishes	Hang a picture	Lock the door	Pick up the toys	

CROSSWORD PUZZLE SOLUTION:

ACROSS: 1 plant, 4 wash, 5 wipe, 6 set, 9 prune, 10 shampoo, 11 replace, 14 vacuum, 15 spray, 16 sweep, 18 weed, 20 take out;

DOWN: 1 polish, 2 tidy, 3 rake, 6 shop, 7 recycle, 8 sort, 9 prepare, 10 shovel, 12 scrub, 13 put away, 17 water, 19 walk

ESL Beginning Level • Pair Practice • Vocabulary Building • Fill In

How much & How many

① Directions: *Read and pronounce the names of the items below.*

water	ice cubes	tickets	wine	sandwiches	oranges	milk	friends	coffee	coins
sugar	people	gas	bananas	dollars	bread	apples	food	rice	hair

Directions: *List the items above under* **HOW MANY?** *or* **HOW MUCH?** *below.*

HOW MANY?
(Count)

ice cubes _____

_____ _____

_____ _____

_____ _____

_____ _____

HOW MUCH?
(Non-count)

water _____

_____ _____

_____ _____

_____ _____

_____ _____

② Directions: *Practice asking and answering questions with another student with* **"How much?"** *and* **"How many?"** *See the examples ▶*

Student 1: *How much/How many* _____ *do you see?*

Student 2: *I see* _____ .

- How much water do you see?
- I see a glass of water.
- How many ice cubes do you see?
- I see three ice cubes.

③ Directions: *Write* **"How much"** *or* **"How many."**

1. How many apples are there? There is one apple.
2. _____ tea do you want? I want one cup of tea.
3. _____ people do you see? I see six people.
4. _____ children are in the photo? There are two.
5. _____ fruit is in the basket? There is much fruit.
6. _____ of this money do you want? I want all of it.

④ Directions: *Write* **"How much"** *or* **"How many"** *in the dialog.*

At the Catering Truck

Customer: How much do two sandwiches cost?
Salesman: They are $4.00 each.
Customer: _____ do these apples cost?
Salesman: 50¢ _____ do you want?
Customer: Two. And I want coffee, too.
Salesman: _____ cups of coffee?
Customer: Two. One for me and one for my friend.
Salesman: Two cups cost $2.00 each. Is that all?
Customer: Yes. _____ does everything cost?

ESL Beginning Level   Pair Practice • Vocabulary Building • Fill In

Teacher's Notes

1 Before distributing the worksheet, begin the lesson with a conversation using "**how much**" and "**how many**" to determine how much the students already know about how these expressions are used.

Distribute the worksheet. Introduce the vocabulary and pronounce the names of the items for each photo. Have the students model the pronunciation of the containers and objects after you. Make sure that the students know the following countable nouns: **glass, carton, cup, bowl, loaf, bottle, bowl, spoon, lock (hair),** and **plate.** Point out that these words are countable and can be used with non-countable words in expressions with "**of**". **Examples:** *glass of water, carton of milk, bowl of rice,* etc.

2 Explain that we use "**how many**" for items that can be counted and "**how much**" for items that cannot be counted. Then, direct the students to list the items in the photos under the columns "**HOW MANY?**" or "**HOW MUCH?**".

3 Introduce the structure by asking questions such as the examples below. Continue asking similar questions about the remaining photos.

> *How much water do you see in the photo?*   *I see a glass of water.*
> *How many ice cubes do you see?*   *I see three ice cubes.*

4 Repeat the same drill substituting "**see**" with "**want**".

5 Have students expand the list of items on the chalkboard by adding their own examples. Continue drilling "**how much**" and "**how many**."

6 Direct students to exercise 3 on the worksheet. Identify the items in the photos and have students repeat them after you. As a oral exercise ask the students to use either "**How much**" or "**How many**" at the beginning of each question below the photos. Expand the activity by asking for volunteers to pose original questions using "**How much**" and "**How many**." Finally, have the students write the expressions on the blank lines provided. (**Answers:** *1. How many, 2. How much, 3. How many, 4. How many, 5. How much, 6. How much.*)

7 Direct the students to exercise 4 at the bottom of the worksheet. Ask the students to read the dialog silently and allow them time to ask about any unfamiliar vocabulary. Be sure to explain the following vocabulary: *catering truck, customer, salesman.* Tell the students to fill in the blank spaces with "**How much**" or "**How many**." Finally Have pairs of volunteers read the dialog in class. As a challenge, ask the students to answer the last question, *"How much does everything cost?"* (Answer: Everything costs $13.00.) Ask for volunteers to write an original dialog modeled on the one on the worksheet.

> **Answers**
> **At the Catering Truck**
> Customer: **How much** do two sandwiches cost?
> Salesman: They are $4.00 each.
> Customer: **How much** do these apples cost?
> Salesman: 50¢. **How many** do you want?
> Customer: Two. And I want coffee, too.
> Salesman: **How many** cups of coffee?
> Customer: Two. One for me and one for my friend.
> Salesman: Two cups cost $2.00 each. Is that all?
> Customer: Yes. **How much** does everything cost?

FOLLOW-UP ACTIVITIES

8 Show that "**how**" can be used with other adjectives in questions such as "*How old?*", "*How big?*", "*How tall?*", "*How long?*", "*How wide?*", "*How heavy?*", "*How high?*", and "*How far?*" Have students ask about size, age, weight, and distance between objects. You can use objects in the classroom or for greater effectiveness you can bring in non-classroom objects.

9 Emphasize the use of such words as "*food,*" "*money,*" "*work,*" "*furniture,*" and "*hair*" with the question "*How much?*" Some students tend to use the question "*How many?*" with these words. It may be useful to drill these in the following types of contrasts:

> How much money?   How many dollars?
> How much work?   How many jobs?

10 Point out that "**no**" can be used to express a zero quantity. Example: *He has **no** money for the movies*.

ESL Beginning & Intermediate Level   Prepositions, Pair Practice, Writing

How with By, With, & On

1 *Read the words below the photos and make sentences with "by," "with," and "on."*

1 Willie	2 Jill	3 Bobby	4 Bill	5 Jim	6 Eric
eat • fork • knife	write • left hand	eat • food • hands	cut • wood • saw	write • pencil	hit • head • hammer
7 Paul & Vera	8 Amy	9 Mrs. Clark	10 Rena & Beth	11 Sue	12 John & Mary
go • school • foot	call • friend • phone	pay • bills • Internet	play • computer	sew • machine	go • school • bus
13 Mr. Jones	14 Jan	15 Olga	16 Maria	17 Harry	18 Jane
pay • bills • mail	sew • clothes	pay • cash	pay • credit card	go • home • car	go • work • bike

2 **Pair-Practice:** *Practice answering and asking questions with another student. See examples.* ▶

How does Willie eat?

He eats with a fork and knife.

Student 1: How does/do _____ ?

Student 2: He/she/they _____ **by/with/on** ____ .

Other Expressions

On	With
on a calculator	with a broom
on a computer	with a brush
on the Internet	with a gun
on the phone	with a hammer
	with a mop
By	with a nail, a tack
by check, cash	with a screw
by hand	with a screw driver
by mail, e-mail	with a spoon
by motorcycle	with a straw
by plane, jet	with glue
by ship, boat	with rope
by taxi, cab	with string
by train, subway	with tape
by truck	with tools

3 **Pair-Practice:** *Practice answering and asking questions with another student. See examples.* ▶ *Use some of the expressions in the box to the right.*

How do you write?

I write with my right hand.

Student 1: How do you _____ ?

Student 2: I _____ **by/with/on** _____ .

4 *Answer the questions in writing. Use "by," "with," and "on" in the answer.*

1. How do you sign your name? *I sign my name with my left hand.*
2. How do you go home? _____
3. How do you eat ice cream? _____
4. How do you wash your clothes? _____
5. How do you pay your bills? _____
6. How do you contact your friends? _____
7. How do you send messages? _____
8. How do you fix your clothes? _____
9. How do you clean your home? _____
10. How do you do math problems? _____

ESL Beginning & Intermediate Level   Prepositions, Pair Practice, Writing

Teacher's Notes

1 Before distributing the worksheet, start the lesson with a conversation. To assess your students' knowledge of the use of "**by**," "**with**," and "**on**." when used with the question word "**How?**", ask personalized questions like the ones below. Use pantomime to elicit short answers.

How do you eat?	(Show your right or left hand.)	*With my right/left hand*
How do you come to school?"	(Walk, get into a car, or get on a bus.)	*By foot, by car, by bus*
How do you put a picture on the wall?	(Hammer a nail into a wall.)	*With a nail and hammer*
How do you talk to your friends?	(Show your cell phone.)	*On the phone.*

2 Distribute the worksheet. Model the following sentences and have the students repeat after you.

WITH	**ON**	**BY**
1. Willie eats with a fork and a knife.	7. Paul and Vera go to school on foot.	12. John and Mary go to school by bus.
2. Jill eats with her right hand.	8. Amy called her friend on a phone.	13. Mr. Jones pays his bills by mail.
3. Bobby ate the food with his hands.	9. Mrs. Clark pays her bills on the Internet.	14. Jan sews clothes by hand.
4. Bill cut the wood with a saw.	10. Rena and Beth play on the computer.	15. Olga paid by cash.
5. Jim writes with a pencil.	11. Sue sews on a machine.	16. Maria paid by credit card.
6. Eric hit his head with a hammer.		17. Harry went home by car.
		18. Jane went to work by bike.

3 Practice the preposition "**with**." Pose the question, "*How does Willie eat?*" Have the students respond with the appropriate answer. After drilling the example several times, introduce similar questions and answers.

4

5 Use the same methodology above to introduce the preposition "**on**." Then, present the preposition "**by**" in the same manner.

After sufficiently drilling "**with**," "**on**," and "**by**" have an individual student ask another student a question using the question word "**How...?**" in a chain drill. The second student must formulate a response based on the photos and the captions.

6 In activity 2, the first pair-practice exercise, direct the students to ask and answers questions using "*How..?*" Model responses using "**with**," "**on**," and "**by**." Have the students continue the activity by working in pairs asking one another questions based on the photos and the captions.

7 Review the prepositional phrases in the box at the right of the worksheet and make sure that the students understand any new vocabulary.

8

9 In activity 3, the second pair-practice exercise, have the students use the question *"How do you...?"* Then, model a few responses using the propositional phrases in the box at the right of the worksheet. Let them work in pairs.

Expand the activity by asking the class personalized questions such as the ones listed in activity 4 at the bottom of the worksheet. Then, encourage the students to ask one another original questions.

10 After reading the questions in activity 4, have students complete the questions in writing.

NOTE:

The usage of the prepositions often varies from individual to individual, For example: *"He paid in cash.", "He paid with cash,"* and *"He paid by cash."*

The expressions "*by accident*" and "*on purpose*" are very useful and may be a logical extension of this lesson.

Expressions with the prepositions "*by*" often do not include any article. Similarly, certain expressions with "*on*" such as ''*on foot*' and "*on purpose*" also lack the article.

Cultural Note: In some countries, there is a taboo against left-handedness. This may be an interesting topic of discussion.

ESL Beginning Level   Household Chores • Present Tense • Ordinal Numbers

Imperative

1 *Read the list of household chores below.*

2 *Help organize Kelly's chores. List in order from first to last.*

FAMILY MESSAGE BOARD

Dear Kelly,
Do not forget your chores.
Make your bed.
Hang up your clothes.
Water the plants.
Take out the garbage.
Do the breakfast dishes.
Mail the letters on the table.

Do you have a game today?
I do not remember.
Close the windows, put the dog outside, turn off the computer, and lock the door. Be home for dinner. Have fun.
         Love, Mom

Kelly

Mom

Kelly's TO DO List

First, _____

Second, _____

Third, _____

Fourth, _____

Fifth, _____

Sixth, _____

Seventh, _____

Eighth, _____

Ninth, _____

Tenth, _____

Eleventh, _____

Twelfth, _____

Thirteenth, _____

3 *List some of your household chores. Compare them with the other students in your class.*

My TO DO List

_____   _____
_____   _____
_____   _____
_____   _____
_____   _____
_____   _____

ESL Beginning Level   Household Chores • Present Tense • Ordinal Numbers

Teacher's Notes

1 Before distributing the worksheet, review ordinal numbers and the following vocabulary:

board	**computer**	**fun**	**list**	**plant**
breakfast	**dinner**	**game**	**lock**	**remember**
chores	**dishes**	**garbage**	**mail**	**table**
close	**door**	**home**	**message**	**turn off**
clothes	**forget**	**letters**	**outside**	**windows**

For effective visual reinforcement, use the chalkboard drawings, flash cards, objects, and photos. Give as many contextual clues and examples of new vocabulary as possible.

2 Read the note on the message board twice as a listening comprehension activity. Then, ask questions to test for general understanding.

3 Disbritute the worksheet and read the note again while students follow along. Direct students to underline any unfamiliar words. Discuss any vocabulary and expressions that students have questions about.

4 Ask some "**True**, **False**, or **I don't know**" inference statements to check for understanding.

> **Examples:** *It's the weekend.*   *The game is today.*
> *Mom is at home.*   *It's Saturday morning.*
> *The windows are open.*   *The dog is inside the house.*

5 Do a *read-and-look-up activity* in which students read a sentence silently, then cover the written sentence and repeat as much of the sentence as they can without looking at the text.

6 Direct the students to help organize Kelly's chores by listing them in order from first to last using ordinal numbers.

7 As a class discussion, talk about the order in which the chores should be done.

8 Ask the students to write some of their own household chores on the blank note paper at the bottom of the worksheet. Ask volunteers to write a list of chores on the board. Correct the spelling and have the students list them on the reverse side of the worksheet.

9 As a follow-up activities, give a dictation based on part of the lists of chores.

ESL Intermediate Level — Will & Won't • Pair Practice • Writing

Time: In, For, Until, By (Expressions of Future)

1 Directions: *Read the items in Jill's cell phone calendars.*

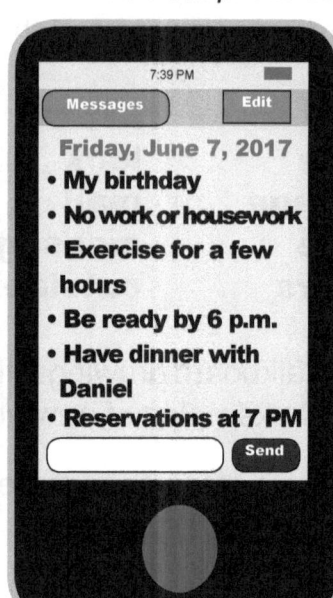

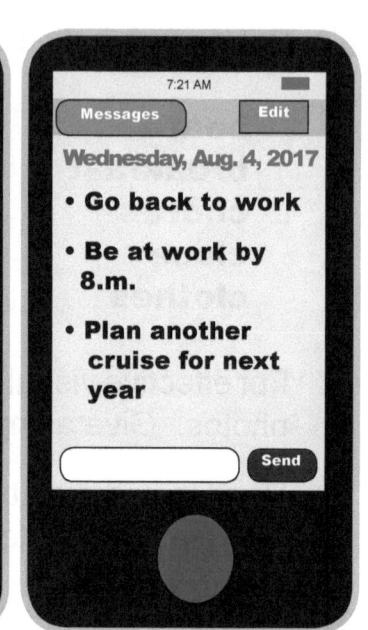

Monday, May 1, 2017 (6:22 PM)
- My birthday is in 5 weeks
- Begin my vacation in 2 months.
- Cruise for 1 month.
- Go back to work on August 4.

Friday, June 7, 2017 (7:39 PM)
- My birthday
- No work or housework
- Exercise for a few hours
- Be ready by 6 p.m.
- Have dinner with Daniel
- Reservations at 7 PM

Tuesday, July 6, 2017 (5:15 PM)
- Begin vacation
- Fly to Florida
- Stay in Miami until July 14
- Board cruise ship to the Caribbean
- Cruise for 3 weeks

Wednesday, Aug. 4, 2017 (7:21 AM)
- Go back to work
- Be at work by 8.m.
- Plan another cruise for next year

2 Pair-Practice: *Practice answering and asking questions with another student. See examples.* ▶

Student 1: **Will Jill _____ ?**

Student 2: **Yes, she will.** or **No, she won't.**

> Will Jill work on June 7?
> No, she won't.

3 Pair-Practice: *Practice answering and asking questions with another student. Use* **When?**, **How long?**, *and* **By what time?** *See examples.* ▶

Student 1: **When/How long/By what time will Jill _____?**

Student 2: **She'll _____ for/until/by _____ .**

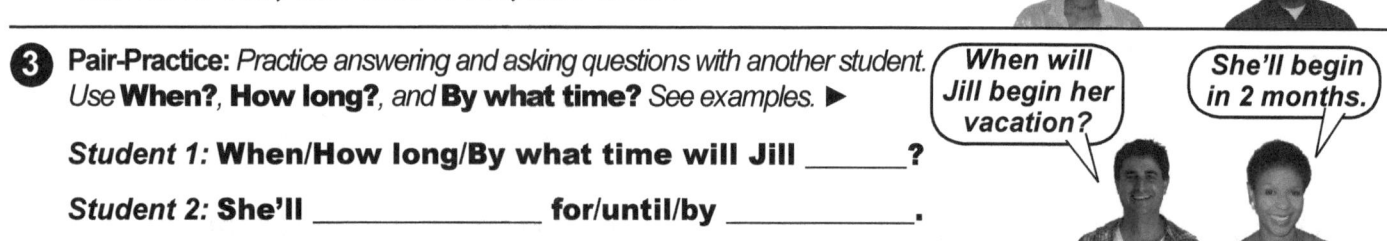

> When will Jill begin her vacation?
> She'll begin in 2 months.

4 Directions: *Answer the questions below. Then, discuss the answers with the other students in class.*

1. When will Jill have her birthday party? _____
2. How long will Jill's vacation be? *(for)* _____
3. Why won't Jill work on Friday, June 7? _____
4. How long will Jill exercise? _____
5. By what time will Jill be ready to go to the restaurant? _____
6. What time will Jill and Daniel arrive at the restaurant? _____
7. How long will Jill stay in Miami? *(until)* _____
8. How long will Jill be in the Caribbean? _____
9. How long will Jill's vacation be? *(until)* _____
10. What time will Jill be at work on August 4? _____

Wed. August 4, 2010 (7:30 AM) — Jill

4 Challenge: *On the back of this worksheet, write four original sentences telling what you* "**will**" *and* "**won't**" *do next week.*

ESL Intermediate Level • Expressions of Time: In, For, Until, By • Will & Won't

Teacher's Notes

1 Before distributing the worksheet, begin the lesson with a conversation using the future tense with "**will**" to determine how much the students already know about expressions of future time. Discuss taking a vacation and ask questions using *"When will you take a vacation?"*, *"How long will be on vacation?"*, and *"How many days will you be on vacation?"*, and *"By what time will you be back?"* Have the students repeat both question and answer. Then direct the question to individual students.

2 Distribute the worksheet. Introduce the vocabulary in the calendar entries by modeling the pronunciation of the phrases on the cell phones. Have the students repeat the pronunciation of the phrases after you. While you are reading, ask the student to underline any unfamiliar words, then explain them.

3 Then model sentences using "**will**" and "**won't**" with the information. For example, drill, *"Jill's birthday will be in 5 weeks,"* and *"She won't work on June 7."* Have students repeat the sentences.

4 Ask yes/no questions beginning with "**will**" having students respond with short answers. **Examples:**

> *Will Jill exercise on June 7?*   Yes, she will.
> *Will she go to a restaurant on May 1?*   No, she won't.
> *Will she or won't she take a cruise?*   She will.

5 Continue drilling similar questions and answers about Jill's other activities. Then, have the students pair up and ask each other.

6 Pose information questions using "**How long**?" Then model the appropriate response using "**for**" or "**until**." Have students repeat both questions and answers. **Examples**:

> *How long will Jill exercise?*   For a few hours.
> *How long will she stay in Miami?*   Until July 14.

7 Continue drilling "**for**" and "**until**" by asking similar questions about the entries on the calendar.

8 Next drill questions with "**When?**" and the corresponding answers with "**in**" and "**by**." **Examples:**

> *When will Jill begin her vacation?*   In two months.
> *When will she be back to work?*   By August 4.

9 On the chalkboard horizontally list the following items:, "**my friend**," "**to the movies**," "**on Saturday**," "**popcorn**" Using the words "**who**," "**where**," and "**what**," pose future tense questions requiring complete answers. **Examples:**

> *Who will you call?*   I'll call my friend.
> *Where will you and your friend go?*   We'll go to the movies.
> *When will you and your friend go there?*   We'll go there on Saturday.
> *What will your friend buy to eat?*   She'll buy popcorn.

10 Stress the contraction of "**will**" ('**ll**) which is normally used in conversation. Vary the written cues on the chalkboard. Wherever possible include information relating to the students in your class. Have students pair up and do exercise 3 using the calendars.

11 Elicit complete responses with the prepositions "**in**," "**by**," "**until**," and "**for**." Make a statement with one of the prepositions, then immediately prompt a response with such questions as *"And you?"*, *"How about you?"*, and *"What about you?"* Examples:

> *I'll be here until 2 p.m. And you?*   *I'll watch TV for an hour. What about you?*
> *My dinner will be ready by 6 p.m.? How about yours?*   *I'll go home in 2 hours. How about you?*

12 Read over the questions at the bottom of the worksheets and direct the students to write their own answers. Discuss the answers as a class discussion. Then direct the students to **Challenge** exercise at the bottom of the worksheet. Have them write four sentences explaining what they will and won't do next weekend.

NOTE

• Explain that "**'ll**" is the contraction of "**will**" and that "**won't**" is the contraction of "**will not**." Show that "**won't**" is also used to express the idea of refusal such as *"I won't eat liver!"* Also point out that "**will**" is followed by the verb and not the infinitive: Contrast "*He will drive a car*," and "*He wants to drive a car.*"

• In some English-speaking countries, "**shall**" is used instead of "**will**" with the pronouns "**I**" and "**we**." In the United States, the use of "**shall**" is limited to questions such as "**Shall we go?**" in which the speaker seeks agreement or concurrence or when referring emphatically to a future time as in *"We shall overcome!"*

• Other common time expressions used with the future: *later, in a little while, next, two days from now, soon, from now on.*

• To clarify the meanings of the prepositions, you may want to use the following definitions:

UNTIL: *up to the time that*   **IN**: *at the end of*   **BY**: *no later than*   **FOR**: *the amount of time spent*

ESL Beginning & Intermediate Levels • Abbreviations • Pair Practice • Writing

In, On, At (Preposition of Location)

1 *Read the addresses.*

1. Miss Susan Hastings
1234½ Kings Road
San Jose, CA 90058

2. Mr. Phil Gleason
1133 Maple Dr. Apt. 6
Washington, D.C. 20020

Regal Book Company
P.O. Box 453
London, Great Britain
S. W. 20 0BH

Dr. Don Leach
6505 St. Denis Blvd., Suite 3
Montreal, Quebec
Canada, G1V 4A8

3. Ms.. Doris Lopez
236 E. Clark Ave., #4
Dallas, Texas 75229

4. Mike Breyer
96 Lake Drive
New York, NY
10001

Mrs. Mary Breyer
2347 St. Thomas Lane
Sydney, N. S. W.
2000 Australia

Paul Hamel
1133 North Clark St., #101
West Hollywood, CA 90069

2 **Pair-Practice:** *Practice answering and asking questions with another student. Use the photos above. See examples.* ▶

What address does Ms. Hastings live at?

She lives at 1234½ Kings Road.

Student 1: What address/city/street _____ in/on/at?

Student 2: _____ in/on/at _____ .

3 *Answer the questions below.*

1. What address does Ms.. Lopez live at? _____
2. What country is the Regal Book Company in? _____
3. What street does Mr. Phil Gleason live on? _____
4. What address is Dr. Don Leach's office at? _____
5. What city does Miss Hastings live in? _____
6. What address does Mr. Gleason live at? _____
7. What post office box is the Regal Book Company at? _____
8. What apartment does Ms.. Lopez live in? _____
9. What suite is Dr. Leach's office in? _____
10. In what apartment does Paul Hamel live in? _____
11. What street do you live on? _____
12. What's your mailing address? _____
13. What city or town do you work in? _____
14. What's country do you live in? _____
15. What state or province do you live in? _____
16. Where's your school's address? _____
17. What's the address of your local library? _____
18. What address do you want to live at? _____

AT, ON, IN

Address
at 1133 Maple Dr.
at P.O. Box 368
at 1234½ Kings Rd.

Apartment, Room, Suite
in Rm. 213
in Ste. 3
in Apt. 6

Street, Corner, Floor
on Maple Dr.
on the corner
on the first floor

City, State, Country
in Dallas
in Texas
in Canada

ESL Beginning & Intermediate Levels • Abbreviations • Pair Practice • Writing

Teacher's Notes

1 Before distributing the worksheet, start the lesson with a conversation. Ask questions that elicit answers using prepositions of location "*in*," "*on*," and "*at*" when reading addresses in the answers to assess your students' knowledge and use of these prepositions.

2 Distribute the worksheet. Read the addresses on the envelopes. Have students repeat them. Then, direct them to the box at the right side of the worksheet and discuss when "*in*," "*on*," and "*at*" are used.

3 Practice the following kinds of questions and answers about the letters. Have students repeat both questions and answers.

What city does Mr. Gleason live in?   *He lives in Washington, D.C.*
What street does he live on?   *He lives on Maple Dr.*
What address does he live at?   *He lives at 496 Maple Dr.*
What apartment does he live in? *He lives in apartment 6.*

4 Have individual students ask questions of other students about the addresses on the envelopes. Expand the activity by having students ask one another personalized questions such as "*What street do you live on?*"

5 In Exercise 2, the pair-practice exercise, direct the students to ask and answers questions using "*What?*" with the preposition at the end of the question. Model responses using the preposition "*in*," "*on*," and "*at*." Have the students continue the activity by working in pairs asking one another questions based on the addresses on the envelopes at the top of the worksheet.

6 In Exercise 3, review the questions 1-10 and possible answers orally. Then, direct the students to answer them in writing.

7 Review the phrases in items 11-18 to make sure that the students understand any unfamiliar vocabulary, then direct them to complete the sentences in their own words. As a class discussion, encourage the students to share their sentences with the rest of the class.

8 You may also wish to drill the following kinds of variations:

In which city does Mr. Gleason live? → **Which** city does he live *in*?   *In what* city does he live → **What** city does he live *in*?

NOTE

The placement of the preposition at the beginning of the question tends to reflect more formal usage.

In English-speaking countries, domestic addresses are traditionally written in the following order:

Line 1: person or name of company
Line 2: street number, street name, apartment number
Line 3: city, state or province, zip or postal code

Two-letter postal codes for states are not technically abbreviations. Therefore, "CA" for California and 'TX" for Texas are not followed by a period.

9 On a subsequent day, have the students bring a postcard or envelope to school. Have them prepare a message to a relative or friend and then address and mail the card or letter. They can also write a comment to the author of this lesson. The address on envelop #4 is my correct address.

CULTURAL NOTE: Make students aware of the street address patterns used in your city. In many English speaking countries, cities are usually organized in blocks. Each block generally contains one hundred addresses. Odd numbers are used on one side of the street and even numbers on the other side. Some cities such as Washington, D.C., utilize a grid system dividing the city into N. E., NW, S. E. and S. W.

10 On the chalkboard, list the abbreviations at the bottom of this page. Drill for pronunciation. Allow the students sufficient time to study the list. Then erase the non-abbreviated forms. Divide the class into two teams. Alternately have one member of a team come to the chalkboard. Select a word from the list of abbreviations and tell the student to write the word beside the corresponding abbreviation. For each correct answer, give one point to the appropriate team. Insist on complete accuracy including spelling and capitalization.

# - Number	Cir. - Circle	Dr. - Drive, Doctor	Mrs. - Misses	P.O. - Post Office	St. - Street, Saint
@ - at	Co. - Company,	E. - East	Ms. - Miss	Pl. - Place	Ste. - Suite
Apt. - Apartment	County	Hwy. - Highway	N. - North	Rd. - Road	S. W. - Southwest
Ave. - Avenue	Ct. - Court	Jr. - Junior	N. E. - Northeast	Rm. - Room	TX - Texas
Blvd. - Boulevard	D.C. - District of	Ln. - Lane	N. W. - Northwest	S. - South	W. - West
CA - California	Columbia	Mr. - Mister	NY - New York	Sr. - Senior	ZIP - Zip Code

ESL Intermediate Level Reading • Writing • Class Discussion

Irregular Adverbs of Manner

1 *Read the story below.*

JOEY'S GARAGE Open Mondays

JOEY

ALFIE'S GARAGE Open Everyday

ALFIE

Alfie and Joey are mechanics. Alfie has a **good** job. He works **hard** every day. He also works **fast**. Alfie has a new car. It's a **fast** car, and it runs **well**. Joey's doesn't have a **good** business. He is a **slow** worker, and he works only on Monday. His car was in a **bad** accident and runs **badly**. It's a very **hard** job. He works **slowly**. Alfie works **hard**, and Joey **hardly** works.

What kind of ...?	How ...?
a **good** job	runs **well**
a **bad** accident	runs **badly**
a **fast** car	works **fast**
a **slow** worker	works **slowly**
a **hard** job	works **hard**

How often ...? **hardly** works

2 *Answer the questions in writing. Use the adjectives and adverbs above.*

1. Does Alfie have a bad job? No, he doesn't. He *has a good job.*
2. Is Alfie a bad worker? No, he isn't. He *is a hard worker.*
3. Does Alfie work slowly every day? No, he doesn't. He _____
4. Is Alfie's car slow? No, it isn't. It _____
5. Does Alfie's car run badly? No, it doesn't. It _____
6. Does Joey have a good business? No, he doesn't. He _____
7. Is Joey a fast worker? No, he isn't. He _____
8. Does Joey's car run well? No, it doesn't. It _____
9. Is Joey's job easy? No, it isn't. It _____
10. Does Joey work fast? No, he doesn't. He _____
11. Does Alfie work slowly? No, he doesn't. He _____

3 **Class Discussion:** *Practice answering and asking questions below with other students in your class. Share the answers with the class.*

1. How do you work? _____
2. What kind of cook are you? _____
3. How do you swim? _____
4. What kind of student are you? _____
5. How do you dance? _____
6. What kind of car do you like? _____
7. What kind of _____ ? _____
8. How do you _____ ? _____

ESL Intermediate Level   Reading • Writing • Class Discussion

Teacher's Notes

It is recommended that you teach lesson "Descriptive Adjectives and Adverbs of Manner" (#0116) before introducing this lesson. This lesson introduces the regular forms of adverbs of manner.

1 Before distributing the worksheet, start the lesson with a conversation. To assess your students' knowledge of the use of descriptive adjectives and adverbs of manner, ask personalized questions like the ones at the bottom of the worksheet.

2 Distribute the worksheet. As a active listening activity, ask the students to underline any unfamiliar vocabulary while you read the text to them. Then explain any new vocabulary.

3 Drill the adjectival and adverbial forms of the words in the boxes to the right of the worksheet. Pose questions beginning with "*How...?*" and "*What kind of...?*" Ask "*How does Alfie work?*" Model the response, "*He works well.*" Ask "*What kind of mechanic is Alfie?*" Model the response, "*He's a good mechanic.*" Have the students repeat both questions and the answers.

4 Continue asking similar questions about the cars, the quality of the work, the kind of cars and the kind of mechanics that Joey and Alfie are. For example,

How does the Alfie's car run?   *What kind of mechanic is Joey?*
What kind of car does Joey have?   *How does Joey work?*

5 Randomly ask yes/no and information questions beginning with "*How...?*" and "*What kind of...?*" Have the students continue the exercise by having individual students ask questions of other students based on the lesson.

6 Expand the activity by asking the class personalized questions such as the ones listed at the bottom of the worksheet. Then, as a class discussion in activity 3, encourage the students to pose original questions.

7 After reviewing the questions in activity 3, have students complete the questions in writing. Ask them to share some answers with the whole class during a class discussion.

NOTE

Explain that adjectives generally precede nouns and the adverbs of manner follow verbs. Point out that many common adverbs are formed by adding the suffix "**-ly**" to adjectives.

Unlike most adverbs, "*well*," "*fast*," and "*hard*" do not end in "*ly*."

8 You may want to review the **Adverbs of Frequency** (Lesson #0115). Practice asking questions beginning with "*How often...?*"

9 Show that "*hard*" is an adverb of manner and' answers the question "*How?*" "*Hardly*" is an adverb of frequency or intensity and answers the question *How often?*" or adds a negative tone. Contrast "*hard*" with "*hardly.*" Pose questions such as "*How does Alfie work?*" Model the response, "*He works hard.*" "*How often does Joe work?*" Model the response, "*He hardly works.*" Additional questions can be patterned after the chalkboard drill given below.

    1. How does Alfie work?   He _____.
    2. How often does Joey work?   He _____.
    3. Is Joey a lazy worker?   No, he's a _____.
    4. How often is Joey's garage open?   It's _____.
    5. Do you work hard or do you hardly work? I _____.

10 Point out that "*hard*" is also used as an adjective meaning "*difficult*" as well as the opposite of "*soft.*" Similarly, "*well*" can also be an adjective meaning "*healthy.*"

You may also want to show that "*well*" can be used with verbs to form compound adjectives such as:

11 *well-mannered person*

    well-done steak   *well-cooked meal*   *well-prepared speech*
    well-written letter   *well-made dress*   *well-dressed woman*
    well-educated man   *well-built house*

ESL Advance Level • Crossword Puzzle • Spelling of Irregular Past Tense Verbs

Irregular Past Tense Verbs 1

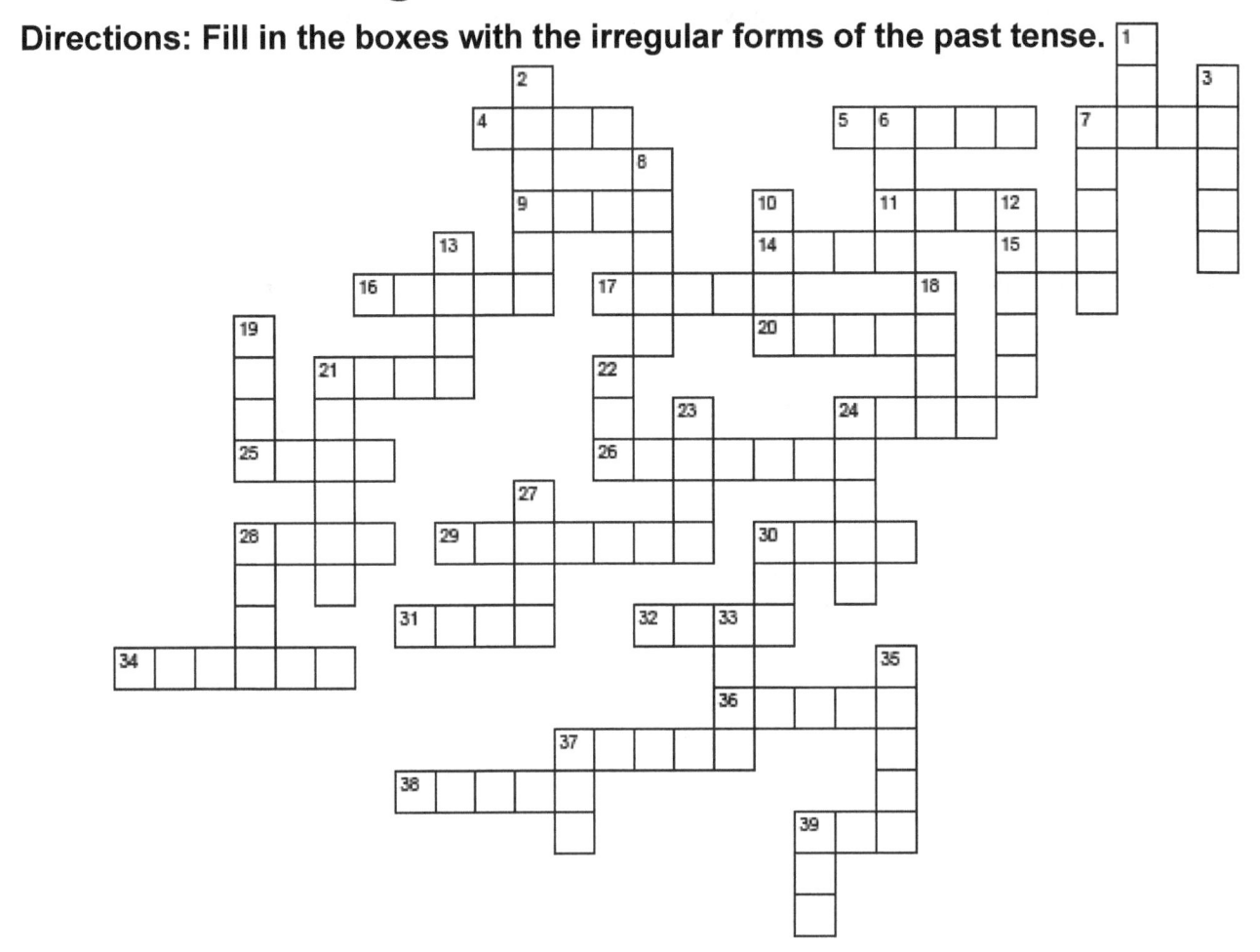

Directions: Fill in the boxes with the irregular forms of the past tense.

ACROSS
4. Billy ___ a model airplane.
5. There was an earthquake yesterday and the earth ___.
7. Yim ___ sick so she went to the hospital.
9. Albert ___ his wife a birthday present.
11. I ___ the newspaper this morning.
14. Jill ___ her friend a dollar to buy some juice.
15. Bob ___ in the race, but he didn't win.
16. The manager ___ all day working on a new project yesterday.
17. Sam ___ his car to work this morning.
20. The soldier ___ a love letter to his girlfriend.
21. Peter ___ the garage door when he arrived home.
24. The couple ___ their house for less than what they paid for it.
25. The job applicant ___ her best clothes for the interview this morning.
26. Mike ___ his job appointment was yesterday, but it was this morning.
28. Amy ___ in the ocean for the first time.
29. Ann ___ a delicious cake to the party.
30. The dog trainer ___ the treat in front of his dog.
31. Helen ___ her new bicycle to school this morning.
32. The witness ___ the truth in the courtroom.
34. Rita ___ to turn off the light before leaving the house.
36. The president ___ to the nation on TV last night.
37. Jose ___ late so he was late for work this morning.
38. Bill ___ an old car rather than a new car.
39. The cat ___ in front of the window all day yesterday.

DOWN
1. Jim ___ dinner with friends last night.
2. My father ___ me how to swim.
3. The kids ___ in the rain while waiting for the school bus.
6. The child ___ himself when he fell off the slide.
7. Jake ___ his long lost ring!
8. Paul ___ a new song on the radio.
10. Yen ___ here from China by airplane.
12. Maria ___ some water after eating hot sauce.
13. My grandfather ___ his money under his mattress.
18. John ___ off his bicycle, but he wasn't hurt.
19. The suspect told the police that he ___ nothing about the crime.
21. The mother ___ some jam on her child's bread.
22. Dad ___ his son use the car to on a date.
23. How much did that ___?
24. Romeo ___ Juliette's heart.
27. Ella ___ up three times last night.
28. Pat ___ in the local band last night.
30. The dog ___ its bone in the back yard.
33. Martha doesn't know where she ___ her ring.
35. Alice ___ to go to the party.
37. Mark ___ the hot plate on the table.
39. We ___ a great movie on TV last night.

ESL Advance Level • Crossword Puzzle • Spelling of Irregular Past Tense Verbs

Teacher's Notes

1 Before distributing the worksheet, point out that many verbs have an irregular form in the past tense. Give a few examples such as see → saw, speak → spoke, write → wrote, etc. See list below.

Present	Past	Present	Past	Present	Past	Present	Past
bring	brought	give	gave	read	read	spend	spent
choose	chose	hear	heard	ride	rode	spread	spread
cost	cost	hide	hid	run	ran	stand	stood
do	did	hold	held	see	saw	steal	stole
drink	drank	hurt	hurt	sell	sold	swim	swam
drive	drove	keep	kept	set	set	teach	taught
eat	ate	know	knew	shake	shook	tell	told
fall	fell	lend	lent	shut	shut	think	thought
feel	felt	let	let	sing	sang	wake	woke
find	found	lose	lost	sit	sat	wear	wore
fly	flew	make	made	sleep	slept	write	wrote
forget	forgot	mean	meant	speak	spoke		

2 Encourage the students to think of other verbs that are irregular in the past tense. Make a list on the chalkboard or whiteboard and give examples of them in context.

3 Distrubute the worksheet and demonstrate how to do a crossword puzzle. Explain the concept of **DOWN** and **ACROSS**. Then, demonstrate how to fill in the puzzle using the clues. Do a few examples with the whole class. This worksheet can be used as a homework activity.

4 Correct the answers by projecting an overhead transparency image directly onto the board on which students can write the answers. See solution below.

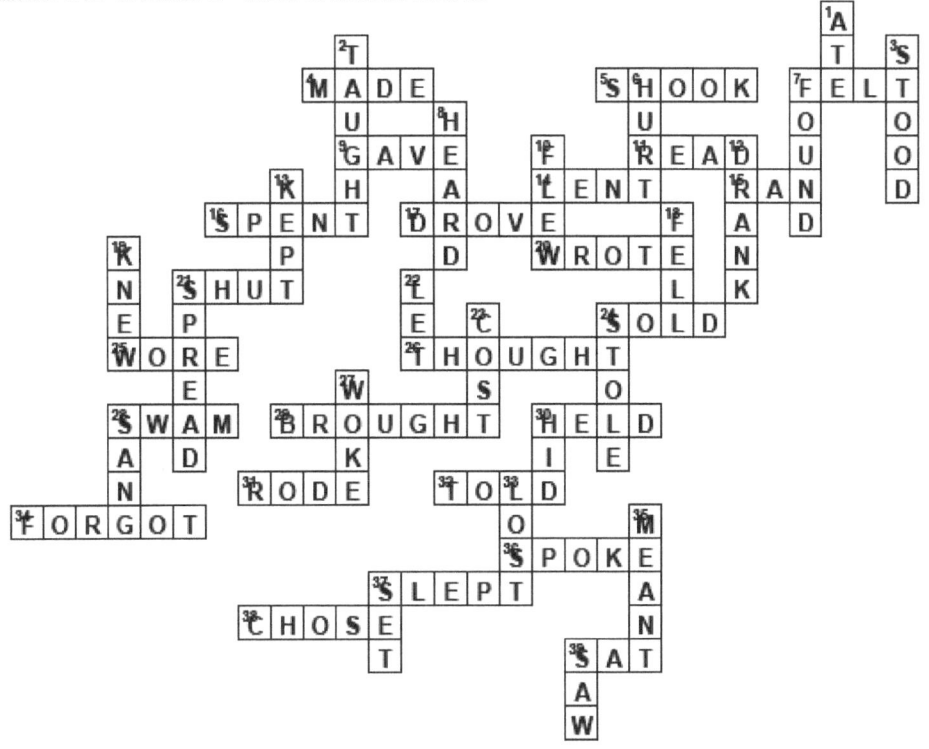

122

Irregular Past Tense Verbs 2

ESL Advanced Level• Crossword Puzzle • Spelling of Irregular Past Tense Verbs

Directions: Fill in the boxes with the irregular forms of the past tense.

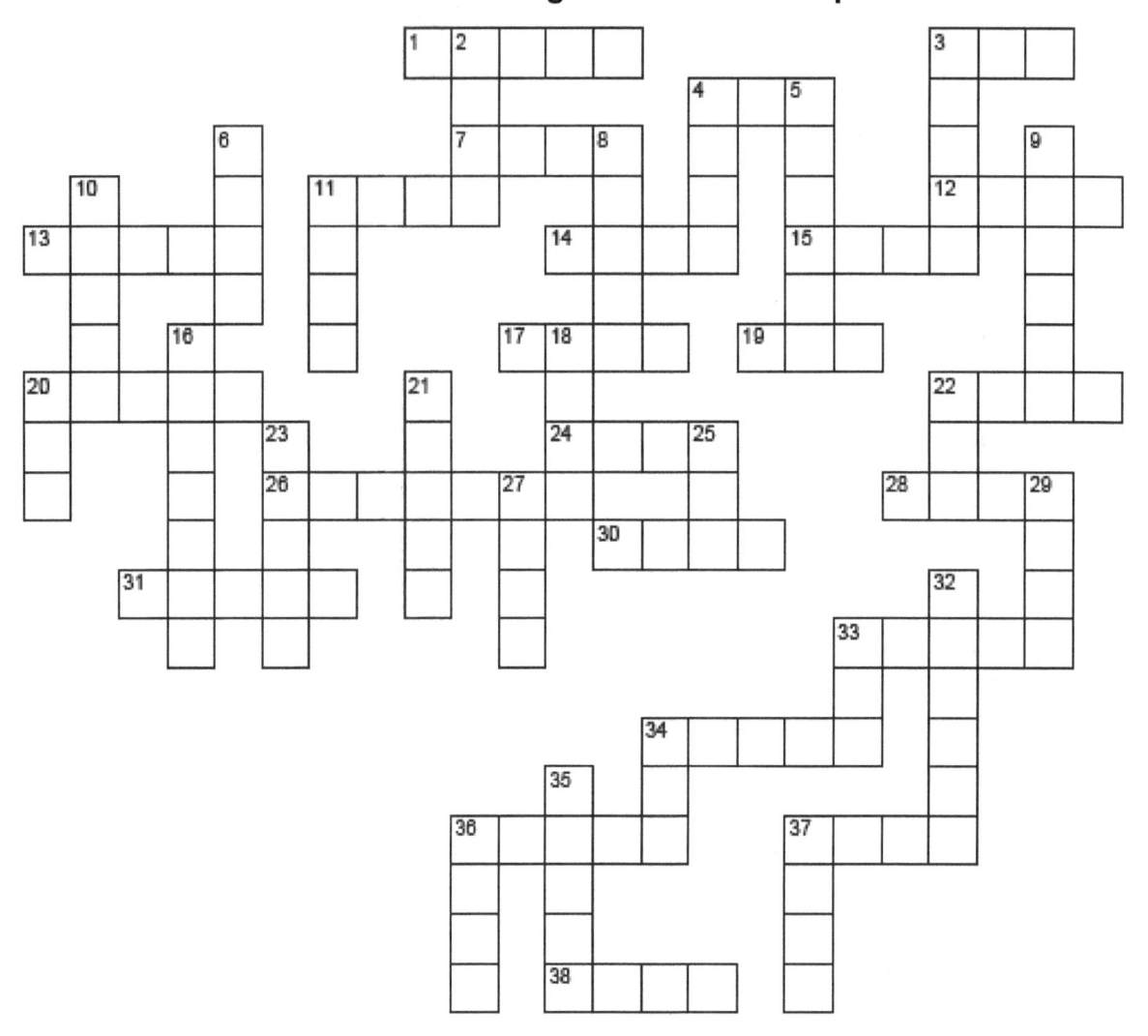

ACROSS
1. choose
3. see
4. let
7. read
11. shut
12. keep
13. drink
14. cost
15. give
17. fly
19. eat
20. hear
22. ride
24. sell
26. think
28. know
30. make
31. shake
33. steal
34. sleep
36. spend
37. feel
38. tell

DOWN
2. hurt
3. speak
4. lend
5. teach
6. wake
8. drive
9. spread
10. write
11. sing
16. bring
18. lose
20. hide
21. find
22. run
23. stand
25. do
27. hold
29. wear
32. forget
33. set
34. sit
36. swim
37. fall

ESL Advanced Level • Crossword Puzzle • Spelling of Irregular Past Tense Verbs

Teacher's Notes

1 Before distributing the worksheet, point out that many verbs have an irregular form in the past tense. Give a few examples such as see → saw, speak → spoke, write → wrote, etc. See list below.

Present	Past	Present	Past	Present	Past	Present	Past
bring	brought	give	gave	read	read	spend	spent
choose	chose	hear	heard	ride	rode	spread	spread
cost	cost	hide	hid	run	ran	stand	stood
do	did	hold	held	see	saw	steal	stole
drink	drank	hurt	hurt	sell	sold	swim	swam
drive	drove	keep	kept	set	set	teach	taught
eat	ate	know	knew	shake	shook	tell	told
fall	fell	lend	lent	shut	shut	think	thought
feel	felt	let	let	sing	sang	wake	woke
find	found	lose	lost	sit	sat	wear	wore
fly	flew	make	made	sleep	slept	write	wrote
forget	forgot	mean	meant	speak	spoke		

2 Encourage the students to think of other verbs that are irregular in the past tense. Make a list on the chalkboard or whiteboard and give examples of them in context.

3 Distribute the worksheet and demonstrate how to do a crossword puzzle. Explain the concept of **DOWN** and **ACROSS**. Then, demonstrate how to fill in the puzzle using the clues. Do a few examples with the whole class. This worksheet can be used as a homework activity.

4 Correct the answers by projecting an overhead transparency image directly onto the board on which students can write the answers. See solution below.

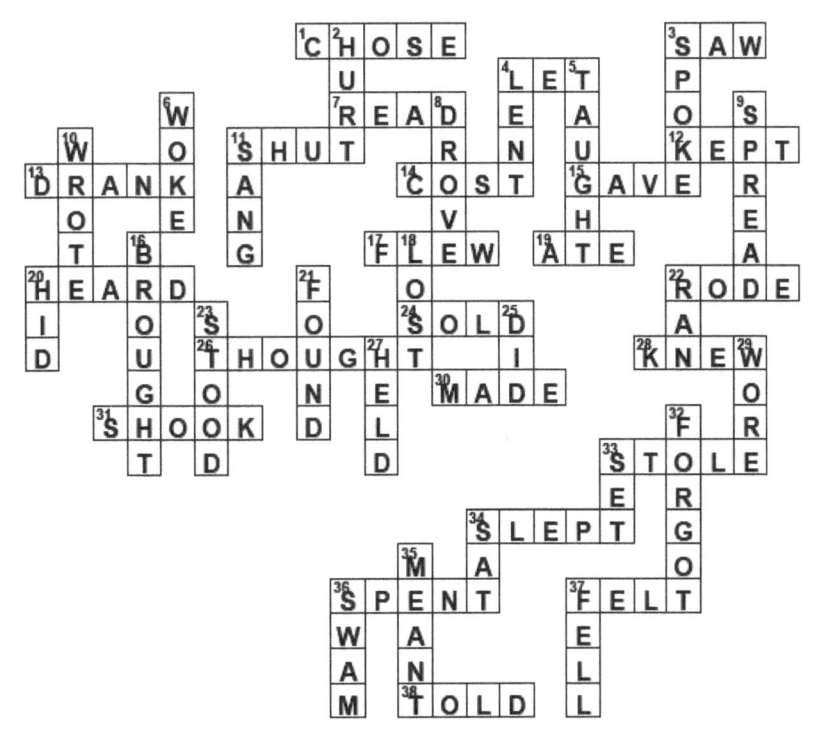

ESL Intermediate & Advanced Levels • Vocabulary Building • Pair Practice • Writing

Job Ads

1 *Study the newspaper ads. Then cover the ads in the middle box. Read the ads on the left side aloud.*

CASHIER p.t/f.t. loc. exp. des. Apply in person, XYZ Co. 321 Main St.	**CASHIER** part time or full time local experience desirable Apply in person, XYZ Company 321 Main St.	**OTHER ABBREVIATIONS USED IN JOB ADS** ad — advertisement appoint. — appointment appl. — application ASAP — as soon as possible avail. — available bkgrnd. — background bus. — business cond. — condition ctr. — center dept. — department dntn. — downtown dr. lic. — driver's license ed. — education equip. — equipment etc. — et cetera ext. — extension eve. — evenings gen. — general hr. — hour immed. — immediate info. — information max. — maximum m/f — male or female off. — office OT — overtime perm. — permanent pri. — private pref. — preferred supv. — supervisor trans. — transportation vac. — vacation @ — at, each # — number % — percent & — and - — minus + — plus = — equals / — or 5' — 5 feet 9" — 9 inches
CARPENTER xlnt. bene. pd. med./den. ins. Call Mr. Wood for appt. 657-8814	**CARPENTER** excellent benefits paid medical and dental insurance Call Mr. Wood for an appointment 657-8814	
CONSTRUCTION gd. work cond. pd. hol. & vac. Send res. to Miss Booker 1133 Clark St.	**CONSTRUCTION** good working conditions paid holidays and vacation Send resume to Miss Booker 1133 Clark Street	
AUTO MECH. min. 2 yrs. exp. hi. sal. Tel. Apex Motors 993-4363 for int.	**AUTO MECH.** minimum 2 years experience high salary Telephone Apex Motors 993-4363 for an interview	
SALESPERSON ref. req. no. exp. nec. Contact Hilec Corp. P.O. Box 105 Centerville, CA	**SALESPERSON** references required no experience necessary Contact Hilec Corporation Post Office Box 105 Centerville, California	

2 *Talk with another student about the ads above.*
Student 1: What does .... mean?
Student 2: It means ....

What does "p.t." mean? / *It means part time.*

3 *Write the complete words for the abbreviations to the left.*

Call for int. _____
xlnt. work cond. _____
gd. sal _____
exp. req. _____
loc. exp. _____

Tel. for appt. _____
p.t./f.t. _____
pd. vac. _____
med. pd. _____
ref. nec. _____

125

ESL Intermediate & Advanced Levels • Vocabulary Building • Pair Practice • Writing

Teacher's Notes

❶ Read the ads to the left. Then read the corresponding ads in the middle box.

Tell the students to cover the ads in the middle box. Ask for volunteers to read the ads using only the abbreviations. (You may want to use an overhead projector to project only the abbreviations.)

❷ Teach the short dialog. Show how to do this activity with the help of a student. Then, have the students continue the exercise by working in pairs or small groups.

❸ Read and explain other common abbreviations and symbols used in job ads in the box at the right of the handout.

Answers:

Call for int.	= Call for an interview
xlnt. work cond.	= excellent working conditions
gd. sal.	= good salary
exp. req.	= experience required
loc. exp.	= local experience
Tel. for appt.	= Telephone for an appointment
p.t./f.t	= part time or full time
pd. vac.	= paid vacation
med. in. pd.	= medical insurance paid
ref. nec.	= references necessary

❹ As a follow-up activity, have the students write an original ad for a job on a piece of paper. Have the students write their names on the back of the paper. Then have the students roll-play interviewing and the ad. The students must discuss the requirements with the author of the ad, who acts as the interviewer.

❺ For more advanced students, you may want to discuss the following topics:
• How should a person dress for an interview?
• What kind of questions are asked during the interview?
• How can a person prepare for an interview?
• What are some do's and don'ts during the interview?
• What are some differences in employment between this country and other countries?
• What kind of information should a person include in a resume.
• In your opinion, what is an acceptable hourly wage?

ESL Advanced Levels Group Discussion • Vocational ESL Vocabulary

Job Interview Questions

1. Are you legally authorized to work?
2. Are you willing to relocate?
3. Are you willing to travel?
4. Are you willing to work nights, weekends, and holidays?
5. Can you describe a time when your work was criticized and how did you handle it?
6. Describe a situation where you had to make a quick decision.
7. Do you have any language abilities that might assist you in performing this job?
8. Do you need additional training?
9. Do you prefer a fixed or flexible work schedule?
10. Do you prefer to work independently or on a team?
11. Have you ever been convicted of a crime?
12. Have you ever had difficulty with a supervisor or teacher? How did you resolve the conflict?
13. How do you feel about taking work home with you?
14. How do you handle stress and pressure?
15. How has your school/work experience prepared you for working at our company?
16. How long do you expect to work for us if hired?
17. How much experience do you have?
18. How would you describe your work style?
19. If you knew your boss was 100% wrong about something, what would you do?
20. Tell me about a major problem you recently handled. Were you successful in resolving it?
21. What are your greatest strengths?
22. What are your salary expectations?
23. What is your greatest achievement?
24. What is your greatest failure and what did you learn from it?
25. What is your greatest weakness?
26. What is your philosophy towards work?
27. What is your style of leadership?
28. What kind of situation do you find stressful?
29. What motivates you?
30. What skills can you bring to this company?
31. What technology are you familiar with?
32. What type of work environment do you prefer?
33. What's the most important thing you learned in school?
34. Where did you work before?
35. Why are you the best person for the job?
36. Why should we hire you?

ESL Advanced Levels — Group Discussion • Vocational ESL Vocabulary

Teacher's Notes

1. Divide the class into groups of three or four.

2. Distribute the sheet of job interview questions.

3. Tell the students to take turns selecting one question.

4. Tell them to read their question aloud and lead their group in discussing the question on the card. (Each student should lead at least one discussion.)

5. Walk around the classroom and join each group for a few minutes and correct the students pronunciation and grammar. (Do not hover over a group, sit down at eye-
6. level.)

7. During the last twenty minutes of the activity, ask volunteers from each group to share which questions their group discussed.

8. Place important vocabulary and expressions on the board.)

9. Ask the students to add to the discussion by providing their own questions.

ESL Beginning & Intermediate Levels • Modal Verbs • Asking Permission • Pair Practice • Writing

May

Read: *Practice the phrases below the photo with another student.*

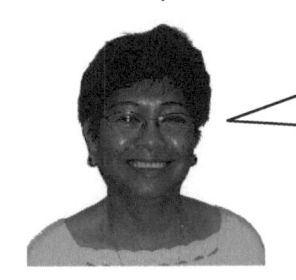

> We use the word **may** to ask permission.
> *Examples:*
> **May** I come in? Yes, you **may**.
> **May** I smoke? No, you **may** not smoke in here.

Pair Practice: *Practice asking and answering questions with the word **may**. See the example to the right. Use the expressions below.*

Student 1: **May I** ...?

Student 2: Yes, You **may**. or No, you **may not**.

... come in?   ... help you?
... go out?   ... show you the way?
... sit down?   ... ask you a question?
... leave the room? ... speak to you for a moment

May I come in?   *Yes, you may.*

Write: *Write polite questions using **may** for the situations below.*

1. May I keep this cat. 
   Bill wants to keep the cat.

2. _____
   He wants to take your order.

3. _____
   He wants to take your photo.

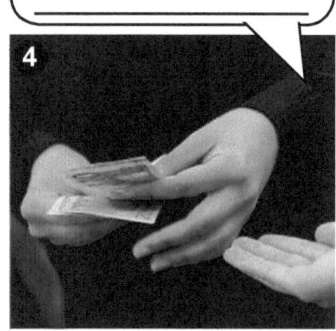

4. _____
   He wants to borrow money.

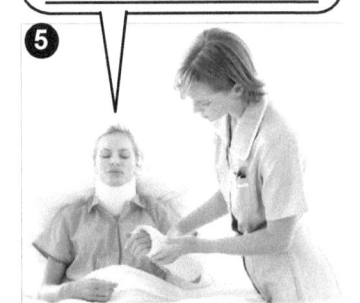

5. _____
   Suzan wants to go home.

6. _____
   Jim wants to use a phone.

7. _____
   Lan wants to turn in his homework tomorrow.

8. _____
   Kim wants a cookie.

129

ESL Beginning & Intermediate Levels • Modal Verbs • Asking Permission • Pair Practice • Writing

Teacher's Notes

1 Read and explain the use of **may** in the box at the top of the page.

Explain that **may** is one of many modal verbs. The most common are: **can**, **could**, **may**, **might**, **shall**, **should**, **will**, **would**, **must**, and **ought to**. Modals do not change form, so we cannot add "-s" to the third person singular. We use modals with the simple form of the verb (an infinitive without "to"). The only exception is "ought to." We place modals in front of the subject to form questions.

2 Read and discuss the vocabulary in the items in the Pair Practice exercise. With the help of a student, demonstrate how to do the pair practice exercise using the phrases. Then have the students continue by working in pairs.

3 As an extension to the Pair Practice exercise, drill asking permission by having students use "may" with the following phrases:

close the window
open the door
turn on the light
close the door
turn off the light
help you

use your telephone
borrow a cup of sugar
come with you
turn in my homework tomorrow
come in
leave now

Examples:

Situation

It is cold in this room.
It's hot in here.
It's dark.

Request

***May** I close the window?*
***May** I open the door?*
***May** I turn on the light?*

4 Explain how to write questions with **may** in the speech balloons on the handout. Correct the answers by having volunteers write them on the chalkboard. Discuss other possible answers.

Follow-Up

5 Explain that we use the word **may** when we want to express indecision. It means "maybe," "not sure," "undecided." **May** often has the same meaning as **might**.

Example: *Today is a nice day. I **may** go to the park, or I **might** go to the beach."*

6 Practice by drilling with the question: *"What are you going to do ..... ?"*

tomorrow
tonight

around ... o'clock
after class

on your vacation
if you win the lottery

ESL Beginning & Intermediate Levels • Modal Verbs • Asking Permission • Pair Practice • Writing

ESL Intermediate Levels • Modal Verb • Expressing Indecision • Pair Practice • Writing

Might

Read: *Practice the phrases below the photo with another student.*

We use the word **might** to express indecision.
Example:
*Today is a nice day. I **might** go to the park or I **might** go to the beach.*

Pair Practice: *Practice asking and answering questions with the word **might**. See the example to the right. Use the expressions below.*

Student 1: What are you going to do ...?
Student 2: I don't know. I might ...

... tonight?
... tomorrow?
... around ... o'clock?
... on the weekend?
... on your birthday?
... later?
... on your vacation?
... after class today?
... if you win the lottery?
... if you lose your job?

What are you going to do tomorrow?

I don't know. I might go to the beach.

Write: *Write polite questions using **could** for the situations below.*

He's thinking of taking a vacation.

Will you go to the company picnic?

What are you going to order for lunch?

What will the children be when they grow up?

Who will you vote for in the next election?

What are you going to do when the war ends?

What are they planning to do?

How long will Bill be at the office today?

ESL Intermediate Levels • Modal Verb • Expressing Indecision • Pair Practice • Writing

Teacher's Notes

1 Read and explain the use of **might** in the box at the top of the page.

Explain that **might** is a modal verb.

- **Might** + verb (simple form) expresses possibility in the future or at present.
- **Might** often has the same meaning as **may**.
- Other modal verbs are: **can**, **could**, **may**, **shall**, **should**, **will**, **would**, **must**, and **ought to**.
- Modals do not change form, so we cannot add "**-s**" to the third person singular. We use modals with the simple form of the verb (an infinitive without "to").

Example: *We **might** go to the movies, or we **might** go to the theater on Saturday.*

2 Read and discuss the vocabulary in the items in the Pair Practice exercise. With the help of a student, demonstrate how to do the pair practice exercise using the phrases. Then have the students continue by working in pairs.

3 Describe situations in which the students must respond with **might**.

Examples:

Stimulus	**Response**
What are you going to order for dinner?	I don't know. I **might** have fish, or I **might** have chicken.
What will you do on your next vacation?	I don't know. I **might** go to Hawaii, or I **might** go to Florida.

4 Explain how to write sentences with **might** on the lines below the photos on the worksheet. Correct the answers by having volunteers write them on the chalkboard. Discuss other possible answers.

5 As a follow-up activity, repeat the pair practice exercise. Contrast "might" and "may" using the following rejoinder:

Student 1: What will you do .... ?

Student 2: I might ..... or I may....

ESL Advanced Level · Giving Advice • Class Discussion

Modal Verbs (Review)

Directions: Write your responses to the situations using modals: should, might, may, would, could.

Dear Wise One:

My neighbor, who I will call Joanna, comes to my home with her three children without calling me first. She is very pleasant and friendly, but I sometimes like my privacy, and I would like to have a chance to clean my home before visitors come over. I'm afraid that if I tell her not to come without calling first, she might get angry and never come again. I don't have many friends and do not want to lose this one. What should I do?

UNHAPPY IN NEW YORK

Dear Wise One:

I'm a woman who has found the most wonderful man in the world. He is kind, generous, and gentle. We have known each other for six months, and we spend many afternoons together. I love him very much. He says that he loves me, too, and wants to marry me. However, there is one problem—he's already married. He says that he doesn't love his wife and plans to divorce her. Every time I ask him about his divorce, he changes the subject. I don't want to wait forever. Please help me.

LOVE SICK IN CHICAGO

Dear Unhappy in New York,

_____
_____
_____
_____
_____
_____
_____

Dear Love Sick in Chicago,

_____
_____
_____
_____
_____
_____
_____

ESL Advanced Level   Modal Verbs • Giving Advice • Class Discussion

Teacher's Notes

1) Introduction

- Bring some newspaper articles that give advice (i.e. Dear Abby) to class.
- Read a few situations and discuss some possible solutions.
- Discuss the following questions:
    - *What kind of problems are presented?*
    - *How often do you agree with the answers given?*
    - *Is the advice helpful? Why or why not?*
    - *What purpose do the articles serve?*
    - *Would you ever write for advice? Why or why not?*

Language Activities

2) Explain polite ways to express a suggestion or give advice using modal verbs:

Should:	You should stop	**Would**:	I would suggest that ....
	You shouldn't continue		If I were you, I would ....
Might:	You might want to	**Could:**	You could try to ....
May:	May I suggest that you		
	You may want to		

3) Before handing out the worksheet, read the two stories to the students as a listening comprehension exercise. Then ask simple questions beginning with question words (what, where, when, why, etc.) to test the students' comprehension. Next, hand out the worksheet and read the stories again while the students circle all unfamiliar vocabulary. Then explain the vocabulary.

4) Discuss possible solutions to the situations.

5) Have the students write their responses to the situations using some of the modals above.

6) After the exercise has been corrected, ask for volunteers to share their solutions with the rest of the class.

Follow-up Activities

7)
- Have students write an anonymous letter asking for advice.
- Distribute the letters to other students in the class.
- Ask students to answer the letters and share their responses.

ESL Beginning Level • Vocabulary Building • Pair Practice • Fill In • Class Discussion

More & Less

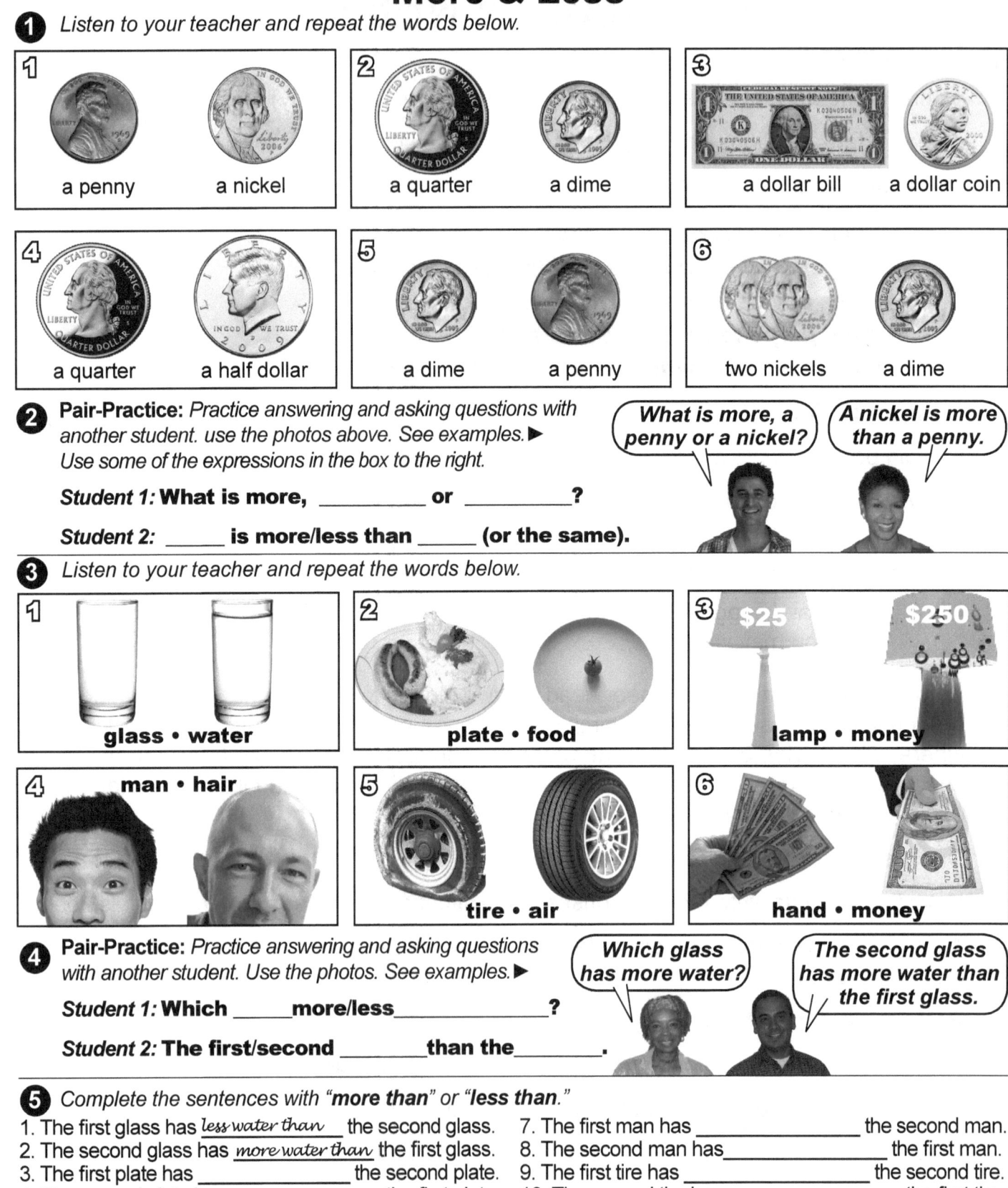

1 *Listen to your teacher and repeat the words below.*

1	2	3
a penny · a nickel	a quarter · a dime	a dollar bill · a dollar coin

4	5	6
a quarter · a half dollar	a dime · a penny	two nickels · a dime

2 **Pair-Practice:** *Practice answering and asking questions with another student. use the photos above. See examples.* ▶
Use some of the expressions in the box to the right.

Student 1: **What is more, _____ or _____?**

Student 2: _____ **is more/less than** _____ **(or the same).**

> What is more, a penny or a nickel?

> A nickel is more than a penny.

3 *Listen to your teacher and repeat the words below.*

1	2	3
glass • water	plate • food	lamp • money $25 / $250

4	5	6
man • hair	tire • air	hand • money

4 **Pair-Practice:** *Practice answering and asking questions with another student. Use the photos. See examples.* ▶

Student 1: **Which** _____ **more/less** _____ **?**

Student 2: **The first/second** _____ **than the** _____ **.**

> Which glass has more water?

> The second glass has more water than the first glass.

5 *Complete the sentences with "**more than**" or "**less than**."*

1. The first glass has *less water than* the second glass.
2. The second glass has *more water than* the first glass.
3. The first plate has _____ the second plate.
4. The second plate has _____ the first plate.
5. The first lamp is _____ the second lamp.
6. The second lamp is _____ the first lamp.
7. The first man has _____ the second man.
8. The second man has _____ the first man.
9. The first tire has _____ the second tire.
10. The second tire has _____ the first tire.
11. The first hand has _____ the second.
12. The second hand has _____ the first.

135

ESL Beginning Level • Vocabulary Building • Pair Practice • Fill In • Class Discussion

Teacher's Notes

1 Bring some examples of U.S. coins to class. Before handing out the worksheet, review the ordinal numbers "*first*" and "*second*" and the names of U. S. currency: **penny**, **nickel**, **dime**, **quarter**, **half-dollar**, **dollar coin**, and **dollar bill**.

2 Ask the question, "*Is a nickel more or less than a penny?*" Model the response, "*It's more.*" Have the students repeat the answer. Continue contrasting the coins by asking similar questions of individual students.

3 Show that the two nickels are the equivalent of a dime. For example, ask the question, "*Are two nickels more or less than a dime?*" Model the response, "*It's the same.*" Continue posing questions eliciting responses with "*more*," "*less*," and "*the same*."

4 Distribute the worksheet. For each picture a the top of the worksheet, ask an information question. such as "*What is more/less, a penny or a nickel?*" Model the response, "*A penny is less than a nickel.*" After having the students repeat the structures, direct questions to individual students.

5 In activity 2, the first pair-practice exercise, direct the students to ask and answer questions using "*What is more/less, _____ or _____?*" Model responses using "*more*", "*less*," or "*the same*." Have the students continue the activity by working in pairs asking one another questions based on the information in the boxes at the top of the worksheet.

6 Direct the students to the activity 3 in the middle of the worksheet. For each photo ask an appropriate question with "*more*" or "*less*." Ask, "*Which has more/less water, the first or the second glass?*" Model the response, "*The second glass has more water than the first glass.*" Continue posing questions eliciting responses with "*more than*" and "*less than*."

7 Have the students fill in the sentences at the bottom of the worksheet. Answers:

1. The first glass has *less water than* the second glass.
2. The second glass *has more water* than the first glass.
3. The first plate has *less food than* the second plate.
4. The second plate has *more food than* the first plate.
5. The first lamp is (cost) *less money than* the second lamp.
6. The second lamp is (cost) *more money than* the first lamp.
7. The first man has *less hair than* the second man.
8. The second man has *more hair than* the first man.
9. The first tire has *less air than* the second tire.
10. The second tire has *more air than* the first tire.
11. The first hand has *more money than* the second.
12. The second hand has *less money than* the first.

ESL Advanced Level   Values Clarification • Discussion • Role Playing

Not Understanding

1 *Read the situation below.*

THE SITUATION

You are in a job training class. Your teacher is explaining something and giving instructions. She is talking fast and using words that you do not understand. What should you do?

2 *Read the possible solutions to the problem above. Rank the solutions in order from the best to the worst. (The top box is the best and bottom box is the worst.) Write your ranking in the column **MY RANKING** to the left below. Please feel free to come up with other practical solutions.*

MY RANKING ← BEST / WORST →

POSSIBLE SOLUTIONS

1. Visit the director of the school and tell him or her your problem.

2. Ask a friend to help you.

3. Do nothing. Just listen and try to understand.

4. Guess what the instructor is saying and try to do it.

5. Wait until the end of the class and tell your teacher that you did not understand.

6. Ask the teacher to slow down and repeat the instructions.

7. (Other)
_____
_____

GROUP RANKING ← BEST / WORST →

3 *Break up into small groups and discuss your ranking with the rankings of the other members in your group. Feel free to discuss other practical possibilities. Finally, decide on a group ranking. Again, rank the possible solutions in order from the best to the worst. All members of the group must agree before you write the numbers in the column **GROUP RANKING**.*

4 *As a whole class, discuss the best and worst solutions to the situation.*

ESL Intermediate Level • Values Clarification: Not Understanding • Discussion

INTRODUCTION

These lessons are appropriate for students in English-as-a-Second-Language (ESL) and Vocational ESL classes as well as for native English speakers entering the work force. The goal of this book is to help people make ethical decisions in the work place. Each lesson presents a commonly-found work situation that requires discussing and clarifying individual and group values. These lessons are not meant to provide a right or wrong response to a decision. They are only a means to clarify an individual's or a group's choices in making an ethically-based decision. Instead of a right or wrong answer, the decision made about a specific situation might be a question between different views of what is right. The lessons help the participants explore the different reasons for their views. Instead of asking the participants to make generalized decisions about ethical questions, the lessons present specific situations in which a variety of good decisions can be made. Some participants may disagree among different versions of what appears right. Participants are encouraged to discuss different perspectives, values, and actions to the same situation. Also be aware that our actions also tend to rely on our experiences, social status, culture, and assumptions. Hopefully, the participants will respond to each other with respect and increase mutual recognition of each other as persons who want to do the right thing.

TEACHING NOTES

1. Before distributing the handout, read the situation and ask basic comprehension questions to check for understanding.

2. Distribute the worksheet to the student, and read the situation to the class. Discuss any unfamiliar vocabulary and expressions.

3. Read the possible solutions to the problem. Again, discuss any unfamiliar vocabulary and ask basic questions to check for understanding. Tell the students that they are free to come up with other practical possibilities in addition to the ones presented.

4. Direct the students to rank the possibilities in order from the best solution to the worst, the best being the box at the top and the worst at the bottom. Have the students prioritize their personal ranking in the column named "**MY RANKING**."

5. Then, gather in groups of four or five students.

6. Tell each group of students to discuss their ranking. Instruct them that they must come up with a single ranking that they must all agree on. Identify one person in each group to record the group's ranking in the column labeled "**GROUP RANKING**." Tell students to talk about what should be done, state the other practical possibilities, and ask about the reasons that support these proposals: observations, values, and assumptions.

7. Have each group report on its ranking to the whole class. You may also want to write the various rankings on the blackboard/whiteboard or overhead transparency for comparison.

8. Discuss other possible solutions with the students and write them on the chalkboard.

8. Finally discuss the pros and cons of each ranking, and lead the class in coming to a general consensus.

9. Write other possible solutions to the problems --on the blackboard as a follow-up exercise.

10. As a follow-up activity, use the exercises as a basis for role playing. When doing a role playing exercise, allow students to .prepare themselves in pairs or small groups before having them perform before the whole class. Give the students the freedom to vary the situation and be creative. Don't over-correct. Note major mistakes; discuss and correct them later. To practice active listening, have the other students in the class note the errors, too. Discuss the role-playing exercises afterwards for students' reaction and interpretations.

ESL Beginning Level   Listening & Reading Comprehension: Numbers

Numbers

LISTENING COMPREHENSION: Directions: *Fold the worksheet on the dotted line. Listen to your partner read the numbers. Then, connect the numbers with a line.*

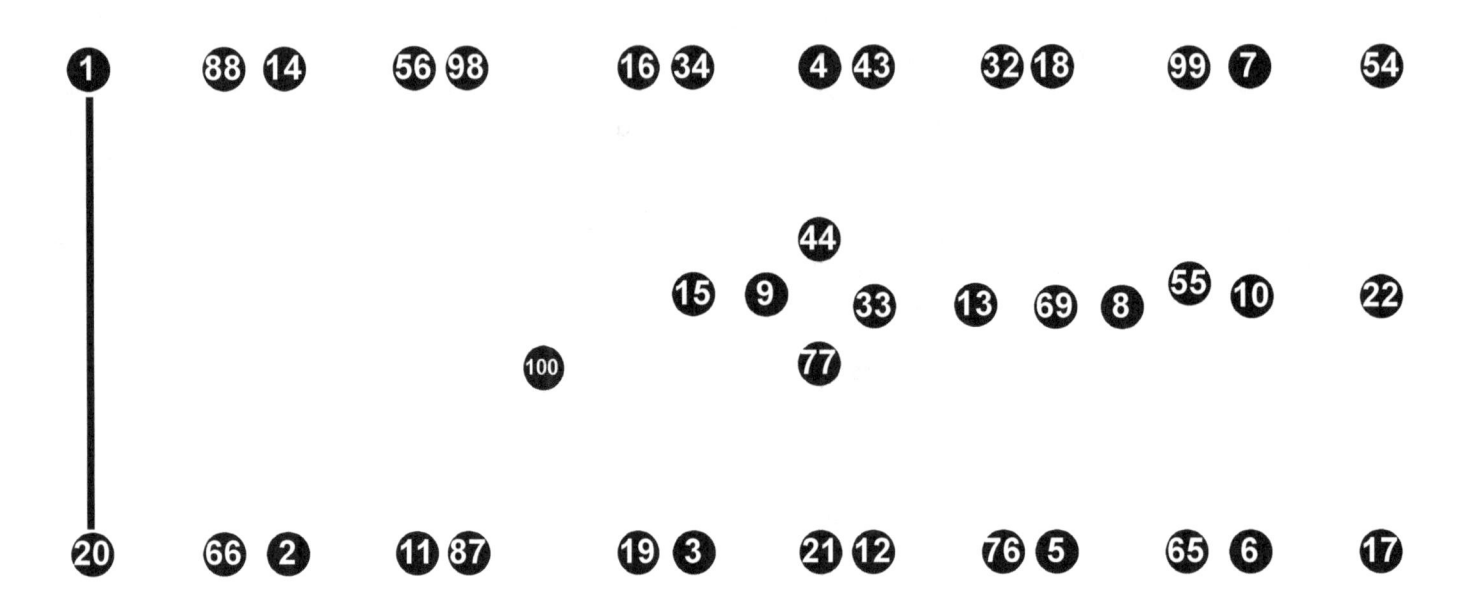

① ⑧⑧ ⑭   ㊾ ㊽   ⑯ ㉞   ④ ㊸   ㉜ ⑱   ⑨⑨ ⑦   ㊾

                                              ㊹
                        ⑮ ⑨   ㉝   ⑬ ㊻ ⑧ ㊾ ⑩   ㉒
                  ⑩⑩   ㊲

⑳   ㊻ ②   ⑪ ㊼   ⑲ ③   ㉑ ⑫   ㊻ ⑤   ㊺ ⑥   ⑰

||||||||||||||||||||||||||||||||||||||||||||◄ **Fold Here** ►|||||||||||||||||||||||||||||||||||||||

READING COMPREHENSION: Directions: *Read the numbers below and connect them with a line in the box above.*

one *to* **twenty**	**eight** *to* **fifty-five**	**fifteen** *to* **three**
thirty-four *to* **four**	**six** *to* **seventeen**	**twelve** *to* **seventy-six**
ten *to* **twenty-two**	**four** *to* **forty-four**	**two** *to* **eleven**
fifty-six *to* **eleven**	**sixty-nine** *to* **eight**	**thirty-three** *to* **twelve**
eighteen *to* **ninety-nine**	**one** *to* **sixty-six**	**sixteen** *to* **nineteen**
three *to* **twenty-one**	**seven** *to* **fifty-four**	**nine** *to* **seventy-seven**
forty-three *to* **thirty-two**	**seventy-seven** *to* **twenty-one**	**eighteen** *to* **sixty-nine**
ninety-eight *to* **eighty-seven**	**thirty-three** *to* **thirteen**	**eighty-eight** *to* **sixty-six**
forty-four *to* **nine**	**sixteen** *to* **one hundred**	**seven** *to* **ten**
thirty-four *to* **fifteen**	**forty-three** *to* **thirty-three**	**ninety-nine** *to* **fifty-five**
twenty-two *to* **seventeen**	**eight** *to* **sixty-five**	**sixty-nine** *to* **five**
ninety-eight *to* **one hundred**	**fifteen** *to* **nine**	**fourteen** *to* **two**

ESL Beginning Level   Listening & Reading Comprehension: Numbers

Teacher's Notes

Use this worksheet as a listening or reading comprehension activity. The students should already be familiar with reading and writing numbers from one to one hundred.

LISTENING COMPREHENSION EXERCISE

1. As a listening comprehension exercise, distribute the worksheet and direct the students to fold the worksheet in half along the dotted line in the center of the page. Explain the word "**connect**." Write a few numbers on the chalkboard and demonstrate how to connect them.

   For example, say *"Connect one to twenty; thirty four to four."*

2. Speak very slowly and repeat each pair of numbers two or three times to allow the students enough time to find and connect the appropriate numbers. Continue reading the numbers until the activity is done.

3. For variety, direct the students to work in pairs by having one student read the numbers and the other connect the numbers on the worksheet.

4. Walk around the classroom and spot check the students' work.

5. Correct the answers by projecting an overhead transparency image directly onto a chalkboard or whiteboard where the students can see the result of the activity.

READING COMPREHENSION EXERCISE

1. Distribute the worksheet and explain that this is a reading activity.

2. As in the listening activity above, explain the word "**connect**." Write a few numbers on the chalkboard and demonstrate how to connect them.

3. If the activity is done in class, walk around the classroom and help the students.

4. Correct the answers by projecting an overhead transparency image directly onto a chalkboard or whiteboard where the students can see the result of the activity.

Solution

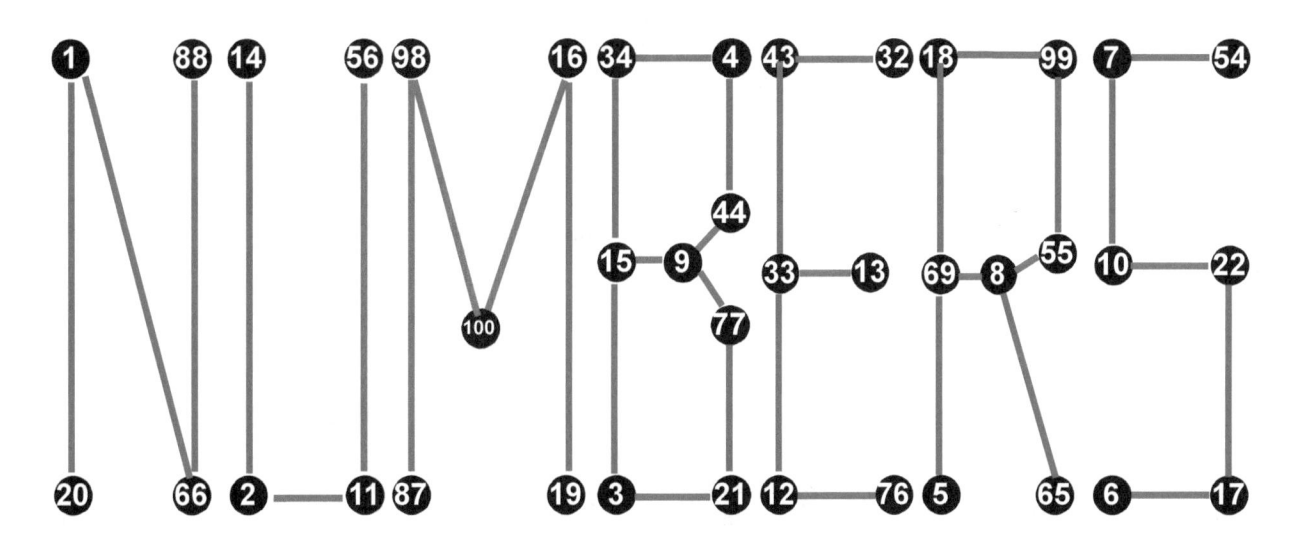

ESL Beginning Level Crossword Puzzle • Vocabulary Building

Occupations

Directions: *Fill in the boxes with the names of the occupations in the photos.*

1 across
5 across *(two words)*
6 across
7 across
11 across
14 across

17 across *(two words)*
18 across
19 across
20 across
21 across
22 across

Crossword grid with 1 across filled in as WAITER and 2 down starting with TAILOR.

2 down
3 down
4 down
5 down *(two words)*
6 down
8 down

9 down
10 down
12 down
13 down
15 down
16 down

141

ESL Beginning Level Crossword Puzzle • Vocabulary Building

Teacher's Notes

1 Before distributing the worksheet, begin the lesson with a conversation. Ask your students general questions about occupations. Ask them to name and describe as many as they can. List them on the board. Make sure that the lists include some of the following items:

baker	bus driver	chauffeur	florist	janitor	soldier
bank teller	butcher	clerk	gardener	maid	tailor
barber	carpenter	farmer	hairdresser	mail carrier	waiter
bartender	cashier	fisherman	painter	mechanic	welder

2 Distribute the worksheet and identify and discuss each photo. Ask simple questions about what people in these occupations do, what they wear, where they work, and any other distinguishing characteristics. For example, ask questions such as:

What does a _____ do?   *When does a _____ work?*
What does a _____ wear?   *Where does a _____ work?*

3 Demonstrate how to do a crossword puzzle. Explain the concept of **DOWN** and **ACROSS**. Then, show the students how to fill in the puzzle using the visual clues. Do a few examples with the whole class.

4 Allow some time for your students to complete the crossword puzzle. You may want to have students work in pairs or assigning it as a homework assignment.

5 Correct the answers by projecting an overhead transparency image directly onto the board on which students can take turns writing the answers on the board. See solution below.

6 Play a crossword puzzle game. Draw or project a grid onto the board or screen as well as a list of the names of occupations. Divide the class into two teams and flip a coin to determine which team goes first. Have the first student of the first team go to the board and write a word that uses one letter of an existing word in the crossword. If the word fits and is correctly spelled, then give one point for every letter of the new word. Then, go on to the first student of the other team. If the word is incorrect, erase it and go to the opposite team.

7 As an additional activity, play Tic-Tac-Toe: Draw a Tic-Tac-Toe grid and fill it in with names of occupations. Divide the class into two teams, each team assigned the symbol "X" or "0." Then flip a coin to determine which team begins. Have the students take turns in an orderly fashion by going down the rows. Tell the first student of the first team to use any word from the grid in a sentence. If the sentence is correct, replace the word with the team's symbol (X or 0), otherwise, leave the word. Go on to the first person on the other team. Continue in this manner until one team wins by having three consecutive X's or 0's in a row vertically, horizontally or diagonally. Keep score by giving one point for each game won. After each game, replace all the words in the grid with different occupations each time.

8 Expand the activity by teaching the names of common professions: *accountant, architect, artist, astronaut, athlete, bank teller, chef, coach, conductor, dentist, doctor, engineer, firefighter, judge, lawyer, musicians, nurse, optometrist, pharmacist, pilot, police officer, politician, teacher,* and *veterinarian*. (See the crossword puzzle for professions #0141)

CROSSWORD PUZZLE SOLUTION:

ACROSS: 1 waiter, 5 bank teller, 6 clerk, 7 soldier, 11 janitor, 14 carpenter, 17 mail carrier, 18 barber, 19 chauffeur, 20 butcher, 21 baker, 22 farmer;

DOWN: 2 tailor, 3 mechanic, 4 welder, 5 bus driver, 6 cashier, 8 maid, 9 bartender, 10 hairdresser, 12 fisherman, 13 painter, 15 florist, 16 gardener

ESL Beginning Level   Opposites • Vocabulary

Opposites

Directions: *Practice the questions and answers orally with another student. Use the words in the box.*

What does big mean? *It means NOT small.*

bad	fat	last	short
big	first	left	small
cheap	full	light	tall
cold	good	long	thick
empty	happy	old	thin
expensive	heavy	right	wrong
down	hot	sad	young

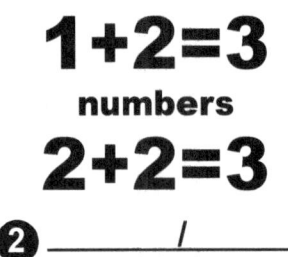

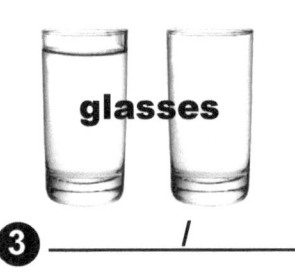

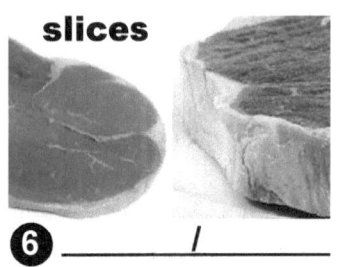

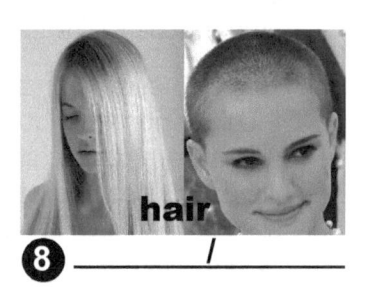

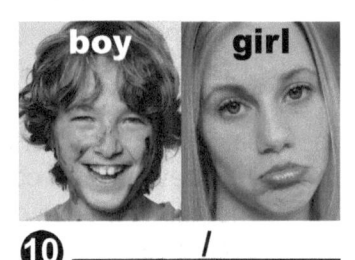

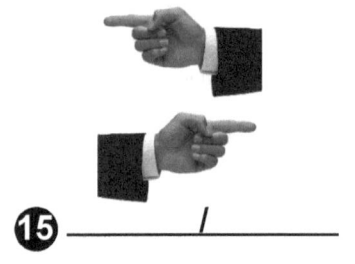

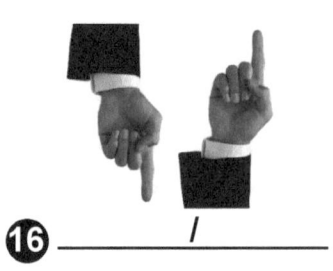

1. balls — big / small
2. numbers — ___ / ___
3. glasses — ___ / ___
4. weights / feather — ___ / ___
5. temperature — ___ / ___
6. slices — ___ / ___
7. lamps ($25 / $250) — ___ / ___
8. hair — ___ / ___
9. A Z letters — ___ / ___
10. boy / girl — ___ / ___
11. woman / girl — ___ / ___
12. angel / devil — ___ / ___
13. men — ___ / ___
14. woman / man — ___ / ___
15. ___ / ___
16. ___ / ___

Write: *Write the opposite words below the pictures.*

143

ESL Beginning Level   Opposites • Vocabulary

Teacher's Notes

1 Distribute the worksheet and review the vocabulary in the photos. *Discourage the students from filling in the words below the photos. This should be a time for oral practice.*

balls	weights	hair	devil
numbers	feather	letters	man
problems	temperature	boy	men
(math)	slices	girl	woman
glasses	meat	woman	first
	lamps	angel	second

2 Teach the opposites below:

bad/good	empty/full	happy/sad	short/tall
big/small	down/up	heavy/light	thick/thin
cheap/expensive	fat/thin	left/right	right/wrong
cold/hot	first/last	old/young	

3 Practice the new vocabulary by having the students use this pattern:
"In photo number one, the first _____ is _____ and the second is _____."
Example: *In photo number one, the first ball is **big** and the second is **small**.*

4 Continue practicing the new vocabulary by having the students use the pattern in the dialog boxes on the worksheet: Student 1: **What does _____ mean?**
Student 2: *It means NOT ___.* Example: *What does **thick** mean. It means **not thin**.*

5 Have the students write the correct words under the photos. Correct the activity by projecting a transparency or projector directly onto the chalkboard or whiteboard on which the students can write, see, and correct their answers.
Answers:

1. big/small	5. hot/cold	9. first/last	13. tall/short
2. right/wrong	6. thin/thick	10. happy/sad	14. thin/fat
3. full/empty	7. cheap/expensive	11. old/young	15. left/right
4. heavy/light	8. long/short	12. good/bad	16. down/up

6 As a follow-up activity, teach additional opposites:

smooth/rough	to/from	more/less	light/dark
narrow/wide	in/out	no/yes	hard/soft
on/off	all/none	high/low	day/night
sharp/dull	many/few	near/far	new/old
		below/above	much/little

Opposites Concepts

ESL Beginning Level — Crossword Puzzle • Vocabulary Building

Directions: *Fill in the boxes with the opposite of the word below the photos.*

Across:
- 1 across: soft
- 5 across: rough
- 7 across: far
- 8 across: night
- 9 across: dark
- 11 across: right
- 13 across: sad
- 14 across: fat
- 16 across: young
- 17 across: wide
- 19 across: above

Down:
- 1 down: low
- 2 down: up
- 3 down: yes
- 4 down: short
- 5 down: dull
- 6 down: thin
- 10 down: cold
- 12 down: empty
- 13 down: light 
- 15 down: old 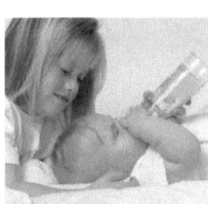
- 18 down: off 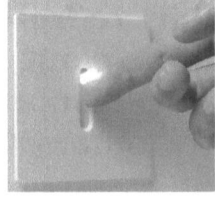
- 19 down: small 
- 20 down: short 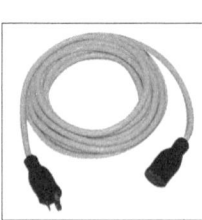

1 across answer shown in grid: HARD (with HIGH going down from H)

ESL Beginning Level Crossword Puzzle • Vocabulary Building

Teacher's Notes

1 Before distributing the worksheet, begin the lesson with a conversation to assess your students' knowledge of some common opposites concepts. Ask questions using the simple present tense such as, "**What is the opposite of _____?**"

Make sure that some of the following opposites concepts are included:

2
below/above	full/empty	high/low	long/short	no/yes	smooth/rough
big/small	happy/sad	hot/cold	narrow/wide	old/young	tall/short
day/night	hard/soft	left/right	near/far	on/off	thin/fat
down/up	heavy/light	light/dark	new/old	sharp/dull	thick/thin

3 Continue practicing the new vocabulary by asking question such as "**What does _____ mean?**" Model the answer, "**It means NOT _____.**" Example: "**What does thick mean. It means not thin.**"

Distribute the worksheet. Identify the opposite concept represented in the photos.

Demonstrate how to do a crossword puzzle. Explain the concept of **DOWN** and **ACROSS**. Then, show the students how to fill in the puzzle using the visual clues. Do a few examples with the whole class. Allow some time for your students to complete the crossword puzzle. You may want to have students work in pairs or assigning it as a homework assignment.

4 Correct the answers by projecting an overhead transparency image directly onto the board on which students can take turns writing the answers on the board. See solution below.

5 Play a crossword puzzle game. Draw or project a grid onto the board or screen as well as a list of opposites. Divide the class into two teams and flip a coin to determine which team goes first. Have the first student of the first team go to the board and write a word that uses one letter of an existing word in the crossword. If the word fits and is correctly spelled, then give one point for every letter of the new word. Then, go on to the first student of the other team. If the word is incorrect, erase it and go to the

6 opposite team.

7 As a follow-up activity discuss additional opposites concepts such as: *cheap/expensive, first/last, to/from, in/out, all/none, many/few, more/less,* and *much/little.*

8 As an additional activity, play Tic-Tac-Toe: Draw a Tic-Tac-Toe grid and fill it in with opposites concepts. Divide the class into two teams, each team assigned the symbol "X" or "0." Then flip a coin to determine which team begins. Have the students take turns in an orderly fashion by going down the rows. Tell the first student of the first team to use any word from the grid in a sentence. If the sentence is correct, replace the word with the team's symbol (X or 0), otherwise, leave the word. Go on to the first person on the other team. Continue in this manner until one team wins by having three consecutive X's or 0's in a row vertically, horizontally or diagonally. Keep score by giving one point for each game won. After each game, replace all the words in the grid with a different group of verbs.

CROSSWORD PUZZLE SOLUTION:

ACROSS: 1 hard, 5 smooth, 7 near, 8 day, 9 light, 11 left, 13 happy, 14 thin, 16 old, 17 narrow, 19 below;

DOWN: 1 high, 2 down, 3 no, 4 tall, 5 sharp, 6 thick, 10 hot, 12 full, 13 heavy, 15 new, 18 on, 19 big, 20 long.

ESL Intermediate Level — Prepositions of Location • Vocabulary Building

Parts of a Car

1) Pair Practice: Practice asking and answering questions with the expressions of location in the box below. See the example to the right.

Student 1: **Where is/are the ...?**
Student 2: **They're ...**

Where are the tires?
They're on the outside of the car.

on the outside of	on the left side of
on the inside of	in front of
on the side of	in the back of
on the right side of	at the corner of

Left labels:
hood
fender
hubcap
tire
speed-ometer
steering wheel
air bag
gear shift
floor mat
break
windshield wipers
grill
headlights
turn signal light

Right labels:
gas cap
handle
door
mirror
glove box
arm rest
dash board
gas pedal
trunk
licence plate
tail light
exhaust
bumper

OUTSIDE INSIDE FRONT BACK

2) Information Search: Identify the items below and explain where you find them. Use the expressions in the box above. Use a dictionary, the Internet, or other photos.

engine	headrest	door lock	reflectors
horn	door handle	gas gauge	antenna
gas tank	floor mat	stick shift	heater
bucket seats	brake light	radio	seat belt

147

ESL Intermediate Level   Prepositions of Location • Vocabulary Building

Teacher's Notes

❶ Read and explain the different parts of the car. Practice the pronunciation of the vocabulary:

OUTSIDE   **INSIDE**

wipers	windshield		gear shift	vent
trunk	tail light		arm rest	gas pedal
hubcap	turn signal light		glove box	speedometer
grill	hood		brake	dashboard
gas cap	fenders		mirror	steering wheel
tire	bumper			
headlights	license plate			

❷ With the help of a student, demonstrate how to do the pair practice exercise using the photos and the list of prepositions. Then have the students continue by working in pairs. Pairing and grouping exercises give students time, especially in large classes, to practice important speaking skills. Organizing students to work together can be somewhat frustrating at the start, but once they clearly understand what you expect of them, subsequent pairing or grouping activities usually proceed smoothly. Most pair practice exercises consist of simple substitution or transformation drills that you can also use for drilling the class as a whole.

• Explain that this kind of exercise is to allow students to practice their speaking skills, not their writing skills. Tell students to put away all writing materials.

• Have each student choose a partner. You will probably have to go around the classroom and pair students up the first few times you do this type of activity. Encourage students to pair up with different partners each time.

• Walk around the classroom, listening to individual students and correcting any errors that you hear. This provides an excellent opportunity to spend time with your weaker students.

❸ Have students do a word search activity telling them to find the following items using a dictionary, the Internet, or other photos to identify the following items:
engine

horn	door handle	gas gauge	antenna
gas tank	floor mat	stick shift	heater
bucket seats	brake light	radio	seat belt
head rest	door lock	sun visor	

❹ Ask the students to identify where the items above are found using the expression of locations. The items may not appear in the photos on the worksheet. Tell them to label the part directly on the worksheet.

❺ You may want to explain that British English use different words for some parts of the car: **hood/bonnet, trunk/boot,** and **gas/petrol.**

ESL Intermediate Level | Crossword Puzzle • Vocabulary Building

Parts of a Car

Directions: *Fill in the boxes with the names of the car parts in the photos.*

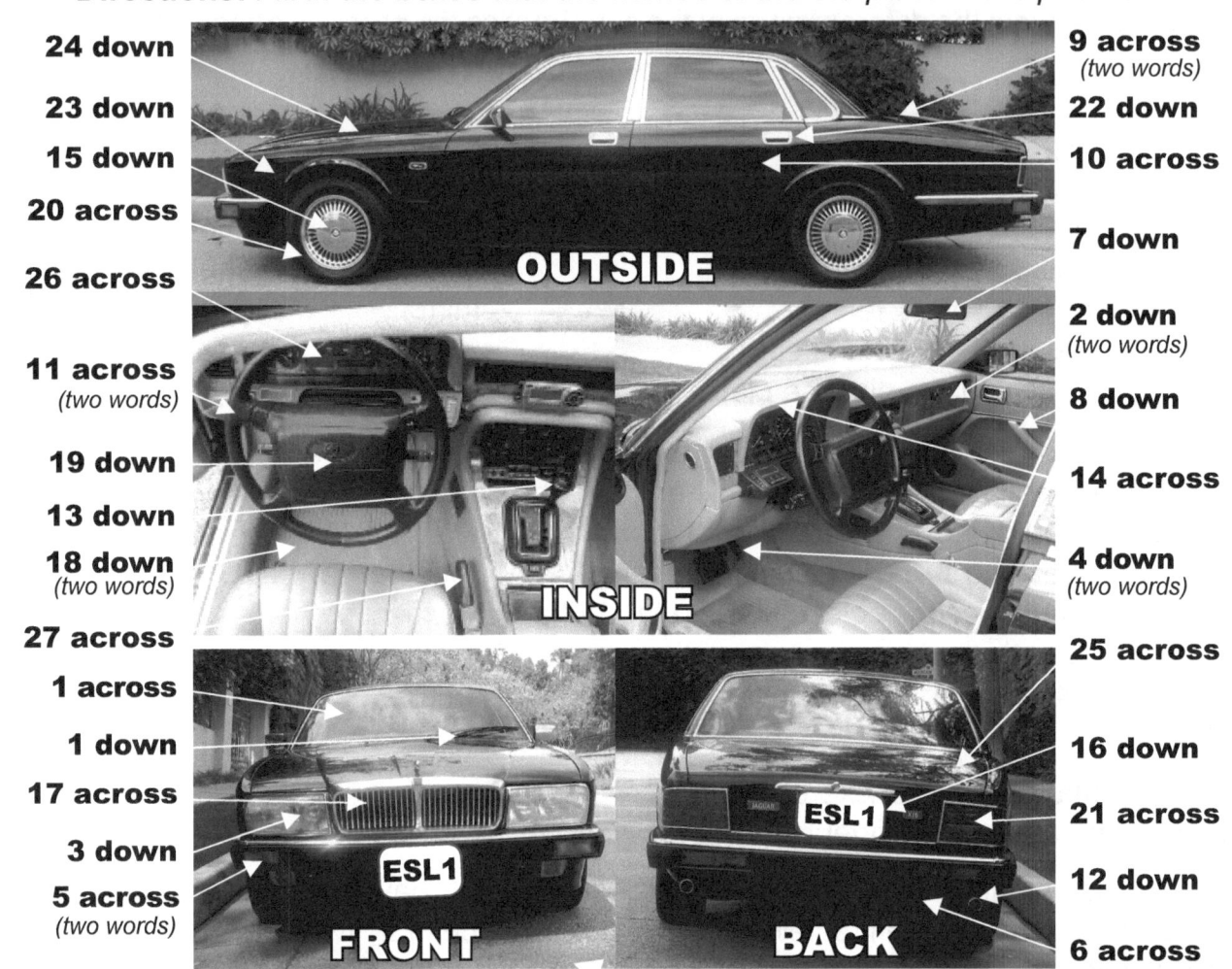

24 down
23 down
15 down
20 across
26 across

11 across (two words)
19 down
13 down
18 down (two words)
27 across
1 across
1 down
17 across
3 down
5 across (two words)

9 across (two words)
22 down
10 across
7 down
2 down (two words)
8 down
14 across
4 down (two words)
25 across
16 down
21 across
12 down
6 across

OUTSIDE
INSIDE
FRONT
BACK

1 across: WINDSHIELD
1 down: WIPER

149

ESL Intermediate Level Crossword Puzzle • Vocabulary Building

Teacher's Notes

1 Before distributing the worksheet, begin the lesson with a conversation. Ask your students general questions about the parts of a car. Ask your students to name and describe as many as they can. List them on the board. Make sure that the lists include some of the following items:

wipers	tire	turn signal light	plate	brake	speedometer
trunk	headlights	hood	gear shift	mirror	dashboard
hubcap grill	windshield	fenders	arm rest	vent	steering wheel
gas cap	tail light	bumper license	glove box	gas pedal	

2 Distribute the worksheet and identify and discuss each item indicated by an arrow. Ask simple questions about their location on or in the car, what the parts are used for, and any other distinguishing features.

3 This activity lends itself well to role playing in which you act as a car salesperson and the students respond as customers. Such role playing presents an excellent opportunity to introduce common questions asked in car shopping for a used car:

How many miles does the vehicle have on the odometer?   *Has the vehicle ever been involved in an accident?*

Is the seller the original owner?   *Can I take the car on a test drive?*

Does the seller have records of repairs and maintenance?   *How many miles does the car get per gallon of gas?*

Does it have air conditioning, power windows, a CD?   *How much is the asking price?*

Why is the owner selling the car?   *Was the owner happy with the car?*

4 Discuss other parts of the car not mentioned in the puzzle:

engine	head rest	door lock	sun visor
horn	door handle	gas gauge	antenna
gas tank	floor mat	stick shift	seat belt
bucket seats	brake light	radio	heater

5 Demonstrate how to do a crossword puzzle. Explain the concept of **DOWN** and **ACROSS**. Then, show the students how to fill in the puzzle using the visual clues. Do a few examples with the whole class.

6 Allow some time for your students to complete the crossword puzzle. You may want to have students work in pairs or assigning it as a homework assignment.

7 Correct the answers by projecting an overhead transparency image directly onto the board on which students can take turns writing the answers on the board. See solution below.

8 Play a crossword puzzle game. Draw or project a grid onto the board or screen as well as a list of the new car part names. Divide the class into two teams and flip a coin to determine which team goes first. Have the first student of the first team go to the chalkboard and write a word that uses one letter of an existing word in the crossword. If the word fits and is correctly spelled, then give one point for every letter of the new word. Then, go on to the first student of the other team. If the word is incorrect, erase it and go to the opposite team.

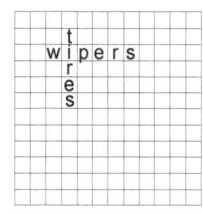

Cultural Note:

9 You may want to explain that British English use different words for some parts of the car: *hood/bonnet, trunk/boot,* and *gas/petrol.*

CROSSWORD PUZZLE SOLUTION:

ACROSS: 1 windshield, 5 turn signal, 6 bumper, 9 gas cap, 10 door, 11 steering wheel, 14 dashboard, 17 grill, 20 tire, 21 taillight, 25 trunk, 26 speedometer, 27 break;

DOWN: 1 wiper, 2 glove box, 3 headlight, 4 gas pedal, 7 mirror, 8 armrest, 12 exhaust, 13 gearshift, 15 hubcap, 16 licence, 18 floor mat, 19 airbag, 22 handle, 23 fender, 24 hood

ESL Beginning Level   Vocabulary Building: Expressions of Time

Parts of the Day

1 *Read and pronounce the expressions of time in the box below.*

| in the morning | in the afternoon | in the evening | at night |

2 *Practice answering and asking questions with another student. See the sample. Use the expressions above.*

Student 1: **When do you .... ?**

Student 2: **I ....**

When do you get up?

I get up in the morning.

I get up _____

We go to school _____

I do homework _____

I watch TV _____

I have lunch _____

I sleep _____

I rest _____

I use a computer _____

I take a shower _____

I go to bed _____

I eat dinner _____

I study _____

3 *Complete the sentences with the words in boxes above.*

151

ESL Beginning Level   Vocabulary Building: Expressions of Time

Teacher's Notes

1 Before distributing the worksheet ask simple questions eliciting the expressions for the parts of the day: **in the morning, in the afternoon, in the evening**, and **at night**. Ask questions using "**when**" and the new vocabulary (**get up, homework, watch, lunch, sleep, rest, use, computer, shower, eat, dinner, sleep,** and **study**). Ask the following questions to determine how much the students already know.

2 Drill the vocabulary and expressions of time by asking Yes/No Questions: Example:

Do you go to school in the morning?   *Yes, I do.*
Do you go to school in the evening?   *No, I don't.*

3 Next, practice asking and answering questions using the question word "**when**," the new vocabulary above, and the expressions of time. Examples:

When do you get up?   *When do you rest?*

When do you go to school?   *When do you use a computer?*

When do you do homework?   *When do you take a shower?*

When do you watch TV?   *When do you go to bed?*

When do you have lunch?   *When do you eat dinner?*

When do you sleep?   *When do you study?*

4 Distribute the handout. Read the names of the parts of the day the box at the top of the page. Have the students repeat the names several times for correct pronunciation.

5 Explain that we use the prepositions "**in**" with *morning, afternoon,* and *evening*; and "**at**" with *night*.

6 Read the directions for the Pair Practice exercise #2, and do a few examples with the whole class. Use the incomplete sentences in the cartoon balloons as cues. Then, have the students continue by practicing in pairs. *(Tell the students not to write; this should be a time for oral practice.)*

7 Expand the activity by asking the students to provide original questions and answers.

8 Next, direct the students to complete the sentences in the balloons in writing, and do a few examples with the whole class. *(You may want to give this as a homework assignment.)*

9 Correct the sentences by projecting a copy of the handout that has been transferred to an overhead transparency directly onto the chalkboard or whiteboard where students can write the correct answers.

10 Follow-Up Activities

On a subsequent day, dictate sentences with the vocabulary and expressions.

• Teach the expression "**at ... o'clock**." Drill the word order.

Example: *I get up at 6 o'clock in the morning.*

• Teach the variations in the abbreviation of "*ante meridian*" and "*post meridian*:" **a.m., p.m., AM, PM**.

ESL Advanced Level — Passive Voice • Listening • Writing

Passive Voice (Past Tense)

Directions: Look at the pictures below as you listen to your teacher's questions. Then, write your answers below each picture.

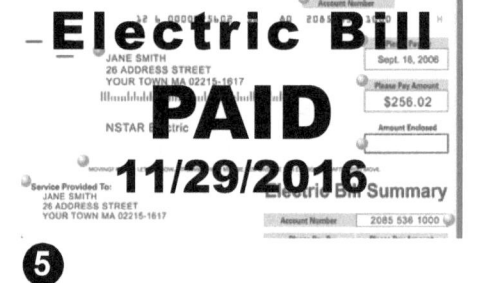

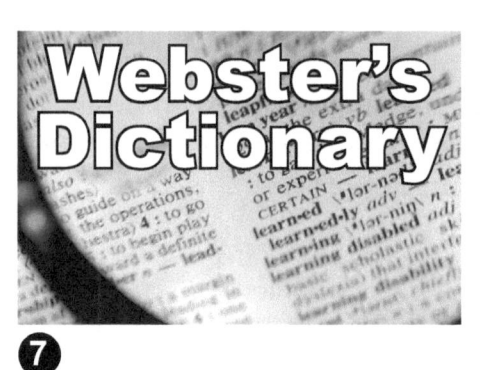

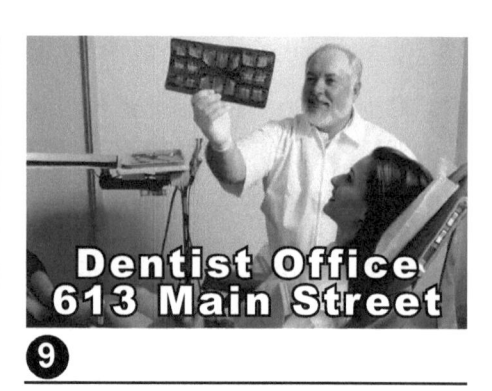

1. Joanne was born on August 7, 1986

2.

3.

4.

5.

6.

7.

8.

9.

ESL Advanced Level　　　　　　　　　　　Passive Voice • Listening • Writing

Teacher's Notes

❶ Explain how the passive voice is formed. We form the passive voice by using the verb **to be** in the appropriate tense and past participle of the main verb. Regular verbs take the ending **-ed**. (See the list at the bottom of this sheet for irregular verbs.) Examples:

	to be	**past participle**	
Joanne	was	born	in 1986
Alex and Clara	were	married	in June.

• Only transitive verbs (verbs that are followed by a object) are use in the passive. We cannot use verbs such as **come** and **happen** in the passive.

❷ Distribute the handout and identify the items on the worksheet. Read the directions with the students. Before having the students write the answers, first do the activity orally. Ask the following questions:

1. When was Joanne born?
2. When were Alex and Clara married?
3. What was sold?
4. Where was the car made?
5. When was the electric bill paid?

6. Who was the lottery won by?
7. Who was the dictionary written by?
8. What animals were lost and found?
9. Where is the dentist's office located?

❸ Repeat the exercise having the students write the answers below the pictures. Finally, correct the answers. You may want to make an overhead transparency of the worksheet that can be projected directly onto a chalkboard or whiteboard on which students can write their answers. Answers:

1. Joanne was born on August 7, 1986.
2. Alex and Clara were married on June 15th.
3. A house was sold.
4. The car was made in Germany
5. The electric bill was paid on Nov. 29 2008.

6. The lottery was won by Paul.
7. Webster wrote the dictionary.
8. A dog was lost and a cat was found.
9. The dentist's office is located at 613 Main St.

❹ Follow-up

• On a subsequent day use the questions and answers as a short dictation.
• Have students come up with sentences using the vocabulary below.

Present	Past	Past Participle	Present	Past	Past Participle
bear	bore	born	buy	bought	bought
begin	began	begun	find	found	found
do	did	done	drink	drank	drunk
eat	ate	eaten	hurt	hurt	hurt
forget	forgot	forgotten	light	lit	lit
freeze	froze	frozen	lose	lost	lost
get	got	got, gotten	make	made	made
give	gave	given	pay	paid	paid
know	knew	known	sell	sold	sold
hide	hid	hid, hidden	spend	spent	spent
see	saw	seen	teach	taught	taught
speak	spoke	spoken	tell	told	told
steal	stole	stolen	win	won	won
take	took	taken			
write	wrote	written			

ESL Advanced Level — Passive Voice • Rewriting Newspaper Headlines

Passive Voice in Newpaper Headlines

Directions: Rewrite the newspaper headlines in the passive voice using complete sentences.

News Daily

1. A bank was robbed; a thief was caught; and a reward was given by the city.

Headlines:
- Bank Robbed; Thief Caught; Reward Given by City
- 1 Building Damaged, 6 Cars Destroyed, Nobody Hurt by Recent Storm
- Man Murdered; Suspect Arrested by Police
- Famous Painting to Be Bought by City Museum
- Miracle Drug Discovered by Local Doctor
- New Tax Law Passed by Senate
- Water Pipe Broken; Main Street to Be Closed for Repairs by City
- New Bridge to Be Constructed by County
- Electricity To Be Produced by Solar Company Here
- Baby Girl Born in Taxi, Doing O.K.
- New Principal Selected by School Board
- Rare Stamp Sold for $100,000 by Local Collector
- Maria Garcia Named Judge by Governor

WRITE: Rewrite the passive sentences above into active sentences using the back of this sheet. Examples:

Passive: *Maria Garcia Named Judge by Governor.*
Active: *The Governor named Maria Garcia judge.*

Passive: *Man Murdered; Suspect Arrested by Police*
Active: *Somebody murdered a man; the police arrested a suspect.*

155

ESL Advanced Level Passive Voice • Rewriting Newspaper Headlines

Teacher's Notes

1 Explain how the passive is formed. We form the passive voice by using the verb **to be** in the appropriate tense and the past participle of the main verb.

	to be	past participle	
The bank	is	located	near a park.
A building	was	damaged	by a recent storm.
A new bridge	will be	built	by the county.

• Only transitive verbs (verbs that are followed by an object) are used in the passive. We cannot use verbs such as **come** and **happen** in the passive.

• In the passive, the object of an active verb becomes the subject (or agent) of the passive voice. The word **by** precedes the subject at the end of the sentence. Examples.

Active: *The governor named Maria Garcia judge.*   Passive: *Maria Garcia was named judge by the governor.*
Active: *We can do the work.*   Passive: *The work can be done by us.*

2 Distribute the worksheet and use the newspaper headlines as a silent reading activity. Explain that the students must read the headlines by themselves and underline all the words that they do not know. Discuss any new vocabulary. Ask basic comprehension questions to insure understanding.

3 Read the directions orally with the students. Then, have the students rewrite the headlines in complete sentences. Correct the activity. Using an overhead transparency works well with this activity. Project the transparency onto a chalkboard or whiteboard on which the students can write the sentences.

Answers:

1. *A bank was robbed; a thief was caught; and a reward was given by the city.*
2. *A man was murdered and a suspect was arrested by the police.*
3. *A new tax law was passed by the Senate.*
4. *A water pipe was broken; Main Street will be closed for repairs by the city.*
5. *Electricity will be produced by a solar company here.*
6. *A rare stamp was sold for $100,000 by a local collector.*
7. *A baby girl was born in a taxi; she is doing O.K.*
8. *Maria Garcia was named judge by the governor.*
9. *A new principal was selected by the school board.*
10. *A new bridge will be constructed by the County.*
11. *A famous painting will be bought by the city museum.*
12. *A miracle drug was discovered by a local doctor.*
13. *One building was damaged, six cars were destroyed, and nobody was hurt by a recent storm.*

4 Read the directions for the activity at the bottom of the worksheet with the students. Have them write active sentences from the passive sentences.

Answers:

1. *A thief robbed a bank; the police caught the thief; the city gave a reward.*
2. *Somebody murdered a man. The police arrested a suspect.*
3. *The Senate passed a new tax law.*
4. *Something broke a water pipe. The city will close Main Street for repairs.*
5. *A local company will produce solar power here.*
6. *A local collector sold a rare stamp for $100,000.*
7. *A woman bore a baby girl in a taxi. (Not commonly used.) She is doing O.K.*
8. *The governor named Maria Garcia a judge.*
9. *The school board selected a new principal.*
10. *The County will construct a new bridge.*
11. *The city museum will buy a famous painting.*
12. *A local doctor discovered a miracle drug.*
13. *A recent storm damaged one building and destroyed six cars. The storm didn't hurt anyone.*

ESL Advanced Level   Passive Voice • Vocational ESL Vocabulary

Passive Voice • Opening a Small Business

1 *Read the text and fill in the blanks with the correct form of the passive voice.*

Past Tense

Ms. Jensen and a friend thought about opening an ice cream shop last year. They knew that they had to do many things. First, they looked for a good location for the shop. They found an area which _____ near a park. The place _____
                                   1. **locate**   2. **choose**
because many people _____ there during the weekends. Naturally, many
                      3. **find**
other things _____ : a loan _____ at the bank; a license
              4. **do**   5. **take out**
_____ by the city government; the building _____; two sales
     6. **give**   7. **inspect**
persons _____; and finally, some equipment _____ .
         8. **hire**   9. **buy**

Present

Today, everything is going well. Business is good. Ms. Jensen's friend did not like this kind of business, so she sold her half. Now the business _____ by Ms. Jensen alone.
                                                                10. **operate**
Because business is doing so well, she wants to open a second store. The new store

Future Tense

_____ at the beach. She hopes that the new shop will open next month.
   11. **locate**
The new store _____ by the assistant manager of the first store, and all the
                   12. **manage**
new sales persons _____ at the first store. To save money, the ice cream
                     13. **train**
_____ at the first store and then it _____ to the new store.
   14. **make**   15. **transport**

2 *Write sentences in the passive voice using the word **must**. What must be done before opening a business? See example.*

1. A building _____   6. Ads _____
2. Money _____   7. Bills _____
3. Licenses _____   8. Problems _____
4. Sales persons _____   9. The product _____
5. Equipment _____   10. Customers _____

3 *Write additional sentences about what must be done to open a business on the back of this worksheet. Share your thoughts with other students in your class.*

ESL Advanced Level Passive Voice • Vocational ESL Vocabulary

Teacher's Notes

1 Explain how the passive voice is formed. We form the passive voice by using the verb **to be** in the appropriate tense and the past participle of the main verb. Examples"

	to be	past participle	
The shop	is	located	near a park.
The shop	was	inspected	by the city.
The shop	will be	sold	at a future time.

Only transitive verbs (verbs that are followed by an object) are used in the passive. We cannot use verbs such as **come** or **happen** in the passive. Regular verbs take the ending **-ed**. Review the irregular forms of the verbs listed below.

Regular Verbs

Present	Past	Past Participle
locate	located	located
inspect	inspected	inspected
hire	hired	hired
operate	operated	operated
locate	located	located
manage	managed	managed
train	trained	trained
transport	transport	transported

Irregular Verbs

Present	Past	Past Participle
choose	chose	chosen
find	found	found
do	did	done
take out	took out	taken out
give	gave	given

Irregular Verbs (continued)

Present	Past	Past Participle
buy	bought	bought
make	made	made
begin	began	begun
eat	ate	eaten
forget	forgot	forgotten
freeze	froze	frozen
get	got	got, gotten
give	gave	given
know	knew	known
take	took	taken
buy	bought	bought
find	found	found
lose	lost	lost
pay	paid	paid
sell	sold	sold
spend	spent	spent

2 Distribute the worksheet and explain how to fill in the words in the text. Read the directions with the students and do a few examples with the whole class.

3 Correct the exercise by having volunteers read parts of the text. You may want to make an overhead transparency of the worksheet that can be projected directly onto a chalkboard or whiteboard where the students can write the answers. **Answers:**

1. was located
2. was chosen
3. were found
4. were done
5. was taken out
6. was given
7. was inspected
8. were hired
9. was bought
10. is operated
11. will be located
12. will be managed
13. will be trained
14. will be made
15. will be transported

4 Explain how we form the passive voice with modals by placing **modal** and **auxiliary verb** before **be** and the **past participle**. Examples: *A store must be located. The building must be rented.*

Read the direction for the exercise at the bottom of the worksheet. Correct the exercise by having the students write their answers on the board. Answers will vary. Discuss other possible answers.

Follow-Up Activity

5 Do a follow-up activity by substituting the following words with **must** in the exercise.

can   has to   ought to   could   have to   should

158

ESL Intermediate Level   Pair Practice • Fill In • Discussion • Role Playing

Past Continuous & Past Tense Review

1 *Read the captions below the photos.*

Everything happened at two o'clock yesterday.

1 Bob had an auto accident while he was talking on his cell phone.

2 The alarm clock rang while Jill was sleeping.

3 A ball broke the window while the students were studying in class.

4 The electricity went out while the family was watching TV.

5 Daniel didn't score a goal while he was playing soccer.

6 Angela made a phone call while she was sitting in the park.

7 Ted didn't hear the phone ring while he was reading the newspaper.

2 **Pair-Practice:** *Practice answering and asking questions with another student. Use the photos above. See examples.* ▶

Student 1: What happened at 2 o'clock yesterday?

Student 2: He/She/They _____.

What happened at 2 o'clock yesterday?
Bob Had an auto accident.

3 **Pair-Practice:** *Practice answering and asking questions with another student. Use the photos and captions above. See examples.* ▶

Student 1: What was _____ doing when ____?

Student 2: He/She/They _____.

What was Bob doing when he had an accident?
He was talking on his cell phone.

4 *Complete the story with the past continuous or the simple past.*

Yesterday was not a great day. While Bob *was driving* his car, he _____ an accident because he _____
                                                                1. drive   **2. have**   **3. talk**

on his cell phone. At the same time, while Jill _____, the alarm clock _____. Then, a ball _____
                                              4. sleep   **5. ring**   **6. brake**

the window of a school while the students _____. While the students _____ at school, the Carter
                                          7. study   **8. be**

family _____ TV at home. Next, the Carter's electricity _____. They wanted to watch Daniel, their
       9. watch   **10. go out**

favorite soccer player. The Carter's and Daniel were disappointed because he didn't _____ a goal while he
                                                                                       11. score

_____ soccer. On Angela's day off, while she _____ in the park, she _____ an important phone
12. play   **13. walk**   **14. make**

call to Ted, but he didn't _____ the phone ring while he _____ the newspaper. What a day!
                         15. hear   **16. read**

ESL Intermediate Level   Pair Practice • Fill In • Discussion • Role Playing

Teacher's Notes

1 Before distributing the worksheet, start the lesson with a conversation. Ask questions that elicit answers using the simple past and past continuous tenses to assess your students' knowledge of these structures. Use some of the following questions:

What were you doing at 4 o'clock this morning?   *What were you doing when you were waiting for the bus?*
What happened when you were coming to school?   *What happened when it started to rain?*

2 Distribute the worksheet. Identify the people and what they are doing in the picture while reviewing the present continuous tense. Ask, "*What's Bob doing?*" Model the response, "*Bob's sleeping.*" Have students repeat both question and answer. Continue asking similar questions about all the people in the picture.

3 Introduce the past continuous tense by posing questions specifically relating to "*4 o'clock yesterday*" Ask, "*What was Bob doing at 4 o'clock yesterday?*" Model the response, "*He was driving.*" or "*He was talking on his cell phone.*" Continue asking similar questions about the other people.

4 Review the regular and irregular forms of the simple past tense. Be sure to cover the following irregular verbs: "**had**," "**rang**," "**went out (electricity)**," and "**broke**." Ask, "*What happened to Bob?*" Model the response, "*He had an accident.*"

5 Pose questions using the present continuous followed by a clause beginning with "*when*." For example, ask, "*What was Bob doing when the accident happened?*" Model the response, "*He was talking on his cell phone.*" Note that the verb following "*when*" is usually in the simple past tense. Continue asking similar questions about the other actions in the photos.

6 Use the methodology above to introduce questions of the type "*What happened while... ?*" For example, ask, "*What happened while Bob was talking on his cell phone?*" Model the response, "*He had an accident while he was talking on his cell phone*." Note that the verb following "*while*" is usually in the past continuous tense.

7 Randomly pose questions of the type "*What was Bob doing when...?*" and "*What happened while... ?*" Elicit responses using the simple past and past continuous tenses.

8 Pose questions eliciting the past continuous in both parts of the sentence. For example, ask, "*What was Bob doing while Jill was sleeping?*" Model the response, "*He was talking on his cell phone while she was sleeping.*"

9 In Exercise 2, the first pair-practice exercise, direct the students to ask and answer questions using "*What happened at 2 o'clock?*" Model responses using the simple past tense. Have the students continue the activity by working in pairs asking one another questions based on the photos and the captions at the top of the worksheet.

10 In Exercise 3, the second pair-practice exercise, have the students use the question "*What was _____ doing when _____?*" Then, model the responses using the past continuous tense. Let them work in pairs until they have covered each photo.

12 As a quiz, have students ask to complete the story with the past continuous or simple past tenses in Exercise 4. *(Answers: 1 was driving, 2 had, 3 was talking, 4 was sleeping, 5 rang, 6 broke, 7 were studying, 8 were, 9 was watching, 10 went out, 11, didn't score, 12 was playing, 13 was walking, 14 made, 15 hear, 16 was reading)*

FOLLOW-UP ACTIVITY

Class Discussion: List the situations below on the board and ask the students to discuss what happened during these situations in the past.

when you fell   *while you were listening to the radio*   *while you were on vacation*
when the telephone rang   *when you got angry*   *when you had an accident*
when the mail arrived   *when it started to rain*   *while you were going home*

NOTE

Explain that the past continuous is used to describe:

a) An action that is interrupted by another action in the past. Example: *Bob was talking on his cell phone when the accident happened.* (b) An action in progress at a specified moment in the past. Example: Bob was talking on his cell phone. (c) Two simultaneous past actions in progress. Example: *Bob was talking on his cell phone while Jill was sleeping.*

Role Playing: Tell the students that the Union Bank was robbed yesterday around 8 p.m. Divide the class into two groups. The first group acts as a squad of detectives and the second group acts as the suspects, One student should be previously selected to be the robber. The detectives must discover the criminal by asking the question, "*What were you doing at 8 p.m. yesterday?*" The teacher should stimulate further conversation by asking follow-up questions.

ESL Intermediate Level   Past Continuous Tense + Pair Practice + Writing

Past Continuous Tense

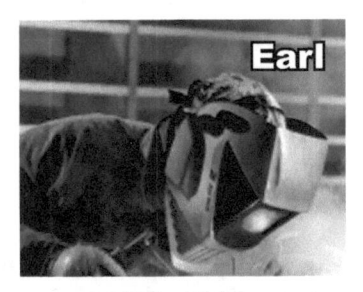

Earl — weld

Bill — work in warehouse

Jim — train a new employee

Leo — make photocopies

Jan — talk on the phone

The managers — have a meeting

① Directions: *Practice asking and answering questions with another student. Use the Past Continuous.*

Student 1: **What was ... doing when the fire started?**

Student 2: **... was ...ing ...**

What was Earl doing when the fire started?

He was welding when the fire started.

FIRE! The fire started at 2:35 p.m.

② Directions: *Fill in the blanks with the simple past or past continuous form of the verbs under the line.*

FIRE REPORT

The fire _____ about 2:35 p.m. at the Pacific Plastics Company in a storeroom at the back of
           begin
the warehouse. Mr. Sam Blazes _____ that he _____ when he accidentally _____ the
                                say   **smoke**   **start**
fire. Mr. Bob Hastings, an employee at the company, _____ the fire department immediately.
                                                      call
Then he _____ the fire to the company security guard. When the fire fighters _____ at 2:55
         report   **arrive**
p.m., some of the employees _____ to put out the fire, the others _____ buildings. The fire
                             try   **evacuate**
fighters _____ the fire quickly and _____ at 3:15 p.m. There _____ no serious injuries
         put out   **leave**   **be**
and damage _____ light. After the fire, while the fire investigators _____ the warehouse
            be   **inspect**
and storerooms, they noticed that there _____ no fire extinguishers or safety signs. The fire
                                         be
investigators _____ the company president that his company _____ ten days to install fire
               tell   **have**
extinguishers and put up safety signs or pay a fine.

ESL Intermediate Level   Past Continuous Tense + Pair Practice + Writing

Teacher's Notes

1 Explain the use of the past continuous tense.

- Use the past continuous to describe an action that interrupts another action in the past.
- Use the simple past tense after words like "**before**," "**when**," and "**after**," and the past continuous after "**while**." *Examples:*

   *They **were fighting** the fire **when** the fire fighters **arrived**.*
   *Mr. Sam Blazes accidentally **set** the fire **while** he **was smoking**.*
   *I **heard** about the fire on the radio **while** I **was driving** here.*

- We also use the past continuous to describe two past actions that were happening at the same time. Example:

   *We **were evacuating** the nearby buildings **while** the fire fighters **were putting out** the fire.*

2 Read the directions for the Pair Practice (#1) activity with the whole class. Do a few examples with the whole class. Then, have students practice in pairs.

3 Practice short "**yes**" and "**no**" questions with the students. *Examples:*

   Question: *Was Earl welding when the fire started?*
   Answer: *Yes, he was.*
   Question: *Was Jim working in the warehouse when the fire started?*
   Answer: *No, he wasn't. He was training a new employee.*

4 Have students fill in the blanks of the FIRE REPORT with the simple past or past continuous form of the word under the line.

5 Check out the pair practice activity on Safety Signs (Item #0009)

Answers to the FIRE REPORT:

FIRE REPORT

The fire **began** about 2:35 p.m. at the Pacific Plastics Company in a storeroom at the back of the warehouse. Mr. Sam Blazes **said** that he **was smoking** when he accidentally **started** the fire. Mr. Bob Hastings, an employee at the company, **called** the fire department immediately. Then he **reported** the fire to the company security guard. When the fire fighters **arrived** at 2:55 p.m., some of the employees **were trying** to put out the fire, the others **were evacuating** buildings. The fire fighters **put out** the fire quickly and **left** at 3:15 p.m. There **were** no serious injuries and damage **was** light. After the fire, while the fire investigators **were inspecting** the warehouse and storerooms, they noticed that there **were** no fire extinguishers or safety signs. The fire investigators **told** the company president that his company **had** ten days to install fire extinguishers and put up safety signs or pay a fine.

ESL Intermediate & Advanced Levels   Past Participle Endings: **-n** or **-en**

Crossword Puzzle: Past Participles

Directions: Fill in the boxes with the past participle of verbs which end in "-n" or "-en."

ACROSS

3. The Korean team was _____ by the Brazilians.
4. White uniforms are usually _____ by nurses.
5. The winner was _____ an expensive prize.
8. Have you ever _____ a horse?
10. The dress was badly _____ by the dog.
11. The baseball was _____ through the window.
13. Ugly graffiti was _____ on the wall.
15. The athlete has _____ the marathon before.
19. The winning ticket was _____ from the bowl.
20. The children have _____ a lot since last year!
22. The students were _____ how to do a crossword puzzle by their teacher.
24. The sun was _____ behind the clouds.
25. All the seats in the bus were already _____.
26. The job applicant has _____ three job offers.
27. The witnesses were _____ to tell the truth.

DOWN

1. The business was _____ many years ago.
2. The U.S. Constitution was _____ in 1789.
3. When were you _____?
4. The lottery was _____ by only one person.
6. How much food have you _____ today?
7. Have you _____ to your family members lately?
9. The patient was _____ to the hospital in an ambulance.
12. Computers have _____ in price in the past year.
14. Some of the passengers have never _____ in an airplane before.
16. Have you ever _____ wallet at home?
17. The criminal was _____ for his crime by his victim.
18. The freezer was full of _____ food.
21. UCLA is a well-_____ university.
22. Have you _____ my key?
23. The sailboat was _____ off course by high winds.

ESL Intermediate & Advanced Levels   Past Participle Endings: **-n** or **-en**

Teacher's Notes

1 Before distributing the worksheet, point out that many irregular past participles end in **-n** or **-en**. List the examples in the box to the right on the board.

2 Encourage the students to think of other words that contain the suffixes **-n** or **-en**. Make a list on the board. Then, ask the students to make as many original sentences as possible using the new words. Past participles should include some of the irregular past participles below:

Present	Past	Past Participle
bear	bore	born
choose	chose	chosen
drive	drove	driven
know	knew	known

beaten	chosen	fallen	frozen	hidden	run	sworn	woken
begun	drawn	flown	gotten	known	seen	taken	worn
blown	driven	forgotten	given	ridden	shown	torn	won
born	eaten	forgiven	grown	risen	spoken	thrown	written

3 Explain that the past participle is used to form the passive voice, present perfect, past perfect tenses, past conditional phrases, and can also be used as adjectives. Most past participles are formed in a regular manner by adding the suffix "-ed" to the present tense. Regular past participles are also identical to the regular forms of the past tense. However there are several dozen irregular forms of the verb that end in "**-n**" or "**-en**." Many of these verbs are also irregular in their past tense forms. Examples:

Present Perfect:	I **haven't <u>seen</u>** that movie yet.
Past Perfect	He **had** already **<u>gone</u>** by the time I arrived.
Passive (past)	Joan **was <u>born</u>** in 2002.
Passive (future)	The kids **will have <u>eaten</u>** dinner by the time I arrive home.
Past conditional phrases:	I **should**n't **have <u>forgotten</u>** my keys.
	She **would have <u>driven</u>** to work if it hadn't been for the storm.
	They **could have <u>spoken</u>** to us about their change of plans, but they didn't.
	Jim **might have <u>gotten</u>** wet crossing the river if it were not for his high boots.
	I'm not sure, but I **may have <u>been</u>** here before.
Adjective:	We have lots of <u>**frozen**</u> food in the freezer.
	UCLA is a well-<u>**known**</u> university.
	The judge asked for a <u>**written**</u> statement.

4 Demonstrate how to do a crossword puzzle. Explain the concept of **DOWN** and **ACROSS**. Then, show the students how to fill in the puzzle using the written clues. Do a few examples with the whole class.

5 Allow some time for your students to complete the crossword puzzle. You may want to have students work in pairs or assigning it as a homework assignment.

6 Correct the answers by projecting an overhead transparency image directly onto the board on which students can take turns writing the answers on the board. See solution below.

CROSSWORD PUZZLE SOLUTION:

ACROSS: 3 beaten, 4 worn, 5 given, 8 ridden, 10 torn, 11 thrown, 13 drawn, 15 run, 19 chosen, 20 grown, 22 shown, 24 hidden, 25 taken, 26 gotten, 27 sworn;

DOWN: 1 begun, 2 written, 3 born, 4 won, 6 eaten, 7 spoken, 9 driven, 12 fallen, 14 flown, 16 forgotten, 17 forgiven, 18 frozen, 21 known, 22 seen, 23 blown

ESL Intermediate Level   Dictation • Pair Practice • Vocabulary Building

Past Tense: Irregular Verbs

Mila

1 Write the phrases that your teacher will dictate to you in the months in the calendar below.

A P R I L	M A Y	J U N E
_____	_____	_____
_____	_____	_____
_____	_____	_____

J U L Y	A U G U S T	S E P T E M B E R
_____	_____	_____
_____	_____	_____
_____	_____	_____
_____	_____	_____

2 Practice the dialog below with another student. Use the calendar pages above.

What did Mila do in April?
She came to the USA.

Student 1: What did Mila do in ...?
Student 2: She ...

3 Practice short answers. Use the calendar.

Did she go to work in June?
Yes, she did.

Student 1: Did she ...?
Student 2: Yes, she did. / No, she didn't.

4 Practice with another student. Use the phrases below:

When did you get a job?
I got a job in June. What about you?
I got a job last March.

Student 1: When did you ...?
Student 2: I ... What about you?
Student 1: I ...

- get a job
- go to work
- buy a car
- come to this city
- begin English classes
- take a break
- have the flu
- leave home
- see a good movie
- leave home
- do your homework
- read a good book
- speak to your family
- wear a tie
- eat ice cream

ESL Intermediate Level   Dictation • Pair Practice • Vocabulary Building

Teacher's Notes

❶ Review the use of the past tense. Explain that we use the base form of the verb (infinitive without "*to*") in the question and negative forms. (Question: ***Did you go to San Francisco?*** Negative: ***No, I didn't go to San Francisco.***) We use "***did***" to signal the question and "***didn't***" to signal the negative. We use the irregular forms only in the affirmative form.

❷ Before handing out the lesson, practice the phrases in the boxes below.

❸ Hand out the lesson and dictate the phrases to the students. Tell students to write the phrases under the appropriate month.

April	**May**	**June**
• left his country	• went to adult school	• found a job
• came to the USA	• took English classes	• began new job
July	**August**	**September**
• met new friend	• bought a car	• got a raise
• took driving lessons	• had the flu	• won the lottery

❹ Correct the dictation. (You may want to project an overhead transparency image directly on to the chalkboard where students can check the answers.) Then, have individual students make complete sentences using the phrases. (i.e., "Mila came to the United States in April.)

❺ Using an overhead transparency, practice the pair practice exercises as whole-class oral drills.

❻ After the students are familiar with the phrases, have them do the pair practice exercises. Pairing exercises give the students time, especially in large classes, to practice important speaking skills. Have each student choose a partner. (The first few times, you will probably have to go around the classroom and pair up students.) Encourage the students to pair up with different partners each time. While students are doing the exercise, walk around the room, listen to individuals, and correct mistakes.

❼ Teach other frequently used irregular verbs:

Present	Past	Present	Past	Present	Past	Present	Past
bring	brought	give	gave	read	read	spend	spent
choose	chose	hear	heard	ride	rode	spread	spread
cost	cost	hide	hid	run	ran	stand	stood
do	did	hold	held	see	saw	steal	stole
drink	drank	hurt	hurt	sell	sold	swim	swam
drive	drove	keep	kept	set	set	teach	taught
eat	ate	know	knew	shake	shook	tell	told
fall	fell	lend	lent	shut	shut	think	thought
feel	felt	let	let	sing	sang	wake	woke
find	found	lose	lost	sit	sat	wear	wore
fly	flew	make	made	sleep	slept	write	wrote
forget	forgot	mean	meant	speak	spoke		

ESL Intermediate Level • Expressions of Time • Pair Practice • Vocabulary Building

Past Tense: Regular Verbs 1

Directions: *Practice making and answering questions orally with a partner about the information in the calendar below. Use the time expressions with the regular past tense.*

```
yesterday                          ago
the day before yesterday           before
last week                          after
```

Examples:

Question: *When did Raphael walk in the park?*
Answer: *He walked in the park three weeks ago.*

Question: *When did Raphael call his grandparents?*
Answer: *He called them the day before yesterday.*

Question: *What did Raphael do before his mother's birthday?*
Answer: *He shopped for a present before his mother's birthday.*

Question: *What happened yesterday?*
Answer: *It rained yesterday.*

Raphael's Calendar

FEBURARY

Sunday	Monday	Tuesday	Wednesday	Thursday	Friday	Saturday
1 Walk in the park	2 Work on computer	3 Shop for birthday present	4 Attend Mom's birthday party	5 Shop for food	6 Cook dinner for friends	7 Clean the apartment
8 Rest	9 Watch special TV program	10 Start new book	11 Pick up dry cleaning	12 Visit Uncle Bill in hospital	13 Play soccer with Daniel	14 Help Dad clean the garage
15 Visit new museum	16 Holiday: Presidents' Day	17 Finish book report	18 Invite Nancy to a movie	19 Wash clothes	20 Attend a concert	21 Wax car
22 Relax	23 Rent Video	24 Visit parents	25 Exercise at the gym	26 Call Grandparents	27 Rain, stay home	28 TODAY

167

ESL Intermediate Level • Expressions of Time • Pair Practice • Vocabulary Building

Teacher's Notes

1 Review the use of the past tense. Explain how to add the **-ed** ending to form the past tense of regular verbs in the affirmative only. We do not use the **-ed** ending with verbs in the question and negative forms. We use **did** with the present tense of the verb to signal the question and **did not** or **didn't** with the present tense of the verb to signal the negative.

2 Explain the meaning of the expressions of time: **yesterday**, **the day before yesterday**, **last week**, **ago**, **before**, and **after**. Then, explain the meanings of the phrases on the calendar.

3 After the students are familiar with the new vocabulary, have them do a pair practice activity. Pairing exercises give the students time, especially in large classes, to practice important speaking skills. Have each student choose a partner. (The first few times, you will probably have to go around the classroom and pair up students.) Encourage the students to pair up with different partners each time. When students are doing the activity, walk around the room, listen to individuals, and correct mistakes.

4 **Follow Up Activity**

Explain the three different ways we pronounce the **-ed** ending.

- When the verb ends in a voiceless sound (except /t/), **-ed** is pronounced as /t/.
- When the verb ends in a voiced sound (except /d/), **-ed** us pronounced as /d/.
- When the verb ends in a /t/ or /d/ sound, **-ed** is pronounced as /id/.

Examples: -ed pronounced as /t/: work**ed**, wash**ed**, cook**ed**, watch**ed**
  -ed pronounced as /d/: open**ed**, clos**ed**, clean**ed**, call**ed**
  -ed pronounced as /id/: rest**ed**, visit**ed**, wait**ed**, paint**ed**

5 Dictate the following words randomly. Then, have individuals come up to the board and write the words in the correct category depending on the sound of the final **-e**d ending.

/t/ sound	/d/ sound	/id/ sound
asked thanked	stayed showed	decided started
danced liked	played arrived	ended painted
dressed washed	called listened	needed visited
finished helped	cleaned lived	rested waited
looked watched	returned loved	wanted
practiced cooked	closed rained	
	opened moved	
	learned	

ESL Intermediate Level   Dictation • Pair Practice • Vocabulary Building

Past Tense: Regular Verbs 2

Mike

1 Write the phrases that your teacher will dictate to you in the boxes in the calendar below.

FEBURARY

Sunday	Monday	Tuesday	Wednesday	Thursday	Friday	Saturday
1	2	3	4	5	6	7
8	9	10	11	12	13	14
15	16	17	18	19	20	21
22	23	24	25	26	27	28

2 Practice the dialog below with another students. Use the calendar above.

Student 1: What did Mike do on ...?
Student 2: He ....

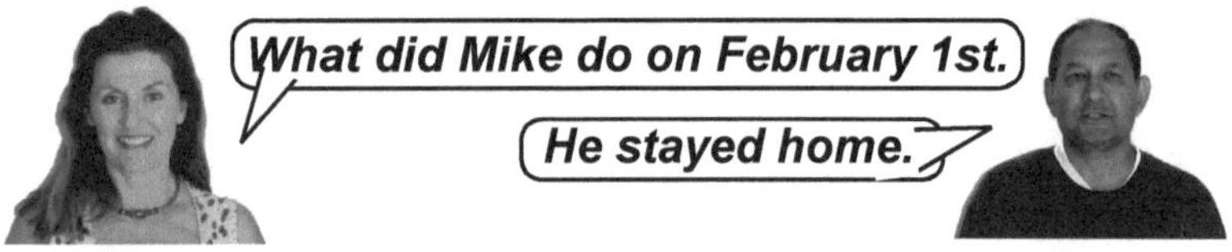

What did Mike do on February 1st.
He stayed home.

3 Practice short answers. Use the calendar.

Student 1: Did he ...?
Student 2: Yes, he did. / No, he didn't.

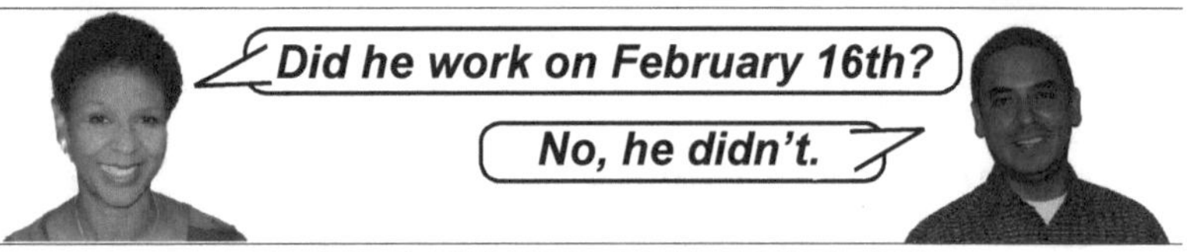

Did he work on February 16th?
No, he didn't.

4 Practice with another student. Use the phrases below:

Student 1: When did you last ...?
Student 2: ... ago. What about you?
Student 1: I ...

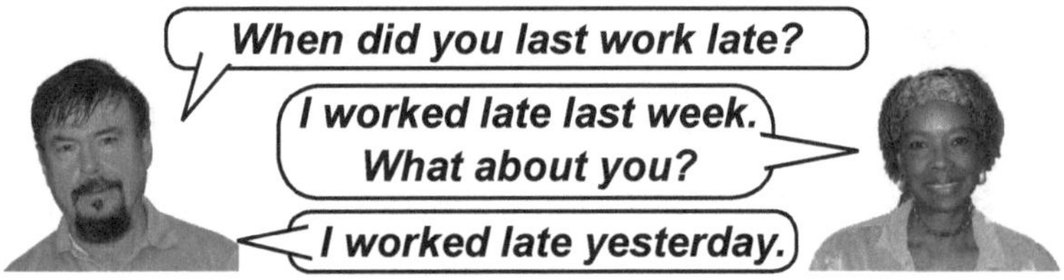

When did you last work late?
I worked late last week. What about you?
I worked late yesterday.

- work late
- finish work early
- wash windows
- call relatives
- clean your apartment
- invite people home
- call a friend
- watch TV
- use your computer
- prepare dinner
- shop for food
- practice English
- exercise
- visit a museum
- volunteer
- relax

169

ESL Intermediate Level   Dictation • Pair Practice • Vocabulary Building

Teacher's Notes

1 Review the use of the past tense. Explain how to add the "*-ed*" ending to form the past tense of regular verbs in the affirmative only. We do not use the "*-ed*" ending with verbs in the question and negative forms. We use "***did***" with the present tense of a verb to signal the question and "***did not***" or "***didn't***" with the present tense of the verb to signal the negative.

2 Before handing out the lesson, practice the phrases below.

3 Hand out the lesson and dictate the phrases. Tell students to write phrases in the boxes.

Feb. 1: stay home	Feb. 11: finish work early	Feb. 21: play tennis
Feb. 2: work late	Feb. 12: wash clothes	Feb. 22: relax at home
Feb. 3: mail package	Feb. 13: cook dinner for friends	Feb. 23: pick up dry cleaning
Feb. 4: invite friends to dinner	Feb. 14: paint living room	Feb. 24: exercise
Feb. 5: answer letters	Feb. 15: call parents	Feb. 25: start work early
Feb. 6: move furniture	Feb. 16: no work	Feb. 26: return library books
Feb. 7: clean apartment	Feb. 17: watch T.V. special	Feb. 27: fix broken door
Feb. 8: shop for food	Feb. 18: visit library	Feb. 28: rain, stay home
Feb. 9: work overtime	Feb. 19: open bank account	
Feb. 10: attend exercise class	Feb. 20: help at senior center	

4 Correct the dictation. (You may want to project an overhead transparency image directly on to the chalkboard where students can check the answers.) Then, have individual students make complete sentences using the phrases. (i.e., "Mike stayed home on February first." or "Mike didn't work on February sixteenth."

5 Using an overhead transparency, practice the pair practice exercises as whole-class oral drills.

6 After the students are familiar with the phrases, have them do the pair practice exercises. Pairing exercises give the students time, especially in large classes, to practice important speaking skills. Have each student choose a partner. (The first few times, you will probably have to go around the classroom and pair up students.) Encourage the students to pair up with different partners each time. While students are doing the exercise, walk around the room, listen to individuals, and correct mistakes.

7 **Follow Up Activity**

Explain the three different ways we pronounce the **-ed** ending.

- When the verb ends in a voiceless sound (except /t/), **-ed** is pronounced as /t/.
- When the verb ends in a voiced sound (except /d/), **-ed** us pronounced as /d/.
- When the verb ends in a /t/ or /d/ sound, **-ed** is pronounced as /id/.

Examples: **-ed** pronounced as /t/: work**ed**, wash**ed**, cook**ed**, watch**ed**
   -ed pronounced as /d/: open**ed**, clos**ed**, clean**ed**, call**ed**
   -ed pronounced as /id/: rest**ed**, visit**ed**, wait**ed**, paint**ed**

8 Dictate the following words randomly. Then, have individuals come up to the board and write the words in the correct category depending on the sound of the final **-e**d ending.

/t/ sound		/d/ sound		/id/ sound	
asked	liked	stayed	showed	decided	painted
danced	washed	played	arrived	ended	visited
dressed	helped	called	listened	needed	waited
finished	watched	cleaned	lived	rested	wanted
looked	cooked	returned	loved	started	
practiced		closed	rained		
thanked		opened	moved		
		learned			

170

ESL Advanced Level • Writing • Past Tense Review • Reading • Listening

Rewrite the Picture Story

1 **Directions:** *Rewrite the story below in the past tense. Replace the photos and symbols with words.*

Last Saturday [Stan] `call` his girlfriend, [Anna] and `invite` her → [dinner] + [a play] x the evening. They `agree` → meet at [Anna] 's [house] at [7:00]. At [7:00] [Stan] `get` x his [car] + `leave` his [house]. Suddenly, his [car] `stop`. The [car] `be` out of [gas]. When [Stan] `search` his [pocket], he `notice` that he ~~have~~ any $. So he `take` out his [phone] + `phone` [Anna]. She `pick` up x her [car] + they `go` → [dinner]. [Anna] `pay` 4 the [dinner] + the [play]. Then, she `drive` [Stan] → his [house]. [Anna] `thank` + `say`, "Let's do this again soon!" [Stan] `think`, "Did he `plan` this evening?"

What do you think?

_____
_____
_____
_____
_____

2 **Vocabulary, Photos & Symbols**

Stan	dinner	pocket	gas	car
Anna	a play	home/house	phone	`drive` change word to the past tense

→ = to   + = and   x = in $ = money   4 = for   ~~have~~ negative

171

ESL Advanced Level • Writing • Past Tense Review • Reading • Listening

Teacher's Notes

1 This is a great way to gage your students' writing especially at the beginning of an intermediate class. It not only tests the use of the past tense, but also details such as the use of articles.

Before distributing the worksheet, the students should already be familiar with the regular and irregular forms of the following verbs:

2 Hand out the worksheet and review the names and symbols at the bottom of the page. Stress that all verbs that appear in the boxes must be changed to the past tense.

3 Ask for a volunteer to read the story, substituting the photos and symbols with words. Students should not be writing at this point. This should be a reading and listening exercise.

4 Explain any unfamiliar vocabulary items.

5 Repeat the exercise two or three times with other volunteers.

6 Ask basic comprehension questions: Who? Where? What? When?

7 Have students rewrite the story replacing the pictures and symbols with words. Compare the students' writing to the story below.

Regular Past Tense Add **-ed** to the present tense of the verb. A consonant is doubled to keep the previous vowel short.	**Irregular Past Tense** The past tense forms are different from the present tense.
call → call**ed** pick up → pick**ed** up thank → thank**ed** invite → invit**ed** stop → stopp**ed** notice → notic**ed** agree → agre**ed** search → search**ed** phone → phon**ed** plan → plann**ed**	leave → **left** put → **put** go → **went** say → **said** be (is) → **was** have → **had** think → **thought** get → **got** drive → **drove**

Last Saturday Stan **called** his girlfriend and **invited** her to dinner and a play in the evening. They **agreed** to meet at Anna's house at six o'clock. At five o'clock Stan **got** in his car and **left** his house. Suddenly, his car **stopped**. The car **was** out of gas. When Stan **searched** his pocket, he **noticed** that he **didn't have** any money. So he **took** out his phone and **phoned** Anna. She **picked** up Stan in her car and they **went** to dinner. Anna **paid** for the dinner and the play. Then she **drove** Stan to his house. Stan **thanked** Anna and **said**, "Let's do this again soon!" Anna **thought**, "Did he **plan** this evening? What do you think?

8

9 Continue the activity by discussing the ending of the story.

Follow-up Activities

• As an additional writing exercise, have students answer the question at the end of the story. Discuss various opinions.

• Ask the students to write their own story using drawings and symbols. Then, have them exchange papers and rewrite the stories.

ESL Advanced Level • Telling a Story • Reading • Writing • Vocabulary Building

Past Tense Review

① Directions: *Fill in the correct form of the past tense of the verbs under the lines.*

A Small Blue Disk

_____
_____
_____
_____
_____
_____
_____

Eric _____ up the ramp into the space craft. He _____ he should not have gone. His curiosity
    walk   **know**
had gotten him into trouble before, but this time it _____ more than curiosity; there _____ some
                                                be   **be**
kind of force pulling him through the door. Inside, he _____ a strange presence; he _____ that
                                                     feel   **sense**
he _____ in a large room. He _____ wonderfully unfamiliar colors dancing on the walls and
    be   **see**
_____ faint musical notes. On the floor next to him, there _____ some small shiny disks that
hear   **be**
_____ out a weak light. He _____ down to pick one up and a human-like figure _____.
give   **bend**   **appear**
Eric _____ still; he _____ not move because a strange force _____ control. The figure
    stand   **can**   **have**
_____ out a hand full of the small pieces of glass, and the boy _____ one. Nervously, Eric
hold   **take**
_____, "Who are you?" The figure _____ nothing. Suddenly the door of the space craft
ask   **say**
_____, and Eric _____ to the floor as the craft _____ and _____ upwards into the sky.
shut   **fall**   **shake**   **move**
He _____ that he would never see his family, friends, or even the Earth again. He _____ to
   think   **begin**
feel panic. The figure _____ closer, _____ to a door, and _____ Eric to follow. As they
                      come   **point**   **signal**
_____ the door, Eric _____ a loud knock. the door _____ and Eric _____ a familiar
approach   **hear**   **open**   **hear**
voice. "Wake up! It's time to get up! Breakfast will be ready in five minutes," his mother _____.
                                                                                       say
Eric _____ his eyes, _____ up in bed and _____ to smile. Getting out of bed, he _____
   open   **sit**   **start**   **pull**
back the blankets and _____ something fall to the floor. He _____ up a small blue disk,
                               hear   **pick**
_____ his head, and _____ where it had come from.
scratch   **wonder**

② Directions: *Write the beginning of the story using the past tense and share it with the class.*

173

ESL Advanced Level • Telling a Story • Reading • Writing • Vocabulary Building

Teacher's Notes

1 Introduction

This lesson is an excellent way to gage your students' use of the regular and irregular forms of the past tense.

2 Before handing out the worksheet, discuss the following questions. Use the past tense.

- *What was the last science fiction movie that you saw? Describe it.*
- *Do you believe that there is intelligent life in outer space?*
- *Have you ever seen or known someone who has seen an unidentified flying object (UFO)?*
- *What would you do if you saw a UFO or alien from another planet?*
- *How do you think the world would greet visitors from another planet?*

Language Activities

3 Review the use of the regular and irregular verbs in the past tense. You may want to drill the verbs with flash cards by writing the present tense on one side and the past tense on the reverse side. To drill the question and negative forms of irregular verbs, show the students the side of the card containing the past tense, then ask them to ask questions using question words (what, where, when, why, how, etc.). The students will be forced to change the verb form and will have to use the word on the reverse side of the card. Ask another student to answer the question. Show the appropriate word for the affirmative or negative answer.

4 Introduce the new vocabulary. You can do this by eliciting the words by means of a sentence in which the last word is not specific. For example, if you want to elicit the word "water," you can say "when I'm thirsty, I drink something. What?" When a student guesses the word, have him or her repeat the original sentence replacing the final word with the specific noun. If nobody can guess the word, say the word and have everybody repeat it in the original sentence. This is a valuable technique because even if the students do not know the word that you are trying to elicit, they are being made aware of the context in which the word is found. It also fosters active listening.

ramp	human-like figure	spacecraft	to scratch
faint (adj.)	presence	to approach	panic
curiosity	escape	Earth	to wonder

5 Before handing out a copy of the story, read it to the students as a listening comprehension exercise. Then ask simple comprehension questions.

6 Hand out the worksheet and read the story again. Discuss any unfamiliar words.

7 Ask the students to change the verbs to the past tense. *(You may want to project a copy of the story that has been put on an overhead transparency directly onto the chalkboard, where students can write the correct answers.)*

8 Discuss several possible beginnings to the story with the students, then ask them to write a beginning to the story.

9 **Follow-up Activities**

- Discuss the possible significance of the piece of glass.
- Have students write an ending to the story.

ESL Beginning Level   Student Mixer • Possessive ('s)

The Possessive ('s)

Pair-Practice: *Practice the questions and answers orally with another student.*
Example: Whose computer is in picture number 1? It's Pearl's computer.

1 Whose computer is this?

It's Pearl's computer.

2 Whose locker is this?

_____

3 Whose backpack is this?

_____

4 Whose book is this?

_____

5 Whose mail is this?

_____

6 Whose photo album is this?

_____

7 Whose pet fish is this?

_____

8 Whose car is this?

_____

9 Whose luggage is this?

_____

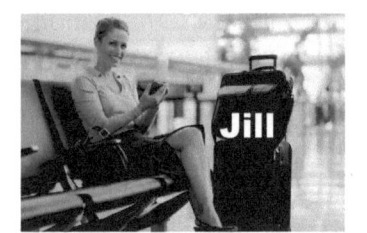

10 Whose office is this?

_____

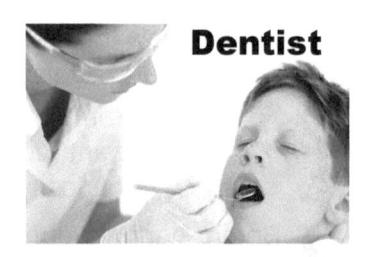

11 Whose restaurant is this?

_____

12 Whose office is this?

_____

Write: Write the answers below each question.

175

ESL Beginning Level Student Mixer • Possessive ('s)

Teacher's Notes

1 Identify and pronounce the names of the people and items on the worksheet.

2 Read and practice the question and answer for item 1. *"Whose computer is it?" "It's Pearl's computer.* Continue the drill substituting the items in the photos. *(Discourage the students from writing. This should be a time for oral practice.)* Continue the substitution drill by pointing to items in the room.

3 Pair up students and have them practice the drill again orally.

Have the students write sentences with the possessive (**'s**) beside each photo.

4 Correct the sentences. You may want to project a copy of the handout that has been transferred to an overhead transparency directly onto a chalkboard or whiteboard on which the students can write the correct answer.

5 **Follow-Up Activities**

- Practice the use of possessive adjectives: **his, her, their.**
  Example: *Pearl. Whose computer is it? It's* **her** *computer.*

- Practice the use of the expression "**belong to.**"
  Example: *Whose cup does it* **belong to**? *It* **belongs to** *Helen.*

- Review the use of the object pronouns: **me, you, him, her, it, us, them**.
  Use them with the expression **belong to**.
  Example: *Whose computer does it* **belong to**? *It belongs to her.* (Point to a woman.)

- Contrast possessive pronouns and adjectives: **my, your, his, her, our, its their**.
  Examples: *This is* **my** *pen. It belongs to* **me**.
  This is **her** *bag. It belongs to* **her**.
  These are **his** *books. They belong to* **him**.

- Practice the short form of the possessive.
  Example: *Whose computer is it? It's* **Pearl's** *computer.*
  Excuse me, whose? **Pearl's.**

Answers:

1. It's Pearl's computer.
2. It's Roger's locker.
3. It's Billy's backpack.
4. It's Rosa's book.
5. It's Mr. Miller's mail.
6. It's grandfather's photo album.
7. It's Helen's pet fish.
8. It's the Jarrett Family's car.
9. It's Jill's luggage.
10. It's the dentist's office.
11. It's Joe's restaurant.
12. It's Mr. Kim's office.

ESL Beginning Level • Prepositions of Location • Pair Practice • Writing

North, South, East, West, Far from, Near, Close To

1 *Read the names of the countries, cities, and directions on the compass below.*

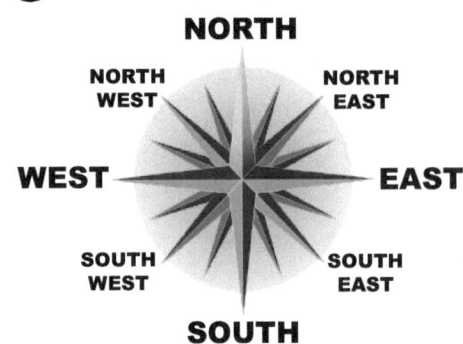

NORTH
NORTH WEST
NORTH EAST
WEST
EAST
SOUTH WEST
SOUTH EAST
SOUTH

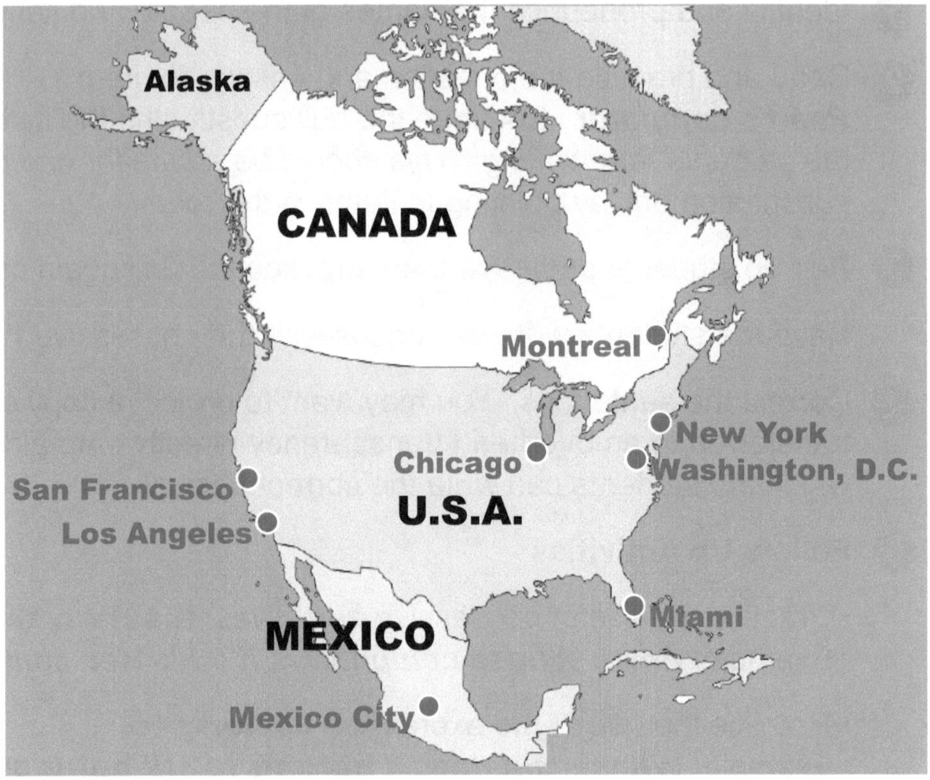

2 Pair-Practice:

Practice answering and asking questions with another student. See examples below. ▼

Student 1: **Where is** _____?

Student 2: **It's** _____.

Student 1: **How far is** _____ **from** _____?

Student 2: **It's** _____ kilometers.

north of
south of
east of
west of
far from
from
near
close to

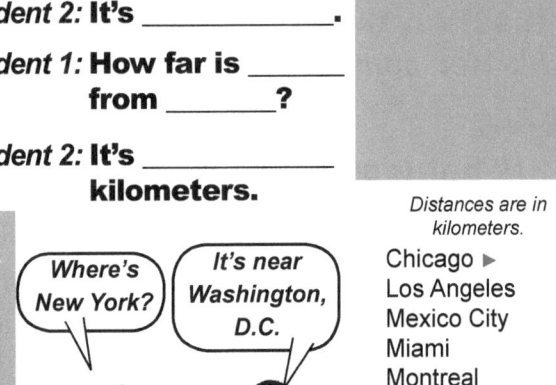

Where's New York?

It's near Washington, D.C.

Distances are in kilometers.	Chicago ▼	Los Angeles	Mexico City	Miami	Montreal	New York	San Francisco	Washington D.C.
Chicago ▶	-------	3371	3332	2188	1353	1356	3522	1109
Los Angeles	3371	-------	3245	4364	4598	4690	648	4251
Mexico City	3332	3245	-------	3574	4579	4219	3892	3855
Miami	2188	4364	3574	-------	2743	2140	4948	1778
Montreal	1353	4698	4579	2743	-------	624	4948	1778
New York City	1356	4690	4219	2140	624	-------	4867	410
San Francisco	3522	648	3892	4948	4877	4867	------	4616
Washington D.C.	1109	4251	3855	1778	965	410	4618	------

3 **Pair-Practice:** *Practice answering and asking questions with another student. Use the graph above. See examples.* ▶

Student 1: **How far is** ____ **from** _____?

Student 2: **It's** ____ **kilometers from** _____.

How far is Miami from Chicago?

It's is 2188 kilometers from Chicago.

4 *Answer the questions in writing.*

1. Where's Canada from Chicago? *Canada is north of Chicago.*
2. Where's Chicago from Washington, D. C. _____
3. Where's Mexico from Canada? _____
4. Where's New York from San Francisco? _____
5. How far is Montreal from New York? _____
6. How far is San Francisco from Los Angeles? _____
7. What's the distance between Montreal and Chicago? _____
8. How many kilometers is it from Miami to Chicago? _____
9. Where's your home from school or work? _____
10. How many kilometers is it from your home to the market? _____

Challenge: How many *miles* is it from your home to the market? _____

ESL Beginning Level • Prepositions of Location • Pair Practice • Writing

Teacher's Notes

1 Before distributing the worksheet, begin the lesson with a class discussion to assess how much your students know about prepositions of location: *north of*, *south of*, *east of*, *west of*, *far from*, *from*, *near*, *to*, and *close to*. You may want to ask some of the questions that are at the bottom of the worksheet.

2 Distribute the worksheet. Identify and pronounce the names of the countries and cities on the map on the worksheet. Ask questions with the question word "*Where?*" such as, "*Where's Montreal?*" Model the response, "*Montreal's in Canada.*" Have the students repeat both question and answer.

3 Introduce "*north of*," "*south of*," "*east of*," "*west of*," "*far from*," "*near*," and "*close to*" by asking questions about the position of one city relative to another. It is recommended that a wall map (or the projection of one onto a screen) be used if possible. Model the sample questions and responses in such as the ones below. Have the students repeat the answers. Examples:

Where's New York?   It's <u>near</u> Washington, D. C.   It's <u>east of</u> Chicago.   It's <u>far from</u> Los Angeles.

4 After modeling the examples, have one student ask a question and another student supply an appropriate answer.

5 Have students practice using the distance chart on the worksheet posing the question, "*How far's Miami from Chicago?*" Show students how to find the answer from the chart. Model and have students repeat the response, "*It's 2188 kilometers.*"

6 Direct the students to exercise 2 and 3. Have your students use the patterns and the examples given in the pair practice activities. With the help of a student, demonstrate how to do the pair practice exercises using the map and the graph on the worksheet. Then have your students continue by working in pairs. Walk around the classroom listening to the pairs of students. Correct their pronunciation as needed.

7 Ask similar questions about places in your city or neighborhood. For example, model a question such as, "*How far's your home from here?*" Have a student respond with an appropriate answer. Be aware that local distances might be expressed in terms of "*blocks*" or "*minutes.*" (Examples: "*I live two <u>blocks</u> from here.*" and "*I live 10 <u>minutes</u> from here.*"

8 Read through the questions in exercise 4 at the bottom of the worksheet as an oral exercise. Then, have students complete the answers in writing.

9 If you have a large wall map, ask your students to speak about additional place names. Expand the exercise to include "*northeast of*," "*northwest of*," "*southwest of*," and "*southeast of*."

10 You might want to practice the following common questions asking about time and distance:

- *What's the distance between [city] and [city]?*
- *How far is it from [city] to [city]?*
- *How many kilometers is it from [city] to [city]?*
- *How long does it take to go from [city] to [city]?*

11 • Show that the adjectives corresponding to "*north*," "*south*," "*east*," and "*west*" are formed by adding the suffix "*-ern*." Using the map, have the students tell you the location of each city. For example, ask, "*In what part of the United States is San Francisco?*" The students should respond, "*It's in the western part.*"

12 The suffix "*-ward*," meaning "*in the direction of*," can be used with "*north*," "*south*," "*east*," and "*west*." Practice the question, "*Where's [city] from here?*" and response, "*It's _____ -ward.*"

13 Here's a device to remember the four points of the compass based on the word "*news*." Show that the initial letters of "<u>*n*</u>orth," "<u>*e*</u>ast," "<u>*w*</u>est," and "<u>*s*</u>outh" spell the word "*news*."

14 Explain that place names are always capitalized.

15 Explain the following abbreviations: **U.S.A.** (United States of America); **N.** (North); **D.C.** (District of Columbia); **E.** (East); **km.** (kilometers); **W.** (West); and **S.** (South)

16 Challenge your students with the last question on the worksheet. Ask them to convert kilometers to miles: To convert kilometers into miles, multiply kilometers by 0.6214. To convert miles into kilometers, multiply miles by 1.609.

17 A compass point such as "*north*" is not capitalized unless it is part of an address or it refers to a specific region.

Compare: He's driving <u>n</u>orth.   He lives in <u>N</u>orth Dakota.
            Go <u>w</u>est two kilometers.   He lives at 103 <u>W</u>est Main Street.
            Turn <u>e</u>ast on Highway 405. Japan's in the Far <u>E</u>ast.

178

ESL Beginning Level   Common Prepositions • Listening, Drawing, Word Building

Prepositions of Location

on between	left right	next to above	below in the middle	over in front of	under behind

Directions: Draw the items listed below in the picture.

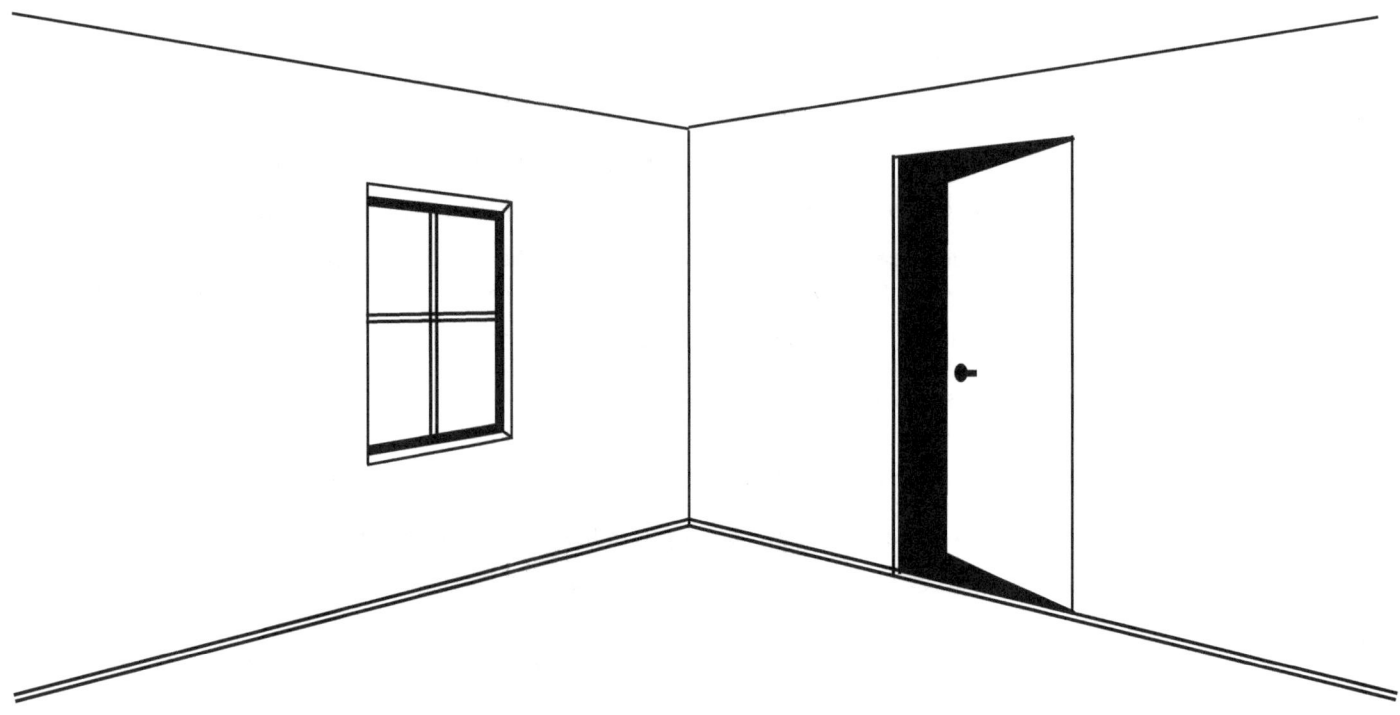

❶ Draw a chalkboard/whiteboard to the left of the window.

❷ Draw a small map of the USA on the chalkboard/whiteboard.

❸ Write "USA" next to the map.

❹ Draw a bulletin board on the right side of the door.

❺ Draw a light switch between the corner and the door.

❻ Draw a little picture above the light switch.

❼ Draw an electrical outlet below the window.

❽ Draw a long table in the middle of the floor/room.

❾ Draw a light on the ceiling over the table.

❿ Draw a chair in front of the table.

⓫ Draw a cat under the chair.

⓬ Draw a dog behind the chair.

ESL Beginning Level   Common Prepositions • Listening, Drawing, Word Building

Teacher's Notes

1 Review the use of common prepositions, adjectives, nouns, and word order. Have the students not only describe where to draw an item, but also how it should look.

Project a copy of the worksheet on an overhead transparency directly onto the chalkboard or whiteboard where the students can draw the items in the picture. You may want to use colored chalk or markers to make the activity more interesting.

2 Have the students read the commands beginning with the word **draw**. Continue the activity by having the students give original commands. A typical dialog should sound something like the following:

Student:	*Please draw a chalkboard/whiteboard.*
Teacher:	*Where?*
Student:	*Near the door.*
Teacher:	*Please repeat.*
Student:	*Please draw a chalkboard/whiteboard near the door.*
Teacher:	*To the left or to the right?*
Student:	*To the left.*
Teacher:	*Please say it all.*
Student:	*Please draw a chalkboard/whiteboard to the left of the window.*
Teacher:	*What kind of chalkboard/whiteboard?*
Student:	*A long chalkboard/whiteboard.*
Teacher:	*Please say it all.*
Student:	*Please draw a long chalkboard/whiteboard near the door to the left.*
Teacher:	*What color?*
Student:	*Green.*
Teacher:	*Please say it all.*
Student:	*Please draw a long green chalkboard/whiteboard near the door to the left.*

3 Continue the activity by having volunteers take turns drawing items in the scene on the board.

4 Reverse the exercise by having the students erase all the items one at a time until nothing is left on the board.

Example: Student 1:   Please erase the chalkboard in the picture.
Student 2:   Where is it?
Student 1: It's at the left of the door.

5 **Follow-up Activity**

Repeat the activity using another scene such as a house on a hill.

ESL Beginning Level • Pair Practice • Writing • Common Verbs • Vocabulary Building

Present Continuous Tense

1 *Read the sentences below the photos.*

1 Jim	2 James	3 Bob, Sue	4 Kim (flower)	5 fish, cat	6 Mark
read, write	sit, wait	play, run	work, plant	swim, watch	stand, sing

7 Amy, Carla	8 Adam	9 Jack, Jill	10 Jan, Ruth (hat)	11 Frank	12 Don, Ed
listen, speak	look at, study	eat, drink	make, wear	paint, smile	laugh, listen

2 **Pair-Practice:** *Practice answering and asking questions with another student. See examples.* ▶

Student 1: **Is/Are** _____[name]_____?

Student 2: **Yes/No,** _____.

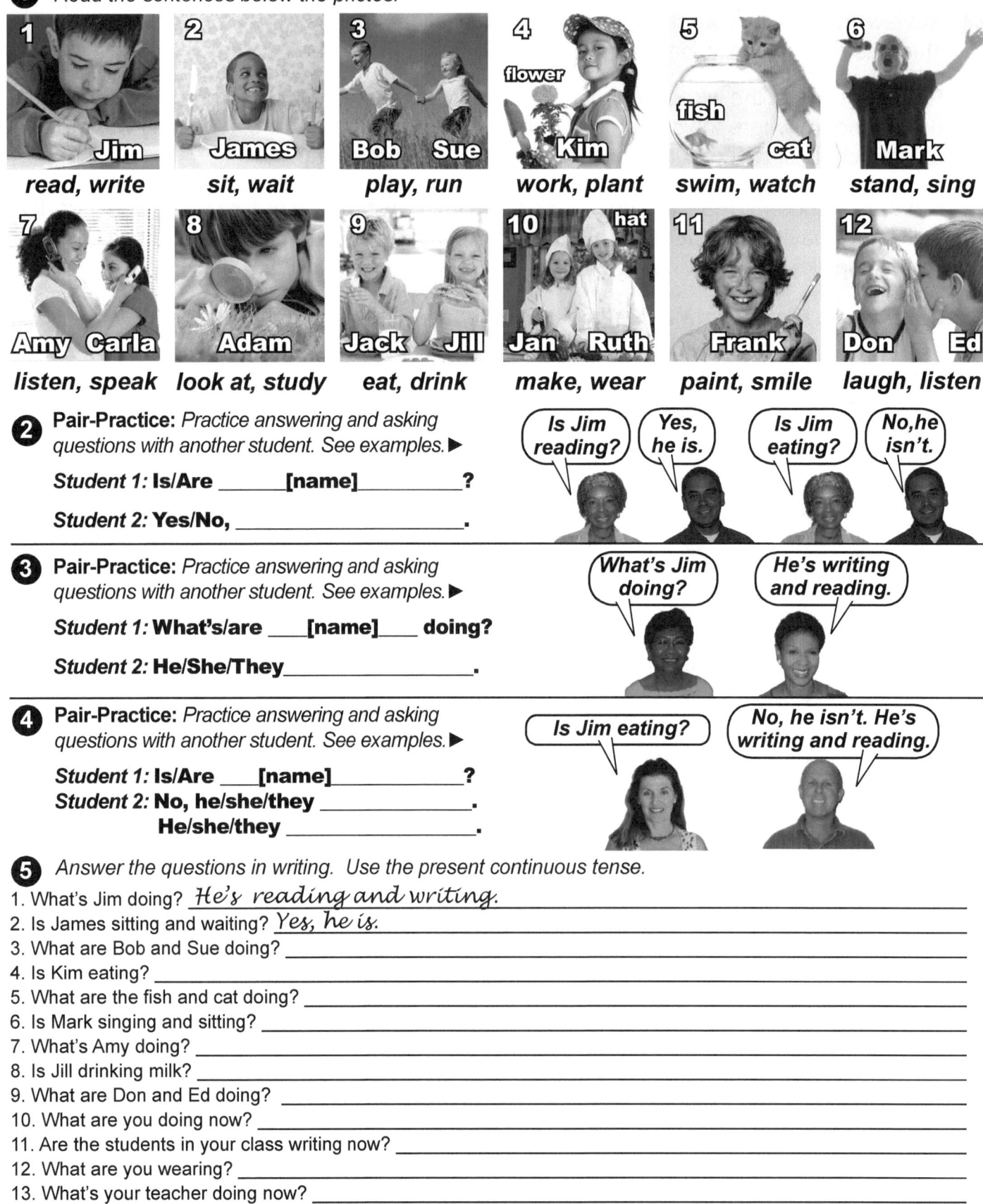

Is Jim reading? — *Yes, he is.*
Is Jim eating? — *No, he isn't.*

3 **Pair-Practice:** *Practice answering and asking questions with another student. See examples.* ▶

Student 1: **What's/are** ___[name]___ doing?

Student 2: **He/She/They** _____.

What's Jim doing? — *He's writing and reading.*

4 **Pair-Practice:** *Practice answering and asking questions with another student. See examples.* ▶

Student 1: **Is/Are** ___[name]___?
Student 2: **No, he/she/they** _____.
         He/she/they _____.

Is Jim eating? — *No, he isn't. He's writing and reading.*

5 *Answer the questions in writing. Use the present continuous tense.*

1. What's Jim doing? *He's reading and writing.*
2. Is James sitting and waiting? *Yes, he is.*
3. What are Bob and Sue doing? _____
4. Is Kim eating? _____
5. What are the fish and cat doing? _____
6. Is Mark singing and sitting? _____
7. What's Amy doing? _____
8. Is Jill drinking milk? _____
9. What are Don and Ed doing? _____
10. What are you doing now? _____
11. Are the students in your class writing now? _____
12. What are you wearing? _____
13. What's your teacher doing now? _____

ESL Beginning Level • Pair Practice • Writing • Common Verbs • Vocabulary Building

Teacher's Notes

1 Before distributing the worksheet, begin the lesson with a conversation to assess your students' use of the present continuous tense. Ask questions such as:

What are you doing? *Are you sitting/standing?*
Is [a student's name] sitting/standing? *Are [two student's names] listening/speaking?*
What are they doing? (pointing to someone? *What am I (the teacher) doing now?*

2 Distribute the worksheet. Identify the people and what they are doing in the photos. Ask the question, "**What's Jim doing?**" Model the response, "**Jim's reading and writing.**" Have the students repeat both question and answer. Continue asking similar questions about the people in the photos.

3 Drill the verb forms "*am*," "*is*," and "*are*" with yes/no questions.

Is James waiting? *Yes, he is.*
Are Bob and Sue swimming? *No, they aren't. They're playing and running.*
Are you sitting? *Yes, I am.* or *No, I'm not.*

4 After modeling the questions and responses several times, have one student ask another student similar questions about the other people in the photos.

5 Tell one student to ask another student a question requiring a negative response. The second student must respond with a short negative answer followed by a statement describing the true activity. For example: Student 1: *Is Jim eating?* Student 2: *No, he isn't. He's writing.* Continue by having one student ask another student a question patterned after one above.

6 For variety, have students ask each other questions with the word "*where*" such as "*Where's James?*" Students should reply, "*He's sitting at the table.*"

7 Ask students questions using "*you*" such as, "*Are you sitting now?*" Have students respond with an appropriate answer. After a while, have the students ask each other original questions using the verbs under the photos.

8 With the help of a student, demonstrate how to do the pair practice exercises 2, 3, and 4 using the photos. Then have the students continue by working in pairs. Walk around the classroom listening to the pairs of students. Correct their pronunciation as needed.

9 Direct your students to exercise 5 at the bottom of the worksheet. Read the questions with the students and ask for volunteers to answer the questions orally using the subject pronouns *(he, she, it, they, we, you)* in place of names. Then, have students complete the questions in writing. Answers: 1 He's reading and writing. 2 Yes, he is. 3 They're playing and running. 4 No, she isn't. She's working. 5 The fish is swimming, and the cat is watching the fish. 6 He's singing. He's not sitting. He's standing. 7 She's listening and speaking. 8 No, she isn't. She's eating. 9 Don's smiling, and Ed's speaking to Don.
10, 11, 12, and 13 (Answers will vary.)

Note the Spelling Rules:

• When a word ends in a consonant-vowel-consonant pattern and the final vowel is stressed, the last consonant is doubled before adding "*-ing.*" A final "*w*," "*x*," or "*y*" is never doubled. The combination "*qu*" is counted as one consonant.

Double Consonants: *swim → swi*mm*ing, sit → si*tt*ing, run → ru*nn*ing*
Single consonants: *drink → drinking, eat → eating, play → playing*

• If the word ends in silent "*e*," drop the "*e*" before adding "*-ing.*" Examples: *make → making, come → coming*

• Exceptions: *lie → lying, die → dying, tie → tying*

• If a word ends in a "*c*," a "*k*" is inserted when adding "*-ing.*" Examples: *picnic → picnicking, panic → panicking*

Note that verbs referring to conditions rather than actions cannot be used in the present continuous. This restriction is especially common with verbs describing mental and physical states. Examples: *want, like, need, know, believe, own, see, hear*

Compare: *I see the sign.* *I'm looking at the sign.* (action)
  I have a car. *I'm having dinner.* (action)
  I like this movie. *I'm enjoying this movie.* (action)

10 Follow Up Activity: Pantomime can be used as a game. Divide the class into two teams. Have the students guess the action. Have a student keep count of each team's correct guesses. Some examples are: **opening a door**, **closing a window**, **reading a book**, and **playing the piano**.

ESL Beginning & Intermediate Levels   Tense Review • Vocabulary Building
Present Continuous & Simple Present Review

1 *Read the captions below the photos.*

1. Mrs. Brown
Mrs. Brown is shopping. She needs oranges.

2. Vera
Vera is using the ATM machine. She wants cash.

3. Jim and Joanne
Jim and Joanne are taking a taxi. They don't own a car.

4. Tamara
Tamara is listening to music. She doesn't hear the traffic.

5. Doctor
The doctor is looking at an X-ray. He doesn't see a problem.

6. Tony
Tony and his friends are watching TV. They like football games.

7. Kevin
Kevin is stealing prescription drugs. He knows it's wrong.

8. Adam
Adam is tying his new shoes. He likes them very much.

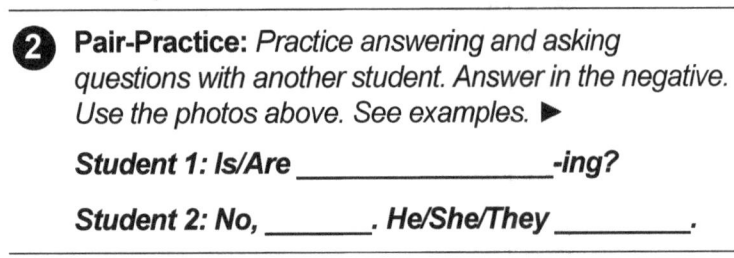

2 **Pair-Practice:** *Practice answering and asking questions with another student. Answer in the negative. Use the photos above. See examples.* ▶

Student 1: Is/Are _____-ing?

Student 2: No, _____. He/She/They _____.

Is Mrs. Brown working?
No, she isn't. She's shopping.

3 **Pair-Practice:** *Practice answering and asking questions with another student. Answer in the negative. Use the photos above. See examples.* ▶

Student 1: Do/Does _____?

Student 2: No, _____. He/She/They _____.

Does Mrs. Brown need apples?
No, she doesn't. She needs oranges.

4 *Answer the questions using the present continuous or simple past tense.*

1. What does Mrs. Brown want? <u>She wants oranges.</u>
2. Is Vera watching TV? <u>No, she isn't.</u>
3. Does Jim own a car? _____
4. Is Tamara watching the traffic? _____
5. Does Tamara like music? _____
6. Is the doctor looking at a problem? _____
7. What is Tony doing? _____
8. Does Tony own a TV? _____
9. Is Kevin stealing cash? _____
10. What does Kevin know? _____
11. Is Adam tying his old shoes? _____
12. Does Adam need new shoes? _____
13. Do you own a car? _____
14. What are you doing now? _____
15. Where are you sitting? _____
16. Do you hear traffic? _____
17. Are you listening to your teacher? _____
18. Why do people steal? _____

183

ESL Beginning Level • Vocabulary Building • Pair Practice • Fill In • Class Discussion

Teacher's Notes

1 Distribute the worksheet. Identify the people and what they are doing in the photos by reading the captions. Ask the question, "*What's Mrs. Brown doing?*" Model the response, "*She is shopping.*" Have students repeat both question and answer. Continue asking similar questions using the present continuous about the people in the photos.

2 As an active listening activity, have the students underline or circle any unfamiliar words as you are reading the captions. Then, explain any unfamiliar vocabulary.

3 Ask the students questions requiring a negative answer. For example, ask "*Is Mrs. Brown working?*" Model the response, "*No, she isn't. She's shopping.*" Continue the activity by asking the following questions with some new vocabulary:

Is Vera using a bank?   *Are Jim and Joanne taking a bus?*
Is Tamara watching TV?   *Is the doctor reading a book?*
Is Kevin stealing money?   *Are Tony and his friends listening to the radio?*
Is Adam playing?   *Is Mrs. Brown eating?*

4 Continue the activity by telling one student to ask another student a question requiring a negative response. The second student must respond with a short negative answer followed by a statement describing the true activity.

5 Next, Introduce the simple present by posing yes/no questions. Ask, "***Does Mrs. Brown need oranges?***" Model the response, "***Yes, she does.***" Have students repeat both question and answer. Continue asking questions such as:

Does Mrs. Brown need oranges?   *Does the doctor see a problem?*
Does Vera want cash?   *Do Tony and his friends like football?*
Do Jim and Joanne own a car?   *Does Kevin know its wrong to steal drugs?*
Does Tamara hear the traffic?   *Does Adam like his new shoes?*

6 Using the same methodology described in activity 2 above, practice the simple present. Pose questions requiring a negative response. Model the responds with a short negative answer followed by a statement describing the true activity. For example, ask "***Does Mrs. Brown need apples?*** Model the response, *"No, she doesn't. She needs oranges."*
Continue with questions such as:

Does Mrs. Brown need tomatoes?   *Does the doctor see a problem?*
Does Vera want a check?   *Do Tony and his friends like TV?*
Do Jim and Joanne own a bus?   *Does Kevin know he is right?*
Does Tamara hear traffic?   *Does Adam have a new hat?*

7 Randomly pose questions about the picture contrasting the use of the simple present and the present continuous. Ask yes/no questions to contrast short answers in the present continuous and the simple present. For example,

Is Mrs. Brown shopping? Yes, she is.   *Does she need oranges? Yes, she does.*
Is she working? No, she isn't.   *Does she need apples? No, she doesn't.*

8 In activity 2, the first pair practice exercise, direct the students to ask and answers questions using "*Is/Are ___[name]___?*" Model responses using a negative short answer followed by a true statement. Have students work in pairs.

9 In activity 3, the second pair practice exercise, direct the students to ask and answer questions using *Do/Does___[name]___?*" Model responses using a negative short answer followed by a true statement.

10 Direct the students to activity 4 at the bottom of the worksheet. Review the questions for understanding and have the students complete sentences in writing.

11 As a class discussion ask the students to share some of their answers to questions 13-18. Continue the activity by asking the students to pose original questions to other students in the class.

NOTE

Verbs referring to conditions rather than actions cannot be used in the present continuous. This restriction is especially common with verbs describing mental and physical states such as "*want,*" "*like,*" "*need,*" "*know,*" "*believe,*" "*own,*" "*see,*" and "*hear.*" Compare:

I see the cat.   *I'm looking at the cat.*
I have a dog.   *I'm having a party.*
I like the party.   *I'm enjoying the party.*

ESL Advance Level • Job Interview • Pair Practice • Writing • Class Discussion
Present Perfect Tense 1

1 Read the job interview questions and answers.

An employer is interviewing Juan for a job.

1. How long have you been in this country? — Since July
2. How long have you lived at your present address? — For 2 months.
3. How long have you worked? — For 10 years.
4. How long have you worked in your present occupation? — Since last year.
5. How long have you had a driver's license? — For two weeks.
6. How long have you studied English? — Since I arrived here.

2 **Pair-Practice:** Practice answering and asking questions with another student. Use the questions above. See examples. ▶

How long has Juan been in this country? Since July.

Student 1: How long has Juan _____?
Student 2: He's _____ for/since _____.

VERB PHRASES
- attended this school
- been in high school/9th grade
- been married, sick, here
- had a boyfriend/girlfriend
- had a checking account,
- worn your watch, your ring
- had a driver's license,
- had glasses, a bicycle, a car,
- cared for a cat, a dog, a pet
- liked ...
- lived in this city
- planned to ...
- played the [musical instrument]
- rented your house/apartment
- shopped at [store name]
- smoked cigarettes
- wanted to ...
- worked at your present job

3 **Pair-Practice:** Practice answering and asking questions with another student. Use some of the phrases in the box to the right. See examples. ▶

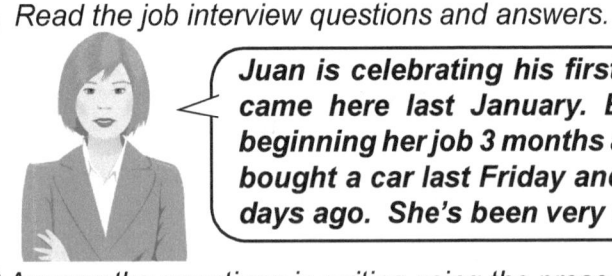

How long have you attended this school? I've attended this school since March.

Student 1: How long have you _____?
Student 2: I've _____ for/since _____.

4 Read the job interview questions and answers.

Juan is celebrating his first year in this city. His sister, Ella, came here last January. Ella started work in April. After beginning her job 3 months ago, she got a driver's license. She bought a car last Friday and moved into her own apartment 2 days ago. She's been very happy ever since!

5 Answer the questions in writing using the present perfect tense with "**for**" and "**since**."
1. How long has Juan lived in this country? _Juan has lived in this country for one year._
2. How long has Ella worked? _____
3. How long has she been at her present job? _____
4. How long has she had a driver's license? _____
5. How long has she had a car? _____
6. How long has she lived in her own apartment? _____
7. How long has she been happy? _____
8. How long have you worked? _____
9. How long have you lived here? _____
10. How long have you studied English? _____

CHALLENGE: Write two original questions. Ask them to other students in your class. Write their answers below.
11. How long have you _____? _____
12. How long _____? _____

ESL Advance Level • Job Interview • Pair Practice • Writing • Class Discussion

Teacher's Notes

1 It is recommended that lesson (*Present Perfect Tense 1, #0107*) be taught prior to this one.

2 Before distributing the worksheet, start the lesson with a conversation. Ask questions that elicit sentences using the present perfect tense to determine how well they can use the verb structure. Use some of the sample questions below:

How long have you lived here?   *How long have you worked?*   *How long have you studied English?*

3 Distribute the worksheet. Read the interview questions in the balloons. Answer the questions in short answers. Read the questions again, but this time respond in complete sentences. For example, ask, "*How long has Juan been in this country?*" Mode the response, "*He's been in this country since July.*" Have students repeat both questions and answers.

4 Ask students personalized questions. Refer to the verb phrases listed in the box at the right of the worksheet. Note that only two irregular verbs have been presented: "*had*," "*been*" and "*worn*." Have the students answer in complete sentences using "*for*." Discuss and explain any new vocabulary in the phrases if needed. Begin the drill with the question, "*How long have you...?*"

5 Repeat the activity above using the question "*How long have you...?*" This time have the students respond using the word "*since*."

6 Repeat the activities above allowing students to respond with short answers beginning with "*for*" or "*since*":

How long has Juan lived in this country?   Since July.
How long have you lived here?   For 6 months

7 Review the formation of the present perfect tense. The present perfect expresses an indefinite time in the past; whereas the simple past implies a specific time. This distinction could be clarified by expanding the activity above. Have students give initial short answers in the present perfect, and then expand their answers in the past tense giving specific time references (*ago*, *last week*, *yesterday*, *on Friday*, *at 8 p.m.*).

Question: *How long have you lived here?*   Response: *For one year.* (and I still live here.)
Question: *How long have you lived here?*   Response: *Since last year.* (and I'm still here.)

NOTE: You may want to point out that "*'s*" is a contraction of "*is*" and "*has*." Compare "*He's working now.*" and "*He's worked for many years.*" Explain that the present perfect is used to express an action that began in the past, continues to the present and will possibly continue into the future. Explain that "*for*" precedes the quantity of time or duration and "*since*" precedes the starting point. You may want to explain this concept graphically on the chalkboard.

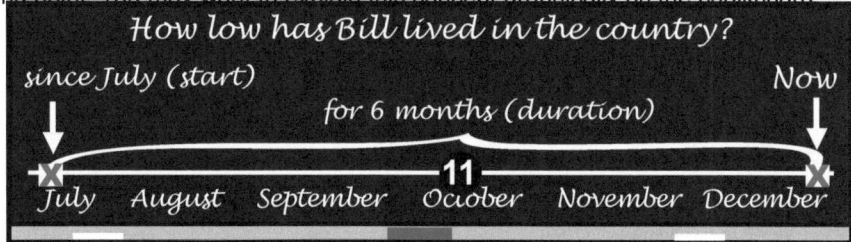

How low has Bill lived in the country?
since July (start)   for 6 months (duration)   Now
July   August   September   October   November   December
11

8 In Exercise 2, the first pair-practice exercise, direct the students to ask and answer questions using "*How long has Juan ...?*" Model responses using "*for*," and "*since*." Have the students continue the activity by working in pairs asking one another questions based on the job interview questions at the top of the worksheet.

9 In Exercise 3, the second pair-practice exercise, use the question "*How long have you...?*" Then, model the responses. Use the verb phrases in the box at the right side of the worksheet as cues. Expand the activity by having the students ask one another original questions using the verb phrases in the box. Have students share some of their questions with the class.

10 For Exercise 4, read the text and point out that it is completely written in the simple past tense, except for the last sentence. Explain the vocabulary as necessary. Then have the students complete the questions in writing. This exercise requires the students to formulate answers in the present perfect which have been logically derived from information in the reading passage. Point out the questions 8, 9, and 10 require original answers.

12 Direct the students to the bottom of the page *(Questions 11 and 12)*. Challenge the students to write two original questions using the phrases in the box to the right of the worksheet. Then, allow a few minutes for the students to get up, walk around the room, and ask another student to answer the questions. Students should write down the answers. Finally, have a class discussion using the students' original question and responses.

On a subsequent day, Use the text in Exercise 3 as a dictation.

ESL Advance Level • Shopping Survey • Pair Practice • Writing • Discussion

Present Perfect Tense 2

1 Read the questions in the supermarket shopping survey.

A store employee is asking Judy Tanaka some shopping survey questions.

Can I ask you a few questions?

Welcome to our store. We have been at your service for 100 years.

1. Have you ever been in this store before? — Yes.
2. Have you ever tried our store brands? — Yes.
3. Have you ever used coupons before? — Yes
4. Have you ever tasted our ice cream? — No.
5. Have you ever purchased our produce? — Yes.
6. Have you ever answered a survey before? — No.

Who? Me? Sure!

2 **Pair-Practice:** Practice answering and asking questions with another student. Use the questions above. See examples. ▶

Have you ever been here before? / Yes, I have.

Student 1: Have you ever _____?

Student 2: Yes, I have. or No, I haven't.

VERB PHRASES
visited your local library?
been to a play?
attended a concert?
visited the zoo?
enjoyed a circus?
used your cell phone today?
listen to your favorite radio station.
helped a friend?
played a musical instrument?
eaten in a Chinese restaurant?
had a bad haircut?

3 **Pair-Practice:** Practice answering and asking questions with another student. Use some of the expressions in the box to the right. See examples. ▶

How many times have you been here? / I've been here a few times.

Student 1: How many times have you _____?

Student 2: I've _____ .

TIME EXPRESSIONS
never ... before   twice
many times   three times
once   a few times

4 Answer the questions in writing using the present perfect tense.
1. Has Judy ever shopped in this store before? _Yes, she has shopped in the store before._
2. Has she ever eaten this store's ice cream? _____
3. Has she ever used coupons before? _____
4. Have you ever answered a shopping survey? _____
5. Have you ever used coupons in a supermarket? _____
6. Have you ever been to an outside farmer's market? _____
7. Has the supermarket clerk ever overcharged you for food? _____
8. Have you ever received samples of new products by mail? _____
9. Have you shopped at the same market for a long time? _____
10. Have you ever worked in the supermarket? _____

5 Fill in the blanks with verbs in the present perfect tense.

Judy Tanaka _has lived_ in this city and _____ in the same market for a very
                 lived   **shop**
long time. This is the first time that anybody _____ her and _____ questions
                            stop   **ask**
about her buying habits. A woman asked her, "_____ you ever _____ our
                                            tasted
ice cream?" Judy answered, "No, I _____ your ice cream, but I _____ in
                      try   **be**
this store many times before."

ESL Advance Level • Shopping Survey • Pair Practice • Writing • Discussion

Teacher's Notes

1 Before distributing the worksheet, start the lesson with a conversation. Ask questions that elicit sentences using the present perfect tense to determine how well they can use the verb structure. Use some of the sample questions below:

Have you ever visited a museum? If so, how many times?   ***Have you ever played an instrument? If so, how often?***
Have you been to the local library? If so, how many times?   ***Have you ever attended a concert? How many times?***

2 Distribute the worksheet. Read the survey questions in the balloons at the top of the worksheet. Model the responses using short answers. For example, ask, *"Have you ever been in this store before?"* Model the responses, *"Yes, I have."* and *"No, I haven't."* Have students repeat both questions and answers.

3 Repeat the exercise by replacing "*you*" with "*Judy*." For example, ask, *"Has Judy ever been in this store before?"* Reply, *"Yes, she has."* or *"No, she hasn't."*

4 In Exercise 2, the first pair-practice exercise, have the students work in pairs asking one another questions based on the survey questions at the top of the worksheet.

5 Drill and ask questions based on the shopping survey using *"How many times?"* Model responses using *"never ... before,"* *"many times,"* *"several times,"* *"once,"* *"twice,"* *"three times,"* and *"a few times."* Examples:

How many times have you been in this store?   ***I've been here twice.***
   I've never been here before.

6 In Exercise 3, the second pair-practice exercise, expand the activity by having the students ask one another original questions using the expressions in the box at the right side of the worksheet.

Direct the students to the writing activity in Exercise 4. Review and discuss the questions to make sure that the students understand the vocabulary. After writing and correcting the answers, encourage the students to pose original questions using the questions modeled after those on the worksheets. Then, have a class discussion based on their questions.

7 As a quiz, have the students fill in the words in Exercise 4. (**Answers:** *has lived, has shopped, has stopped, has asked, Have ... tasted, haven't tried, I've been*)

FOLLOW-UP ACTIVITIES

8 On a subsequent day, use some of the students' original questions as a dictation.

9 Review the forms of the verb "*to have*" in the present tense (*have, has*).

10 Show that the present perfect tense is formed by combining the present tense of "*have*" and the past participle. This lesson only introduces the two irregular forms "*been*" and "*eaten.*"

11 Ask various questions relating to the students' experiences. Use some of the questions in the box to the right of the worksheets as models.

NOTE

The present perfect expresses an indefinite time in the past; whereas the simple past implies a specific time. This distinction could be clarified by expanding the activity above. Have students give initial short answers in the present perfect, and then expand their answers in the past tense giving specific time references (*ago, last week, yesterday, on Friday, at 8 p.m.*).

   Question: *Have you ever visited the local library?*
   Response: *Yes, I have. I visited it last week.*

You may want to point out that "*'s*" is a contraction of "*is*" and "*has*." Compare "*He's working now.*" and "*He's worked for many years.*"

Explain that the word "*ever*" is not echoed in an affirmative response. However, it is used for emphasis after the superlative as in "***This is the best book that I've ever read.***"

In the United States, there is usually a grammatical distinction between "*have*" as a primary verb and "*have*" as an auxiliary verb. Examples:

   Do you have any sisters?   *Yes, I do.*
            I don't have any sisters.

   Have you called your brother?   *Yes, I have.*
            I haven't called my brother.

ESL Advanced Level — Dealing With AIDS • Group Discussion • Writing

Past Perfect Tense

1 Directions: *Read and discuss the grammar rules below.*

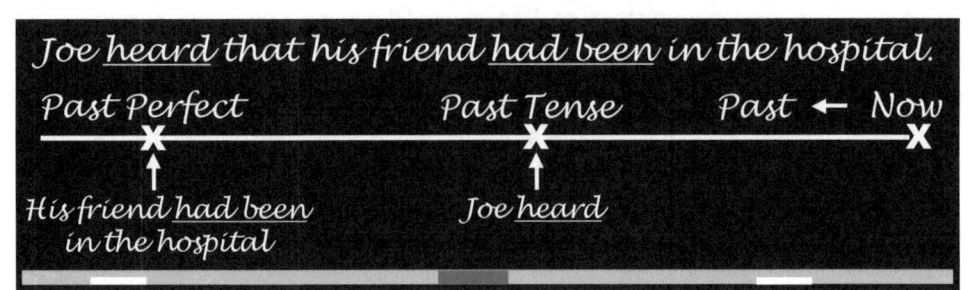

> Joe <u>heard</u> that his friend <u>had been</u> in the hospital.
>
> Past Perfect — Past Tense — Past ← Now
>
> His friend <u>had been</u> in the hospital   Joe <u>heard</u>

We use the past perfect tense to show a past action that came before another past action. See the example to the left.

2 Directions: *Read the story below. Circle and discuss any unfamiliar words.*

Best of Friends

Because Joe Blanc had transferred to Union School in the middle of the term, he had not been able to make many friends. One of the few friends he had made was Tom Rogers, who, although friendly and bright, seemed isolated from the other students. Joe and Tom often studied and went places together after school.

One day, Joe was waiting at his locker for Tom, when Doug Cuff came up to him and said, "Joe, there's something you should know about Tom."

"What's that?" asked Joe, surprised and curious.

"Tom was in the hospital with AIDS. Everyone here at school knows it. That's why they stay away from him. If you keep being seen with him, they'll stay away from you, too."

Doug turned away and left abruptly as Tom came up.

"What's up?" Tom asked Joe, whose face had turned a deep red.

3 Directions: *Practice making sentences using the verbs in the box below.*

Common verbs used before the present perfect tense			
... realized that ...	... told me that ...	... felt that ...	... heard that ...
... explained that ...	... thought that ...	... knew that ...	... reminded me that ...

4 Directions: *Write an ending using the past perfect. Use some of the verbs in the box above.*

_____
_____
_____
_____
_____
_____

ESL Advanced Level • Dealing with AIDS • Past Perfect Tense • Discussion • Writing

Teacher's Notes

1 Begin the lesson with a discussion. Do not distribute the worksheet yet. Use the following questions as a guide:

*   ***What do you know about AIDS?***
    (According to the Center for Disease Control, Aids/HIV is the leading cause of death of people in the US between the ages of 25-44.)
*   ***What do the letters stand for?***
    (Acquired Immune Deficiency Syndrome)
*   ***What is the difference between AIDS and HIV?***
    (HIV is the virus that may cause AIDS. HIV belongs to a subset of viruses called retroviruses or slow virus. This is because it is a progressive disease. HIV is entered through the body through the mucous membranes or thru blood to blood contact. Once you get the virus it slowly begins to attack the immune system, killing off healthy immune system cells. The deterioration and destruction of immune function leads to AIDS.)
*   ***Do you know anyone who has AIDS?***
*   ***How would you feel if you found out that one of your closest friends had AIDS?***
*   ***Would you treat him or her differently?***
*   ***Is it okay to discriminate against those with AIDS or any other disease?***

2 Distribute the worksheet and review the use of the past perfect tense at the top of the sheet. Explain that we use the past perfect tense to show a past action that came before another past action.

3 Do an active listening comprehension exercise by having the students circle any unfamiliar words in the story as you are reading it. You may want to review the following vocabulary: **transfer, term, although, isolated, locker, stay away, abruptly, "What's up?"** Then ask simple questions beginning with question words (what, where, when, why, etc.) to test the students' comprehension.
Practice the use of the past perfect orally by having the students finish the sentences with common verbs that are often followed by the past perfect tense:

I realized that ...	I felt that ...	I explained that ...	I knew that ...
I told him ...	I heard that ...	I thought that ...	I reminded her that ...

4 Repeat the exercise above. Change the sentences to negative, then questions. Substitute the pronouns with real names.

5 Discuss the story by asking students how they would continue it.

6 Have students write an ending to the story using examples of the past perfect tense.

7 After the exercise has been corrected, ask for volunteers to share their stories with the class.

Follow-up Activity

8 Choose one of the best endings to the story and use it to prepare a handout with some of the words missing as in a **cloze*** exercise. Read the text aloud and have the students fill in the missing words as they read along. As an additional activity, have them write in the missing words as homework.

* A **cloze** exercise is a technique in which words are deleted from a passage. You can delete every seventh word, all prepositions, verbs, new vocabulary, etc. Then the students are required to insert the missing words. Students must construct the meaning from the context of the text.

ESL Beginning Level — Present Tense (Does) • Household Chores

Present Tense & Household Responsibilities

1 *Read the list of household chores. Then, divide the chores between Nancy and Ron. Write the chores on the lists below.*

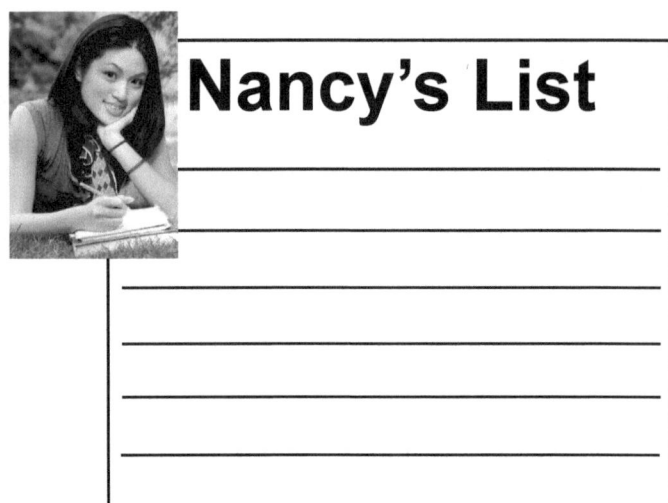

- Replace a light bulb.
- Fix the clock.
- Hang a picture.
- Water the plants.
- Clean the bathroom.
- Wash the windows.
- Sweep the hallway.
- Wax the floor.
- Change the sheets.
- Wash and dry the clothes.
- Iron the clothes.
- Shop for food.
- Dust the furniture.
- Empty the garbage.
- Shake the carpet.
- Vacuum the drapes.
- Wash the car.
- Cut the lawn.

Nancy's List

Ron's List

2 **Pair Practice:** *Talk with another student. Practice asking and answering questions about the household chores above. See example.*

"What does Nancy do?"

"She waters the plants"

3 *Make a list of your household chores on the back of this sheet. Then, discuss them with the other students in the class.*

ESL Beginning Level   Present Tense (Does) • Household Chores

Teacher's Notes

1 Read and explain the new vocabulary:

replace	sweep	dust	picture	sheets
fix	wax	empty	plants	clothes
hang	change	shake	bathroom	furniture
water	dry	vacuum	window	garbage
clean	iron	light bulb	hallway	carpet
wash	fold	clock	floor	drapes

2 Have students demonstrate any previous knowledge of the words. Ask general questions to determine how much the students know about the vocabulary. Use Wh-questions. (Who, What, Where, When, Why, How, What kind, etc.)

• Elicit new words whenever you can. A simple way of doing this is by means of a sentence in which the last word is not given. For example, If you want to elicit the word "water," you might say, *"When I'm thirsty, I drink...."* Students try to guess the word. This is a valuable technique because even if the students cannot guess the new word, they learn the context in which it is used when they do hear it.

You can also collect some magazine, newspaper, or internet pictures to illustrate the vocabulary.

3 Direct the students to divide the household chores between Nancy and Ron. Have them write the sentences on the worksheet.

4 As a pair-practice exercise, have the students practice asking and answering questions using **does** and the **-s** ending of the third person singular of the verbs.

5 Discuss what kind of household duties are done by men and women in your students' countries.

6 Have the students make a list of their household chores on the back of the handout. Discuss and compare the students' chores in class.

7 As a follow-up activity, you may want to teach expressions beginning with **do**:

do the housework	do the laundry	do the dusting
do the dishes	do the ironing	do the vacuuming
do the cooking	do the bathroom	do the windows
do othe work	do the shopping	do nothing
do a good job	do the cleaning	

ESL Beginning Level   Student Mixer • Present Tense • Personal Information

Present Tense

Directions: Walk around the room and find the students with the information below. Write the students' names on the lines.

1 _____
has a job.

2 _____
doesn't work.

3 _____
has a brother.

4 _____
has a sister.

5 _____
takes the bus to school.

6 _____
doesn't speak my language.

7 _____
lives near school.

8 _____
is handsome.

9 _____
is pretty.

10 _____
drives a car.

11 _____
doesn't smoke.

12 _____
is a good student.

ESL Beginning Level   Student Mixer • Present Tense • Personal Information

Teacher's Notes

❶ Use this group activity as a mixer exercise in which students have to talk to each other to get the necessary information. This is an excellent way for students to get to know one another especially at the beginning of a new term. Have the students get up and walk around the room to collect the names of other students who match the personal information on the worksheet. Allow at least 15 minutes.

❷ Distribute the worksheet and read the directions at the top of the handout to the students.

❸ Review the vocabulary below:

is	**work**	**school**	**handsome**	**smoke**
has	**brother**	**speak**	**pretty**	**good**
doesn't	**sister**	**live**	**drive**	**student**
job	**bus**	**language**	**car**	

❹ Review and practice the following phrases:

What's your name?   *Who is .... ?*
Please spell it.   *Who .... + (present tense)?*
Do you .... ?   *Does he/she .... ?*
Are you .... ?   *Is he/she .... ?*

❺ Read the directions at the top of the worksheet with the students.

Have the students practice asking and answering questions about the information collected.

Who has a .... ?
Who doesn't .... ?
Who is .... ?

❻ Follow-Up Activities

Have the students make up an additional list of other kinds of personal information such as ... is married, is single, has children, can sing, etc. and repeat the exercise.

ESL Beginning Level · Crossword Puzzle • Vocabulary Building

Professions

Directions: *Fill in the boxes with the names of the professions in the photos.*

1 across

4 across

6 across

8 across

9 across *(two words)*

13 across

16 across *(two words)*

18 across

20 across

21 across

22 across

23 across

Crossword grid with 1 across filled in as ASTRONAUT and 1 down filled in as ATHLETE.

1 down

2 down

3 down

5 down

7 down

10 down

11 down

12 down

14 down

15 down

17 down

19 down

ESL Beginning Level   Crossword Puzzle • Vocabulary Building

Teacher's Notes

1 Before distributing the worksheet, begin the lesson with a conversation. Ask your students general questions about the names of some professions. Ask them to name and describe as many as they can. List them on the board. Make sure that the lists include some of the following items:

accountant	athlete	conductor	firefighter	nurse	police officer
architect	bank teller	dentist	judge	optometrist	politician
artist	chef	doctor	lawyer	pharmacist	teacher
astronaut	coach	engineer	musicians	pilot	veterinarian

2 Distribute the worksheet and identify and discuss each photo. Ask simple questions about what people in these professions do, what they wear, where they work, and any other distinguishing characteristics. For example, ask questions such as:

What does a _____ do?   *When does a _____ work?*
What does a _____ wear?   *Where does a _____ work?*

3 Demonstrate how to do a crossword puzzle. Explain the concept of **DOWN** and **ACROSS**. Then, show the students how to fill in the puzzle using the visual clues. Do a few examples with the whole class.

4 Allow some time for your students to complete the crossword puzzle. You may want to have students work in pairs or assigning it as a homework assignment.

5 Correct the answers by projecting an overhead transparency image directly onto the board on which students can take turns writing the answers on the board. See solution below.

6 Play a crossword puzzle game. Draw or project a grid onto the board or screen as well as a list of the names of various professions. Divide the class into two teams and flip a coin to determine which team goes first. Have the first student of the first team go to the board and write a word that uses one letter of an existing word in the crossword. If the word fits and is correctly spelled, then give one point for every letter of the new word. Then, go on to the first student of the other team. If the word is incorrect, erase it and go to the opposite team.

7 As an additional activity, play Tic-Tac-Toe: Draw a Tic-Tac-Toe grid and fill it in with names of professions. Divide the class into two teams, each team assigned the symbol "X" or "0." Then flip a coin to determine which team begins. Have the students take turns in an orderly fashion by going down the rows. Tell the first student of the first team to use any word from the grid in a sentence. If the sentence is correct, replace the word with the team's symbol (X or 0), otherwise, leave the word. Go on to the first person on the other team. Continue in this manner until one team wins by having three consecutive X's or 0's in a row vertically, horizontally or diagonally. Keep score by giving one point for each game won. After each game, replace all the words in the grid with a different group of professions.

8 Expand the activity by teaching additional vocabulary items such as in the area of occupations: *baker, bank teller, barber, bartender, bus driver, butcher, carpenter, cashier, chauffeur, clerk, farmer, fisherman, florist, gardener, hairdresser, painter, janitor, maid, mail carrier, mechanic, soldier, tailor, waiter,* and *welder. (See the crossword puzzle for occupations on page 141.)*
CROSSWORD PUZZLE SOLUTION:

ACROSS: 1 astronaut, 4 nurse, 6 pilot, 8 chef, 9 bank teller, 13 artist, 16 police officer, 18 coach, 20 pharmacist, 21 architect, 22 teacher, 23 engineer;

DOWN: 1 athlete, 2 accountant, 3 musicians, 5 firefighter, 7 veterinarian, 10 judge, 11 optometrist, 12 politician, 14 conductor, 15 dentist, 17 lawyer, 19 doctor

ESL Intermediate Level • Question Words • TV and Movie Surveys • Discussion

Question Word Review

1 Read the questions in the TV Questionnaire Survey.

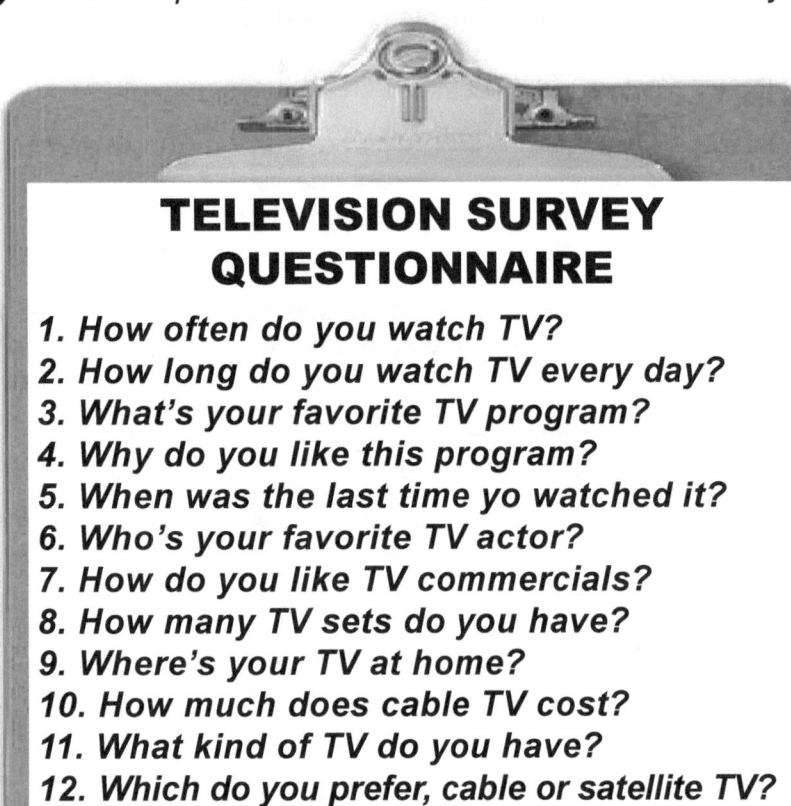

Excuse me. May I ask you a few questions?

Who? Me? Sure!

TELEVISION SURVEY QUESTIONNAIRE

1. How often do you watch TV?
2. How long do you watch TV every day?
3. What's your favorite TV program?
4. Why do you like this program?
5. When was the last time yo watched it?
6. Who's your favorite TV actor?
7. How do you like TV commercials?
8. How many TV sets do you have?
9. Where's your TV at home?
10. How much does cable TV cost?
11. What kind of TV do you have?
12. Which do you prefer, cable or satellite TV?

2 Write questions for a movie survey questionnaire. Use the questions above as samples.

MOVIE SURVEY QUESTIONNAIRE

1. How often _____?
2. How long _____?
3. What _____?
4. Why _____?
5. When _____?
6. Who _____?
7. How many _____?
8. Where _____?
9. How _____?
10. How much _____?
11. What kind of _____?
12. Which _____?

ESL Intermediate Level • Question Words • TV and Movie Surveys • Discussion

Teacher's Notes

1 Before distributing the worksheet, begin the lesson with a conversation using different question words: *How often?*, *How long?*, *What?*, *Why?*, *When?*, *Who?*, *How many?*, *Where?*, *How?*, *How much?*, *What kind of?*, and *Which?* as if you were conducting a TV questionnaire survey. Use questions modeled after some of the questions that appear on the worksheet to determine how well the students know the vocabulary and structures in the survey and how well they are able to answer the questions orally.

2 Distribute the worksheet. Have the students repeat the questions in the television survey. Make sure that the students understand the vocabulary and the grammatical structures. Avoid discussing the answers at this point.

3 As a class discussion, have an individual student ask another student the first question in the survey. After the answer has been given, solicit other possible responses. Have students practice each subsequent question in the same manner.

4 Direct students to the movie survey questionnaire in exercise 2. Have them write original questions similar to those in the first activity. Walk around the room and assist the students.

5 Pair up students and have them ask each other the questions in their movie survey. Circulate from group to group, and check for pronunciation and structural errors.

6 Have students exchange worksheets and answer the questions in the movie and/or television surveys in writing.

7 Have each student prepare an oral or written report based on his or her partner's answers.

8 Again, as a class discussion, have the students ask one another questions. After completing the activity, have the students direct their original questions to you for an answer. Try to elicit as many question variations as possible.

9 Have the students develop another survey about one of the following subjects:

cars	travel	radio	cooking
art, music	hobbies	Internet	food
sports	books	computers	clothing styles
games	magazines	cell phones	fashions

10 Identify and discuss different types of movies and TV programs

animated films	educational	musicals	movies	telethons
cartoons	programs	mystery movies	serials	tragedies
comedies,	game shows	reality shows	soap operas	travel films
crime dramas	horror films	religious	sports	variety shows
documentaries	love stories	programs	suspense	westerns
dramas	monster movies	science fiction	thrillers	wildlife adventures

11 You may want to discuss television in different countries. Possible topics include:

- *Favorite shows*
- *Channels, national networks*
- *Role of commercials (frequency, purpose, influence)*
- *Program scheduling*
- *Types of sponsorship (commercial, subscription, governmental, public)*
- *Television technology (DVD players, DVRs, cable, satellite TV)*
- *Government regulations, censorship*

ESL Intermediate Level — Reading • Discussion • Vocabulary Building

Reading a Newspaper • Information Search

Directions: *Answer the questions about the information in the newspaper below.*

1. How old is the newspaper? 
2. How much does the newspaper cost? 
3. How often is the paper published? 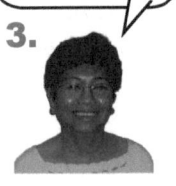
4. Are cats allowed in the apartment in the classified ads? 
5. Where can you find sports news?
6. On what pages are the classified ads?
7. Will it rain tonight?
8. What's a good TV program for children tonight?
9. What kind of accessories does the car in the ads have?
10. How long is the movie "War & Pizza?"
11. How long is the shoe store open on Wednesdays?
12. Does Mr. Booth still work in any of his pervious occupations?
13. When did Mr. Booth begin tutoring?

THE SMALL TOWN NEWS

Serving the Community Since 1945 — Free

November 29, 2010 — Daily — 6 pages

SHOES
UP TO **75% OFF**
TOMMY'S
450 Ocean St.
Hours:
Mon.- Fri. 9-6
Sun. 10-3
323-436-9876
newshoes.com

MAN OF THE YEAR

The city council has named Mr. Carl Booth, 72 years old and retired, has been a volunteer tutor in the English-as-a-second language classes in the local adult school for the past five years. As part of his rich experience, he has been a boxer, soldier, pilot, barber, and painter. He speaks fluent Spanish and Russian and is now learning Chinese. Mr. Booth is a sports enthusiast, who gets up at 4:30 a.m. every day to exercise and ride his bicycle several miles before he goes to school. School officials say that Mr. Booth is extremely helpful and effective, especially with older students. He serves as an example of an active and productive senior citizen.

TV TONIGHT'S BEST PICKS
Channel   7 pm
2   local news
4   national news
7   Movie • Buddies
8   Football game
9   Cartoon program
See page 4 for more listings.

WEATHER
Today: Mostly clear. Tonight: Cloudy with possibility of rain tomorrow. *Go to page 4 for more weather.*

MOVIES
WAR & PIZZA  
Show Times:
5:30, 7:15, 9:00, & 10:45
King Theater, 123 Main Street.
Call for info. 431-645-0987

SPORTS
Winning Team
Fairfax High School football team won the state championship over rival Hamilton High. *See details on page 5.*

COMICS — By Paul J. Hamel
That's English
— You're the right man for the job.
— You can begin tonight on graveyard.
DICTIONARY: GRAVEYARD: A work shift from midnight to 8 a.m.

INDEX
Local News   2
Business   3
Sports   4
Weather   5
Want Ads   6

CLASSIFIED ADS *Go page 6 for more ads.*

APARTMENT
2bdrm. A/C, new cpts/drps, stv., pkg., no pets. Call 321-435-0978

JOBS
Sales person, no exp. nec., good sal. + bene. Call for appt. at 986-321-6734

CARS
2008 Ford, exlt. cond., A/C, CD player, blue. Make offer, Call 243-452-9800

FURNITURE
Sofa-bed, gold color, gd. cond., Best Offer. Call Mike at 546-980-1232

199

ESL Intermediate Level   Reading • Discussion • Vocabulary Building

Teacher's Notes

1 This lesson is meant to be an introduction to learning the vocabulary used when reading a newspaper.

Distribute the worksheet and point out and explain the following vocabulary:

newspaper	advertisement	comics	index
headline	classified ads	photograph	weather
movies	column	article	sports

2 Also practice the following expressions of location:

upper right hand	on the right side	top/bottom
in the middle/center	corner to the right	to the left
lower left hand	on the left side	above/below

3 Draw a square on the chalkboard and practice the vocabulary above. For example, demonstrate by drawing an "X" in the square to show the following locations:

- the upper/lower right hand corner
- the upper lower left hand corner
- the center of the middle
- the top or bottom

4 Ask volunteers to read the various parts of the newspaper orally. Discuss any unfamiliar vocabulary and abbreviations. Be sure to include the following items:

bdrm. - bedroom	nec. - necessary	dr. - door	sto. - stove
pkg. - parking	cond. - conditions	drps. - drapes	oppt. - appointment
exlt. - excellent	cpt. - carpets	bene. - benefits	
A/C - air conditioning	sal. - salary	gd. - good	

5 As a reading comprehension exercise, have the students answer the questions in the balloons. Encourage them to work in pairs or small groups. Tell them that they have to find the answers from the information given in the newspaper. Walk around the classroom and check the students' work. To correct the activity, have volunteers explain how they found the answers.

6 As a follow-up activity, have students bring in a local newspaper. Prepare questions similar to those on the worksheet and ask the students to find the answers.

7 Check out other worksheets that deal with abbreviations: Reading Apartment Ads (Item #0047) and Job Ads (Item #0048).

Answers to the Questions

1. How old is the newspaper? Have students subtract this year from 1945 when it started.
2. How much does the newspaper cost? It's free.
3. How often is the newspaper published? It is published daily.
4. Are cats allowed in the apartment in the classified ads? No pets are allowed.
5. Where can you find sports news? Sports news is found on page 4.
6. On what pages are the classified ads? They are on page 6.
7. Will it rain tonight? No, but there is a possibility of rain for tomorrow.
8. What's a good TV program for children tonight? The cartoon program.
9. What kind of accessories does the car in the ads have? Air conditioning and a CD player.
10. How long is the movie "War & Pizza?" One hour and forty- five minutes.
11. How long is the shoe store open on Wednesdays? It's open from 9 am to 6 pm.
12. Does Mr. Booth still work in any of his previous occupations? No, he is retired.
13. When did Mr. Booth begin tutoring? He began five years ago.

ESL Intermediate & Advance Level   Reading • Discussion • Vocabulary Building

Reading Body Language

Class Discussion

1. When you meet someone for the first time, how do you greet him or her?
2. Do you use the same greeting for men as for women?
3. How do you greet your friends?
4. How do you greet a friend of the opposite sex?
5. How do you greet members of your family: children, adults, old people?
6. What are some good/insulting gestures that you can show the class?
7. Can you think of some gestures that have different meanings in different cultures?
8. Have you ever made a social mistake using wrong gestures? Explain what happened.
9. Do you know of any gestures that are unique to certain cultures?
10. Do you know of any universal gestures that are understood by everybody in the world?

What is Body Language?

Body language is all the body gestures and signals you give by voluntary or involuntary body movement or placement. Body language includes head movements, facial expressions through your eyebrows, eyes, nose, lips, tongue, and jaw; overall body posture using your shoulder movements, arm placements, hand and finger gestures, leg and feet placement; handling and placement of objects such as pens, papers, etc); and eye-contact. Reading the signals that people send out with their body language is a very useful social skill.

Research has shown that communication is made up of the words we use (7%), non-verbal communication (55%), and our tone of voice (38%).

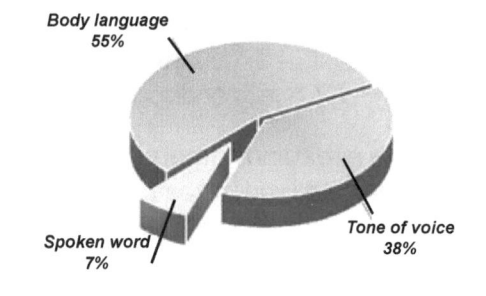

Because many non-verbal messages are 'culture specific', they can cause a lot of misunderstanding between people from different backgrounds. Gestures such as pointing, waving, shaking or nodding the head are common human gestures, but they do not always mean the same in every culture.

Can you guess the meanings of these hand gestures?

1
2
3
4
5

6
7
8
9
10

201

ESL Intermediate & Advance Level   Reading • Discussion • Vocabulary Building

Teacher's Notes

1 Distribute the *Introduction to Body Language* handout and begin the activity by discussing some of the questions that appear at the top of the page.

2 Continue the activity by reading the section "*What is Body Language*" on the worksheet.

3 Then, ask the students to try to guess the meanings of the gestures in the photos at the bottom of the page.

Lead a group discussion by asking students to share body language from their cultures.

5 Make a list of emotions on the board and ask the students to come up with appropriate body language. The list should include words like happy, say, tired, excited, lazy, etc.

6 Play a pantomime game in which a student comes in front of the class and expresses an emotion. The rest of the class must guess the meaning the body language.

7 Improvised Role Playing: Divide the class into small groups. Ask the groups to create a role play that involves ONLY body language and NO talking. Each group takes its turn at presenting their scene in front of the whole class.

Some suggestions:

• You are meeting the leader of your country.
• It's 11:55 on New Years Eve.
• You are late for a dinner party.
• It's the end of a party. You are the last people left.
• You are all friends at a funeral.
• You and family members had a big fight on your way back from a vacation.

8 Have the students continue by providing their own scenarios.

Answers

1. Hang loose - An Hawaiian gesture of frendship and understanding 2. Bang bang you're dead 3. Call me 4. Check please 5. Good job! Well done! 6. Dislike, rejection 7. A-OK Everything's fine 8, Peace (can also mean "V" for victory 9. Good luck 10. F-You!

ESL Beginning & Intermediate Levels • Vocabulary Building • Pair Practice Dictation

Safety Signs

❶ *Fold the page on the dotted line. Look at your side of the worksheet only. Compare your signs after you finish the exercise.*

❷ *Write the words that your partner reads to you in the blank signs below.*

❷ *Read and spell the words on the signs below to your partner.*

Student 1

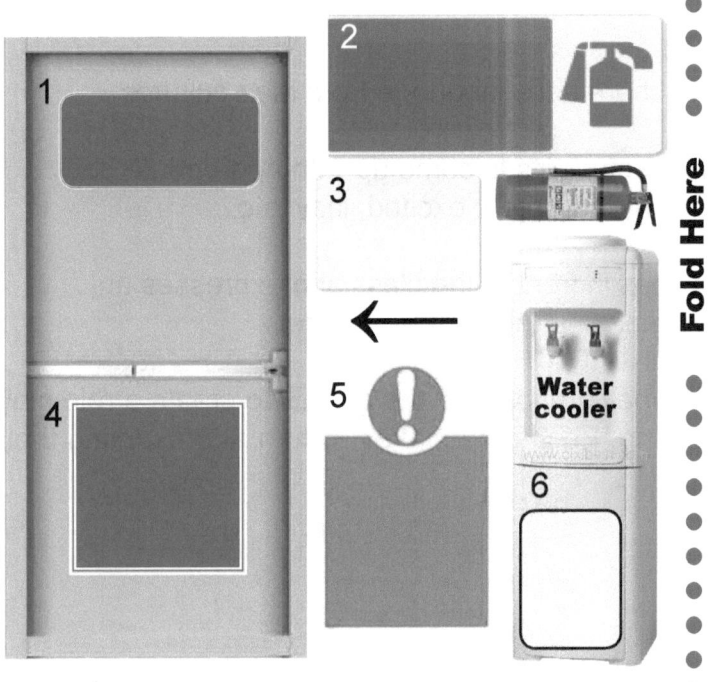

Student 2

Fold Here

1.
2.
3.
4.
5.
6. Water cooler

1. RESTRICTED AREA
2. FIRE EXTINGUISHER
3. FIRE ESCAPE
4. EMERGENCY EXIT
5. Fire door keep shut
6. OUT OF ORDER / Water cooler

❸ *Read and spell the words on the signs below to your partner.*

❸ *Write the words that your partner reads to you in the blank signs below.*

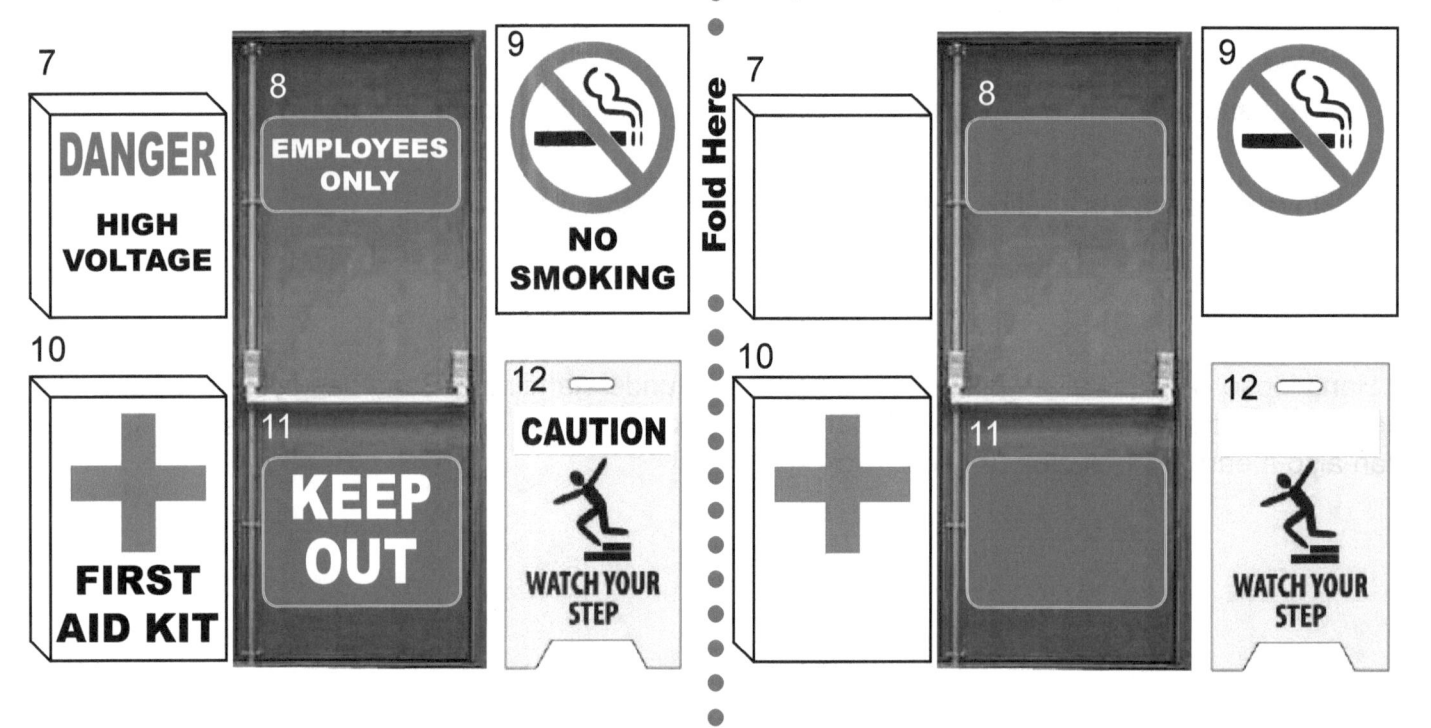

Fold Here

7. DANGER HIGH VOLTAGE
8. EMPLOYEES ONLY
9. NO SMOKING
10. FIRST AID KIT
11. KEEP OUT
12. CAUTION WATCH YOUR STEP

7.
8.
9. NO SMOKING (image)
10. (first aid cross)
11.
12. WATCH YOUR STEP

203

ESL Beginning & Intermediate Levels • Vocabulary Building • Pair Practice Dictation

Teacher's Notes

1 Before distributing the handout, review some prepositions:

near	to the left	above	under
next to	to the right	below	over

2 Review the names of the objects on the handout:

wall cabinet	fire	sign	water cooler
door	extinguisher	wall	

3 Explain that there are different kinds of safety signs:

- **PROHIBITION SIGNS:** These signs are used to prohibit actions to prevent personal injury and the risk of fire.

- **MANDATORY SIGNS:** Mandatory signs convey action that must be taken e.g. procedures in case of fire.

- **WARNING SIGNS**: These signs are to inform personnel of possible dangers in the workplace.

- **SAFE CONDITIONS SIGNS:** To show directions to areas of safety and medical assistance and to include safe exit.

- **FIRE EQUIPMENT SIGNS:** To show location of fire equipment and compliance with fire precautions.

4 Distribute the worksheet. Direct the students to fold the page on the dotted line. Tell them to look at their side of the page only. Explain that the students must full in the blank signs that their partner describes and dictates the words. Also explain that they will have the opportunity to compare their signs after both finish the exercise.

5 As a follow-up activity, you may want to teach the meanings of other safety signs:

Asbestos	Eye protection	No diving	Slippery when
Authorized	required	No eating in	wet
personnel only	Fire hose	area	Strictly no
Beware of dog	Flammable	No life guard on	admittance
Biohazards	Goggles must	duty	Visitors must
Blasting keep	be worn	No loitering	report to the
away	Handicapped	No pets	office
Corrosives	Hard hat area	Notice	Warning
Do not block	Hazard	Poison	Wash hands
Do run	Hazardous	Radiation	Wet paint
Electric shock	waste	Radioactive	Wheelchair
risk	High pressure	Safety first	accessible
Eye protection	Lazer danger	Safety glass	Workers
must be worn	Look out	required	overhead

6 For an additional lesson, use a similar exercise using traffic signs in the collection of *Bundle of Tricks*. See *Traffic Signs, ESL Beginning & Intermediate Levels, Vocabulary building, Pair Practice, Dictation.*

ESL Intermediate Level   With Present Tense • Past Tense • Infinitive • Writing

Say & Tell

Directions: Read the rule for using **say** and **tell**.

> The words **say** and **tell** have the same meaning, but they are used in different ways.
> We use **say** when we say **something** (to someone).
> Example: The teacher is saying "Pay attention" (to the students.)
> We use **tell** when we tell **someone something**.
> Example: The teacher is telling the students "Pay attention."
> We also use **tell** in expressions such as "tell a story, a lie, or a joke.

Activity 1: Describe what the people are saying. Use the verb **say** and **tell** in the present tense.
　　Examples: What **is** the teacher **saying**? She **is saying** "Pay attention!"
　　What **is** the teacher **telling** the students? She **is telling** the students "Pay attention!"

Activity 2: Repeat the exercise using the past tense: **said** and **told**.
　　Examples: What **did** the teacher **say**? She **said** "Pay attention."
　　What **did** the teacher **tell** the students? She **told** the students "Pay attention."

Activity 2: Repeat the exercise using the past tense: **said** and **told** and the infinitive of the verb.
　　Examples: What **did** the teacher **say**? She **said to** pay attention.
　　What **did** the teacher **tell** the students? She **told** the students **to** pay attention.

1 Pay attention!
Say: _The teacher said to pay attention._

2 Beth — Drive carefully! — Steve
Tell: _Beth told Steve to drive carefully._

3 Take a card. — Ray, Rita
Say: _____

4 Dance slowly. — Alice, Joe
Tell: _____

5 Please come in. — Driver
Say: _____

6 Prepare for take-off. — Pilot, Copilot
Tell: _____

7 Troy — Smile for the camera.
Say: _____

8 Jack — Follow me.
Tell: _____

9 David — CALL ME
Say: _____

10 Be careful. — Nurse
Tell: _____

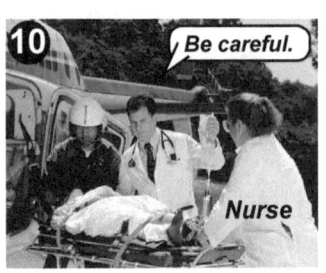

11 Please be seated. — Speaker
Say: _____

12 Jim, Bill, Bob — Tell me the secret, too.
Tell: _____

205

ESL Intermediate Level   With Present Tense • Past Tense • Infinitive • Writing

Teacher's Notes

1 Before distributing the handout explain the use of **say** and **tell**. Read the rules at the top of the worksheet with the students.

2 Pronounce the names (and occupations) of the people in the photos and discuss the meanings of the words in the balloons on the worksheet:

Pay attention	**Please come in.**	**Call me.**
Drive carefully!	**Prepare for take-off**	**Be careful**
Take a card.	**Smile for the camera.**	**Please be seated.**
Dance slowly.	**Follow me.**	**Tell me the secret, too.**

3 Do **Activity 1** by asking the students to describe what is happening in the photos. Drill the use of **say** orally using the pictures.

Example: *Student 1: What is the teacher saying?*
Student 2: The teacher is saying, "Pay attention!"

Next repeat the drill using **tell** with the same pictures.

Example: *Student 1: What is the teacher telling the student?*
Student 2: The teacher is telling the student, "Pay attention!"

4 Do **Activity 2** by repeating the oral exercise using the past tense of **say** and **tell**. See examples on the worksheet.

5 Do **Activity 3** by using say and tell with the infinitive **to + verb**. See examples on the worksheet.

6 Have students write sentences on the worksheet using **say** and **tell** as a classroom exercise or as homework.

Answers:

1. The teacher said to pay attention.

2. Beth told Steve to drive carefully.

3. Rita said to take a card (to Ray).

4. Alice told Joe to dance slowly.

5. The driver said to please come in (to the passenger).

6. The pilot told the copilot to prepare for take-off.

7. Troy said to smile for the camera (to his parents).

8. Jack told the children to follow him.

9. David said to call him.

10. The doctor told the nurse to be careful.

11. The speaker told the audience to be seated.

12. Jim told Bill and Bob to tell him the secret, too.

ESL Beginning Level   Vocabulary Building • Pair Practice

How Do You Spell / Say / Pronounce...?

① Directions: *Practice asking and answering questions with another student. Use the words (verbs) in the box below. See the example below.*

Student 1: *How do you pronounce "............?"*

Student 2: *We say "..............."*

come	give	see	take
do	hold	say	tell
eat	know	sit	think
drink	make	speak	walk
find	read	teach	write

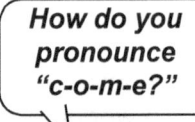

How do you pronounce "c-o-m-e?"

We say [kuhm].

② Directions: *Practice saying the names of the letters in the alphabet. Then practice asking and answering questions with another student. Use the words in the box above. See the example below.*

Student 1: *How do you spell "_____?"*

Student 2: *We spell it "_ _ _ _ _."*

English Alphabet

a b c d   l m n   t u v
e f g   o p   w x
h i j k   q r s   y z

How do you spell "come?"

We spell it "c-o-m-e."

③ Directions: *Practice asking and answering questions. Use the words in the box. See the example below.*

Student 1: *How do you say "_____" in __(language)__?*

Student 2: *We say "_____"*

English	Yes	No	Thank You
French	Oui	Non	Merci
Italian	Si	No	Gracie
Spanish	Si	No	Gracias
German	Ya	Nein	Bitte
Russian	Da	Niet	Spaceeba

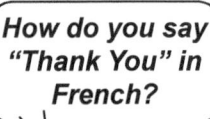

How do you say "Thank You" in French?

We say "Merci."

④ Directions: *Practice asking and answering questions with another student who doesn't speak your language. Use the expressions in the box. See the example below.*

Student 1: *How do you say "_____" in your language?*

Student 2: *We say "_____"*

Hello	Man	One
Good-bye	Woman	Two
Thank You	Child	Three
Yes	Book	I'm hungry.
No	Please	I don't understand.

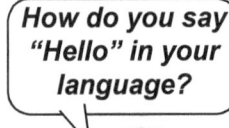

How do you say "Hello" in your language?

We say "Bonjour."

ESL Beginning Level • How do you say/pronounce/spell...? • Vocabulary Building • Pair Practice

Teacher's Notes

1 Before distributing the worksheet, review the following verbs:

come	drink	hold	read	sit	take	walk
do	find	know	see	speak	tell	write
eat	give	make	say	teach	think	

2 Introduce the vocabulary. You can do this by eliciting the words by means of a sentence in which the last word is not specific. For example, if you want to elicit the word "water," you can say, "When I'm thirsty, I drink something. What?" When a student guesses the word, have him/her repeat the original sentence replacing the final word with the specific noun. If nobody can guess the word, give the word and have everybody repeat the word in the original sentence. This is a valuable technique used in presenting new vocabulary because even if the students do not know the word that you are trying to elicit, they are being made aware of the context in which the word is found. Naturally, this cannot be done with very low level classes. In this case, explain the words through pictures, flash cards, or by other means, and simply have the students repeat the words after you.

3 Distribute the worksheet and read through the verbs in the box in Exercise 1. Have students give examples for each verb.

4 Teach the question: **How do you pronounce the word "_____?"** *(Do not spend time writing the phonetic spelling. It's more important that the students be able to understand and simply pronounce the words.)*

5 Review the names of the letters in the English alphabet. You may want to teach the Alphabet song in which the letters are sung in small groups. See the box in Exercise 2 and the music with lyrics below.

6 Continue by practicing the question: **How do you spell "_____?"** Use the verbs in the box in Exercise 1.

7 Next, teach the question: **How do you say "_____" in __(language)__?** Use the words and expressions in the box in Exercise 3. Expand the exercise by asking how to say words in the students' native languages.

8 Review the meanings of the words and expressions in the box in Exercise 4. Teach the question: **How do you say "_____" in your language?** Use the words and expressions in the box in Exercise 4.

9 Expand the activity by encouraging the students to supply new words and continue the activity.

ESL Beginning Level   Crossword Puzzle • Vocabulary Building

School Items

Directions: *Fill in the boxes with the names of the school items in the photos.*

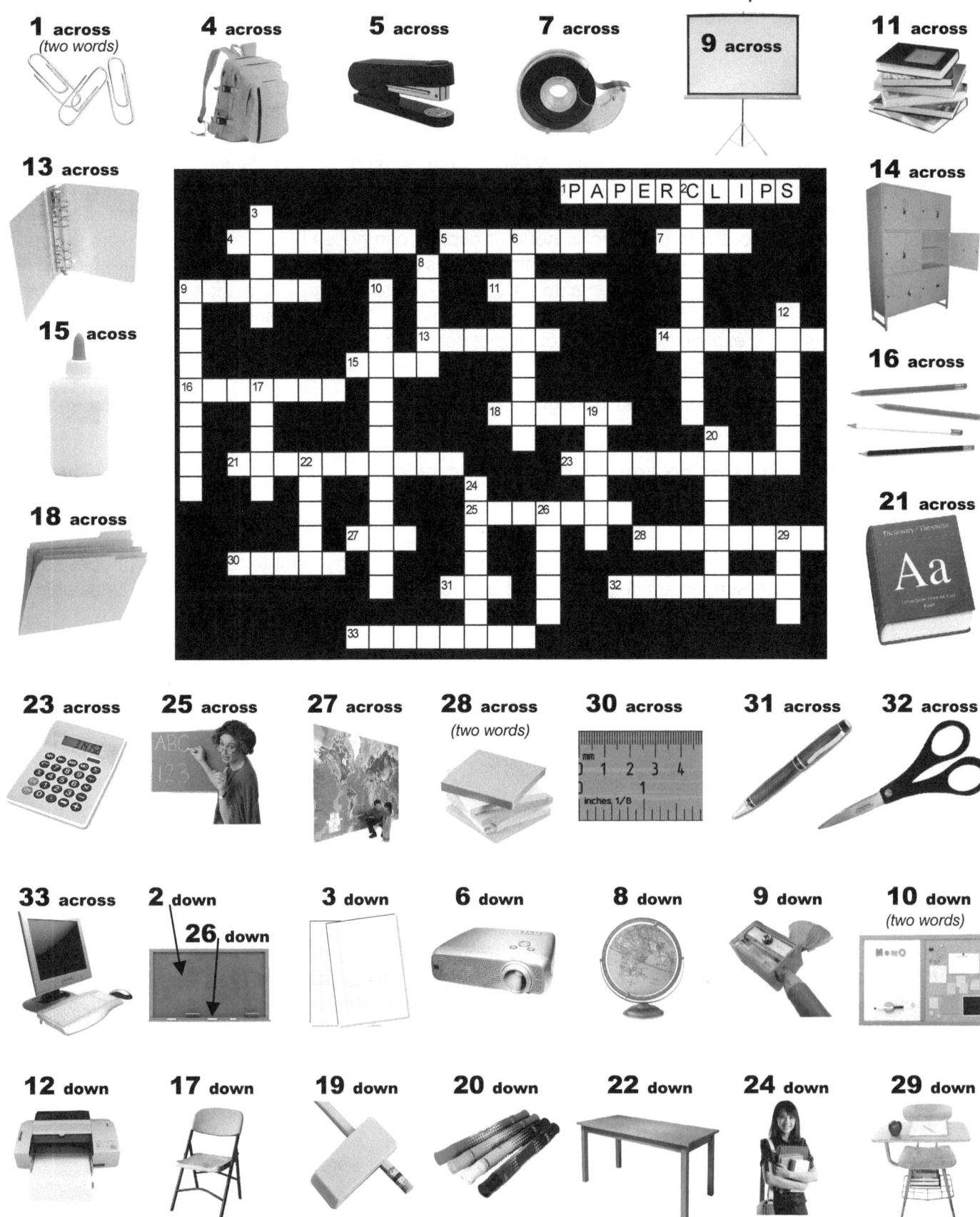

- 1 across (two words)
- 4 across
- 5 across
- 7 across
- 9 across
- 11 across
- 13 across
- 14 across
- 15 acoss
- 16 across
- 18 across
- 21 across
- 23 across
- 25 across
- 27 across
- 28 across (two words)
- 30 across
- 31 across
- 32 across
- 33 across
- 2 down
- 26 down
- 3 down
- 6 down
- 8 down
- 9 down
- 10 down (two words)
- 12 down
- 17 down
- 19 down
- 20 down
- 22 down
- 24 down
- 29 down

1 across: PAPERCLIPS

ESL Beginning Level   Crossword Puzzle • Vocabulary Building

Teacher's Notes

1 Before distributing the worksheet, begin the lesson with a conversation. Ask your students general questions about common classroom items. Ask them to name and describe as many as they can. List them on the board. Make sure that the lists include some of the following items:

backpack	calculator	computer	folder	map	paper clips	projector	sharpener	tape
binder	chair	desk	globe	markers	pen	ruler	stapler	teacher
books	chalk	dictionary	glue	note pads	pencils	scissors	student	
bulletin board	chalkboard	eraser	lockers	paper	printer	screen	table	

2 Distribute the worksheet and identify and discuss each clothing and accessory item. Ask simple questions about size, color, use, and any other distinguishing features.

3 Review and practice the following phrases:

Where is/are the _____?   *Show me where the _____ is/are?*
What color is/are the _____?   *Give the _____ to [person's name].*
Who has a _____?   *Why do you use _____?*

4 Demonstrate how to do a crossword puzzle. Explain the concept of **DOWN** and **ACROSS**. Then, show the students how to fill in the puzzle using the visual clues. Do a few examples with the whole class.

5 Allow some time for your students to complete the crossword puzzle. You may want to have students work in pairs or assigning it as a homework assignment.

6 Correct the answers by projecting an overhead transparency image directly onto the board on which students can take turns writing the answers on the board. See solution below.

7 Play a crossword puzzle game. Draw or project a grid onto the board or screen as well as a list of the school items. Divide the class into two teams and flip a coin to determine which team goes first. Have the first student of the first team go to the chalkboard and write a word that uses one letter of an existing word in the crossword. If the word fits and is correctly spelled, then give one point for every letter of the new word. Then, go on to the first student of the other team. If the word is incorrect, erase it and go to the opposite team.

8 As an additional activity, play Tic-tac-toe: Draw a tic-tac-toe grid and fill it in with school items. Divide the class into two teams, each team assigned the symbol "X" or "0." Then flip a coin to determine which team begins. Have the students take turns in an orderly fashion by going down the rows. Tell the first student of the first team to use any word from the grid in a sentence. If the sentence is correct, replace the word with the team's symbol (X or 0), otherwise, leave the word. Go on to the first person on the other team. Continue in this manner until one team wins by having three consecutive X's or 0's in a row vertically, horizontally or diagonally. Keep score by giving one point for each game won. After each game, replace all the words in the grid with a different group of animal names each time.

CROSSWORD PUZZLE SOLUTION:

ACROSS: 1 paperclips, 4 backpack, 5 stapler, 7 tape, 9 screen, 11 books, 13 binder, 14 lockers, 15 glue, 16 pencils, 18 folder, 21 dictionary, 23 calculator, 25 teacher, 27 map, 28 note pads, 30 ruler, 31 pen, 32 scissors, 33 computer;

DOWN: 2 chalkboard, 3 paper, 6 projector, 8 globe, 9 sharpener, 10 bulletin board, 12 printer, 17 chair, 19 eraser, 20 markers, 22 table, 24 student, 26 chalk, 29 desk

ESL Intermediate Level • Modal Verbs • Giving Opinions & Advice • Pair Practice • Writing

Should

Read: *Practice the phrases below the photo with another student.*

We use the word **should** when we want to express an opinion or give advice. **Should** is sometimes a polite form of **must**.
Examples:
You **shouldn't** *smoke. It's bad for you.*
You **should** *come to school early to get a good seat.*

Pair Practice: *Practice asking and answering questions with the word should. See the example to the right. Use the expressions below.*

Student 1: What **should** you do ...
Student 2: You **should** ...

... to find a job?
... to learn English?
... to learn English well?
... to make friends?
... to keep friends?
... if you see an accident?
... if you are very sick?
... if you can't go to work?

What should you do to find a job?

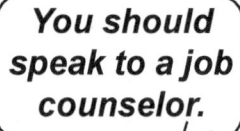

You should speak to a job counselor.

Write: *What should the people in the photos do? Write your opinion under each photo. Use* **should**.

❶ They should get married.

❷ _____

❸ _____

❹ _____

❺ _____

❻ _____

❼ _____

❽ _____

211

ESL Intermediate Level • Modal Verbs • Giving Opinions & Advice • Pair Practice • Writing

Teacher's Notes

1 Read and explain the use of **should** in the box at the top of the page.

Explain that **should** is a modal verb.

• **Should** generally has the same meaning as **ought to**.

2 • Other modal verbs are: **can**, **could**, **may**, **might**, **shall**, **should**, **will**, **would**, **must**, **ought to**.

• Modals do not change form, so we cannot add the **-s** ending to the third person singular. We use modals with the simple form of the verb (an infinitive without **to**)

3 Example: *We should come early to get a good seat.*

• We place modals in front of the subject to form questions.

Example: **Should** *we go to the beach?*

Read and discuss the vocabulary in the items in the Pair Practice exercise. After the students are familiar with the phrases, have them do the pair practice exercises. Pairing exercises give the students time, especially in large classes, to practice important speaking skills. Have each student choose a partner. (The first few times, you will probably have to go around the classroom and pair up students.) Encourage the students to pair up with **4** different partners each time. While students are doing the exercise, walk around the room, **5** listen to individuals, and correct mistakes.

Describe situations in which the students must respond with **should**.

6 Examples:

Stimulus	Response
It's my mother's birthday.	*I should get her a present.*
Jim smokes too many cigarettes.	*Jim should stop smoking.*
7 *Pablo can't speak English.*	*Pablo should go to school.*

Correct the answers by having volunteers write them on the chalkboard. Discuss other possible answers.

As a follow-up activity, repeat the pair practice exercise. Contrast **should** and **ought to** using the following rejoinder:

Student 1: What **should** *you do .... ?*
Student 2: You **ought to** *.....*

ESL Beginning Level   Vocabulary Building • Role Playing

Social Language

Directions: *Practice the dialogs below with another student.*

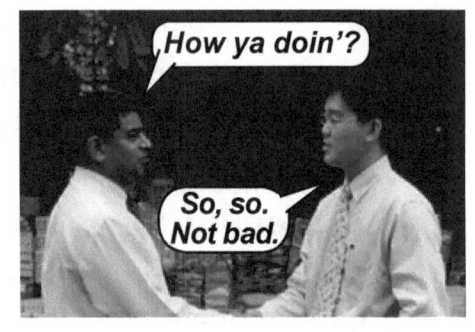

- Pleased to meet you.
- Pleased to meet you, too.

- How are you doing?
- Fine, and you?
- Great!

- How ya doin'?
- So, so. Not bad.

- What's new?
- Nothing much.

- How's it going?
- OK.
- Fantastic!

- What's up?
- Nothing. What about you?

- Can I borrow a dollar?
- Sure. Here you are.
- I'll pay you back tomorrow.

- Are you using this?
- No, I'm not. You can use it.

- What does this mean?
- It means "danger."

- Excuse me. I'm sorry.
- No problem.

- Do you understand?
- Uh-huh.

- Thank you.
- You're welcome.

- So long.
- Bye.

- See you later!
- Take care!

- Nice talking to you.
- I have to go. Bye.

ESL Beginning Level — Vocabulary Building • Role Playing

Teacher's Notes

1 Directions

Before handing out the worksheet, teach the fifteen mini-dialogs with actions using as much body language as possible to show their correct context.

Example: Shaking hands while saying, *"Pleased to meet you."*

2 Have the whole class repeat each line of the mini-dialogs after you have modeled the sentences. Break up longer sentences into segments, or use a backward-buildup technique, starting at the end of the sentence and working toward the beginning. Here is a demonstration of the technique.

Instructor	Students
you.	you.
meet you.	meet you.
to meet you.	to meet you.
Pleased to meet you.	Pleased to meet you.

3 Teach the second line (the rejoinder) of the mini-dialog in the same manner. Repeat the first line and have a student respond with the rejoinder. Then reverse roles.

4 Select two students to repeat the two lines. Continue with a chain drill in which one student asks a question or makes a statement and another student makes an appropriate rejoinder.

5 Distribute the worksheets and have the students practice the mini-dialogs in pairs.

6 Using an overhead projector or chalkboard, help the students write several of the mini-dialogs to create several longer ones.

7 Then encourage the students to present the new original dialogs in front of the class.

8 Encourage the students to write their own 8-line dialog using some of the expressions and vocabulary in the lesson.

Follow-up Activities

9
• Write the first part of the rejoinder on the chalkboard and have the students come up to write the second part.

• Give several mini-dialogs as a dictation on a subsequent day.

ESL Intermediate Level   Reading • Pair Practice • Ordering from a Menu

Some & Any 1

❶ *Read the menu.*

MENU

BREAKFAST
- Cereal, milk, fresh fruit
- Eggs with bacon or ham
- Toast with jam, orange juice

LUNCH

SANDWICHES
- Hamburger with French fries
- BLT (Bacon, lettuce, and tomato)
- Turkey and bean sprouts
- Tuna salad

SALADS
- Leafy green garden salad

(Assorted dressings available: Ranch, Thousand Island, Blue Cheese, French, oil and lemon)
- Pasta salad
- Fresh fruit salad

DINNER
- Baked chicken with mash potatoes
- Fresh fish, french fried potatoes
- Fried chicken and vegetables
- Roast beef with baked potatoes
- Seafood plate with rice
- Vegetarian vegetable plate

DESSERTS
- Fresh fruit plate
- Hot apple pie
- Chocolate layer cake
- Ice cream

BEVERAGES
- Coffee or tea
- Mineral water
- Diet & regular sodas
- Wine & beer

❷ *Talk with a student. Use the menu. Practice with the sample dialog below.*

Student 1: **What would you like to order?**
Student 2: **I'd like some**...

(What would you like to order?) (I'd like some chicken.)

❸ *Talk with a student. Use the menu. Use the the words and the sample dialog below.*

Student 1: **Does the restaurant have any ...?**
Student 2: **Yes, it has some** ....
    or
No, it doesn't have any ...

(Does the restaurant have any hot dogs.) (No, it doesn't have any hot dogs.)

hot dogs	turkey
hamburgers	milk
omelets	carrots
fish	soft drinks
salad	pasteries
cookies	roast beef

215

ESL Intermediate Level   Reading • Pair Practice • Ordering from a Menu

Teacher's Notes

1 Read the items on the menu and explain the types of food.

Explain the use of **some** and **any**.

- Use **some** as an indefinite article or pronoun in the affirmative. Example: *I'd like **some** chicken.*

- We usually use **any** in questions and in negative sentences. Example: ***Does the restaurant have any** cookies? No, it doesn't have **any** cookies. or It doesn't have **any**.*

2 Practice the use of some and any. Gather groups of small items such as paper clips, coins, and buttons, which can be concealed in the palm of the hand. Randomly distribute the items to several students (ideally fifty percent of the class). Make sure that these students have several of each item. Drill the structure by having individual students ask questions of other students. For example:

Student 1: Do you have any paper clips?
Student 2: Yes, I have some. (The student shows the item.)

Student 3: Do you have any coins?
Student 4: No, I have some buttons. (The student shows a different item.)

Student 5: Do you have any buttons?
Student 6: No, I don't have any. (The student shows that he has nothing.)

3 Teach the mini-dialog in the Pair Practice activities and demonstrate how to do this exercise with the help of a student. Then, have the students continue the exercise by working in pairs.

4 This activity lends itself well to role playing in which you act as the waiter or waitress and the students respond as customers. Such role playing presents an excellent opportunity to introduce common expressions used in restaurants:

May I help you?	**Check, please.**
Are you ready to order?	**Would you like any ...?**
	I'd like some ...
Anything else?	**Could you bring me some ...?**
	Do you have any ...?

5 **Cultural Note**
Depending on the geographical area of the United States, the meals of the day are known as either breakfast, lunch, and dinner; or breakfast, dinner, and supper. The word brunch is a combination of words breakfast and lunch and refers to a late-morning meal especially on weekends.

6 Discuss other American type food such as the following:

Buffalo Wings	Cookies	Fish & chips	Onion rings	Sherbet
Caesar salad	Corned beef	French toast	Patty melt	Shrimp cocktail
Cheese cake	Cottage cheese	Lemonade	Pickles	Sundae
Chili	Donuts	Milk shake	Pizza	Yogurt
Coleslaw	Fish & Chips	Nachos	Potato chips	

7 As a follow-up activity ask students to make a menu of their favorite national or ethnic foods and explain them to the other students in the class.

ESL Intermediate Level • Reading a Menu • Pair Practice • Fill In Vocabulary Building

Some & Any 2

1 Read the menu. The restaurant does **NOT** have any of the crossed out items.

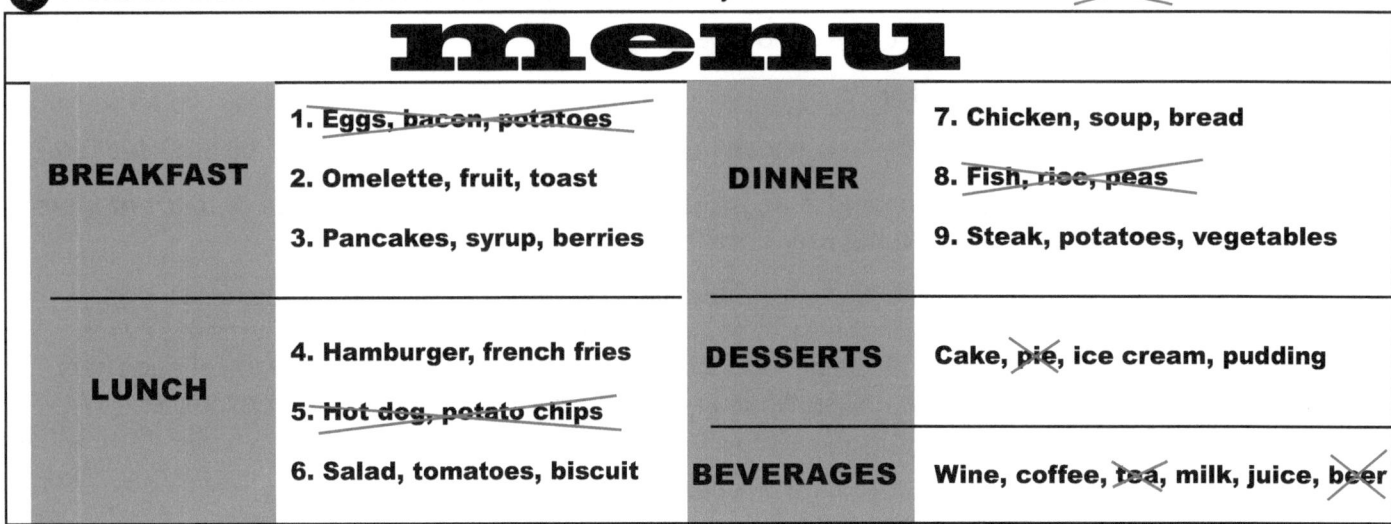

menu

BREAKFAST	1. ~~Eggs, bacon, potatoes~~ 2. Omelette, fruit, toast 3. Pancakes, syrup, berries	**DINNER**	7. Chicken, soup, bread 8. ~~Fish, rice, peas~~ 9. Steak, potatoes, vegetables
LUNCH	4. Hamburger, french fries 5. ~~Hot dog, potato chips~~ 6. Salad, tomatoes, biscuit	**DESSERTS**	Cake, ~~pie~~, ice cream, pudding
		BEVERAGES	Wine, coffee, ~~tea~~, milk, juice, ~~beer~~

2 **Pair-Practice:** *Practice answering and asking questions with another student. Use the menu. See examples.* ▶

Student 1: **Do you have any _____?**

Student 2: **Yes, we have some _____ .**

Student 1: **Do you have any _____?**

Student 2: **We don't have any _____ , but we have some _____ .**

Do you have <u>any</u> cake? — Yes, we have <u>some</u> cake.

Do you have <u>any</u> tea? — We don't have <u>any</u> tea, but we have <u>some</u> coffee.

3 Complete the sentences below.

1. No, <u>we</u> <u>don't</u> <u>have</u> <u>any</u> pie, but we have <u>some</u> cake.
Do you have <u>any</u> pie?
Troy wants some pie.

2. No, _____ _____ tea, but _____ _____ coffee.
Do _____ _____ tea?
Alice wants some tea.

3 No, _____ _____, but _____ _____ chicken.
Do _____ _____ fish?
Kim wants some fish.

4. No, _____ _____, but _____ .
Do _____ _____ ?
Beth wants a hot dog.

5. No, _____ _____, but _____ .
Do _____ _____ ?
James wants some beer.

6. No, _____ _____, but _____ .
Do _____ _____ ?
Rex wants some eggs.

ESL Intermediate Level • Reading a Menu • Pair Practice • Fill In Vocabulary Building

Teacher's Notes

1 Before distributing the worksheet, begin the lesson with a class discussion to assess how much your students know about using "*some*" and "*any*." You may want to ask questions about what you have hidden in your hands. In one hand place a few paper clips and in the other you should have nothing. Ask "***Do I have any paper clips in my hands?***" Open you hand and show that there are some paper clips. Respond "***Yes, I have some paper clips.***" Ask another question, "***Do I have any coins in my hands?***" Open your hands and show that there is nothing in your hands and say "***No, I don't have any coins in my hands***.

2 Gather groups of small items such as paper clips, coins, and buttons which can be concealed in the palm of the hand. Randomly distribute the items to several students (ideally fifty percent of the class). Make sure that these students have several of each item. Drill the structures by having individual students ask questions of other students. For example:

Ray: ***Do you have any paper clips?*** Alice:
Jim: ***Yes, I have some.*** (The student has the item.)

Irene: ***Do you have any coins?***
Paul: ***No, but I have some buttons.*** (The student has different items.)

Steve: ***Do you have any buttons?***
Clara: ***No, I don't have any.*** (The student has nothing.)

3 Take three paper cups and invert them on a table placing two small identical objects under one of the cups. Rapidly slide the cups changing their relative position. Ask, "***Are there any beans under the second cup?***" The students should respond either, "***Yes, there are some.***" or "***No, there aren't any.***"

4 Distribute the worksheet and explain the items in the menu at the top of the page. Have students repeat the items after you. Note that crossed-out items indicate that the restaurant is out of this food item. Teach the short dialog below.

Customer: ***Do you have any fish?***   Waiter: ***No, we don't have any fish, but we have some chicken.***

5 Vary the dialog above by substituting different food items. Prompt the new vocabulary for the dialog by oral cue, by picture, by flash card, by object, or by written cue on the chalkboard.

6 This activity lends itself well to role playing in which you act as the waiter and the students respond as customers. Such role playing would present an excellent opportunity to introduce common expressions used in a restaurant:

May I help you?	**Would you like any_____?**	**Are you ready to order?**
I'd like some _____.	**Anything else?**	**Could you bring me some?**
Check please.	**Do you have any_____?**	**Would you please bring me ____?**

7 Direct the students to exercise 2 in the middle of the worksheet. Have your students use the patterns and the examples given in the pair practice activities. With the help of a student, demonstrate how to do the pair practice exercises using the menu. Then have your students continue by working in pairs. Walk around the classroom listening to the pairs of students. Correct their pronunciation as needed.

8 Have your students go to exercise 3 at the bottom of the worksheet. Show them how to fill in the blanks modeled after the examples shown in the pair practice activity in exercise 2.

NOTES:

• Specifically drill the spelling of "*some*" and "*any*." As a memory aid you might point out that the last three letters of "*any/many*" and "*some/come*" are identical.

• "*Any*" is also used with the meaning "*all*," for example, "***Any fish can swim.***" This usage should be introduced at a much higher level. "*Some*" is occasionally used in a question when the speaker is expecting an affirmative answer.

• Use "*some*" as an indefinite article or pronoun in the affirmative. Example: ***I'd like some chicken.***

• We usually use "*any*" in questions and in negative sentences. Example: "***Does the restaurant have any cookies?*** "***No, it doesn't have any cookies.***" or "***It doesn't have any.***"

Cultural Note: Depending on the geographical area, the meals of the day are known as either "***breakfast, lunch, and dinner,***" or "***breakfast, dinner, and supper.***" The word "***brunch***" is a combination of the words "***breakfast***" and "***lunch***" and refers to a late-morning meal especially on the weekend.

ESL Advanced Level • Crossword Puzzle • Vocabulary Building: Words with Silent Letters

Spelling Words with Silent Letters

Directions: *Fill in the boxes with words containing silent letters.*

ACROSS

1. Potatoes, peas, cabbage
3. The past tense of "throw"
4. What _____ you do if you had a million dollars?
6. I'm right and you are _____.
7. She likes to read _____.
8. It's hard to _____ a tall mountain.
11. Obey the traffic _____.
12. Mr. and Mrs. Landry have a son and a _____.
14. The past tense of "can"
16. An _____ is surrounded by water.
19. It's dark in here; please turn on the _____.
21. I don't _____ the answer.
22. Another word for "Fall"
24. The ball came _____ the window and broke it.
26. The middle of your leg.
27. Did yo hear the train _____?
28. Spoon, fork, and _____.
29. The first day of the weekend.

DOWN

2. The past tense of "see"
3. The past tense of "think"
4. A day in the middle of the week.
5. People you know very well.
8. A religious holiday
9. I _____ food at the market yesterday.
10. A hamburger is a type of a _____.
13. A woman is pretty and a man is _____.
15. I don't drive to work; I _____ there.
17. _____ carefully to the directions.
18. She _____ her hair after she washed it.
20. One, _____, three, four
21. A noise you make on a door.
23. We learn English as a Second _____.
25. My _____ is 5 feet, 9 inches.

ESL Advanced Level • Crossword Puzzle • Vocabulary Building: Words with Silent Letters

Teacher's Notes

1 Demonstrate how to do a crossword puzzle. Explain the concept of DOWN and ACROSS. Then, show how to fill in the crossword puzzle boxes using the clues.

2 Do a few examples with the whole class. This activity serves as an excellent homework assignment.

3 Correct the answers by projecting an overhead transparency image directly onto a chalkboard or whiteboard where the students can write the answers to the puzzle.

4 As a follow-up activity, you may want to expose the students to other common words with silent letters besides those in the crossword puzzle:

Silent B	**Silent G**	where	**Silent K**	**Silent P**	**Silent U**
crumb	champagne	whether	knock	psychiatrist	guess
dumb	feign	why	knowledge	pneumonia	guidance
				psychotic	guitar
Silent D	**Silent GH**	**Silent H** *(at*	**Silent L**		guest
handkerchief	light	*the beginning*	calm	**Silent S**	
	might	*of word)*	half	isle	**Silent W**
Silent E	right	hour	salmon		wrap
hope	fight	honest	talk	**Silent T**	write
drive	weight	honor	should	castle	who
gave		heir		fasten	whose
write	**Silent H**	herb	**Silent N**	often	whom
site	what		autumn	whistle	
	when		hymn		

5 Play a crossword puzzle game. Draw or project a grid onto the chalkboard or whiteboard as well as a list of other words with silent letters. *(See list above.)* Divide the class into two teams and flip a coin to determine which team goes first. Have the first student of the first team go to the chalkboard and write a word that uses one letter of an existing word in the crossword. If the word fits and is correctly spelled, then give one point for every letter of the new word. Then, go on to the first student of the other team. If the word is incorrect, erase it and go to the opposite team.

6 As an additional activity, play Tic-tac-toe: Draw a tick-tack-toe grid and fill it in with the words containing silent letters. Divide the class into two teams, each team assigned the symbol "X" or "0." Then flip a coin to determine which team begins. Have the students take turns in an orderly fashion by going down the rows. Tell the first student of the first team to use any word from the grid in a sentence. If the sentence is correct, replace the word with the team's symbol (X or 0), otherwise, leave the word. Go on to the first person on the other team. Continue in this manner until one team wins by having three consecutive X's or 0's in a row vertically, horizontally or diagonally. Keep score by giving one point for each game won. After each game, replace all the words in the grid with a different group of words containing silent letters each time.

CROSSWORD PUZZLE SOLUTION:

ACROSS: 1 vegetables, 3 threw, 4 would, 6 wrong, 7 read, 8 climb, 11 sign, 12 daughter, 14 could, 16 island, 19 light, 21 know, 22 autumn, 24 through, 26 knee, 27 whistle, 28 knife, 29 Saturday

DOWN: 2 saw, 3 thought, 4 Wednesday, 5 friends, 8 Christmas, 9 bought, 10 sandwich, 13 handsome, 15 walk, 17 listen, 18 comb, 20 two, 21 knock, 23 foreign, 25 height

ESL Intermediate Level — Present Perfect • Pair Practice • Writing • Discussion

Still, Anymore, Just, Ago, Already, Yet

1 Read the photo captions.

Family Photos

1. René Landry in 1974 
2. René Landry now 
3. Eric and Michelle Landry in 1999 
4. Michelle with Erin and new baby 
5. René's house in 1964. 
6. René's home today. 
7. Eric, Michelle, Erin, and Paige today 
8. The Landry's future home?

Aurélie: My grandfather, René Landry, was a postal clerk many years ago. He doesn't work in the post office anymore. He's retired, but he's still works part time. Now he paints and sells his own art work. He still lives in the same house that he bought in 1964.

My cousin, Eric, got married to Michelle a few years ago, and just became a father again. They already have enough money to buy their own home, but they haven't bought one yet. They put a deposit on a new house, but they don't know if the bank has approved the home loan yet.

2 Answer the questions in writing using "*still*," "*anymore*," "*just*," "*ago*," "*already*," and "*yet*."

1. Is René Landry still a postal clerk? _No, he isn't a postal clerk anymore._
2. When was René a clerk? _____
3. Does René still work? _____
4. René doesn't want to buy a house. Why not? _____
5. When did Eric and Michelle get married? _____
6. Are Eric and Michelle still married? _____
7. What did Eric just become? _____
8. Do Eric and Michelle have enough money to buy a home? _____
9. Did Eric and Michelle buy a new home? _____
10. Has the bank approved their home loan yet? _____

3 Fill in the blanks with "*still*," "*anymore*," "*just*," "*ago*," "*already*," and "*yet*."

Richard: My dad was an electronics salesman many years _ago_. He's _____ a salesman, but he doesn't sell electronics _____. Now, he sells cars. He _____ has the same car that he bought in 1999. I am his son, Richard, and took my driver's test a week _____, and I _____ received my driver's license in the mail. I _____ have enough money to buy my own car, but I haven't brought one _____. I _____ ride my bike!

ESL Intermediate Level   Present Perfect • Pair Practice • Writing • Discussion

Teacher's Notes

1 Before beginning the lesson, review the use of the present perfect tense.

2 Before distributing the worksheet, start the lesson with a conversation. Ask questions that elicit answers using "*still*," "*anymore*," *just*," "*ago*," "*already*," and "*yet*" to determine how well they can use them. Use some of the sample questions below:

> *Do still ride a bike? (still/not anymore)*   *When did we begin this lesson? (just)*
> *When did you come here? (ago)*   *Have you eaten lunch yet? (already/not yet)*

3 Distribute the worksheet and identify the people in the Family Photos. Read the text aloud twice. The second time have the students repeat each sentence after you.

Clarify the vocabulary with the definitions below:
  ago: *at a past time*   **just**: *moment or short time ago*   **still**: *continuing now*
  already: *before now completed*   **(not) yet**: *(not) up to now*   **anymore**: *continuing now*

4 Model the following questions and answers having the students repeat:

Is René Landry still a postal clerk?   *No, he isn't a postal clerk anymore.*
Does he still work?   *Yes, he still works as a painter.*

5 Elicit the structures by asking individual students. Note that the word "*still*" follows the verb "*be*," or a modal such as "*can*" or an auxiliary such as "*have*" in perfect tenses.

6 Drill the following questions and answers: *(Note that "still" precedes single verbs.)*

Does René still live in the same house?   *Yes, he still lives in the same house.*
Does René work at the post office?   *No, he doesn't work at the post office anymore.*

7 Ask personalized questions with "*still*" and "*anymore*" Use the, appropriate vocabulary below to make questions such as *"Do you still ride a bike?"* You may want to list the following verbs on the board.

  ride a bike   play with [object]   live in/with   be single/married
  remember [event]   smoke   like (to)   have...
  drink [beverage]   work   go to   enjoy [event]

8 Using the photos, drill the following questions and answers with "*just*" and "*ago*":

  When did René work in the post office?   *He worked there many years ago.*
  When did Eric and Michelle get married?   *They got married a few years ago.*
  When did Eric and Michelle put a deposit on a new house.   *They just put a deposit on a new house.*

9 Ask personalized questions eliciting "*just*" and "*ago*" such as *"When did the bell ring?"* List the following verbs on the board.

  ring   begin this lesson   sit down   move to this city
  get up   eat lunch   clean your room   get married
  be born   have a birthday   speak to...   buy...

10 Using the family photos, drill the following questions and answers with "*already*" and "*yet*."

  Does Eric and Michelle have enough money to buy a home?   *Yes, they already have enough money.*
  Has Eric and MIchelle bought a house yet?   *No, they haven't bought one yet.*

11 Ask personalized questions with "*already*" and "*yet*" such as *"Have you eaten breakfast yet?"* List the verbs on the board.

  eat lunch   get married   graduate   buy a car
  do your homework   see [movie title]   read (the newspaper)   find a job
  learn to swim/dance   be in the ___ grade   be ____ o'clock   get a driver's license

12 Direct the students to the writing activity in Exercise 2. Review and discuss the questions to make sure that the students understand the vocabulary. After writing and correcting the answers, encourage the students to pose original questions using the questions modeled after those on the worksheets. Then, have a class discussion based on their questions.

13 As a quiz, have the students fill in the words in Exercise 3. (**Answers:** *ago, still, anymore, still, ago, just, already, yet, still.*)

FOLLOW-UP ACTIVITIES

On a subsequent day, use the text in Exercise 1 as a dictation.

Drill short answers, *"He still is," "He still does," "Not anymore," "A week ago," "He just did," "He already does,"* and *"Not yet."*
Drill the following variations of "*anymore*": "*no longer*," "*no more*" and "*any longer.*"

ESL Intermediate Level • Giving Street Directions • Pair Practice • Vocabulary Building

Street Directions

Directions: *Fold the page in half on the dotted line and choose the top or bottom of the worksheet. Do this activity with a partner. Look at your side of the handout only. Compare your maps only after you both finish giving the directions.*

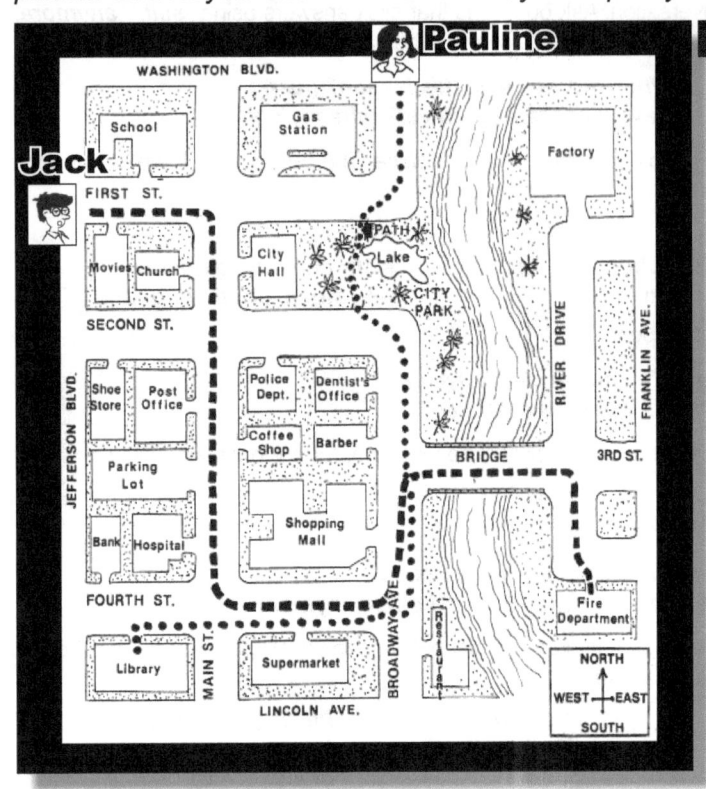

Student 1

Directions: *Give directions to your partner. Tell your partner to trace on his or her map how the Jack and Pauline go from one place to another on the map.*

Some Useful Expressions:

1. How can I go/get to ...?
2. Please give me directions to ...
3. Turn right/left at _(building)_.
4. Turn right/left on _(street)_.
5. Go straight ahead. or Go down the street.
6. Keep going until you get to ...
7. Follow _(street)_.
8. Go _(number)_ block.
9. Go pass _(building or street)_.
10. Go across/over the bridge.
11. Go around the corner.
12. Take a right/left at ...

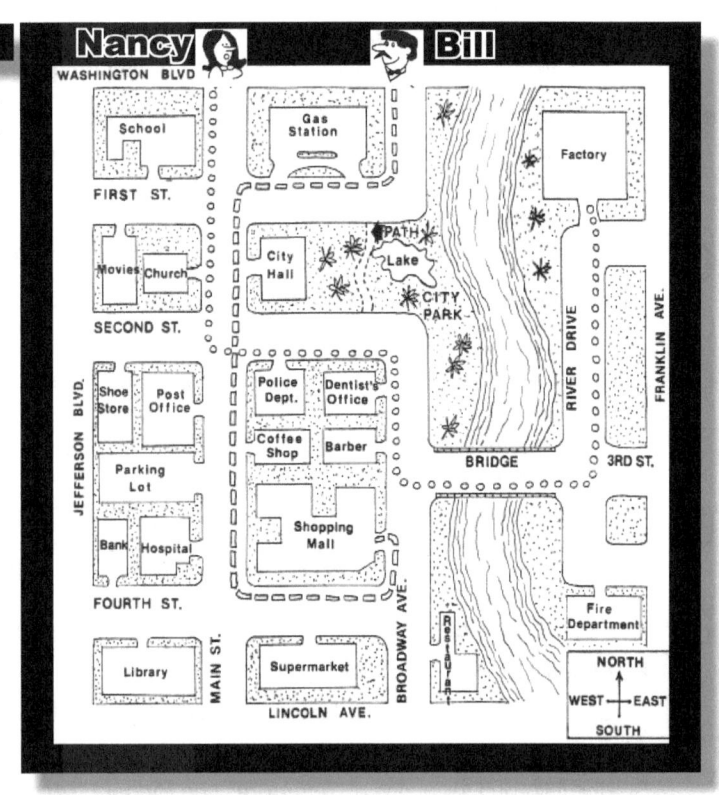

• **Fold Here** •

Student 2

Directions: *Give directions to your partner. Tell your partner to trace on his or her map how the Nancy and Bill go from one place to another on the map.*

Some Useful Expressions:

1. How can I go/get to ...?
2. Please give me directions to ...
3. Turn right/left at _(building)_.
4. Turn right/left on _(street)_.
5. Go straight ahead. or Go down the street.
6. Keep going until you get to ...
7. Follow _(street)_.
8. Go _(number)_ block.
9. Go pass _(building or street)_.
10. Go across/over the bridge.
11. Go around the corner.
12. Take a right/left at ...

ESL Intermediate Level • Giving Street Directions • Pair Practice • Vocabulary Building

Teacher's Notes

1 Hand out the worksheet and help students familiarize themselves with the map by finding the following locations:

school	barber	movies	hospital
shoe store	fire dept.	bank	supermarket
dentist's office	factory	shopping	path
restaurant	parking lot	mall	city hall
gas station	coffee shop	lake/park	police department
post office	bridge	church	library
			river

2 Tell the students to find the places above by indicating the street they are located on as well as the direction from the nearest cross street. For example:

Question: *Where's the shoe store?*
Answer: *It's on Second Street, west of Main Street.*
Question: *Where's the dentist's office?*
Answer: *It's on Broadway Avenue, north of 3rd. St.*

3 Explain any unfamiliar vocabulary and abbreviations on the map.

4 Drill the use of the expressions at the bottom of the worksheet. Let each desk or table in the classroom represent a city block and each aisle, a street. Have individuals stand up and follow your directions.

For example, say, *"Go straight ahead two blocks,*
turn right and go three blocks,
turn left and go straight until you come to..."

5 Have the students continue the activity by letting one student give directions to another. Have students choose partners, and make sure that each partner fold the worksheet in half. Explain that each worksheet contains different people as well as routes represented by dotted and broken lines.

6 Explain the following rules:

a. Students must how each other their maps.
b. Students must indicate orally how the people on their maps get to their destination.
c. Students must draw a line from the start to the final destination.
d. Students can compare their maps only after all the lines have been drawn from start to finish.

7 Tell students to expand the activity by giving one another additional directions from one place to another.

Walk around the room and check the students' work.

8 Follow-up Activities

• Ask the students to give directions on how to go from the school to certain locations in your community.

• Play a game, Mystery Location. Give directions to a location in your community and students must guess what is found there. Let students continue the activity by letting them give each other directions to the mystery location.

• Have students write original dialogs about giving directions.

• Have students actually role-play their dialogs in front of the class.

9 Check out other worksheets dealing with Street Signs (#0009) and Safety Signs (#0010).

ESL Beginning & Intermediate Levels Vocational ESL Vocabulary • Fill In

Suffixes used in Occupations

Read: *Read the rule below.*

We can form many names of occupations by adding the ending "-er" to a verb. Examples:

work → work**er**
teach → teach**er**
paint → paint**er**

Read: *Write the name of the occupation using the ending "-er."*

1. A _____ teaches children.
2. A _____ farms the land.
3. A _____ robs money.
4. A bus _____ drives a bus.
5. A _____ sings songs.
6. A _____ plays basketball.
7. A _____ manages a store.
8. A _____ waits on tables.
9. A _____ writes books.
10. A _____ reports the news.
11. A _____ paints pictures.
12. A _____ speaks to people.

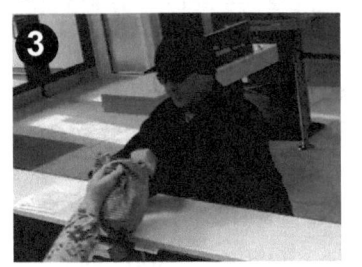

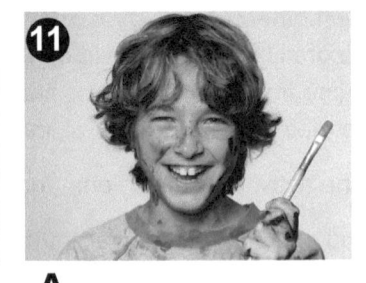

Read: *Read other suffixes used in occupations:*
-ist: typ**ist**, art**ist**, dent**ist**, chem**ist**
-or: doct**or**, direct**or**, instruct**or**, act**or**
-ess: steward**ess**, waitr**ess**, actr**ess**, host**ess**
-man or **-woman**: police**man**, police**woman**, sales**man**, sales**woman**

Write: *How many occupations can you name using the suffixes above?*

_____ _____ _____ _____
_____ _____ _____ _____
_____ _____ _____ _____

Write: *Walk around the room and make a list of the occupations of the students in your class.*

225

ESL Beginning & Intermediate Levels Vocational ESL Vocabulary • Fill In

Teacher's Notes

1 Read the rule and examples in the box at the top of the lesson.

2 Ask the students to identify other words that follow the rule, and write them on the chalkboard. Some words:

manager	builder	programmer	swimmer
reporter	painter	teacher	reader
waiter	writer	driver	speaker
worker	learner	runner	listener

3 Explain how to fill in the words in the WRITE exercise. Read the directions and do a few examples with the whole class.

4 Practice the words in the exercise and from the list on the chalkboard by asking and answering questions such as:

Question: *Who teachers children?*
Answer: *A **teacher** teaches children. or A **teacher** does.*

5 Read through the other suffixes in the second READ exercise.

6 Next, have the students write as many occupations that they can find using "**-ist**," "**-or**," "**-ess**," "**-man**," and "**-woman**."

Discuss the different occupations. Have volunteers write the words on the chalkboard and drill the correct pronunciation of each.

7 Use the last exercise as a group activity. Tell the students to stand up, walk around the room, and ask other students in class for their occupations. Have students write the occupations on the board.

8 As a follow-up activity on a subsequent day, dictate the sentences in the first WRITE exercise as a short quiz.

ESL Beginning Level — Telling Time • Pair Practice • Fill In

Telling Time

Read: *Practice reading the times in the clocks below.*

| two o'clock |  two fifteen |  two thirty |  two forty-five |  two to two |

Pair Practice: *Practice telling time with another student. Use the photos below.*

Excuse me. What time is it?
It's five o'clock.

Expressions of Time

What time is it?	a.m. / p.m.
quarter to	noon
quarter past/after	midnight
half past	o'clock

1. It's five o'clock
2. It's eleven twenty. / It's twenty past eleven. 
3. _____ 
4. _____ 
5. _____ 
6. _____ 
7. _____ 
8. _____ 
9. _____ 
10. _____ 
11. _____ 
12. _____ 
13. _____ 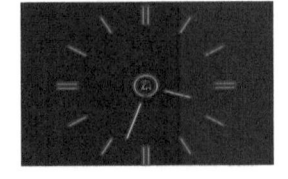
14. _____ 
15. _____ 

Write: *Practice writing the time in words below the pictures.*

ESL Beginning Level Telling Time • Pair Practice • Fill In

Teacher's Notes

1 Review how to pronounce and write numbers one to sixty.

2 Distribute the worksheet and read the times on the clocks at the top of the worksheet. Point out that **to** and **two** are pronounced the same.

3 Practice telling time using a paper clock with movable hands or even a real clock.

4 Teach the vocabulary: **clock**, **watch**, **clock tower**, and **digital clock**.

5 Read and practice the question and answer in the speech balloons on the worksheet. Student 1: *Excuse me, What time is it?* Student 2: *It's five o'clock.*

6 Have the students say the times in the photos on the worksheet. *(Discourage students from writing. This should be a time for oral practice.)*

7 Pair up students and have them repeat the activity orally.

8 Have students write sentences indicating the time below each photo on the first line. *(Leave the second line blank for the time being.)*

9 Correct the sentences. You may want to project a copy of the worksheet directly onto a chalkboard or whiteboard on which the students can write, see, and correct their answers.

1. It's five o'clock.
2. It's eleven twenty.
3. It's ten fifty-four.
4. It's twelve twenty-eight.
5. It's eleven o'clock.
6. It's ten twenty-seven.
7. It's eleven fifty-two.
8. It's one fifty.
9. It's seven fifteen.
10. It's nine thirty.
11. It's ten o seven.
12. It's six thirty-five.
13. It's three thirty-three.
14. It's twelve forty-five.
15. It's eight thirty-five p.m.

10 Teach other expressions of time (See Expressions of Time at the right of the worksheet.)

o.clock   **quarter after**   **noon**
quarter to   **half past**   **midnight**
quarter of   **a.m. (ante meridiem)**
quarter past   **p.m. (post meridiem)**

11 Repeat the oral and written exercises again using the new expressions of time.

12 Have the students use the second line below each photo to write sentences with the new vocabulary. *(See example in photo number 2.)* Then have the students correct their answers in the same way as the first activity. **Answers:**

1. It's five o'clock.
2. It's twenty after/past eleven.
3. It's six to eleven.
4. It's twenty-eight after/past twelve.
5. It's eleven o'clock.
6. It's twenty-seven after/past seven.
7. It's eight minutes to eleven.
8. It's ten to two.
9. It's fifteen after/past seven.
10. It's half past nine.
11. It's seven after/past ten.
12. It's twenty-five to seven.
13. It's twenty-seven minutes to three.
14. It's a quarter to twelve.
15. It's twenty-five to nine p.m.

ESL Intermediate Level • Relative Pronoun: That • Vocational ESL • Pair Practice • Writing

That • Relative Pronoun

Directions: *Practice the phrases below the photo with another student.*

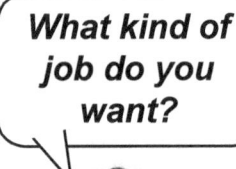

What kind of job do you want?

I want a job that pays well.

Student 1: **What kind of job do you want?**
Student 2: **I want a job that ...**

1. pays well
2. is near my home 
3. provides training 
4. has medical benefits 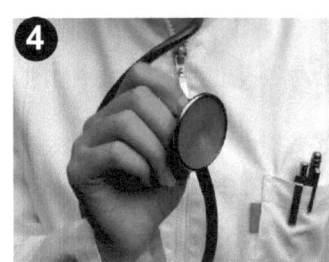 
5. has good working conditions 
6. gives me the chance to advance 
7. has a good work schedule 
8. isn't boring 
9. offers paid vacations 
10. has a good retirement plan 
11. pays for my education 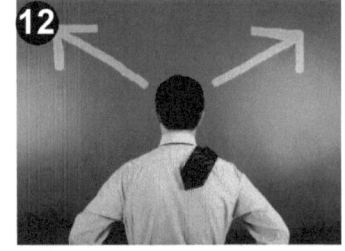
12. allows me to make decisions

Write: *Write sentences with* **that**. *Begin with* **I want a job that ...**
Example: *I want a job that is enjoyable.*

1. _____
2. _____
3. _____
4. _____

229

ESL Intermediate Level • Relative Pronoun: That • Vocational ESL • Pair Practice • Writing

Teacher's Notes

1 Before distributing the worksheet, explain the use of the relative pronoun "**who**" for people and "**that**" for things.

Examples:

2 There are many people **who** need work.

Ella is looking for a job **that** is near her home.

Review the new vocabulary:

3
pays well	**has good working conditions**	**offers paid vacations**
is near my home	**gives me the chance to advance**	**has a bood retirement plan**
provides training	**has a good work schedule**	**pays for my education**
has medical benifits	**isn't boring**	**allows me to make decisions**

Distribute the worksheet. Read the directions with the students and do the **Pair Practice** drill orally in class.

4 Discuss other qualities that a person might look for in a job:

flexible
enjoyable
pays for mileage
pays for holidays

listens to your suggestions
5 **hires helpful employees**

6 Write the new phrases on the chalkboard and repeat the drill using them.

Have the students write three original sentences using **that**. Read the example at the bottom of the page.

Correct the sentences. You may want to project a copy of the handout that has been transferred to an overhead transparency directly onto the chalkboard where students can write their sentences.

7 Follow-Up

Teach that relative pronouns can be used as the subject or object of a sentence, but when we use them as the object, they can be deleted.

Examples:

*The owner is the person **who** you want to see.*

The owner is the person ~~who~~ you want to see.

*This is the job **that** I want.*

This is the job ~~that~~ I want.

230

ESL Beginning Level   Pair Practice • Vocabulary Building • Fill In

To Be: Short Answers
Are you ...? Yes, I am. / No, I'm not.

① Read: *Practice the dialog.*

> Are you a student?
> No, I'm not.
> Are you the teacher?
> No. I'm not.
> Well, what are you?
> I'm a visitor.

② Pair Practice: *Practice the dialog with another student.*

Student 1: *Are you a/an ...?*   **Student 2:** *Yes, I am. / No, I'm not.*

student	 teacher	 man	 woman	 teenager
 minor	 citizen	 immigrant	 tourist	 friend
 kid	 senior citizen	 husband	 wife	 adult
 brother	 sister	 mother	 father	 grand parent

③ Write: *Answer the questions.* Write **Yes, I am.** or **No, I'm not.**

1. Are you a student? ___Yes, I am.___
2. Are you a tourist? ___No, I'm not.___
3. Are you a teacher? _____
4. Are you an adult? _____
5. Are you a citizen? _____
6. Are you a brother? _____
7. Are you a sister? _____
8. Are you a kid? _____
9. Are you a minor? _____
10. Are you an immigrant? _____

231

ESL Beginning Level   Pair Practice • Vocabulary Building • Fill In

Teacher's Notes

1 Before distributing the worksheet, begin the lesson with a conversation to assess your students' knowledge of the terms used for family and community relationships. On the chalkboard list as many terms as you can elicit from your students. Make sure that you include some of the phrases below:

student	*woman*	*senior citizen adult*		*immigrant*
teacher	*teenager*	*husband*	*minor*	*tourist*
man	*kid*	*wife*	*citizen*	*visitor*
brother	*sister*	*mother*	*father*	*grand parent*

2 Distribute the worksheet. Identify the people by reading the word below each photo. Model the pronunciation of the words and have your students repeat them. Next, practice the use of the indefinite article "*a*" and "*an*" with each word. Continue practicing the vocabulary words by writing the article in front of each word and modeling the pronunciation of the article and nouns.

3 Ask questions that elicit short answers. Ask questions such as "*Are you a student?*" Model the response, "*Yes, I am.*" and "*Are you a teacher? No, I'm not.*" Gradually direct students to ask one another question with a similar pattern.

4 Direct the students to the short dialog at the top of the page. Model the questions and responses and have your students repeat them after you. Continue practicing the dialog by having several pairs of students perform for the rest of the students.

5 Have the students continue the activity by having them work in pairs. Walk around the room and monitor their pronunciation especially in using the articles "*a*" or "*an*.")

6 Direct the students to the questions at the bottom of the worksheet. Read the sentences and ask individual students to respond. Then, show how to write the answers using the examples provided. Have the students finish the writing exercise on their own or as a homework assignment.

7 In correcting the exercise, try projecting a copy of the worksheet onto a chalkboard on which the students can write their answers.

Follow-Up Activities:

8 As a student mixer activity, have the students stand up, walk around the room, and ask other students "*Are you a/an ....?*" Allow five minutes for the activity. Then, ask your students to share any information they want to share about their classmates. (For this activity students should be familiar with the use of "*He's ...,*" *She's* ...," and "*They're ....*")

9 As a follow-up exercise, repeat the exercise substituting the vocabulary below:

Professions: *cashier, accountant   , manager, apartment manager, nurse, truck driver, police officer, electrician, engineer , salesperson , student, plumber*

Adjectives: *single, strong, honest, cold, married, friendly, hungry, warm, widowed, smart, thirsty, healthy*

Phrases: *in the class, at home, near the window, from Europe, at school, near the door, from Mexico, at work, at your desk*

10 Repeat the activity by having the students answer with "*Yes, we are.*" or "*No, we aren't.*"

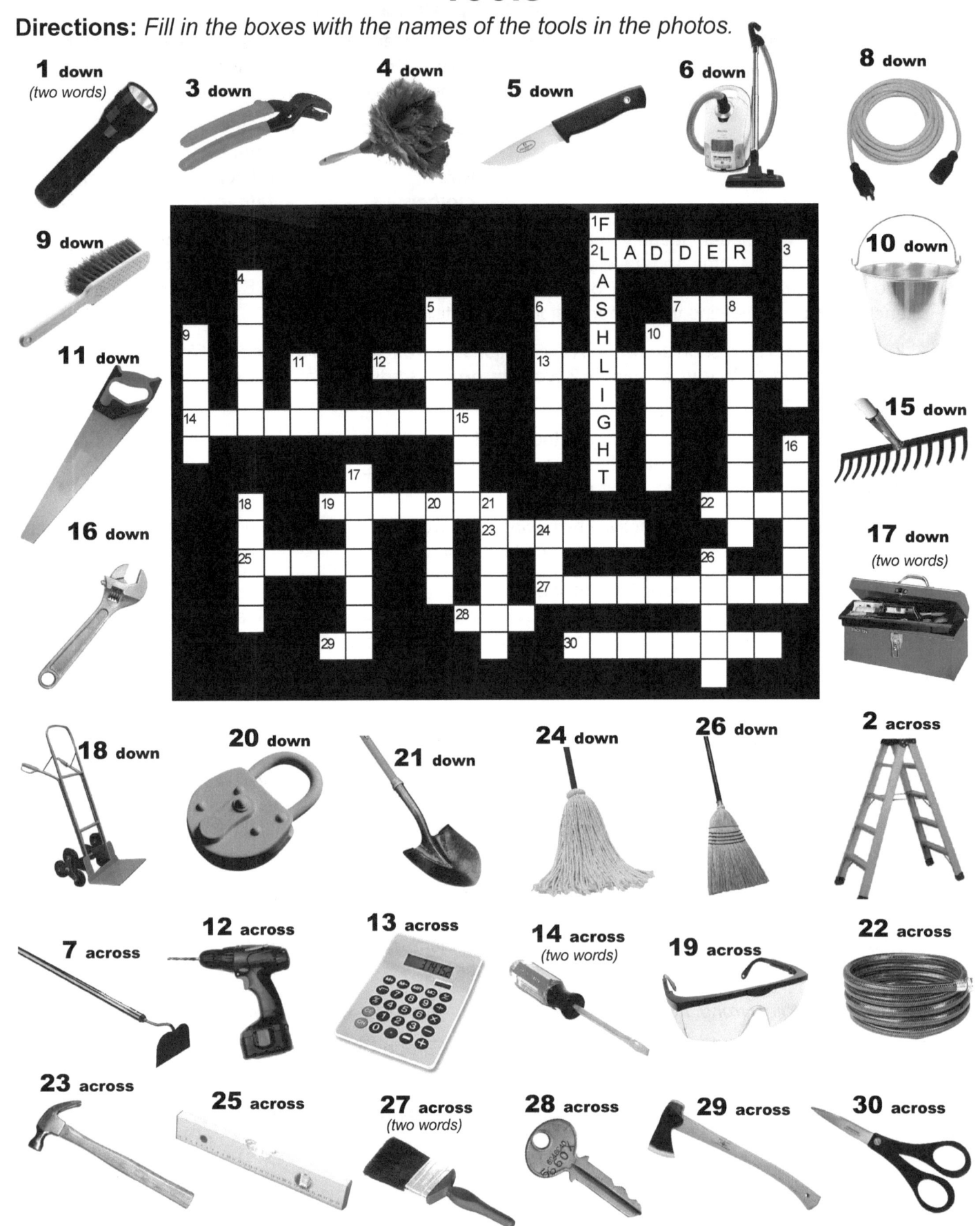

ESL Beginning Level
Crossword Puzzle • Vocabulary Building
Tools

Directions: *Fill in the boxes with the names of the tools in the photos.*

1 down (two words)
3 down
4 down
5 down
6 down
8 down
9 down
10 down
11 down
15 down
16 down
17 down (two words)
18 down
20 down
21 down
24 down
26 down
2 across
7 across
12 across
13 across
14 across (two words)
19 across
22 across
23 across
25 across
27 across (two words)
28 across
29 across
30 across

233

ESL Beginning Level Crossword Puzzle • Vocabulary Building

Teacher's Notes

1 Before distributing the worksheet, begin the lesson with a conversation. Ask your students general questions about common household tools. Ask them to name and describe as many as they can. List them on the board. Make sure that the lists include some of the following items:

ax	calculator	extension cord	hoe	ladder	paint brush	scissors	vacuum
broom	dolly	flash light	hose	level	pliers	screw driver	wrench
brush	drill	goggles	key	lock	rake	shovel	
bucket	duster	hammer	knife	mop	saw	tool box	

2 Distribute the worksheet and identify and discuss each tool. Ask simple questions about their use, shapes, sizes, and any other distinguishing features.

3 Extend this activity by having the students think of as many different gerunds as possible for each item on the worksheet. List the new vocabulary on the board or overhead transparency.

Examples: *A flash light is used for seeing in the dark.*
A broom is used for sweeping.
A lock is used for protecting valuables.
An extension cord is used for connecting a distant electrical item to an outlet.
A shovel is used for digging.
A hose is used for watering.
A dolly is used for moving heavy items.
A ladder is used for climbing.
A calculator is used for adding, subtracting, multiplying, and dividing numbers.

4 Ask the students to think of other tools that they use such as box cutter, dust pan, putty knife, rake, and tape measure. Have your students write the names of the tools on the worksheet. Then, have them explain what the tools are used for. You may want to make an overhead transparency of the handout that can be projected onto the board where students can write the list of tools and their uses.

5 Demonstrate how to do a crossword puzzle. Explain the concept of **DOWN** and **ACROSS**. Then, show the students how to fill in the puzzle using the visual clues. Do a few examples with the whole class.

6 Allow some time for your students to complete the crossword puzzle. You may want to have students work in pairs or assigning it as a homework assignment.

7 Correct the answers by projecting an overhead transparency image directly onto the board on which students can take turns writing the answers on the board. See solution below.

8 Play a crossword puzzle game. Draw or project a grid onto the board or screen as well as a list of the new tools. Divide the class into two teams and flip a coin to determine which team goes first. Have the first student of the first team go to the chalkboard and write a word that uses one letter of an existing word in the crossword. If the word fits and is correctly spelled, then give one point for every letter of the new word. Then, go on to the first student of the other team. If the word is incorrect, erase it and go to the opposite team.

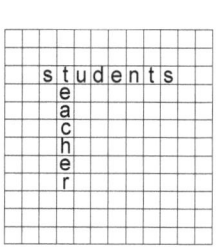

CROSSWORD PUZZLE SOLUTION:

DOWN: 1 flashlight, 3 pliers, 4 duster, 5 knife, 6 vacuum, 8 extension, 9 brush, 10 bucket, 11 saw, 15 rake, 16 wrench, 17 toolbox, 18 dolly, 20 lock, 21 shovel, 24 mop, 26 broom;

ACROSS: 2 ladder, 7 hoe, 12 drill, 13 calculator, 14 screwdriver, 19 goggles, 22 hose, 23 hammer, 25 level, 27 paintbrush, 28 key, 29 ax, 30 scissors

ESL Advanced Level • Should • Group Discussion

Topics for Converstion 1
LAW • EDUCATION • GOVERNMENT • ENVIRONMENT

Law
1. Should people have the right to keep guns at home?
2. Should marijuana be legalized?
3. Should pornography be banned?
4. Should the alcohol drinking age be increased or lowered?
5. Should pit bull dogs be banned?
6. Should abortion be legal?
7. Should adultery be a criminal offense?
8. Should there be capital punishment?

Education
9. Should a university education be free to all?
10. Should English be the only official language in the U.S.?
11. Should there be a world language?
12. Should parents be required to send their children to school?
13. Should religion be taught in school?

Government
14. Should governments spend money exploring outer space?
15. Should everyone be taxes at the same rate?
16. Should illegal immigrants be detained in jails?
17. Will there ever be a world government?
18. Should military service be voluntary?
19. Should governments limit the number of children couples can have?

Environment
20. Are there too many people on this planet?
21. Should the dead be buried or cremated?
22. Is climate change real?

ESL Advanced Level — Should • Group Discussion

Teacher's Notes

1. Distribute the handout to the students.

2. Divide the class into groups of three or four.

3. Tell the students to take turns selecting one of the topics on the handout.

4. Tell them to read their question aloud and lead their group in discussing the question. If a group does not feel comfortable discussing a topic, encourage them to choose another topic. (Each student should lead at least one discussion.)

5. Walk around the classroom and join each group for a few minutes and correct the students pronunciation and grammar. (Do not hover over a group, sit down at eye-level.)

6. During the last twenty minutes of the class, ask volunteers from each group to share which questions their group discussed. (Place important vocabulary and expressions on the board.)

7. Continue this activity by asking the students to come up with original questions. Discuss possible answers with the whole class.

ESL Advanced Level   Group Discussion
Topics for Converstion 2 • Business

1. Are international corporations too big?
2. Is business spying a major problem?
3. Is identity theft a serious problem?
4. Should animals be used in product research?
5. Are we too dependent on computers?
6. Do flexible work schedules work?
7. Should businesses monitor their employee's e-mails?
8. Are CEOs paid too much?
9. Should there be a minimum wage law?
10. Is climate change man-made?
11. Is a 40-hour work week too long?
12. Should business profits be shared with employees?
13. Are you optimistic or pessimistic about the future world economy?
14. Should some office workers be allowed to work at home?
15. Can solar and wind power solve our energy problems?
16. Should internet sales be taxed like other businesses?
17. Do ethics play an important part in business?
18. Are businesses taxed too much?
19. Do environmental laws work?
20. Are cell phones dangerous?
21. Should the retirement age be extended?
22. Do import and export taxes hurt or help businesses?
23. Should governments regulate banks?
24. Should all employees be drug tested?
25. Should marketing companies target children?
26. Should employees belong to unions?
27. Should undocumented immigrants be allowed to work?
28. Should businesses pay for their employees' health care?
29. Should health care be public or private?
30. Should business contribute to their employee's pension plan?

ESL Advanced Level Group Discussion

Teacher's Notes

1 Distribute the handout to the students.

2 Divide the class into groups of three or four.

3 Tell the students to take turns selecting one of the topics on the handout.

4 Tell them to read their question aloud and lead their group in discussing the question. If a group does not feel comfortable discussing a topic, encourage them to choose another topic. (Each student should lead at least one discussion.)

5 Walk around the classroom and join each group for a few minutes and correct the students pronunciation and grammar. (Do not hover over a group, sit down at eye-level.)

6 During the last twenty minutes of the class, ask volunteers from each group to share which questions their group discussed. (Place important vocabulary and expressions on the board.)

7 Continue this activity by asking the students to come up with original questions. Discuss possible answers with the whole class.

ESL Advanced Level — Group Discussion

Topics for Converstion 3 • Personal

1. Are you satisfied with your cell phone company? Why or why not?
2. Have you ever been married? Explain.
3. How can you improve your quality of life here?
4. How different is your living condition here from where you used to live?
5. How do get around the city/town?
6. How do you deal with different cultures?
7. How easy/hard has it been making friends here?
8. How have your eating habits changed since you've been here?
9. How informed are you about what's happening in the world?
10. How often should you be in contact with your family abroad?
11. How will your experience here help shape your future?
12. Tell us something that most people don't know about yourself.
13. What do you like/dislike about your current living conditions?
14. What do you think you'll be doing ten years from now?
15. What is the weirdest thing that has ever happened to you?
16. What is your favorite hobby or pass time?
17. What is/was your favorite subject at school?
18. What surprised you most about this city?
19. What's the best way to get internet connection at home?
20. What's the best way to get money from your country?
21. What's the cheapest way to call your family overseas?
22. What's the longest period of time you've been away from home?
23. Where have you traveled in the world?
24. Who can you talk to if you need personal advice?

ESL Advanced Level Group Discussion

Teacher's Notes

1 Distribute the handout to the students.

2 Divide the class into groups of three or four.

3 Tell the students to take turns selecting one of the topics on the handout.

4 Tell them to read their question aloud and lead their group in discussing the question. If a group does not feel comfortable discussing a topic, encourage them to choose another topic. (Each student should lead at least one discussion.)

5 Walk around the classroom and join each group for a few minutes and correct the students pronunciation and grammar. (Do not hover over a group, sit down at eye-level.)

6 During the last twenty minutes of the class, ask volunteers from each group to share which questions their group discussed. (Place important vocabulary and expressions on the board.)

7 Continue this activity by asking the students to come up with original questions. Discuss possible answers with the whole class.

ESL Beginning & Intermediate Levels • Vocabulary Building • Pair Practice Dictation

Traffic Signs

1 *Fold the page on the dotted line. Look at your side of the worksheet only. Compare your signs after you finish the activity.*

2 *Write the words that your partner reads to you in the blank signs below.*

2 *Read and spell the words on the signs below to your partner.*

Student 1

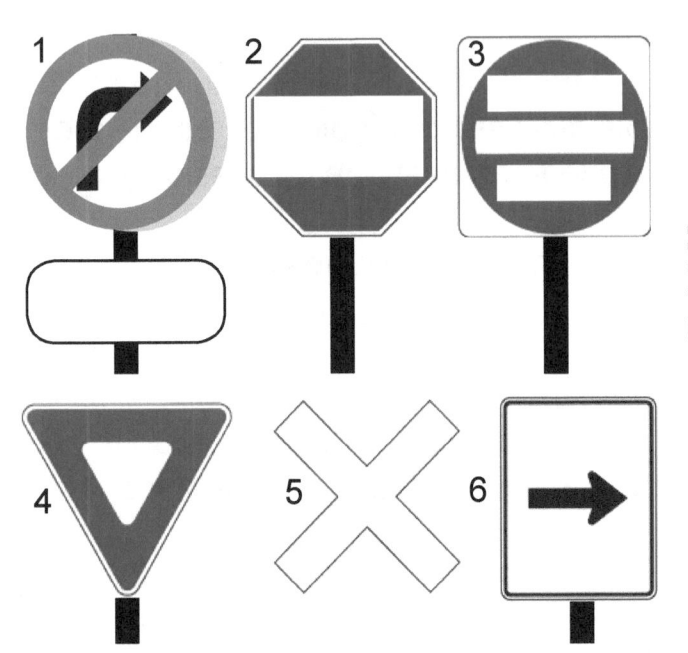

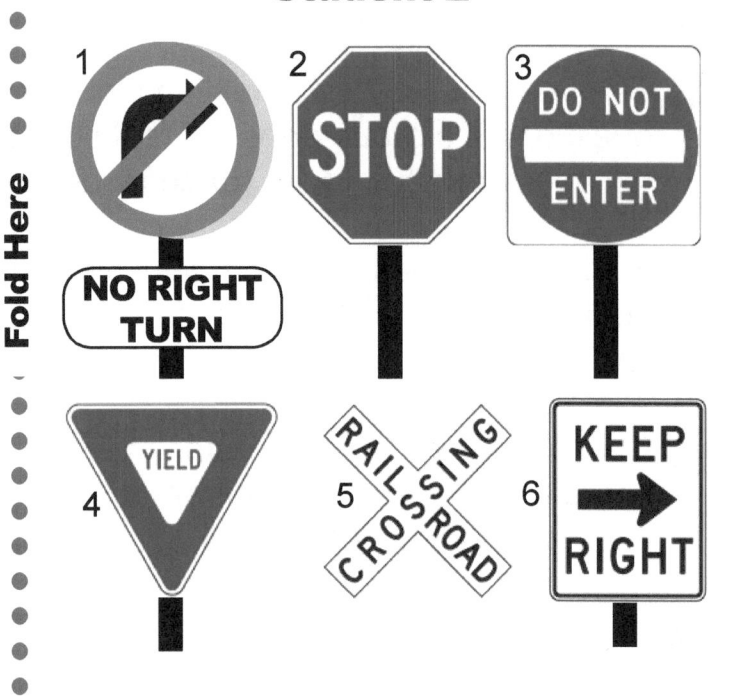

Student 2

Fold Here

3 *Read and spell the words on the signs below to your partner.*

3 *Write the words that your partner reads to you in the blank signs below.*

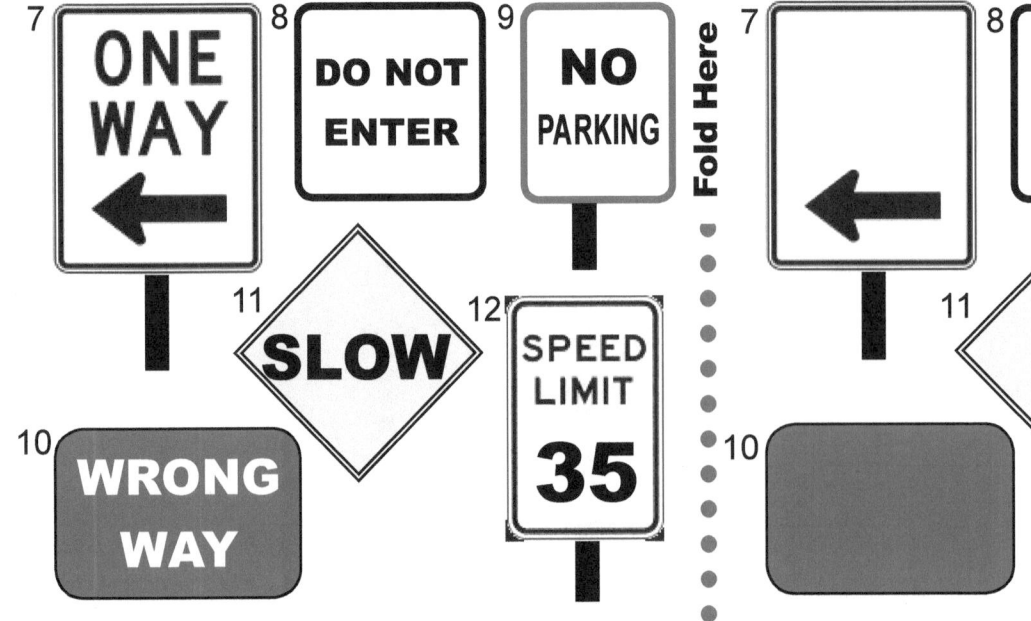

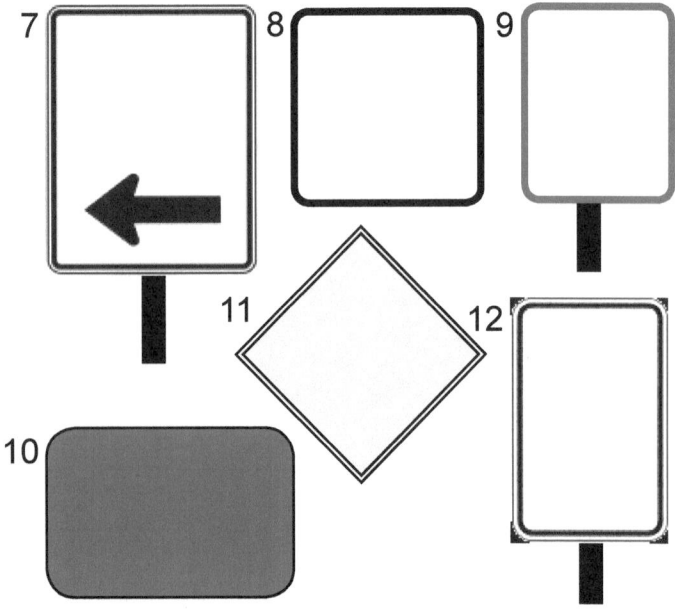

Fold Here

ESL Beginning & Intermediate Levels • Vocabulary Building • Pair Practice Dictation

Teacher's Notes

1 Before distributing the handout, review shapes and meanings of the various traffic signs. (You may wan to contact your local Department of Motor Vehicles for a driver handbook that contains illustrations of all traffic sighs.)

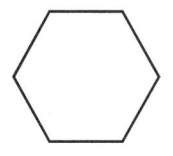

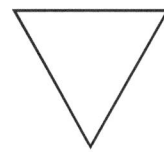

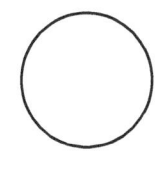

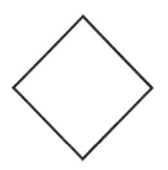

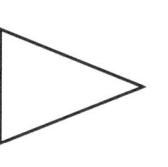

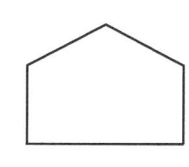

STOP   **YIELD**   **RAILROAD CROSSING**   **WARNING**   **TRAFFIC**   **NO PASSING**   **SCHOOL**

2 Review the colors and their meanings:

    red   = danger, stop   blue   = service
    orange = construction   white = traffic rules
    yellow = general warning   brown = public recreation areas
    green = direction and distance   black = night speed limit

3 On the chalkboard or white board, draw the signs and write their meanings below them. Do repeat and drill exercises for pronunciation. Then, erase the meanings. Divide the class into two teams. Alternately have one member of a team come to the board. Have him/her select a sign and then write the meaning under it. For each correct answer, give one point to the appropriate team. Insist on complete accuracy.

4 Review prepositions of location using **top**, **bottom**, **middle**, **right**, and **left**. *For example,* **top left**, **bottom right**, **middle left***, etc.*

5 Distribute the worksheet. Then, have students fold the page on the dotted line. Tell them to look at their side of their page only. Explain, that the students must fill in the blank signs that their partner describes and dictates. Also, explain that they will have the opportunity to compare pictures after they both finish the exercise.

6 As a follow-up activity, you may want to teach the meanings of other signs:

NO STOPPING ANY TIME	RIGHT LANE MUST TURN RIGHT	DIP
TRUCK ROUTE	BUSSES AND CAR POOLS ONLY	FLOODED
NO PED CROSSING	GAS FOOD LODGING	SLIDE AREA
NO PARKING ANY TIME	NEXT SERVICE 22 MILES	BUMP
SPEED CHECKED BY RADAR	REST AREA	FALLING ROCKS
NO BICYCLES	SOFT SHOULDER	ROUGH ROAD
DO NOT PASS	PAVEMENT ENDS	LOW CLEARANCE
SLOWER TRAFFIC KEEP RIGHT	NARROW BRIDGE	NOT A THROUGH STREET
TOW AWAY ZONE	TUNNEL	DETOUR AHEAD
EMERGENCY PARKING ONLY	PED XING	OPEN TRENCH
PARK PARALLEL	NO OUTLET	FLAGMAN AHEAD
PASSING LANE AHEAD	SLIPPERY WHEN WET	ROAD WORK AHEAD
BEGIN FREEWAY	THUR TRAFFIC MERGE LEFT	BRIDGE OUT
USE CROSSWALK	ISLANDS	ROAD CLOSED
3-WAY SIGNAL	HILL	PREPARE TO STOP

ESL Beginning Level   Crossword Puzzle • Vocabulary Building

Transportation

Directions: *Fill in the boxes with the names of the modes of transportation in the photos.*

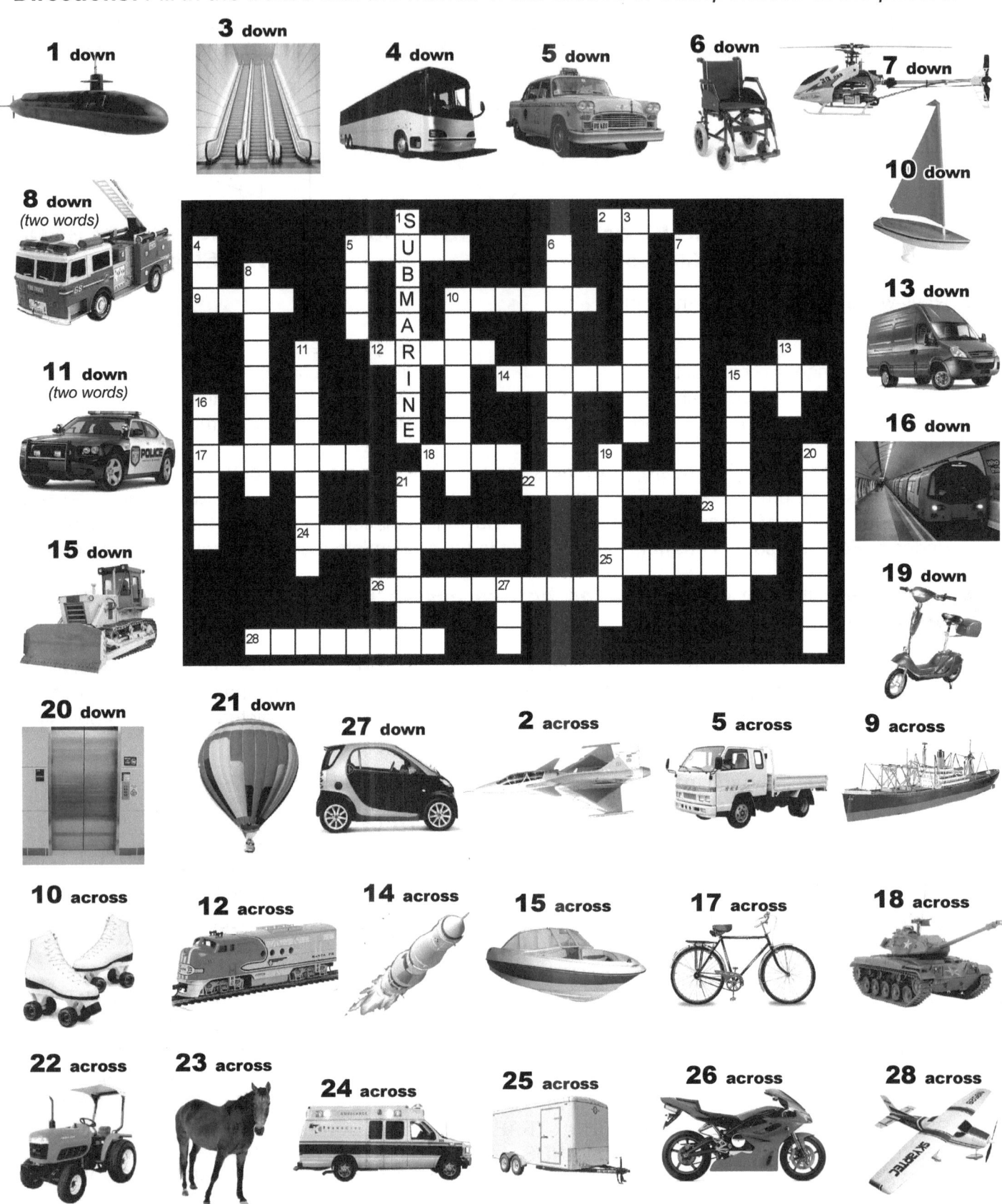

1 down
3 down
4 down
5 down
6 down
7 down
8 down (two words)
10 down
11 down (two words)
13 down
15 down
16 down
19 down
20 down
21 down
27 down
2 across
5 across
9 across
10 across
12 across
14 across
15 across
17 across
18 across
22 across
23 across
24 across
25 across
26 across
28 across

243

ESL Beginning Level · Crossword Puzzle • Vocabulary Building

Teacher's Notes

1 Before distributing the worksheet, begin the lesson with a conversation. Ask your students general questions about different modes of transportation. Ask them to name and describe as many as they can. List them on the board. Make sure that the lists include some of the following items:

airplane	boat	elevator	horse	rocket	skates	taxi	truck
ambulance	bulldozer	escalator	jet	sailboat	submarine	tractor	van
balloon	bus	fire truck	motorcycle	scooter	subway	trailer	wheelchair
bicycle	car	helicopter	police car	ship	tank	train	

2 Distribute the worksheet and identify and discuss each mode of transportation. Ask simple questions about their use, speed, size, and any other distinguishing characteristics. Also discuss the terms for those who operate them. For example, ask questions such as:

Who operates a _____?   *How fast can a _____ go?*
Where can you see a _____?   *Why do we use a _____?*

3 Demonstrate how to do a crossword puzzle. Explain the concept of **DOWN** and **ACROSS**. Then, show the students how to fill in the puzzle using the visual clues. Do a few examples with the whole class.

4 Allow some time for your students to complete the crossword puzzle. You may want to have students work in pairs or assigning it as a homework assignment.

5 Correct the answers by projecting an overhead transparency image directly onto the board on which students can take turns writing the answers on the board. See solution below.

6 Play a crossword puzzle game. Draw or project a grid onto the board or screen as well as a list of the names of the various modes of transportation. Divide the class into two teams and flip a coin to determine which team goes first. Have the first student of the first team go to the board and write a word that uses one letter of an existing word in the crossword. If the word fits and is correctly spelled, then give one point for every letter of the new word. Then, go on to the first student of the other team. If the word is incorrect, erase it and go to the opposite team.

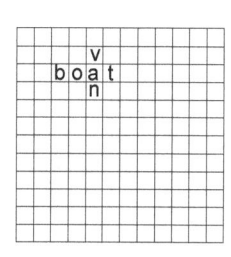

7 As an additional activity, play Tic-Tac-Toe: Draw a Tic-Tac-Toe grid and fill it in with names of modes of transportation. Divide the class into two teams, each team assigned the symbol "X" or "0." Then flip a coin to determine which team begins. Have the students take turns in an orderly fashion by going down the rows. Tell the first student of the first team to use any word from the grid in a sentence. If the sentence is correct, replace the word with the team's symbol (X or 0), otherwise, leave the word. Go on to the first person on the other team. Continue in this manner until one team wins by having three consecutive X's or 0's in a row vertically, horizontally or diagonally. Keep score by giving one point for each game won. After each game, replace all the words in the grid with a different group of animal names each time.

8 Expand the activity by teaching additional vocabulary items such as: *canoe, cruise ship, dump truck, jet fighter, freighter, jet ski, motorboat, sports car, wagon, golf cart, and kayak.*

CROSSWORD PUZZLE SOLUTION:

DOWN: 1 submarine, 3 escalator, 4 bus, 5 taxi, 6 wheelchair, 7 helicopter, 8 fire truck, 10 sailboat, 11 police car, 13 van, 15 bulldozer, 16 subway, 19 scooter, 20 elevator, 21 balloon, 27 car;

ACROSS: 2 jet, 5 truck, 9 ship, 10 skates, 12 train, 14 rocket, 15 boat, 17 bicycle, 18 tank, 22 tractor, 23 horse, 24 ambulance, 25 trailer, 26 motorcycle, 28 airplane

ESL Advanced Level
Game • Group Discussion
Trivia 1 Game Questions and Answers

1. How long is a round in boxing? (3 minutes)
2. How many colors are there in a rainbow? There are seven colors: red, orange, yellow, green, blue, indigo, and violet.--Wikipedia
3. How many lanes does an Olympic swimming pool have? (8)
4. How many legs does a spider have? (8)
5. How many players are there on a volleyball team? (6)
6. In what language does "*obrigado*" mean "thank you?" (Portuguese)
7. In which city is Hollywood? (Los Angeles)
8. What are the first three words of the bible? (In the beginning...)
9. What are the five colors of the Olympic rings and what do they symbolize? The colors are red, yellow, green, blue, and black. They symbolize the continents.
10. What colors make purple? (red and blue)
11. What do you use to take a cork out of a bottle? (a corkscrew)
12. What horoscope sign has a crab? (Cancer)
13. What is the capital of Australia? (Canberra)
14. What is the first letter on a keyboard? (Q)
15. What country has the largest population? (China)
16. What money do they use in Japan? (Yen)
17. What's the biggest country in the world? (Russia)
18. What year did Christopher Columbus go to America? (1492)
19. What's the capital of Brazil? (Brasilia)
20. What's the capital of Finland? (Helsinki)
21. What's the capital of Ecuador? (Quito)
22. What's the world's longest river? (Nile)
23. On what continent is Cameroon? (Africa)
24. What's the capital of Kenya? (Nairobi?
25. What's the hardest rock? (Diamond)
26. What's the highest mountain in Africa? (Kilimanjaro)
27. What's the highest mountain in the world? (Everest)
28. What's the largest city in India? (Bombay)
29. What's the most important book in the Muslim religion? (Koran)
30. What's the name of the famous big clock in London? (Big Ben)
31. What's the real name of Siddartha Gautama? (Buddha)
32. What's the smallest country in the world? (Vatican City)
33. When did the first man go into space? (1961)
34. When did the First World War start? (1914)
35. When did the Second World War end? (1945)
36. Where does the American president live? (The White House)
37. Where is the smallest bone in the body? (Ear)
38. Where was Christopher Columbus born? (Genoa, Italy)
39. Which fast food restaurants were established by Ray Kroc? (McDonald's)
40. Which is the largest ocean? (Pacific)
41. Which is the most spoken language? (Chinese)
42. Which is the only mammal that can't jump? (Elephant)
43. Which is the smallest ocean? (Arctic)
44. Which planet is nearest the sun? (Mercury)
45. Which river goes through London? (Thames)
46. What state is known as the "Golden State?" (California)
47. What does "D.C." mean in Washington, D.C.? (District of Columbia)
48. Who gave his name to the month of July? (Julius Caesar)
49. Who invented the electric light bulb? (Thomas Edison)
50. Who invented the telephone? (Bell)
51. Who painted the Mona Lisa? (Da Vinci)
52. Who said E=mc2 (Einstein)
53. Who said, "I think, therefore I am"? (Descartes)
54. Who said, "Vini, vidi, vici"? (Caesar)
55. Who starts first in chess? (White)
56. Who was the first man in space? (Gagarin)
57. Who was the first man on the moon? (Neil Armstrong)
58. Who was the first president of the United States? (Washington)
59. Who is Mickey Mouse's girlfriend? (Minnie Mouse)
60. What is the biggest city in the United States? (New York)

ESL Advanced Level   Game • Group Discussion

Teacher's Notes

❶ Divide the class into three or four groups.

❷ Ask them to choose a name for their team.

❸ Write the names on the board.

❹ Read a trivia question aloud twice.

❺ Let the students to discuss the question and a possible answer.

❻ Have each group choose a spokesperson to give the answer.

❼ Ask each group for their answer. If the answer is correct that group gets a point. Mark it on the board under each team chosen name.

❽ At the end of the activity add up the points.

❾ Have everybody stand up and give the winning team a round of applause.

❿ Distribute a copy of the handout containing the list of all the trivia questions.

ESL Advanced Level
Game • Group Discussion
Trivia 2 Game Questions and Answers

1. Where is the lowest point of the western hemisphere? Death Valley, California
2. What Canadian province divides Alaska from the rest of the USA? British Columbia
3. In what state is Chicago? Illinois
4. In which Canadian province is French the official language? Quebec
5. In which state is the Grand Canyon? Arizona
6. Which state has the highest island mountain?
7. Hawaii - Mauna Kea 4,205 m (13,796 ft)
8. What is the capital of California? Sacramento
9. What is the smallest state in size? Rhode Island
10. Which state has the smallest population? Wyoming population: 568,000
11. Who became the first US President to resign in office? Richard Nixon
12. What do the stripes on the American flag symbolize?
13. The 13 original colonies
14. On August 18, 1920 who got the right to vote? Women
15. Where is the Silicon Valley? Santa Clara County and San Jose, CA
16. What does the US motto "E Pluribus Unum" mean? Out of Many, One
17. What is the second most popular sport in the world? Cricket
18. Whose picture is on a one hundred dollar bill? Benjamin Franklin
19. On the bottom of the US seal is MDCCLXXVI? What does it mean? 1776, the year the USA declared its independence from England
20. The Statue of Liberty in New York harbor was a gift from what country? France
21. What is the supreme law of the United States? The Constitution
22. What are the two parts of the U.S. Congress? The Senate and House of Representatives
23. How many U.S. Senators are there? 100, two from each state
24. In what month do Americans vote for their president? The first Tuesday in November
25. What is the name of the Vice President of the United States now? Joe Biden
26. What title does the wife of the president have? First lady
27. What are the three branches of the US government? Executive (President), Judicial (Supreme Court), and Legislative (Senate and the House of Representatives)
28. What is the former name for Istanbul, Turkey? Constantinople
29. Who is the current governor of California? Governor Jerry Brown
30. How old do US citizens have to be to vote? 18 years old
31. Where is the city of Washington located? In the District of Columbia
32. In what year was slavery abolished in the United States? 1863
33. What did the USA purchase from Russia for $7,200,000 in 1887? Alaska
34. Where would you go to see the Coliseum? Rome
35. Where would you go to see the Parathion? Athens, Greece
36. Where would you go to see the Taj Mahal? India
37. Where would you go to see Mount Kilimanjaro? Kenya, Africa
38. Where would you go to see the Stonehenge? England
39. Where would you go to see the Leaning Tower? Pisa, Italy
40. Which animal has the most neck bones? A swan
41. What country does tennis come from? France
42. What is the largest city in Europe? Moscow
43. What is the tallest tree found in North America? Sequoia, Redwood
44. Who was America named after? A map maker, Amarigo Vespucci, from Italy (1451-1512)
45. What is the world's largest city? Tokyo with 34,700,000 people
46. What country was the first to give women the right to vote? New Zealand in 1893
47. On a pair of dice how many spots are there in total? 21 in total
48. Where can we find the Dome of The Rock? Jerusalem, The oldest Muslim building which has remained intact in its original form
49. Where can we find the Sistine Chapel? In the Vatican, Rome
50. What is the chemical symbol for gold? Ag
51. Oscar De La Hoya is known for which sport? Boxing
52. What is the largest group of animals? Insects - There are about 900 thousand known species of insects, and that's more than all the other species combined.
53. What is the world's most expensive spice? Saffron - It's harvested by hand, from the saffron crocus.
54. In Greek mythology Poseidon is the god of what? The sea
55. Besides humans what is the most intelligent animal in the world? Chimpanzee
56. What country has no rivers? Saudi Arabia
57. What substance can melt a pearl? Vinegar
58. What animal lays the largest eggs in the world? Ostrich
59. What kind of mosquito does not bite? Males
60. The largest eyes belong to what animal? Giant squid
61. What common food can dogs die from? Chocolate
62. What do the stars on the US flag represents? The 50 states
63. What is the population of the City of Los Angeles? City: 3,800,000 (County: 9,830,000)
64. Which state has the largest population? California population: 37,000,000
65. What's the capital of Denmark? Copenhagen
66. Where is the deepest point in the ocean? Mariana trench
67. Who said "If you give me a lever and a place to stand I can move the world." Archimedes
68. What is the longest river in China? The Yangtze River (3,720 mi or 5,263 km)
69. What is the most famous landmark in Moscow? Red Square
70. What is the largest rain forest in South America? Amazon
71. How do you say "yes" and "no" in Russian? "Nyet" and "Da"
72. Which two countries share the Iberian Peninsula? Spain and Portugal
73. Which is the lowest point on Earth? The Dead Sea
74. Name a famous Egyptian queen. Cleopatra
75. Who wrote "Hamlet?" William Shakespeare
76. How many teeth do humans have? 32
77. Name the planets of the solar system? Mercury, Venus, Earth, Mars, Jupiter, Saturn, Uranus, and Neptune (Pluto was taken off the list in 2006.)
78. How many kilometers separate Russian from the USA? 86 kilometers (53.44 miles)

ESL Advanced Level																														Game • Group Discussion

Teacher's Notes

❶ Divide the class into three or four groups.

❷ Ask them to choose a name for their team.

❸ Write the names on the board.

❹ Read a trivia question aloud twice.

❺ Let the students to discuss the question and a possible answer.

❻ Have each group choose a spokesperson to give the answer.

❼ Ask each group for their answer. If the answer is correct that group gets a point. Mark it on the board under each team chosen name.

❽ At the end of the activity add up the points.

❾ Have everybody stand up and give the winning team a round of applause.

❿ Distribute a copy of the handout containing the list of all the trivia questions.

ESL Advanced Level — Group Discussion

Trends: Current and Future

trend: *definition* - a general direction in which something tends to move

Discuss some of the following trends and their implications for the future.

1. hair styles
2. cigarette smoking
3. renewable energy
4. university costs
5. use of technology
6. cost /standard of living
7. personal liberty/freedom
8. employment opportunities
9. entertainment choices
10. climate change
11. life expectancy
12. clothes and fashion
13. food production
14. social networking
15. family size
16. gas and energy prices
17. genetic engineering
18. global economy
19. personal security
20. robots
21. housing costs
22. human rights
23. amount of personal privacy
24. income disparity
25. interest rates
26. interior design
27. internet use
28. life expectancy
29. curing diseases
30. availability of health care
31. shopping
32. news coverage
33. pace of life
34. parties and celebrations
35. kinds of personal relationships
36. political views
37. population growth
38. racial and ethnic harmony
39. real estate prices
40. recreational activities
41. religious beliefs
42. stock market growth
43. acceptance of homosexuality
44. surveillance
45. tattoos
46. terrorism
47. tourism
48. modes of transportation
49. use of marijuana
50. war

ESL Advanced Level Group Discussion

Teacher's Notes

1 Start the lesson with a question: Why Study Trends?

Explain that trends mean change, and change will influence our future.

Discuss a few truths about change:
- Change is inevitable.
- Change is continual.
- Change shapes our professional and personal lives.
- Change rearranges the world around us.
- Change begins and ends opportunities.
- Change helps us spot many hidden opportunities.
- Change can be uncomfortable.
- Most people don't like change.
- Evolve by embracing change.

Discuss what to consider when studying trends:
- Avoid studying fads, whims, and crazes.
- Look for patterns.
- Trends are long term.
- Continually evaluate how trends will impact your life.

2 Distribute the handout to the students.

3 Divide the class into groups of three or four.

4 Tell the students to take turns selecting one of the topics on the handout.

5 Tell them to read their topic aloud and lead their group in discussing it. If a group does not feel comfortable discussing a topic, encourage them to choose another topic. (Each student should lead at least one discussion.)

6 Walk around the classroom and join each group for a few minutes and correct the students pronunciation and grammar. (Do not hover over a group, sit down at eye-level.)

7 During the last twenty minutes of the class, ask volunteers from each group to share which topics their group discussed. (Place important vocabulary and expressions on the board.)

8 Continue this activity by asking the students to come up with additional topics. Discuss possible answers with the whole class.

ESL Intermediate & Advanced Levels • Values Clarification • Discussion • Role Playing

Understanding Directions

1 *Read the situation below.*

THE SITUATION

Your boss needs a letter in an hour and tells you to type it in a certain way, but you don't understand her directions. You ask her to repeat the directions, but you still don't understand. What should you do?

2 *Read the possible solutions to the problem above. Rank the solutions in order from the best to the worst. (The top box is the best and bottom box is the worst.) Write your ranking in the column* **MY RANKING** *to the left below. Please feel free to come up with other practical solutions.*

MY RANKING ←—BEST   WORST—→

POSSIBLE SOLUTIONS

1. Ask a co-worker to type the letter for you.

2. Type the letter the way you usually do it even if it is wrong.

3. Do not type the letter.

4. Ask your boss again specifically how to do it and ask questions if you are not sure.

5. Pretend that you did not hear your boss's request.

6. Tell the boss that you are too busy and that she should ask another person to type the letter.

7. (Other)

_____
_____

GROUP RANKING ←—BEST   WORST—→

3 *Break up into small groups and discuss your ranking with the rankings of the other members in your group. Feel free to discuss other practical possibilities. Finally, decide on a group ranking. Again, rank the possible solutions in order from the best to the worst. All members of the group must agree before you write the numbers in the column* **GROUP RANKING**.

4 *As a whole class, discuss the best and worst solutions to the situation.*

251

ESL Intermediate & Advanced Levels • Values Clarification • Discussion • Role Playing

INTRODUCTION

These lessons are appropriate for students in English-as-a-Second-Language (ESL) and Vocational ESL classes as well as for native English speakers entering the work force. The goal of this book is to help people make ethical decisions in the work place. Each lesson presents a commonly-found work situation that requires discussing and clarifying individual and group values. These lessons are not meant to provide a right or wrong response to a decision. They are only a means to clarify an individual's or a group's choices in making an ethically-based decision. Instead of a right or wrong answer, the decision made about a specific situation might be a question between different views of what is right. The lessons help the participants explore the different reasons for their views. Instead of asking the participants to make generalized decisions about ethical questions, the lessons present specific situations in which a variety of good decisions can be made. Some participants may disagree among different versions of what appears right. Participants are encouraged to discuss different perspectives, values, and actions to the same situation. Also be aware that our actions also tend to rely on our experiences, social status, culture, and assumptions. Hopefully, the participants will respond to each other with respect and increase mutual recognition of each other as persons who want to do the right thing.

TEACHING NOTES

1. Before distributing the handout, read the situation and ask basic comprehension questions to check for understanding.

2. Distribute the worksheet to the student, and read the situation to the class. Discuss any unfamiliar vocabulary and expressions.

3. Read the possible solutions to the problem. Again, discuss any unfamiliar vocabulary and ask basic questions to check for understanding. Tell the students that they are free to come up with other practical possibilities in addition to the ones presented.

4. Direct the students to rank the possibilities in order from the best solution to the worst, the best being the box at the top and the worst at the bottom. Have the students prioritize their personal ranking in the column named "**MY RANKING**."

5. Then, gather in groups of four or five students.

6. Tell each group of students to discuss their ranking. Instruct them that they must come up with a single ranking that they must all agree on. Identify one person in each group to record the group's ranking in the column labeled "**GROUP RANKING**." Tell students to talk about what should be done, state the other practical possibilities, and ask about the reasons that support these proposals: observations, values, and assumptions.

7. Have each group report on its ranking to the whole class. You may also want to write the various rankings on the blackboard/whiteboard or overhead transparency for comparison.

8. Discuss other possible solutions with the students and write them on the chalkboard.

8. Finally discuss the pros and cons of each ranking, and lead the class in coming to a general consensus.

9. Write other possible solutions to the problems --on the blackboard as a follow-up exercise.

10. As a follow-up activity, use the exercises as a basis for role playing. When doing a role playing exercise, allow students to .prepare themselves in pairs or small groups before having them perform before the whole class. Give the students the freedom to vary the situation and be creative. Don't over-correct. Note major mistakes; discuss and correct them later. To practice active listening, have the other students in the class note the errors, too. Discuss the role-playing exercises afterwards for students' reaction and interpretations.

ESL Advanced Level　　　Information Search • Discussion • Writing

Using The Library, Internet, or New Media

Directions: *Find and write the answers to the questions below. Also write the source you used or how you to found the information. There are 100 possible points.*

1 *Who was the 16th president of the United States?*
Answer: _____
Source _____ **10** points

2 *How is the word "psyche" pronounced?*
Answer: _____
Source _____ **5** points

3 *What year did the Internet start?*
Answer: _____
Source _____ **15** points

4 *What is the population of your town or city?*
Answer: _____
Source _____ **5** points

5 *What year did the country of Cameroon become independent?*
Answer: _____
Source _____ **10** points

6 *What is the telephone number of your local police station?*
Answer: _____
Source _____ **5** points

7 *What time will sunrise and sunset be tomorrow?*
Answer:　Sunrise: _____　Sunset: _____
Source _____ **10** points

8 *What is the time difference betwen Tokyo and your city?*
Answer: _____
Source _____ **10** points

9 *What is an oenophile?*
Answer: _____
Source _____ **5** points

10 *What countries border Brazil?*
Answer: _____
Source _____ **10** points

11 *What does Wikipedia do?*
Answer: _____
Source _____ **5** points

12 *What is another word for "plethora?"*
Answer: _____
Source _____ **10** points

Total Points: _____ points

ESL Advanced Level Information Search • Discussion • Writing

Teacher's Notes

1 This exercise uses a scavenger hunt type of game as a learning tool. The objective of this activity is to allow students to visit, use, and explore a library in addition to the Internet and other news media such as a newspaper.

2 Contact the school or city librarian and arrange a time for your class to visit the library, preferably when no other students are there. If no library is available you may want to bring some reference materials into the classroom: an encyclopedia, an atlas, a dictionary, a newspaper, a telephone book, a thesaurus, an almanac, a computer, and cell phone. While it is possible to do the exercise this way, it is more involved than visiting a library.

The Activity

3 While in the library, hand out the worksheet and read the directions and all the questions making sure that the students completely understand all the vocabulary and know what to do. Show the location of the reference materials, the card catalog, magazine and newspaper section, reference area, computer lab, etc.

4 Tell the students that they have 45 minutes to find all the information and write their answers on the worksheet.

5 Explain that the person or team who gets the most points will win a prize (e. g., a book, a dictionary, or even a piece of candy). If there is limited time, consider allowing students to work in teams. In case of a tie, flip a coin or choose the neatest paper to determine the winner.

During the activity, the teacher should act as a consultant who may give clues, but no answers. The teacher should also provide hints to direct students to the correct resources.

6 After the time is up, assemble the class, have students exchange papers, and correct the activity. Applaud the winner and present the prize. **Answers:**

1. Abraham Lincoln *(Sources will vary.)*
2. SI-Kee *(Source: Dictionary)*
3. 1882 *(Source: Wikipedia)*
4. Answers will vary. *(Source: U.S. Census Bureau)*
5. 1960 *(Sources will vary.)*
6. Answers will vary. *(Source: Telephone Directory)*
7. Answers will vary. *(Source: Newspaper)*
8. Answers will vary. *(Sources will vary.)*
9. A connoisseur of wine. *(Source: Dictionary)*
10. Colombia, Venezuela, Guyana, Suriname, French Guyana, Uruguay, Argentina, Paraguay, Bolivia, and Peru.
11. Wikipedia is an online encyclopedia.
12. Overabundance, excess, glut, surplus (Source: Thesaurus)

7 **Follow-up Activity**

• Hand out blank index cards.

• Ask students to write a question on one side of a white index card and write the answer and the source in which it was found on the back of the card. Have the students write their names on the card.

• Collect the cards and use them as the basis of a game. Divide the class into two teams. Teams take turns answering the questions and telling where the information can be found. If a student is asked his or her own question, pass to the next question. If the answer is correct, the team collects a point. The team with the most points wins.

ESL Beginning Level — Crossword Puzzle • Vocabulary Building

Vegetables

Directions: *Fill in the boxes with the names of vegetables in the photos.*

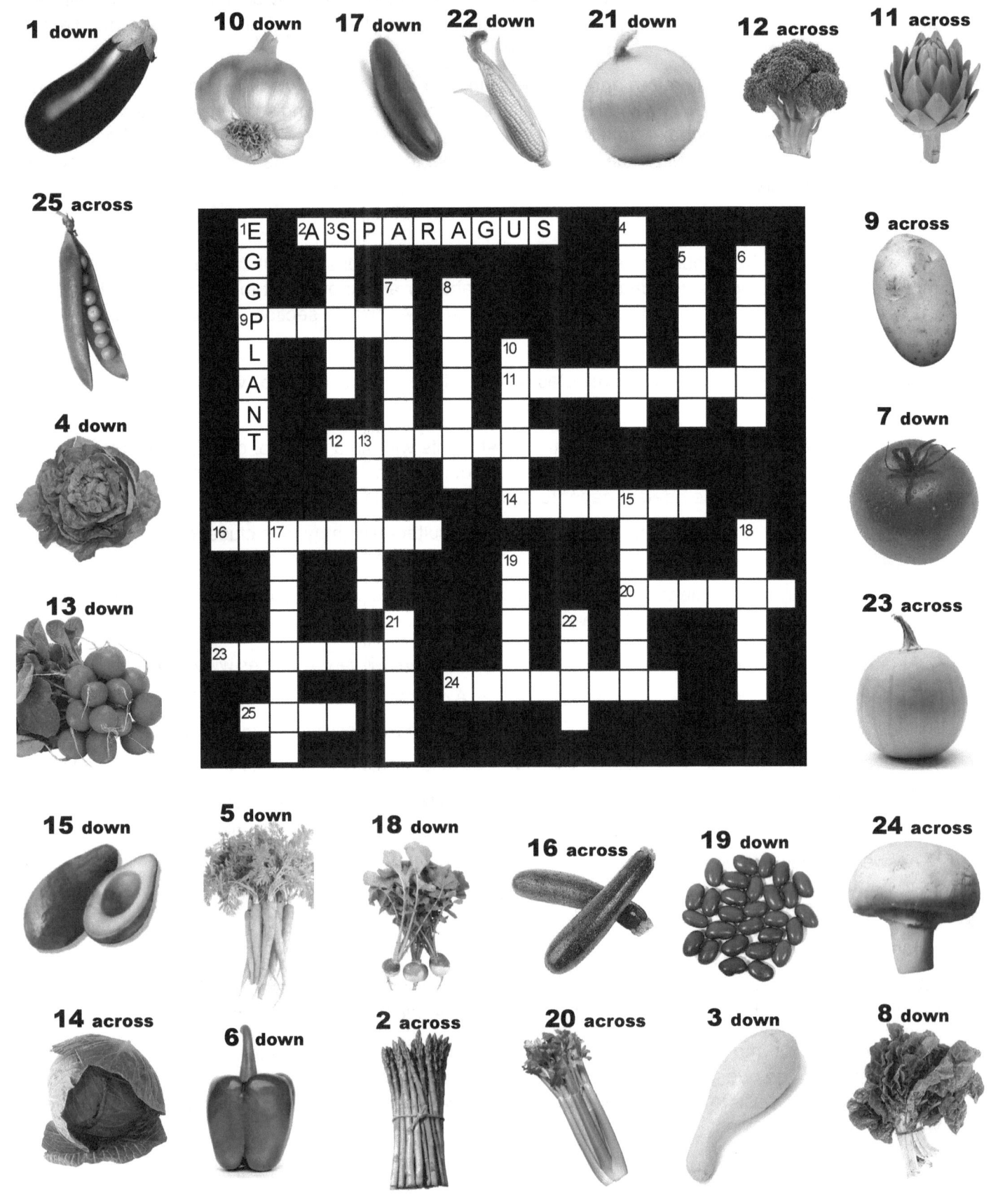

1 down
10 down
17 down
22 down
21 down
12 across
11 across

25 across
9 across

4 down
7 down

13 down
23 across

15 down
5 down
18 down
16 across
19 down
24 across

14 across
6 down
2 across
20 across
3 down
8 down

255

ESL Beginning Level   Crossword Puzzle • Vocabulary Building

Teacher's Notes

1 Before distributing the worksheet, ask the students general questions about vegetables such as which ones they eat at home. Ask them to name and describe as many as they can and list them on the chalkboard or whiteboard. Make sure that the lists include the following vegetables.

Artichoke	Beet	Corn	Mushroom	Radish	Turnips
Avocado	Cauliflower	Cucumber	Onion	Spinach	Zucchini
Asparagus	Cabbage	Eggplant	Pepper	Squash	
Broccoli	Carrot	Garlic	Potato	Peas	
Bean	Celery	Lettuce	Pumpkin	Tomato	

2 Distribute the worksheet and identify and discuss each vegetable. Ask simple questions about their shapes, sizes, colors, and tastes.

3 Demonstrate how to do a crossword puzzle. Explain the concept of **DOWN** and **ACROSS**. Then, show the students how to fill in the puzzle using the visual clues. Do a few examples with the whole class.

4 Correct the answers by projecting an overhead transparency image directly onto the board on which students can write the answers. See solution below. Consider giving this worksheet as a homework assignment.

5 Encourage the students to think of as many other vegetables that they can name, especially those from other cultures. Make a list on the chalkboard or whiteboard. You may want to list some common vegetables not listed in the crossword puzzle.

Beets	Chickpeas	Garbanzo	Leeks	Radicchio	Watercress
Bok Choy	Chili Peppers	Beans	Lima Beans	Red Cabbage	Yams
Brussel	Collard	Green beans	Okra	Rhubarb	
Sprouts	Greens	Jicama	Parsley	Rutabagas	
Cauliflower	Endive	Kale	Parsnips	Sweet Potato	

6 Play a crossword puzzle game. Draw or project a grid onto the chalkboard or whiteboard as well as a list of vegetable names. Divide the class into two teams and flip a coin to determine which team goes first. Have the first student of the first team go to the chalkboard and write a word that uses one letter of an existing word in the crossword. If the word fits and is correctly spelled, then give one point for every letter of the new word. Then, go on to the first student of the other team. If the word is incorrect, erase it and go to the opposite team.

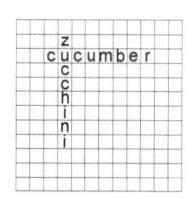

7 As an additional activity, play Tic-tac-toe: Draw a Tic-Tac-Toe grid and fill it in with the names of vegetables. Divide the class into two teams, each team assigned the symbol "X" or "0." Then flip a coin to determine which team begins. Have the students take turns in an orderly fashion by going down the rows. Tell the first student of the first team to use any word from the grid in a sentence. If the sentence is correct, replace the word with the team's symbol (X or 0), otherwise, leave the word. Go on to the first person on the other team. Continue in this manner until one team wins by having three consecutive X's or 0's in a row vertically, horizontally or diagonally. Keep score by giving one point for each game won. After each game, replace all the words in the grid with a different group of vegetable names each time.

CROSSWORD PUZZLE SOLUTION:

ACROSS: 2 asparagus, 9 potato, 11 artichoke, 12 broccoli, 14 cabbage, 16 zucchini, 20 celery, 23 pumpkin, 24 mushroom, 25 peas;

DOWN: 1 eggplant, 3 squash, 4 lettuce, 5 carrot, 6 pepper, 7 tomato, 8 spinach, 10 garlic, 13 radish, 15 avocado, 17 cucumber, 18 turnip, 19 beans, 21 onion, 22 corn

ESL Beginning Level Infinitive • Vocabulary Building

Want & Want to

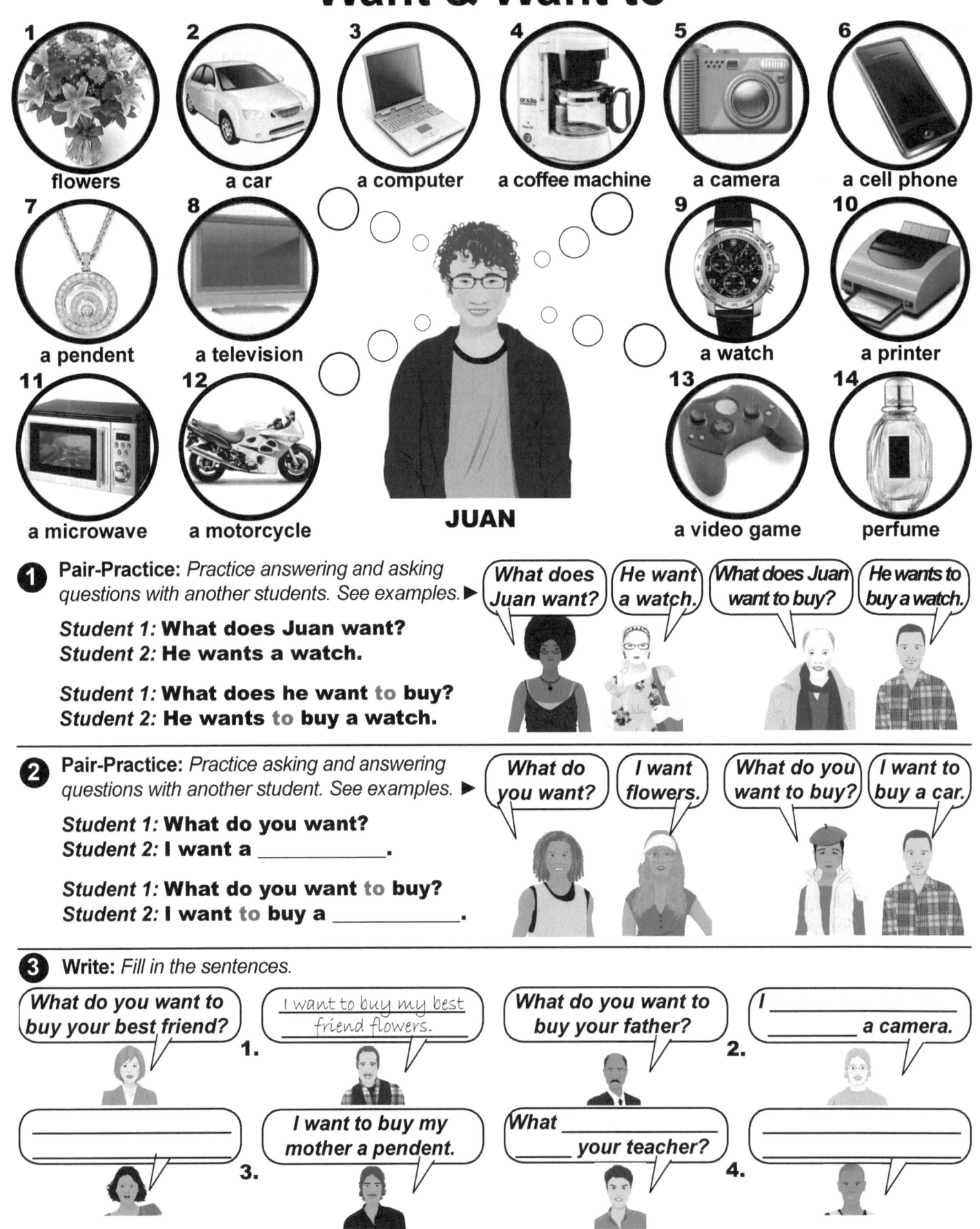

1. flowers
2. a car
3. a computer
4. a coffee machine
5. a camera
6. a cell phone
7. a pendent
8. a television
9. a watch
10. a printer
11. a microwave
12. a motorcycle
13. a video game
14. perfume

JUAN

1 **Pair-Practice:** *Practice answering and asking questions with another students. See examples.* ▶

What does Juan want? / He want a watch. / What does Juan want to buy? / He wants to buy a watch.

Student 1: **What does Juan want?**
Student 2: **He wants a watch.**

Student 1: **What does he want to buy?**
Student 2: **He wants to buy a watch.**

2 **Pair-Practice:** *Practice asking and answering questions with another student. See examples.* ▶

What do you want? / I want flowers. / What do you want to buy? / I want to buy a car.

Student 1: **What do you want?**
Student 2: **I want a _____.**

Student 1: **What do you want to buy?**
Student 2: **I want to buy a _____.**

3 **Write:** *Fill in the sentences.*

What do you want to buy your best friend?

I want to buy my best friend flowers.
1.

What do you want to buy your father?

I _____ a camera.
2.

_____

I want to buy my mother a pendent.
3.

What _____ your teacher?

_____
4.

257

ESL Beginning Level Infinitive • Vocabulary Building

Teacher's Notes

1 Before distributing the worksheet, begin the lesson with a conversation about common gifts. Ask general questions to determine how many gift items the students can already name. Make a list on the chalkboard or whiteboard. Be sure to include the following items: ***car, television (TV), a motorcycle, a cell phone, a computer, a microwave oven, a computer printer, a coffee maker, a watch, a pendent, flowers, a video game.***

2 Distribute the worksheet. Introduce the vocabulary and pronounce the names of the items below each photo with the whole class. Introduce the structure by asking yes/no questions such as *"Do you want a car?"* Model the response, *"Yes, I do."* or *"No, I don't."* Continue posing questions to individual students. Expand the activity by having an individual students ask *"What do you want?"* to another student who must supply an appropriate answer.

3 Use the same methodology above to introduce **"want to"** in the question, *"What does Juan want to buy?"* and *"What do you want to buy?"* (Note: In rapid conversation, the pronunciation of **"want to"** is **"wanna."** Students should at least have a passive recognition of this form.)

4 Alternately ask students questions contrasting **"want"** and **"want to buy."**

5 With the help of your students, make a list on the chalkboard or whiteboard of holidays and special occasions when gifts are given. This list might include birthdays, weddings, anniversaries, religions holidays, Mother's Day, Father's Day, births, baby showers, going-away parties, retirement parties, and other holidays specific to the native or resident country of the students.

6 Ask the question, *"What does Juan want to buy for his father's birthday?"* or *"What does Juan want to buy his father for his birthday?"* (Point out the use of the **'s** for singular possessives and **s'** for plural possessives.)

7 Have one student ask another student a similar question using a holiday or occasion. The second student should supply an appropriate answer. Encourage students to continue the exercise by expanding the list to include original answers. Drill the question, *"What present/gift do you want to buy for your...?"* with the following vocabulary: ***brother, friend, mother, father, sister, husband, wife, children, grandparents,*** and ***teacher***.

8 Review the sentences in the balloons in Exercise 3 at the bottom of the page and explain how to fill in the missing words in the questions and answers. Encourage students to continue the activity by providing original sentences, which can be written on the board.

FOLLOW-UP ACTIVITIES

9 Drill the use of **"to"** as part of the infinitive with **"like to," "need to,"** and **"hope to."**

ESL Beginning and Intermediate Levels • Emotions • Pair Practice • Writing

Was & Were

1 *Read the names and phrases below the photos.*

the robbery

#	Name	Emotion	Place
1	Cat	Afraid	at home
2	Jasmine	Relaxed	at a hotel
3	players	Confused	at the game
4	Maria Rex	Patient	at the park
5	Jan Judy	Angry	at the playground
6	Mark	Depressed	at school
7	Carla	Tired	at the library
8	Roy	Happy	at the hospital
9	Bozo	Sad	at the circus
10	Ramona	Surprised	at a restaurant
11	Fred	Worried	at the bank
12	Ann Fred	Nervous	at the wedding

2 **Pair-Practice:** *Practice answering and asking questions with another student. Use the photos above. See examples.* ▶

Student 1: **How was/were ____ [name] ___?**

Student 2: **He/She/It/They was/were_____.**

> How was the kitten?
>
> It was afraid.

3 **Pair-Practice:** *Practice answering and asking questions with another student. Use the photos above. See examples.* ▶

Student 1: **Where was/were _____ during the robbery?**

Student 2: **He/She/It/They was/were _____.**

> Where was the kitten during the robbery?
>
> It was at home.

4 *Write "was" or "were" on the lines below.*

What _were_ the cat and people doing during the robbery? The cat _was_ at home, and it _____ afraid. Jasmine _____ at a hotel. The players _____ at a football game, and they _____ angry because the referee _____ confused. At the same time, Maria _____ at the park with her dog. The dog and Maria _____ patient. Jan and Judy _____ at the playground. They _____ not very happy. Mark _____ at school. He _____ depressed because he _____ not at the football game. Carla _____ at the library. It _____ late and Carla _____ tired. Roy was at the hospital when his son _____ born. He _____ very happy. Bozo _____ at the circus. Ramona and her boyfriend _____ at a restaurant. Fred _____ at the bank. He_____ nervous because there _____ no money in his bank account. Ann and Fred _____ happy and nervous because they were at their wedding. The people at the wedding _____ happy for them.

5 *Answer the questions with "was" and "were."*

1. Where were you yesterday? _I was at school._ _____
2. How were you on the first day of school? _____
3. Where were you on your birthday?_____
4. How were you yesterday? _____
5. Where were you and your family when you were young?_____
6. Where were you _____? _____
7. How were you _____? _____

ESL Beginning and Intermediate Levels • Emotions • Pair Practice • Writing

Teacher's Notes

1 Before distributing the worksheet, start the lesson with a conversation. To assess your students' knowledge of the use of "*was*" and "*were*," ask personalized questions like the ones at the bottom of the worksheet.

2 Distribute the worksheet. Read the names and explain the phrases below the photos.

3 Drill the emotion illustrated in the first photo by asking the question, "*How was the cat?*" Model the response, "*It was afraid.*" Continue asking similar questions about each picture. Have students repeat both the question and answer.

4 Ask a yes/no question for picture one such as, "*Was the cat happy?*" Model the response, "*No, it wasn't. It was afraid.*" Have students repeat the question and answer for each photo. Have one student ask a similar question and another student give an appropriate response.

5 Ask individual students personal questions such as, "*How were you on your birthday?*", "*How were you on the first day of school?*", or "*How were you yesterday?*" For variety, ask students, "*When was the last time you were [emotion]?*" Continue this activity with students asking each other similar questions.

6 Make a statement using "*was*" or "*were*" such as, "*I was home on Sunday.*" Tell students to ask you a yes/no question based on your statement. For example, a student could ask, "*Were you at home on Saturday, too?*" or "*Were you at home alone?*" Answer the student's question with a short negative answer such as, "*No, I wasn't.*" followed by an explanation.

7 Have individual students ask original questions using "*was*" and "*were*." Use examples such as, "*Where were you last night?*" and "*Was yesterday Saturday?*"

8 Tell students that you are a detective conducting an investigation about a bank robbery. Tell them that they have to answer your questions. Question individuals as to where they were at a specific time. For example, ask:

When were you at the bank?   *Where were you at midnight?*
When was the last time you were at the bank?   *Where were you on Friday night?*

9 In activity 2, the first pair-practice exercise, direct the students to ask and answer questions using "*How was [name]?*" Model responses using "*was*" and "*were*." Have the students continue the activity by working in pairs asking one another questions based on the information in the phrases below the photos.

10 In activity 3, the second pair-practice exercise, have the students use the question "*Where was/were [name] during the robbery?*" Then, model a few responses as examples. Let the students continue working in pairs. Walk around the room listening for and correcting the students' pronunciation.

11 Next, direct the students to exercise 4 and 5. Have them read the text and the questions silently and ask them to point out any unfamiliar vocabulary. After explaining any new words, have them fill in the text and answer the questions with "*was*" and "*were*." Ask for volunteers to read the text and answer the questions.

12 Finally, challenge the students to write two original questions using "*How*" and "*Where*" with "*was*" and "*were*" at the bottom of the worksheet. As a class discussion, ask the students to share their questions and answers with the class.

13 As a follow-up activity, have students explain how they feel when the following things happen. Have students use the structure "*What do you feel when you ..... ?*" Have the students respond with "*I feel [emotion] when I .....*"

see a mouse   *get a letter from home*   *find money*
hear about an accident   *see a horror film*   *save money*
meet new people   *go on vacation alone*   *dance*
give a speech   *see a comedy*   *see a movie 10*
attend the first day of school *see an old friend*   *times*
make a mistake   *say goodbye to an old friend*   *hear a bad singer*
go to a wedding   *win money*   *cry*

14 *have children*
On subsequent days introduce some of the following emotions: *amazed, annoyed, ashamed, bored, brave, calm, cheerful, confident, confused, courageous, enlightened, delighted, disappointed, disgusted, excited, exhausted, frustrated, funny, hopeful, impatient, interested, jealous, lonely, nervous, patient, proud, puzzled, satisfied, scared, shocked, sorry, tense, terrified, tolerant, timid, uncertain, unhappy, worried.*

Note that "*how*" can also be used in exclamations such as "*How sad!*" and "*How embarrassing!*"

ESL Beginning Level • Expressions of Time • Appointment Book • Pair Practice • Fill In

Where, When, What time

1 Read Roberto's appointment book.

Monday, May 5th
Club Meeting
Community Center
7 P.M.

Tuesday, May 6th
Birthday Party
Bob's house
7 o'clock in the evening

Wednesday, May 7th
Dentist Appointment
143 Main Street
3 P.M.

Thursday, May 8th
Lecture on China
School Auditorium
7:30 in the afternoon

Friday, May 9th
Job Interview
Employment Agency
9 o'clock in the morning

Saturday, May 10th
Soccer Game
Central City Park
9 A.M.

Sunday, May 11th
Doctor's appointment
Good Health Hospital
10:15 in the morning

Monday, May 12th
Volunteer meeting
Senior Activity Center
8 A.M.

Roberto's Appointment Book

2 Practice the dialogs below with another student. Use the calendar above.

Student 1: Where's the _____?
Student 2: It's at the _____

> Where's the club meeting?
> It's at the community center

Student 1: When's the _____?
Student 2: It's on _____?

> When's the club meeting?
> It's on Monday, May 5th.

Student 1: What time's the _____?
Student 2: It's at _____?

> What time's the club meeting?
> It's at 2:30 in the afternoon.

3 Complete the questions and answers. Use the information in the appointment book above.

1. When _'s_ the club meeting? It's at _7 p.m._ Is it in the morning? No, it isn't. It's _in the evening_ .
2. _____'s the Birthday party? It's at Bob's house. _____'s the party? It's at 7 o'clock in the evening.
3. _____ _____'s the dentist appointment? _____ at 3 P.M.
4. _____ the lecture on China in the morning? No, it _____. It's _____.
5. _____'s the doctor's office? It's at Good Health Hospital. Is the appointment at 10:15 A.M.? Yes, it ___.
6. ____ the volunteer meeting at the Community Center? No, it ____. It's at the _____.
7. What time is it now? _____.
8. What's today's date? _____.
9. When's your school open? _____.
10. Where's your home? _____.

261

ESL Beginning Level • Expressions of Time • Appointment Book • Pair Practice • Fill In

Teacher's Notes

1 Numbers in a date are spoken as ordinal numbers. For example: "*May 5*" is read as "*May fifth.*" It can also be written as "*May 5th.*" It might be useful to review ordinal numbers prior to beginning this lesson.

2 Pose the question, "*When's the club meeting?*" Model the answer, "*It's on Monday, May 5th.*" Have students repeat both the question and answer. Then ask the same question to individual students prompting the appropriate answer as necessary. Drill this structure several times by posing similar questions about other entries in the appointment book.

3 Use the methodology above to introduce the question word "*where.*" Present the question word "*what time*" in the same manner.

4 Only after drilling each question word separately, begin posing questions randomly about the appointment book using "*where,*" "*when,*" and "*what time.*"

5 With the help of a student, demonstrate how to do the pair practice exercises using the appointment book. Then have the students continue by working in pairs.

6 For additional practice, ask questions using "*what*" such as, "*What's on Monday, May 5th?*" or "*What's at the community center?*" Model the response, "*The club meeting is.*" Continue this exercise by having students ask each other similar questions.

7 Direct your students to exercise 3 at the bottom of the worksheet. Tell the students that the exercise is based on the appointment book to the left of the exercise. Have the students complete the questions and answers in writing.

Answers:
1. When's the club meeting? It's at 7 P.M. Is it in the morning? No, it isn't. It's in the evening.
2. Where's the Birthday party? It's at Bob's house. When's the party? It's at 7 o'clock in the evening.
3. What time's the dentist appointment? It's at 3 P.M.
4. Is the lecture on China in the morning? No, it isn't. It's in the afternoon.
5. Where's the doctor's office? It's at Good Health Hospital. Is the appointment at 10:15 A.M.? Yes, it is.
6. Is the volunteer meeting at the Community Center? No, it isn't. It's at the Senior Activity Center.
7. What time is it now? (Answers will vary.)
8. What's today's date? (Answers will vary.)
9. When's your school open? (Answers will vary.)
10. Where's your home? (Answers will vary.)

NOTE

• Note the variations in the abbreviation of *ante meridian* and *post meridian*: a.m., p.m., AM, PM.

• As a variation, a date such as "*on May 5th*" can also be expressed as "*on the 5th of May*" In the United States, the Independence Day holiday is known as "*the Fourth of July.*"

• When used as prepositions of time, "*at*" is used with clock time; "*on*" is used to indicate days or dates; and "*in*" is used with longer periods of time such as years, months, and seasons.

AT	ON	IN
at 9 (o'clock)	on Monday	in 1980
at 2:30 (p.m.)	on May 5th	in May
at noon	on a holiday	in (the) summer
at lunch (time)	on the weekend	in the 1990s

• For parts of the day, use "*in the morning,*" "*in the afternoon,*" "*in the evening,*" and "*at night.*"

8 As a follow up activity, have students make a list of times and places for their own activities. As a class discussion, ask the students to ask you, the teacher, and other students about some common daily activities using "*where,*" " *when,*" and " *what time.*"

ESL Intermediate Level   Which? • Pair Practice • Writing • Discussion

Who & That (Relative Pronouns)

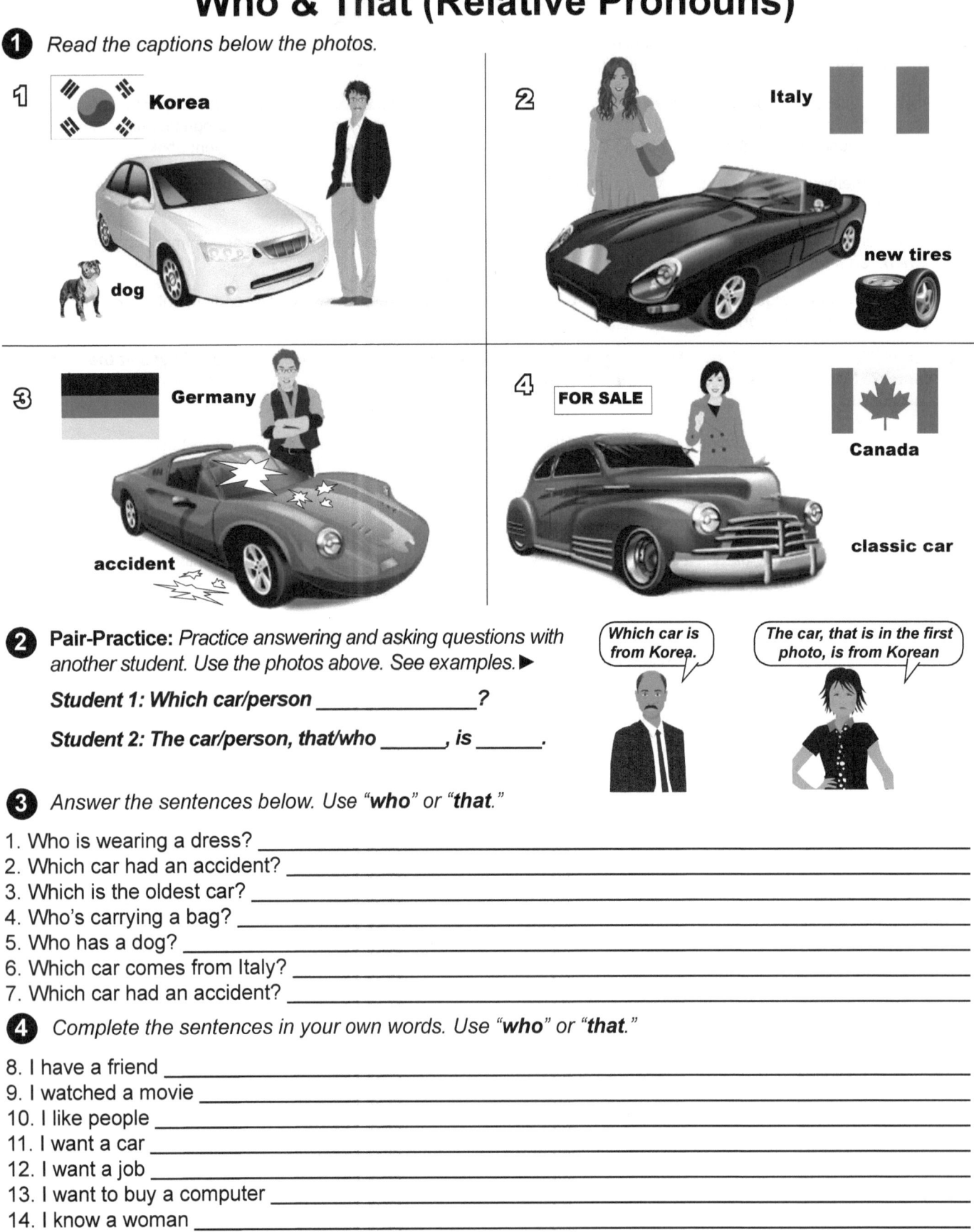

1 Read the captions below the photos.

1. Korea — dog
2. Italy — new tires
3. Germany — accident
4. FOR SALE — Canada — classic car

2 **Pair-Practice:** *Practice answering and asking questions with another student. Use the photos above. See examples.* ▶

Student 1: Which car/person _____?

Student 2: The car/person, that/who _____, is _____.

> Which car is from Korea.

> The car, that is in the first photo, is from Korean

3 *Answer the sentences below. Use "who" or "that."*

1. Who is wearing a dress? _____
2. Which car had an accident? _____
3. Which is the oldest car? _____
4. Who's carrying a bag? _____
5. Who has a dog? _____
6. Which car comes from Italy? _____
7. Which car had an accident? _____

4 *Complete the sentences in your own words. Use "who" or "that."*

8. I have a friend _____
9. I watched a movie _____
10. I like people _____
11. I want a car _____
12. I want a job _____
13. I want to buy a computer _____
14. I know a woman _____
15. I see a person _____

263

ESL Intermediate Level   Which? • Pair Practice • Writing • Discussion

Teacher's Notes

1 Before distributing the worksheet, start the lesson with a conversation. Ask questions that elicit answers using "*who*" and "*that*" as relative pronouns in the answers to assess your students' knowledge of these structures.

2 Distribute the worksheet. Identify the following through questions and answers:

- *The origin of the cars (Korea, Italy, Germany, and Canada)*
- *The color of the cars (yellow, black, red).*
- *The people (by their clothing).*
- *Other objects in the photos (For sale sign, dog, new tires, accident)*
- *The relative positions of objects (next to, beside, in front of, in back of, behind).*

3 Ask the question to familiarize the students with the vocabulary in the photos. For example, ask "**Where's the dog?**" Model the response, "**It's next to the car in photo 1.**" Continue asking similar questions such as "**Who wants to sell a car?**", "**Which car has new tires?**", and "**What-kind of car is from Canada?**"

4 Ask questions using the words "**Which?**" and "**Who?**" prompting answers with the relative pronouns "**that**" and "**who.**" For example:

- *Which car's from Korea? The car, <u>that's in photo number one</u>, is from Korea.*
- *Which car has new tires tire? The car, <u>that comes from Italy</u>, has new tires.*
- *Who's standing next to a car? The man, <u>who has the dog</u>, is standing next to his car.*
- *Who has a classic car? The woman, <u>who is from Canada</u>, has a classic car.*

5 Have students repeat both questions and answers. Note that the contractions "**who's**" and "**that's**" are normally used in conversation.

6 In Exercise 2, the pair-practice exercise, direct the students to ask and answers questions using "**Which?**" and "**Who?**" Model responses using "**that**" or "**who.**" Have the students continue the activity by working in pairs asking one another questions based on the photos at the top of the worksheet.

7 In Exercise 3, go over the questions 1-7 and possible answers orally. Then, direct the students to answer them in writing.

8 Review the phrases in items 8-15 to make sure that the students understand any unfamiliar vocabulary, then direct them to complete the sentences in their own words.

9 As a class discussion, encourage the students to share their sentences with the rest of the class.

NOTE

10 Explain that the word "**that**" is generally used for people and objects, but "**who**" is exclusively used for people. In more formal English "**which**" is often used for objects.

Note that the combination of "**who**" or "**that**" with the verb "*to be*" can often be deleted. Examples:

The car (that's) from Germany was in an accident.
The man (who was) dancing with Kim fell down.

12 For advanced classes, this lesson can be used to practice the deletion of the relative pronoun followed by the verb "*to be*" For further practice you may want to use the following chalkboard activity:

Cross out the word "**that**" or "**who**" and the verb "*to be*" *(am, is, are)* when appropriate.

1. The man ~~who is~~ standing next to the yellow car drives a car from Korea.
2. Mr. Green wants to buy's car that doesn't use a lot of gas.
3. The woman ~~who lives~~ in the big house ~~that is~~ on the corner is Mrs. Bell.
4. Please sell me the car ~~that is~~ from Canada.
5. Do you know the student who works after school in the small shoe store ~~that is~~ across the street?

ESL Beginning Level   Reading an Office Directory • Pair Practice • Fill In

Who & What

① Directions: *Read information in the office directory.*

② Pair-Practice: *Practice asking and answering questions with another student. Use the directory See examples.* ▶

Student 1: **Who's the _____ ?**

Student 2: **_____ is.**

Who's the president?

Maria Garcia is.

VALLEY FURNITURE COMPANY
OFFICE DIRECTORY

POSITION	NAME	EXTENSION
President	Maria Garcia	349
Vice President	John Smith	643
Foreman	Boris Popov	112
Secretary	Kim Park	395
Receptionist	Carlo Caruso	401
Accountant	Kumiko Ito	213
Supervisor	Hans Muller	569
Shipping Clerk	Annette Duval	670
Security Office	Ali Ahmed	899
Salesperson	Quang Nguyen	740

③ Pair-Practice: *Practice asking and answering questions with another student. Use the directory. See examples.* ▶

Student 1: **What's his/her extension?**

Student 2: **It's _____.**

What's her extension?

It's 349.

④ Directions: *Complete the questions and answers below.*

1. Who's__ the ___Principal___ ? Mr. Commings is.

2. Mrs. Willis is the Assistant Principal. ___What__'s his extension? It's _____.

3. _____'s the counselor? She's _____.

4. _____'s Mary Willis? She's the _____.

5. Who____ the Financial Manager? Mrs. Mlla Madamba _____.

6. Miss Jerrett is the _____. _____'s her extension? It's _____.

WESTSIDE ADULT SCHOOL

NAME	POSITION	EXT.
MR. FRED COMMINGS	PRINCIPAL	514
MRS. MARY WILLIS	ASSISTANT PRINCIPAL	630
MS. PATTY HENRY	COUNSELOR	769
MISS VERA JERRETT	SECRETARY	286
MRS. MILA MADAMBA	FINANCIAL MANAGER	413
MR. CLARENCE BOOKER	OFFICE CLERK	301
MISS ANNA ELAM	SECURITY OFFICER	198

7. _____ 's the Office Clerk? It's _____. His _____ is 301.

8. What___ Miss Anna Elam? She's the _____, and her extension is _____.

9. Who__ your principal or director? _____ is. What___ his/her telephone number? It's _____.

10. _____'s the counselor at your school? _____ is. _____'s his/her extension? It's _____.

265

ESL Beginning Level   Reading an Office Directory • Pair Practice • Fill In

Teacher's Notes

1 Before doing this activity, students should already know how to use possessive pronouns: "*his*" and "*her*" and reading numbers.

2 Before distributing the worksheet, begin the lesson with a conversation using "*who*" and "*what*" in questions to determine how well they can use them. Ask questions such as *"Who is the principal or director of this school?"*, *"What's his/her phone number?"* and *"What's [staff member's name]?"* *"He/She is the [position]."* Have the students repeat both question and answer. Then direct the question to individual students.

3 Distribute the worksheet and read the information in the office directory at the top of the page. Introduce the vocabulary by modeling the pronunciation of the names, positions, and extensions for each person in the office directory. Have the students repeat the pronunciation of the words after you. While you are reading, ask the student to underline any unfamiliar words, then explain them. Clarify the job titles as necessary.

4 Pose the question, "*Who's the president of the company?*": Model the answer, "*Maria Garcia is.*" Have the students repeat both the question and answer. Then ask the question to individual students prompting the answer as necessary. After drilling this example several times, pose similar questions about the remaining names in the directory.

5 Use the methodology described in item above to introduce and drill the question, "*What's his/her extension?*" Numbers for telephone extensions are normally read as single digits. Zero is read as the letter "0."

6 Randomly pose questions about the directory using "*who*" and "*what*."

7 Repeat the same methodology for the directory for Westside Adult School. Drill the structures and vocabulary by having individual students ask questions using "*who*" or "*what*" and by having other students supply the appropriate answers.

8 In exercise 2, the first pair-practice exercise, direct the students to ask and answer questions using "*Who's the [position]?*" Model responses "*[Name] is.*" Have the students continue the activity by working in pairs asking one another questions based on the information in the office directory.

9 In activity 3, the second pair-practice exercise, have the students use the question *"What's his/her extension?"* Then, model a few responses as examples. Let the students continue working in pairs. Walk around the room listening for and correcting the students' pronunciation.

10 Have the students do exercise 4 in writing. Tell them that the activity is based on the directory for the Westside Adult School. When correcting the exercise, emphasize the punctuation and capitalization.

Answers:
1. Who's the Principal? Mr. Commings is.
2. Mrs. Willis is the Assistant Principal. What's his extension? It's 349.
3. Who's the counselor? She's Mrs. Patty Henry.
4. Who's Mary Willis? She's the Assistant Principal.
5. Who's the Financial Manager? Mrs. Mlla Madamba is.
6. Miss Jerrett is the secretary. What's her extension? It's 286.
7. Who's the Office Clerk? It's Mr. Clarence Booker. His extension is 301.
8. What's Miss Anna Elam? She's the Security Officer, and her extension is 301
9. Who's your principal or director? (Answer will vary) is. What's his/her telephone number? It's (Answers will vary.
10. Who's the counselor at your school? (Answer will vary) is. What's his/her extension? It's (Answer will vary).

11 On the chalkboard, write a list of persons and a separate list of inanimate objects. Ask the single-word questions "*Who?*" and "*What?*" Have students answer with an appropriate word from the board.

12 Have students alphabetize by last name the persons in the directory for the Valley Furniture Company.

13 Write a directory of key personnel in your school on the board. Use the directory for drilling "*who*" and "*what*."

NOTE

"*Miss*" is not an abbreviation and does not utilize a period.

"*Ext.*" is an abbreviation of "*extension*."

ESL Intermediate Level • Relative Pronoun: Who • Vocational ESL • Pair Practice • Writing

Who: Relative Pronoun

Directions: *Practice the phrases below the photo with another student.*

What kind of person is the owner looking for?

The owner is looking for a person WHO is honest.

Student 1: *What kind of person is the owner looking for?*
Student 2: *The owner is looking for a person **who** ...*

1 is honest
2 is good with numbers
3 has training
4 can use a computer
5 handle money well
6 works well with people
7 isn't lazy
8 is well-dressed
9 is punctual
10 is friendly
11 is bilingual (Buenos dias.)
12 is helpful

Write: *Write sentences with **who**. Begin with **I am a person who** ...*
Example: *I am a person who is reliable.*

1. _____
2. _____
3. _____
4. _____

ESL Intermediate Level • Relative Pronoun: Who • Vocational ESL • Pair Practice • Writing

Teacher's Notes

1 Before distributing the worksheet, explain the use of the relative pronoun **who**. Explain that we usually use **who** for people and **that** for things.

Examples: *The owner of the store is looking for a person **who** is honest.*
*Jim is looking for a job **that** is near his home.*

2 Review the new vocabulary:

honest	computer	punctual
numbers	handle	friendly
training	lazy	bilingual
use	well-dressed	helpful

3 Distribute the handout. Read the directions with the students and do the Pair Practice Drill orally in class.

Discuss other qualities that the owner might want in an employee:
reliable

trustworthy	clean	has experience	likes to do a good job
knowledgeable	well-groomed	energetic	doesn't argue
listens well	speaks English	learns quickly	can make change
intelligent	polite	accurate	can work on weekends
neat	courteous	lives nearby	Write the words on the

4 chalkboard and repeat the drill using the new words.

5 Have the students write three original sentences using "who." Read the example at the bottom of the page.

6 Correct the sentences. You may want to project a copy of the handout that has been transferred to an overhead transparency directly onto the chalkboard where students can write their sentences.

Follow-Up

7 Teach that relative pronouns can be used as the subject or object of a sentence, but when we use them as the object, they can be deleted.

Examples:

*The owner is the person **who** you want to see.*

The owner is the person ~~who~~ you want to see.

*This is the job **that** I want.*

This is the job ~~that~~ I want.

8 For additional practice with relative pronouns, refer to the worksheet and lesson plan **Relative Pronoun: That** (Item #0030).

"Would" Used in Hypothetical Questions

1. If electricity weren't invented yet, how would your life be different?
2. If only one book existed, which book would you like it to be?
3. If you could ask God any one question, what would it be?
4. If you could be an animal, what animal would you be?
5. If you could be another person for a day, who would you be?
6. If you could change one thing about your life, what would it be and why?
7. If you could change one thing in the world, what would it be?
8. If you could date a celebrity, who would you choose?
9. If you could eat only one food for the rest of your life what food would you choose and why?
10. If you could give a charity a million dollars, what organization would you help?
11. If you could go anywhere in the world for a vacation, where would you go?
12. If you could go back to any moment in history, where would you go?
13. If you could live anywhere in the world, where would you live?
14. If you could only listen to one song for the rest of your life, which song would you choose?
15. If you could travel back in time, where would you go?
16. If you found a suitcase full of $1,000,000, what would you do?
17. If you got into a traffic accident, what would you do first?
18. If you could be invisible for a day what would you do and why?
19. If you knew now what you knew ten years ago, what would you do differently?
20. If you saw a colleague stealing at work, would you report him/her?
21. If you were an English teacher, what would you do to improve your students' English?
22. If you were given three wishes, what would you wish for?
23. If you were president, what would you change about your country?
24. If you were the President of the USA for a day, what would you do?
25. If your spouse cheated on you, what would you do?
26. What if you could relive any moment in your life which moment would it be and why?
27. If you could change one thing about yourself, what would it be?
28. If you had to spend 100 days on a desert island, what five things would you take with you and why?
29. If a classmate asked you for the answer to a question during an exam while the teacher was not looking, what would you do?
30. If you had to choose between love and no money or money and no love for the rest of your life, which would you choose?
31. If you bumped your car into another car, but nobody saw you do it, would you leave your name and address?

ESL Advanced Level — Discussing Hypothetical Questions with "Would" • Discussion

Teacher's Notes

❶ Introduction
• Before distributing the worksheet, start the lesson with a conversation. Ask questions that elicit sentences using the conditional with "would" to determine how well they can use the verb structure. Use some of the sample questions below:

If you could choose a new name, what would it be?
If you won the lottery, what would you do with the money?
If you could visit any place in the world, where would you go?

❷ Grammar Review
• Students should already be familiar with the use of the conditional with "would" before doing this exercise.

As a review, teach the following short dialogs to the whole class. Substitute common verbs such as "*swim, play football*, and *cook*" for the first dialog and common adjectives such as "*rich, happy,* and *nervous*." Tell the students to use the same dialogs when answering the question on the question cards.

Dialog 1
Student 1: Can you ...?
Student 2: No, I can't.
Student 1: But, if you could ..., what would you do?
Student 2: I would ... What about you?
Student 1: I would ...

Dialog 2 *(with the verb TO BE)*
Student 1: Are you ...?
Student 2: No, I' not.
Student 1: But, if you were ..., what would you do?
Student 2: I would ... What about you?
Student 1: I would ...

❸ Distribute the handout to the students.

❹ Divide the class into groups of three or four.

❺ Tell the students to take turns selecting one of the questions on the handout.

❻ Tell them to read their question aloud and lead their group in discussing the question. If a group does not feel comfortable discussing a topic, encourage them to choose another one. (Each student should lead at least one discussion.)

❼ Walk around the classroom and join each group for a few minutes and correct the students pronunciation and grammar. (Do not hover over a group, sit down at eye-level.)

❽ During the last twenty minutes of the class, ask volunteers from each group to share which questions their group discussed. (Place important vocabulary and expressions on the board.)

❾ Continue this activity by asking the students to come up with original questions. Discuss possible answers with the whole class.

ESL Intermediate Level — Pair Practice • Writing • Discussion

Why? (Because, To, For)

1 Read the captions below the photos.

1. Mrs. Brown went to the market. She needed to buy some food.

2. Mila and Roy had dinner. They wanted to celebrate their anniversary.

3. Vera went to the ATM. She wanted to get some cash.

4. Ann visited the hairdresser. She needed to get a haircut.

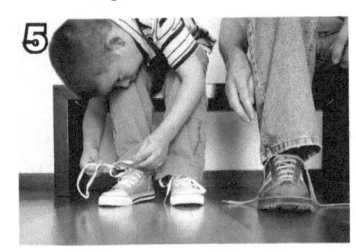

5. Adam went to the department store. He needed to have shoes.

6. Mary goes to the local gym. She needs to exercise more.

7. These students attend school. They want to improve their English.

8. Tony turned on the TV. His friends wanted to watch a soccer game.

2 **Pair-Practice:** Practice answering and asking questions with another student. Use the photos above. Answer with *"because"*. See examples. ▶

Why did Mrs. Brown go to the market?
Because she needed to buy some food.

Student 1: Why _____?
Student 2: Because _____.

3 **Pair-Practice:** Practice answering and asking questions with another student. Answer with *"to"* or *"for."* See examples. ▶

Why did Mrs. Brown go to the market?
To buy some food.
For food.

Student 1: Why _____?
Student 2: To _____. or For _____.

4 Complete the sentences. Use the photos above.

1. Mrs. Brown went to the market to _buy food._
2. Mila and Roy had dinner because _____
3. Vera went to the ATM for _____
4. Ann visited the hairdresser to _____
5. Adam went to the department store because _____
6. Mary goes to the local gym for _____
7. The students go to school because _____
8. Tony turned on the TV to _____
9. I came to this school _____

Challenge: Write three original questions using "Why?" Answer them with **"because," "to,"** and **"for."**

10. Why _____? Because _____
11. Why _____? To _____
12. Why _____? For _____

ESL Intermediate Level   Pair Practice • Writing • Discussion

Teacher's Notes

1 Before distributing the worksheet, start the lesson with a conversation. Ask questions with "*Why?*" that elicit sentences using "*because*," "*to*" *(in order to)*, and "*for*" to assess your students' knowledge of these structures. Use some of the sample questions below:

Why do you study English?   Why did you come to this city? Why are you wearing a watch?

2 Distribute the worksheet. Identify the people and what they are doing in the photos by reading the captions. Have the students repeat the captions after you. As a active listening activity, tell the students to underline or circle any unfamiliar vocabulary, which should be explained.

3 Ask questions using "'*why*" and model responses with "*because*." For example, ask, "*Why did Mrs. Brown go to the market?*" Respond, "*She went to the market because she needed to buy some food.*" Continue posing similar questions about the remaining pictures.

4 Using the same method above, repeat the activity, but this time model responses using "*to*." For example, drill "*Mrs. Brown went to the market to buy some food*" After drilling "*to*" with each photo, introduce responses using "*for*." For example, practice, "*Mrs. Brown went to the market for some food.*"

5 After sufficiently drilling "*for*," "°*to*," and "*because*" have an individual student ask another student a question using "*why*" in a chain drill. The second student must formulate a response based on the photos.

6 In Exercise 2, the first pair-practice exercise, direct the students to ask and answers questions using "*Why...?*" Model responses using "*because*." Have the students continue the activity by working in pairs asking one another questions based on the photos and the captions at the top of the worksheet.

7 In Exercise 3, the second pair-practice exercise, have the students use the question "*Why?*" Then, model the responses using either "*to*" and "*for*." Let them work in pairs.

8 Expand the activity by asking the class personalized questions such as the ones listed below. Then, encourage the students to ask one another original questions. Here are some sample questions that you might want to list on the board:

Why do you go to the library, barber, hairdresser, drugstore?
Why do you sleep, eat, exercise, study, read?
Why do people work, save money?
Why do you wear shoes, a watch, glasses, a coat?
Why do we have police, fire-fighters, doctors, friends?
Why do we need laws, newspapers, cell phones, computers, books?

9 Have students complete the sentences in Exercise 4 in writing. (Answers: 1 to buy food, 2 because they wanted to celebrate their anniversary, 3, for cash, 4 to get a haircut, 5 because he needed to have new shoes, 6 for exercise, 7 they want to improve their English, 8 to watch a soccer game, 9 *Answers will vary*.)

10 Next, challenge the students to write three original questions, which they must ask other students. Then, they must write the other students' responses using "*because*," "*to*," and "*for*" on the worksheet.

12 Finally, have a class discussion based on the questions and answers.

NOTES

Point out that "*to*" is a shortened form of "*in order to*."

You may want to practice the structure "*What. . . for?*" It is commonly used in conversation.

    Example: "*What did Mrs. Brown go to the market for?*"

"*How come?*" is often used in conversation. Students should at least have a passive recognition of this form.

Note that "*How come?*" does not take the normal question pattern. Compare:

    a) *How come she went home?*   b) *Why did she go home?*

Students tend to have great difficulty with the spelling of "*because*." Stress the vowel combination by underlining, by highlighting with colored chalk or by identifying the individual words "*be*" and "*cause*."

272

ESL Intermediate Level • Taking a Trip • Pair Practice • Vocabulary Building

Will (Future Tense)

1 Read Ruth's itineary.   *Ruth*

Saturday, June 1
- leave Los Angeles
- fly to Denver
- walk in the mountains

Tuesday, June 4
- fly to Chicago
- visit art museums
- have dinner with cousin Joe

Friday, June 7
- fly to Boston
- rent a car
- see historic places

Monday, June 11
- take a bus to New York
- visit United Nations building
- attend Broadway show

Sunday, June 16
- sail to Miami on a cruise ship
- swim in the ocean
- write post cards

Thursday, June 20
- take a train home
- take photos of the views
- relax on the train

Tuesday, June 25
- arrive in Los Angeles
- take a taxi home
- check phone messages

Wednesday, June 26
- return to work
- bicycle to the office
- share photos with co-workers

Ruth will take a trip across the United States.

2 Practice the dialogs below with another student. Use the calendar above.

Student 1: Where will Ruth ...?
Student 2: She will ...

> Where will Ruth go on June 1st?
> She will fly to Denver.

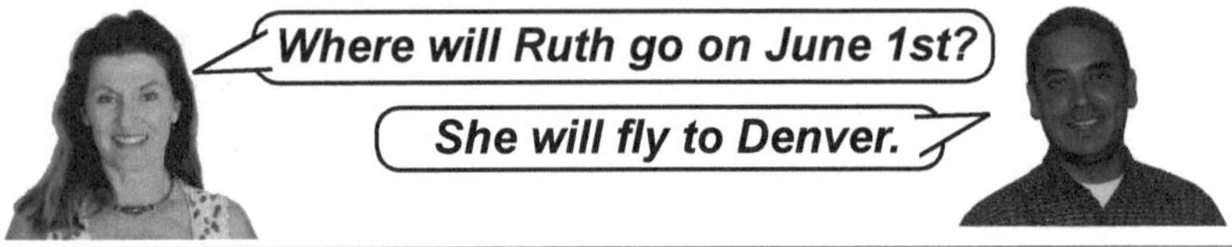

Student 1: When will Ruth ...?
Student 2: She will ...

> When will Ruth fly to Chicago?
> She will fly on Tuesday, June 4th.

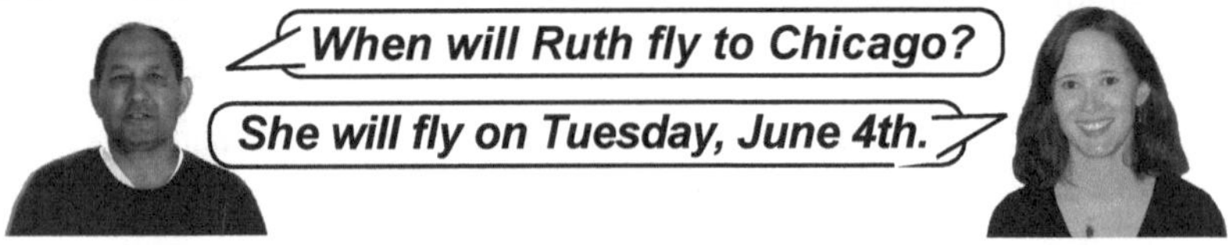

Student 1: What will Ruth ... ?
Student 2: She will ...

> What will Ruth do in Boston?
> She will rent a car.

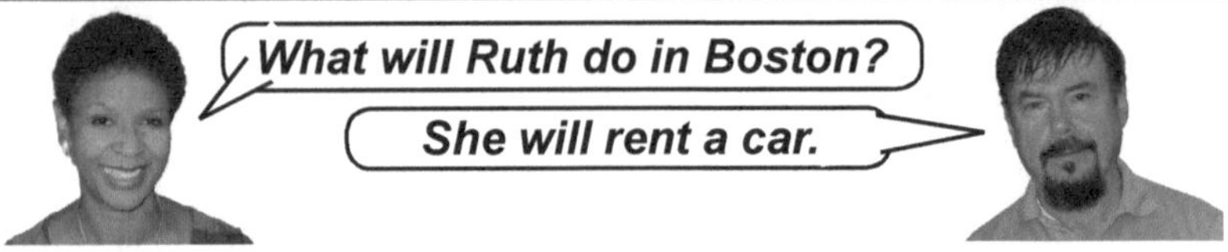

3 Draw lines from the names of the cities to the correct location on the map.

Chicago   Boston

Denver   New York

Los Angeles   Miami

ESL Intermediate Level • Taking a Trip • Pair Practice • Vocabulary Building

Teacher's Notes

1 Read the itinerary and explain the vocabulary. Also review the pronunciation of ordinal numbers (*June first, forth, seventh, eleventh, etc.*)

2 Explain the use of the future with **will** and **won't**:

- Use **will** and **won't** to show future time, especially of plans and promises.

- **Won't** is the contraction of **will not**, and "**ll**" is the contraction of **will**.

- **Will** is a modal. We form the affirmative, question, and negative forms of **will** in the same way as for **can** and **must**.

- Show that **won't** is also used to express the idea of refusal such as "*I won't eat liver!*" Also point out that **will** is followed by the verb and not the infinitive: Contrast "*He will drive a car.*" and "*He wants to drive a car.*"

- In some English-speaking countries, **shall** is used instead of **will** with the pronouns "I" and "we." In the United States, the use of **shall** is limited to questions such as "**Shall we go?**" in which the speaker seeks agreement or concurrence.

- Common time expressions used with the future: **later**, **in a little while**, **next**, **two days from now**, **soon**, **from now on**.

3 With the help of a student, demonstrate how to do the pair practice exercises using the itinerary. Then have the students continue by working in pairs.

4 Have students draw lines from the names of the cities to the correct places on the map. Then, correct the exercise with the answers below.

Chicago — Boston
Denver — New York
Los Angeles — Miami

5 As a follow-up activity, make two lists of sentences on the chalkboard indicating what students **will** and **won't** do on their birthday:

On my birthday I **will** ...	On my birthday I **won't** ...
1. *I'll have a party.*	1. *I won't work.*
2.	2.
3.	3.

6 Have students make an itenerary of their next vacation.

ESL Intermediate Level   When • How • Pair Practice • Writing • Discussion

Word Order • When • How

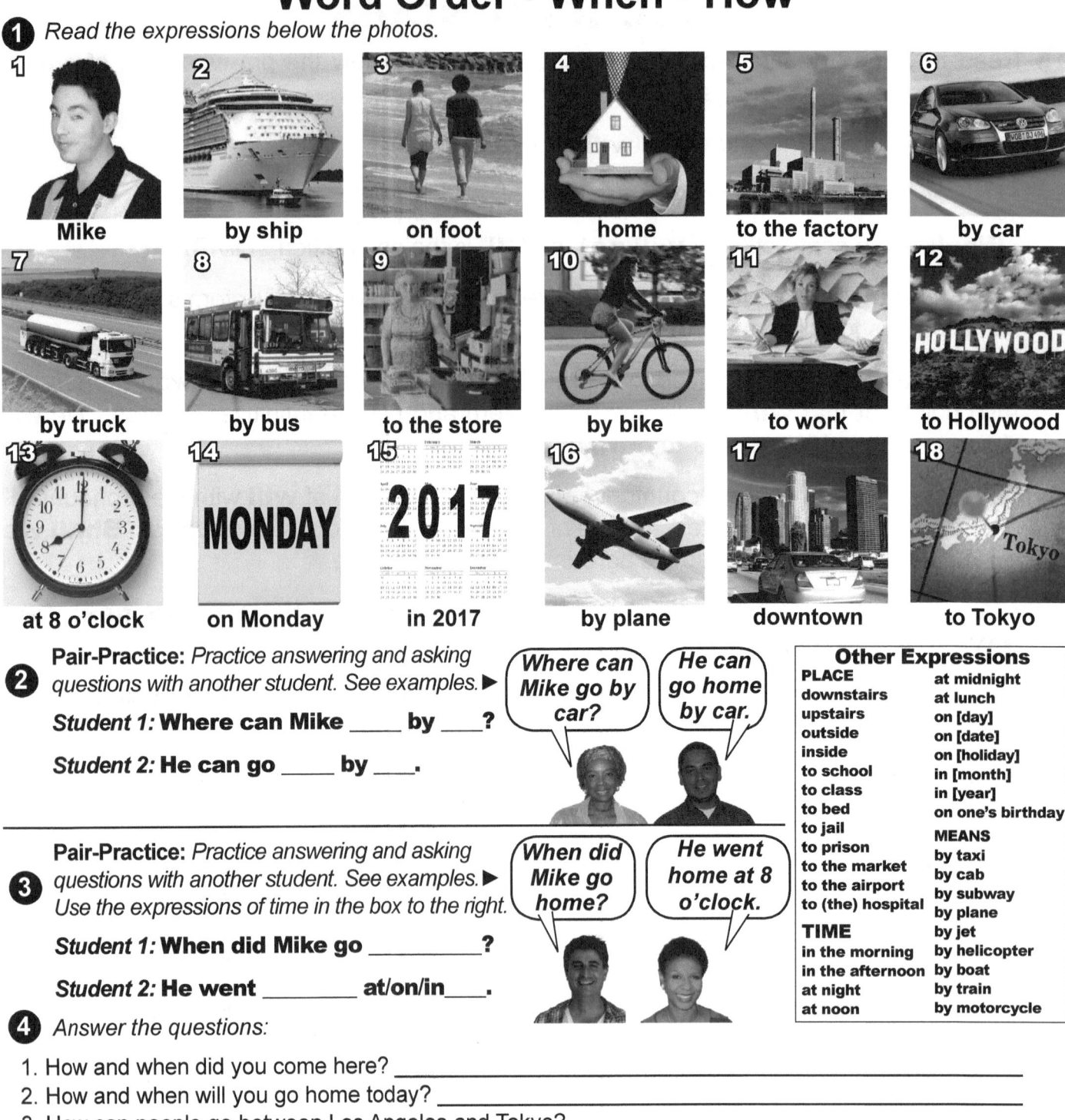

1 *Read the expressions below the photos.*

1	Mike
2	by ship
3	on foot
4	home
5	to the factory
6	by car
7	by truck
8	by bus
9	to the store
10	by bike
11	to work
12	to Hollywood
13	at 8 o'clock
14	on Monday
15	in 2017
16	by plane
17	downtown
18	to Tokyo

2 **Pair-Practice:** *Practice answering and asking questions with another student. See examples.* ▶

Where can Mike go by car?
He can go home by car.

Student 1: **Where can Mike _____ by _____?**

Student 2: **He can go _____ by _____.**

Other Expressions

PLACE
downstairs
upstairs
outside
inside
to school
to class
to bed
to jail
to prison
to the market
to the airport
to (the) hospital

at midnight
at lunch
on [day]
on [date]
on [holiday]
in [month]
in [year]
on one's birthday

MEANS
by taxi
by cab
by subway
by plane
by jet
by helicopter
by boat
by train
by motorcycle

TIME
in the morning
in the afternoon
at night
at noon

3 **Pair-Practice:** *Practice answering and asking questions with another student. See examples.* ▶ *Use the expressions of time in the box to the right.*

When did Mike go home?
He went home at 8 o'clock.

Student 1: **When did Mike go _____?**

Student 2: **He went _____ at/on/in_____.**

4 *Answer the questions:*

1. How and when did you come here? _____
2. How and when will you go home today? _____
3. How can people go between Los Angeles and Tokyo? _____
4. How do you go to the movies? _____
5. Where, how, and when did you go on your last vacation? _____
6. When and how will you go to school? _____
7. How, where, and when do you go shopping? _____
8. How do products travel from the factory to stores? _____
9. Where and when were you born? _____
10. How can you travel from your home to the airport? _____